The Best AMERICAN SPORTS WRITING 1993

The Best AMERICAN SPORTS WRITING 1993

EDITED AND WITH

AN INTRODUCTION BY

Frank Deford

Glenn Stout, SERIES EDITOR

HOUGHTON MIFFLIN COMPANY

BOSTON · NEW YORK   1993

ISSN 1056-8034
ISBN 0-395-63324-9
ISBN 0-395-63323-0 (pbk.)

Printed in the United States of America

AGM 10 9 8 7 6 5 4 3 2 1

For the memory of Arthur Ashe

Contents

Foreword

"WHERE'S the story on Magic Johnson?"

As more people become aware of this series, and of my role in its preparation, I am often asked about a variety of sports issues and events and the resulting stories these events have spawned in the sporting press of the United States and Canada.

I understand the question and I appreciate the attention. It is gratifying to know that *The Best American Sports Writing* is now considered, as its title implies, to be the most likely source for the best sports writing in a given year. As series editor, I read more writing on sports than anyone else I can imagine. While much of my reading, by editorial necessity, lags a month or two behind the present, I am relatively certain that I will see virtually all the significant writing on a given topic within the sports year.

"So where's the story on Magic Johnson?"

I have been asked this question a number of times, and as with similar questions concerning other notable occurrences in sports, my answer is usually, "I don't know . . . yet." This reply puzzles some people, yet I believe my answer to that question explains much of what *The Best American Sports Writing* tries to accomplish and recognize.

A writer is only an accumulation of craft, experience and practice, his or her own life combined with what one learns about the world, filtered through the keyboard and reported to others by way of the word. This reportage can result in a variety of responses — fiction, poetry, nonfiction, and each response can be formed in an infinite number of ways. The writer's task is to choose the right one, the way that best communicates his or her intention.

The writer cannot necessarily control the response any more precisely than a hitter in baseball can fully control his swing. The million practice swings taken in batting practice might result in a ninth-inning home run to win the game. They might also result in a checked swing grounder to third, or an ignominious whiff on a pitch down the middle. The million words previously written might result in the instant classic, in something competent but unmemorable, or in the trash can.

There can be no doubt that Magic Johnson's 1991 revelation that he was infected with the HIV virus was one of the most significant and important sports stories of that year. His subsequent appearance in the 1991–92 NBA All-Star game, and his appointment as a spokesperson for AIDS and as a member of the 1992 U.S. Olympic basketball team added to the prescience of Johnson's story. It received, and deserved, massive attention from the press. Literally thousands of stories have been written in the past two years concerning Johnson.

But this book is not a collection of the best stories. It is a collection of the best writing. And Magic Johnson is not a human being defined solely by one moment, or one story in his life, but a human being whose life is the collection of many moments. In 1978, when he led Michigan State University to the NCAA basketball championship, Magic Johnson was one of the big sports stories of that year. Just as Johnson has gone on to add to his résumé and evolve as a human being, so too does the writer grow and add to his or her experience. While I have read many stories about Johnson over the past two years, some of which have been superb, none struck me as the best writing to appear in either year. Hence my response to the question is "I haven't seen it."

". . . Yet." Johnson's tragic situation forced many sports writers to look at issues that most had previously shied away from — the epidemic of AIDS, human sexuality, the athlete's role in regard to both — and to integrate Johnson's plight into their own experience. This propelled them to react to these issues in different terms, provoking a new response in their own writing, in ways not possible before. That is where the qualifier "yet" comes into play. The "best" Magic Johnson story, the one I'm looking for, may be still to come.

This transformation is not unique to the writer's experience with Magic Johnson. In 1925 Babe Ruth experienced a prolonged slump that at the time was blamed on his consumption of too many hot dogs. Today it is generally believed that Ruth suffered from the combined effects of too much alcohol and venereal disease. The writer's perception about Ruth has evolved and changed. Similarly, of the modern athlete, perhaps none has provoked such a wide variety of reactions as Muhammad Ali. As writers learn more, and as society changes, so too do their stories on Ali. What may have appeared to be a definitive story on Ali thirty years ago seems hopelessly myopic today. What is considered "the best" changes from year to year.

This is not to say that it is either impossible or unlikely for a wonderful story to be written immediately following a significant event. There are some talented and dedicated writers who pull it off regularly. But now, more than ever before, I do believe it is more difficult to do so immediately following the event. Television often strips the experience of its immediacy, making the writer's task more difficult to start with. And it often takes time to sort out and accurately judge an experience. Writers know this feeling as well, if not better, than anyone else. The act of writing is an act of learning; most writers know how it feels to start writing about one topic, thinking they know precisely what they want to say, only to discover they feel quite differently and then write about something else entirely.

So, where is the Magic Johnson story? In a sense, it may be in this volume after all. Peter Richmond's delicate profile of Dodger Manager Tommy Lasorda's son Tommy Jr., "Tangled Up in Blue," is a story whose beginnings can be traced to Johnson's 1991 announcement. Its genesis can be followed through the thousands of stories that Johnson's admission spawned, resulting in a writer who had the ability and desire to tell a story that is both full of joy and full of pain, told well and with sensitivity, and to a magazine that published in 1992 what it probably would not have published in 1990.

I hope, through my attempt to select the "best" sports writing of any given year, that this experience is repeated, and that each

year I find sports writing that demonstrates the ability to evolve
with its readership. Thus far, I've had no real difficulty finding
writing that has been up to that challenge. Were it not so, I would
grow tired of looking, and I have not. The work continues to en-
lighten and inform. That is my own Magic Johnson story.

Each season I personally survey more than 350 magazines,
newspapers and other publications from the United States and
Canada in search of stories for possible inclusion in *The Best
American Sports Writing*. Since it is impossible for a single individual to read every publication that may include a story of merit,
several hundred additional publications are asked to submit material for consideration.

This year, in addition to my own surveys of published work, I
was pleased to receive submissions from more than 125 publications, editors and individuals, including many stories that I otherwise might have missed. Guest editor Frank Deford received
only the very best of these thousands of stories. His challenging
task was to select the few that appear in this volume.

Anyone — editors, writers, even interested readers — is welcome to submit stories for consideration in the next edition of
The Best American Sports Writing. To be considered for inclusion
in *The Best American Sports Writing 1994*, each nonfiction story
must have been published in 1993 and must be column length
(approximately 1,000 words) or longer. Reprints or book ex-
cerpts are not eligible. All stories must be received by me no later
than February 1, 1994, and should include author name, publication name and date. Publications that want to make certain
their contributions will be considered for the next edition should
make sure to include this anthology on their subscription list.
Submissions or subscriptions should be sent to Glenn Stout, *The
Best American Sports Writing*, P.O. Box 963, Back Bay Annex, Boston, Massachusetts, 02117.

Once again I must thank the staff of the Boston Public Library
for being so responsive and considerate of the unique needs of
this project. I am also indebted to Doe Coover, Alan Andres,
Steve Lewers, Larry Cooper and Marnie Patterson for the growing success of this series. I am also grateful to John Dorsey for his
friendship and support, and Siobhan, who graciously shares my
company with several thousand magazines and newspapers for

much of each year. Guest editor Frank Deford approached his task with the same enthusiasm, sensitivity and intelligence one has grown accustomed to in his other projects. Yet it is the writers themselves, who write with such craft and concern on such a diffuse subject, that merit the greatest thanks. Their labor alone gives credence to the title of this volume.

GLENN STOUT

Introduction

VOCATIONALLY, the first thing I was was a newspaperman. Well, a newspaper boy. Not of the sort that flings them up the front walk — but a newspaper boy, because, as a boy I started putting out newspapers. First, one for my elementary school class, then one for my family. I ran the high school newspaper and then the college newspaper, and summers I worked for somebody else's newspaper, Mencken's old place, the *Baltimore Evening Sun*. I was attracted to the grown-up possibility of staying on there, eschewing college, making money doing what I had happily always done for free, but my mother quickly bashed that notion out of my foolish mind, and off I went to higher education, and thence to magazines.

Books followed. And other things — other *mediums*. Apart from ever authoring Chinese fortune cookies, I have written, with varying success, for just about all the other possible communication groups — magazines and books, fiction and nonfiction, movies, radio and television. But never newspapers. There were a couple of attractive opportunities that came along, but I never got back to newspapers, to my origins, until one fine day, in the lee of my fiftieth birthday, one of the richest men in the world invited me to help invent for him the first American daily sports newspaper.

The *National Sports Daily* went on the newsstands in 1990, coincidentally the year that this series began, celebrating the best in sports writing. One of us is still left. The *National* was out of business before the first edition of *The Best American Sports Writing* came out . . . with four selections from our *National* writers prominently included.

I remember how very proud that made me then. We were out of business, gone forever, but there was the cold comfort that, even in death, we were being remembered for our excellence. No other publication earned four selections in *The Best American Sports Writing*.

Of course, it is also true that all the other publications honored by having their work included are still in business. So, you can make of that what you will.

I hope you will indulge me if I bend your ear some about the *National* here. Typically, in this space, you would expect some sort of graceful essay on sports writing, the art. That's a finite subject, though (I'm awfully glad I'm not going to be, say, the seventeenth annual editor to muse here about sports writing, the art), and, anyway, I've already done that myself a maximum once, having put down my complete thoughts about sports writing, the art, in an introduction to my own collection a few years ago.

But the *National* was loved — I certainly loved it — and just enough time has elapsed since it was scuttled to permit those of us involved to become terribly nostalgic about it. So, if you don't give a hoot about hearing the prattling on from an old sea dog, wailing about how his schooner went down, him clinging to the tiller, in the great recession of '91, then I understand, and you may just skip ahead to the prize selections that follow.

Before you leave me, though, understand that the *National Sports Daily* was a newspaper that cared about good writing and sought (to the bitter end) to live by the premise that sports and good writing deserve to go together.

I would just like to get that on the record.

But then, maybe the record speaks for itself. All our surveys showed that sports fans were crazy about the *National*. Once, as a matter of fact, the polling company we hired felt obliged to go back and poll again because they doubted their own results; they had never found a publication so impossibly adored. But the re-survey produced the same statistically impossible raves.

Then, right after that, we folded.

It wasn't the recession that did us in, either. Certainly, we couldn't have picked a worse time to inaugurate a new newspaper — a new anything — than 1990. Advertising started plummeting everywhere in journalism approximately on the very day we opened. Still, we knew all along that the advertisers loved what we did and lusted after our prime audience of demographically correct young men. If we could have built the numbers, the advertisers would have come. But we couldn't, and they didn't.

Of course, since we folded, I have been surprised to discover that I have never met a male American who does not assure me that he devoured the *National* every waking day. We have come, I believe, to be reminiscent of Wilt Chamberlain's one-hundred-point game, which he put up against the New York Knicks. To this day, folks still come up to Wilt and tell him they were there at Madison Square Garden that unforgettable night he went for the hundred. And Wilt smiles and thanks them. The game he scored a hundred against the Knicks was played in Hershey, Pennsylvania. But those fans *wanted* to have been at Wilt's big game. Our fans *wanted* to read our paper every day. I trust them.

No, the *National* failed simply because we couldn't distribute the product. We had no idea what a daunting task it was to get out a national paper so that it could be on people's doorsteps when they awake in the morning — every morning — a *news*paper that not only comes every morning, as advertised, but that has all the results and the box scores and the updated statistics.

The inspiration for the *National* was the extraordinary, sustained success of such sports dailies in countries as disparate as France and Italy, Mexico and Japan. Unfortunately, what we didn't take into consideration was that as different as all those countries were in so many ways, they were also similar in one vital respect: each takes up only one time zone. Maybe if the United States didn't go across, but if it just went up and down, like Chile or the Philippines or Norway, maybe then we could have made a go of it. But, unfortunately, just as all those explorers hunting for the Northwest Passage found out three hundred years ago, America is terribly horizontal. The *National* was in good company, too, in dealing with this nagging happenstance: *USA Today* is a billion dollars in red ink trying to put out a national paper. The fact is, that of the species, the only one that has ever worked is the *Wall Street Journal*, which, of course, doesn't have to ever worry about any night games messing up its deadlines.

I hope I don't sound like I'm whining, though. This logistical stuff was not hard to figure out after the fact, and it should have been just as obvious to us going in.

Anyway, quite apart from all the business to-do, what surprised me most as an editor, as a journalist, was how suspicious, and even negative, others in the profession were to our stated objectives to emphasize quality — especially to emphasize "good writing." Almost from the first, the general response from the newspaper community was that quality was a pretty eccentric thing for a newspaper to concern itself with. The consensus we heard was that Americans no longer valued good writing, and . . . certainly they didn't if it took up more space than a "sound bite," and . . . even more certainly they didn't if it involved the déclassé subject of sports.

The saddest part of this assessment is how it came, almost exclusively, from the people in the business, the people putting out newspapers themselves. Readers, on the other hand, almost never complained that our stories were too highbrow or too long or had too many big words or what-have-you. In fact, readers were pretty laissez faire about the content of the whole paper. If someone wasn't interested in ice hockey, he skipped over the ice hockey standings; if someone wasn't interested in reading some long, thoughtful profile, he just turned that page. No one ever likes everything in a newspaper, but they do — I'm sure — like seeing a paper with lots of choices. The readers' response to our mix always reminded me of my favorite sports book review, one written by a John Duxbury about Joyce Carol Oates's book *On Boxing* for the *Sporting News,* to wit: "The award-winning author explains her interest in boxing in a book that is a blend of history, sociology and psychology. But be advised, it's difficult reading in many places and much of it was far above my intellectual level."

I am something of a contrarian when it comes to sports writing, anyhow. Whereas most critics assume that sports writing must be a home for clichés and awkward syntax, a retreat for writers who can't manage anything else, I've come to hold an opposing belief — that sports writing should be held to a higher standard than that generally imposed on the columns and stories that deal with more serious subjects. After all, sports is a game, a natural drama, peopled by characters who are good for our emotions, but not by the serious and somber "issues" that clutter up the rest of the world. There is more room to write and better material. Certainly, sports is rarely significant in the grand scheme of things, but sports *writing* should always be the most distinguished in any journal.

Regardless of the subject, there has grown abroad in the newspaper business — and magazines, too, for that matter — an almost pathological fear of length. Not all of this editorial support for the soul of wit is misguided, but what is so awfully wrong in this manic determination to minimalize everything is that the campaign is carried out for the wrong syllogistic reasons. Essentially, editors are not arguing that shorter articles are intrinsically better or even that the reader is better served that way, but simply on behalf of this rationale: television is short; television is powerful; ergo everything must be shorter if it is to compete and succeed in a television world.

The signal problem with the assumption (strictly from a business point of view) is that suddenly you have agreed to play by television's rules, and therefore into television's hands. If Aesop were alive today, I'm sure he would find this terribly fertile territory for his next fable. *USA Today*, which has been an important influence on other newspapers, most particularly uses television as its model . . . even as it loses oodles of money as a newpaper. But ultimately, no matter how accomplished *USA Today* can be at aping television, at borrowing the best of television, the fact is that *USA Today*, that no newspaper, can ever be as good at television as television itself. It is no surprise to me that *USA Today*'s sports pages are read for the box scores and stats — the agate numbers — which also happen to be the principal things that television does not supply the fan.

My reasoning is that if print beats television by supplying good sports numbers, and print can also supply good sports writing that television can't, then print should emphasize good writing rather than dismissing it.

I found, however, that, in the newspaper business, this is a decidedly minority view.

There are also specific factors at work on the sports pages

which lessen the attention to good writing. There are simply so many more teams out there, so many more games for any newspaper to cover. As a consequence, the best stories from years past are the sort never even assigned today.

Ah, and something else is in the wind. In sports, where disputation is the heart of the whole enterprise — bunt; hit away; who do you like?; my team is better than your team; sez who?; betcha — the dubious advancement of human dialogue in the form of the all-sports radio station has furthered that breathless state we find so common to all news reporting today. The print medium seems almost embarrassed to go at its own best pace, and more and more the sports pages are given over to breaking news to the exclusion of features.

In a curious way, too, this absolutely reverses the process that had been set in motion only a short while ago, one which celebrated sports writing and put aside space for the best of it. This began to transpire after the war, as newspapers began to merge and fold. The usual casualties were the afternoon papers, which had tended to be the more leisurely editions, the sort that Dad could put up his slippered feet with and read after a hard day at the office while Mom finished cooking the pot roast. The best of the afternoon writers were snapped up by the prevailing morning paper, and these surviving dailies had enough classified ads to turn over editorial space for long and thoughtful feature stories. As time went on, the genre was encouraged by the success of *Sports Illustrated,* which showcased lengthy, intelligent pieces, the sort that had previously only appeared in general interest magazines such as the *Saturday Evening Post* and *Collier's.*

Television was vital to the new equation, too. As readers were suddenly able to *see* games on TV, there was less demand for newspapers to carefully track play-by-play. Writers were encouraged to go behind the scenes, to better explain the games and the people playing them. In that sense, in the beginning television helped liberate sports writing.

Till this time, the sports writer was more limited in his choices. He could aspire to be a columnist, turning out an incendiary few well-chosen words several times a week (usually, it seemed, about whether or not to fire the manager) or to travel on sleeper trains with tobacco-chewing baseball teams. Many of the really fine sports writers — Ring Lardner, Paul Gallico, Damon Runyan and Jimmy Breslin — had to get out of sports to satisfy themselves. "Nothing on earth is more depressing than an old baseball writer," wrote Ring Lardner, who had been a young baseball writer.

The most renowned of the sports writers who stayed in the business tended not to be identified with writing, not even, in any real sense with journalism. Instead, they became regional liege lords. The worst of them were baldly corrupt, extracting tribute from whatever sports promoter hoped to do business in that territory. The most distinguished became a sort of unofficial sports mayor of their city, well-known civic treasures. In San Diego, they even named the new stadium after a sports editor, Jack Murphy. Can you imagine anything like that elsewhere in journalism? Can you imagine them naming a government building after a city hall reporter?

The new post-TV sports pages found a space for longer pieces, though — known in the trade as "takeouts" or "readers." The takeout writer became a prominent part of every sports section of any note. Moreover, a beautifully written monthly magazine, *Inside Sports,* was introduced as artistic competition for *Sports Illustrated,* and even the hoary old *Sporting News* cut back on the minor league box scores in order to run some profiles. Likewise, as television made more familiar heroes of sports stars, men's and general interest magazines began to feature more good sports stories.

It was in this tradition that we at the *National* planned to run what we called our Main Event, a four-page centerpiece that appeared most every day. As daunting a challenge as this was for a daily newspaper — especially for the two inspired editors in charge, Rob Fleder and David Granger — there never was any dearth of stories to fill up the Main Event. The only task was logistical, finding time enough for the writers and support photographers to turn out such original quality day in and day out.

One had to recall Mencken's observation that there are no dull subjects, only dull writers. The readers loved this special treat; it not only gave them a bonus, but it also signaled to them, I think, how seriously we took sports, how much we valued them. Still, right to the end the drumroll of criticism continued from other journalists, maintaining that Main Events were space-wasting, an anachronism, far too long for an impatient America that watches television with a clicker in its sweaty palm.

And, anyhow, I would have to admit that takeouts were going out of fashion even before the _National_ came into existence. There is no doubt that we were bucking the tide, taking the hems down when every other designer was taking them up. While there remain a few takeout specialists left on the most conscientious sports-writing sections, few of them are permitted as much time to work on a piece as they were in the happy days of yore, and virtually no one is hired anymore primarily for good writing skills.

There's a contraction in the scope of the subject matter, too. Newspapers and magazines alike used to pride themselves on colorful characters, on discovering the offbeat. But now that acreage has been ceded altogether to Charles Kuralt, and takeouts are only permitted to be written about the most obvious candidates, namely, the star quarterback, the coach, or the owner. It is unfortunate enough that newspapers are unduly influenced by television on matters of length and substance, but even worse, I think, by the unwritten corollary, Don't dare write about anything that isn't on TV. (Sometimes I think I'd like to start a magazine entitled _Stuff Not on Television_. What do you think of that?)

It is revealing, I'm afraid, that of the five stalwart writers and the two editors who performed the most regular work for the Main Event, most of them had to go to work in magazines after we folded. The only one who could find a newspaper job in the United States went to the _Washington Post_ — one of the very few papers left that regularly runs long readers. And sadly, as you will see from the index of this year's collection — and from the past two, as well — very few of the selections come from newspapers. "There isn't even any room left to run takeouts on Sundays," says one sports editor I know. Instead: too many games, scouting reports, charts, summaries and columns that . . . read . . . like . . . this . . . _all the way_ . . . through . . . with ellipses and bold type where normal punctuation once thrived.

It distresses me that while there is so much written these days in newspapers about sport, and there are so many good writers at work in our profession, so few of the best sports pieces come from that realm. Now, I did not get involved with the *National* primarily out of evangelical instincts. I never had any foolish literary illusions for our paper. I understood that foremost we had to deliver the scores and the stats and the contentious comment — the humor and the scolding alike — that makes up any lively sports page. Nonetheless, I also believed that we could bring to newspapers the highest possible literary component to tag along in the sidecar with the journalism.

And I think we succeeded.

Well, not in life after death. Newspaper competitors aped a great deal that we had done, but none of them saw fit to copy our emphasis on our long, well-written features. If anything, in fact, it seems obvious that the decline in that honorable old newspaper staple has been accelerated in the two years since the *National* went by the boards. Instead, the newspaper-that-would-be-a-TV-set grows in fashion, and the chance for young men and women to write — to really write well — for the everyday public fades. And, after a while, everybody may forget that there were newspaper *stories* once upon a time.

Sports writing is certainly not a higher calling, but it is, perhaps, a genuine form of literature. There isn't much you can get away with, writing sports, because too many of your readers are well informed on the subject at hand. It's such an honest audience, and, perhaps even more important, it's an *enthusiastic* audience. People who love sports will stay with a sports article and give it more of a chance, and so editors are wrong not to be more demanding.

The outfielder Charley Maxwell was always celebrated foremost for coming from the euphonious town of Paw Paw, Michigan. Maxwell was a reliable player, with enough longball skills to stick around for a number of years and play in a variety of cities, all of which boasted, at the time (a generation ago), a considerable newspaper presence. Dueling with one particularly persistent reporter once, who was trying to con Maxwell into saying something controversial, Maxwell finally replied: "I'll bet more people have gone to sleep reading newspapers than they have watching ball games."

Yes, Charley, I'll agree with that. But not sports sections. Nobody ever went to sleep reading a sports section. And I'm posi-

tive nobody ever nodded off reading the *National*. It breaks my heart still that we couldn't make it, and I just hope that if you particularly like any one of the wonderful sports stories that follow, you'll raise your eyes toward heaven and murmur lovingly, "Why, that would have been good enough for the old *National*."
Play ball.

FRANK DEFORD

The Best
AMERICAN
SPORTS
WRITING
1993

PETER RICHMOND

Tangled Up in Blue

FROM GQ

NIGHTTIME IN LOS ANGELES, on a quiet street off Melrose Avenue. An otherwise normal evening is marked by an oddly whimsical celestial disturbance: Baseballs are falling out of the sky.

They are coming from the roof of a gray apartment building. One ball pocks an adjacent apartment. Another bounces to the street. A third flies off into the night, a mighty shot.

This is West Hollywood in the early eighties, where anything is not only possible but likely. West Hollywood shakes its head and drives on by.

But if a passerby's curiosity had been piqued and he'd climbed to the roof of a neighboring building to divine the source of the show, he would have been rewarded by a most unusual sight: a man of striking looks, with long blond hair, startlingly and wincingly thin, hitting the ball with a practiced swing — a flat, smooth, even stroke developed during a youth spent in minor-league towns from Pocatello to Albuquerque.

This is not Tommy Lasorda, Jr.'s, routine nighttime activity. A routine night is spent in the clubs, the bright ones and dark ones alike.

Still, on occasion, here he'd be, on the roof, clubbing baseballs into the night. Because there were times when the pull was just too strong. Of the game. Of the father. He could never be what his father was — Tommy Lasorda's own inner orientation made that impossible — but he could fantasize, couldn't he? That he was ten, taking batting practice in Ogden, Utah, with his dad, and Garvey, and the rest of them?

And so, on the odd night, on a night he was not at Rage, or the Rose Tattoo, he'd climb to the roof, the lord of well-tanned West Hollywood, and lose himself in the steady rhythm of bat hitting ball — the reflex ritual that only a man inside the game can truly appreciate.

"Junior was the better hitter," recalls Steve Garvey. "He didn't have his father's curveball, but he was the better hitter."

"I cried," Tom Lasorda says quietly. He is sipping a glass of juice in the well-appointed lounge of Dodgertown, the Los Angeles baseball team's green-glorious oasis of a spring-training site. It's a place that heralds and nurtures out-of-time baseball and out-of-time Dodgers. A place where, each spring, in the season of illusion's renewal, they are allowed to be the men they once were.

On this February weekend, Dodgertown is crowded with clearly affluent, often out-of-shape white men, each of whom has parted with $4,000 to come to Dodgers fantasy camp. In pink polo shirts and pale-pink slacks — the pastels of privilege — they are scattered around the lounge, flirting with fantasy lives, chatting with the coaches.

"I cried. A lot of times. But I didn't cry in the clubhouse. I kept my problems to myself. I never brought them with me. I didn't want to show my family — that's my family away from my house. What's the sense of bringing my problems to my team?

". . . I had him for thirty-three years. Thirty-three years is better than nothing, isn't it? If I coulda seen God and God said to me 'I'm going to give you a son for thirty-three years and take him away after thirty-three years,' I'd have said 'Give him to me.' "

His gaze skips about the room — he always seems to be looking around for someone to greet, a hand to shake, another camper to slap another anecdote on. Tom Lasorda floats on an ever-flowing current of conversation.

"I signed that contract [to manage the Dodgers] with a commitment to do the best of my ability," he says. "If I'm depressed, what good does it do? When I walk into the clubhouse, I got to put on a winning face. A happy face. If I go in with my head hung down when I put on my uniform, what good does it do?"

These are words he has said before, in response to other inquiries about Tommy's death. But now the voice shifts tone and the words become more weighted; he frames each one with a new meaning.

And he stops looking around the room and looks me in the eye.

"I could say 'God, why was I dealt this blow? Does my wife — do I — deserve this?' [But] then how do I feel, hunh? Does it change it?" Now the voice grows even louder, and a few fantasy campers raise their eyebrows and turn their heads toward us.

"See my point?"

The words are like fingers jabbed into my chest.

"Hunh?"

Then his eyes look away and he sets his face in a flat, angry look of defiance.

"You could hit me over the head with a fucking two-by-four and you don't knock a tear out of me," he says.

"Fuck," he says.

The word does not seem to be connected to anything.

He was the second of five sons born, in Norristown, Pennsylvania, a crowded little city-town a half-hour north of Philadelphia, to Sabatino Lasorda, a truckdriver who'd emigrated from Italy, and Carmella Lasorda.

By the age of twenty-two, Tom Lasorda was a successful minor league pitcher by trade, a left-hander with a curveball and not a lot more. But he was distinguished by an insanely dogged belief in the possibility of things working out. His father had taught him that. On winter nights when he could not turn the heat on, Sabatino Lasorda would nonetheless present an unfailingly optimistic face to his family, and that was how Tom Lasorda learned that nothing could stomp on the human spirit if you didn't let it.

Tom Lasorda played for teams at nearly every level of professional ball: in Concord, New Hampshire; Schenectady, New York; Greenville, South Carolina; Montréal; Brooklyn (twice, briefly); Kansas City, Missouri; Denver; and Los Angeles. Once, after a short stay in Brooklyn, he was sent back to the minors so the Dodgers could keep a left-handed pitcher with a good fastball named Sandy Koufax, and to this day Lasorda will look you in the eye and say "I still think they made a mistake" and believe it.

The Dodgers saw the white-hot burn and made it into a minor-league manager. From 1965 to 1972, Lasorda's teams — in Pocatello, Ogden, Spokane, then Albuquerque — finished second, first, first, first, second, first, third and first. Sheer bravado was the tool; tent-preaching thick with obscenities the style.

In 1973, the Dodgers called him to coach for the big team, and he summoned his wife and his son and his daughter from Norristown, and they moved to Fullerton, California, a featureless sprawl of a suburb known for the homogeneity of its style of life and the conservatism of its residents.

In 1976, he was anointed the second manager in the Los Angeles Dodgers' nineteen-year history. His managing style was by instinct, not by the book, and his instincts were good enough to pay off more often than not. In his first two years, the Dodgers made the World Series. In 1981, they won it. In 1985, they didn't make it because Lasorda elected to have Tom Niedenfuer pitch to St. Louis's Jack Clark in the sixth game of the playoffs, against the odds, and Jack Clark hit a three-run home run. In 1988, though, he sent a limping Kirk Gibson to the plate and gave us a moment for history.

From the first, Lasorda understood that he had to invent a new identity for this team, the team that Walter O'Malley had yanked out of blue-collar-loyal Brooklyn-borough America and dropped into a city whose only real industry was manufacturing the soulless stuff of celluloid fantasy. His clubhouse became a haunt for show-business personalities, usually of distinctly outsized demeanor — Sinatra, Rickles — and he himself became the beacon of a new mythology, leader of the team that played in a ballpark on a hill on a road called Elysian, perched above the downtown, high and imperious. Because, really, aren't there too many theme parks to compete with in Los Angeles to manage your baseball team as anything other than another one?

In sixteen years, the tone of the sermon has seldom faltered, at least not before this year. This year, through no fault of Tom Lasorda's, his fielders have forgotten how to field, in a game in which defense has to be an immutable; and if this is anyone's fault, it's that of the men who stock the farm system. His pitching is vague, at best. So the overwhelming number of one-run games — most of which the Dodgers lost — is, in fact, testament, again, to Lasorda's management. No one has questioned his competence.

His spirit has flagged considerably, but his days, in season and out, are as full of Dodger Blue banquet appearances as ever, with impromptu Dodgers pep rallies in airport concourses from Nashville to Seattle. Unlike practitioners of Crystal Cathedral pulpitry, Lasorda the tent-preacher believes in what he says, which, of course, makes all the difference in the world. Because of his faith, Dodger Blue achieves things, more things than you can imagine. The lights for the baseball field in Caledonia, Mississippi; the fund for the former major leaguer with cancer in Pensacola: Tom showed up, talked Dodger Blue, raised the money. Tom's word maintains the baseball field at Jackson State and upgraded the facilities at Georgia Tech.

"I was in Nashville," Tom says, still sitting in the lounge, back on automatic now, reciting. "Talking to college baseball coaches, and a buddy told me nine nuns had been evicted from their home. I got seven or eight dozen balls [signed by Hall of Fame players], we auctioned them, and we built them a home. They said, 'We prayed for a miracle, and God sent you to us.' "

Nine nuns in Nashville.

In the hallway between the lounge and the locker room hang photographs of Brooklyn Dodgers games. Lasorda has pored over them a thousand times, with a thousand writers, a thousand campers, a thousand Dodgers prospects — identifying each player, re-creating each smoky moment.

But on this day, a few minutes after he's been talking about Tommy, he walks this gauntlet differently.

"That's Pete Reiser," Tom Lasorda says. "He's dead." He points to another player. He says, "He's dead." He walks down the hallway, clicking them off, talking out loud but to himself.

"He's dead. He's dead. He's dead. He's dead. He's dead. He's dead."

Back in his suite, in the residence area of Dodgertown, I ask him if it was difficult having a gay son.

"My son wasn't gay," he says evenly, no anger. "No way. No way. I read that in a paper. I also read in that paper that a lady gave birth to a fuckin' monkey, too. That's not the fuckin' truth. That's not the truth."

I ask him if he read in the same paper that his son had died of AIDS.

"That's not true," he says.

I say that I thought a step forward had been taken by Magic Johnson's disclosure of his own HIV infection, that that's why some people in Los Angeles expected him to . . .

"Hey," he says. "I don't care what people . . . I know what my son died of. I know what he died of. The doctor put out a report of how he died. He died of pneumonia."

He turns away and starts to brush his hair in the mirror of his dressing room. He is getting ready to go to the fantasy-camp barbecue. He starts to whistle. I ask him if he watched the ceremony on television when the Lakers retired Johnson's number.

"I guarantee you one fuckin' thing," he says. "I'll lay you three to one Magic plays again [in the NBA]. Three to one. That Magic plays again."

As long as he's healthy, I say. People have lived for ten years with the right medication and some luck. Your quality of life can be good, I say.

Lasorda doesn't answer. Then he says, "You think people would have cared so much if it had been Mike Tyson?"

On death certificates issued by the state of California, there are three lines to list the deceased's cause of death, and after each is a space labeled TIME INTERVAL BETWEEN ONSET AND DEATH.

Tom Lasorda, Jr.'s, death certificate reads:

IMMEDIATE CAUSE: A) PNEUMONITIS — 2 WEEKS
DUE TO: B) DEHYDRATION — 6 WEEKS
DUE TO: C) PROBABLE ACQUIRED IMMUNE DEFI-
CIENCY SYNDROME — 1 YEAR.

At Sunny Hills High School, in Fullerton, California — "the most horrible nouveau riche white-bread high school in the world," recalls Cat Gwynn, a Los Angeles photographer and filmmaker and a Sunny Hills alumna — Tommy Lasorda moved through the hallways with a style and a self-assurance uncommon in a man so young; you could see them from afar, Tommy and his group. They were all girls, and they were all very pretty. Tommy was invariably dressed impeccably. He was as beautiful as his friends. He had none of his father's basset-hound features; Tommy's bones were carved, gently, from glass.

"It was very obvious that he was feminine, but none of the jocks nailed him to the wall or anything," Gwynn says. "I was en-amored of him because he wasn't at all uncomfortable with who he was. In this judgmental, narrow-minded high school, he strut-ted his stuff."

In 1980, at the Fashion Institute of Design and Merchandis-ing, Cindy Stevens and Tommy Lasorda shared a class in color theory. Tommy, Stevens recalls, often did not do his homework. He would spend a lot of his time at Dodgers games or on the road with the team. At school, they shared cigarettes in the hall-way. Tommy would tell her about the latest material he'd bought to have made into a suit. She'd ask him where the money came from. Home, he'd say.

"He talked lovingly about his father and their relationship — they had a very good relationship," Stevens says now. "I was sur-prised. I didn't think it'd be like that. You'd think it'd be hard on a macho Italian man. This famous American idol. You'd figure it'd be [the father saying] 'Please don't let people know you're my son,' but it was the opposite. I had new respect for his father. There had to be acceptance from his mom and dad. Tommy had that good self-esteem — where you figure that [his] parents did something right."

In the late seventies, Tommy left Fullerton, moving only an hour northwest in distance — though he might as well have been crossing the border between two sovereign nations — to West Hollywood, a pocket of gay America unlike any other, a com-munity bound by the shared knowledge that those within it had been drawn by its double distinction: to be among gays, and to be in Hollywood. And an outrageous kid from Fullerton, ready to take the world by storm, found himself dropped smack into the soup — of a thousand other outrageous kids, from Apple-ton, and Omaha, and Scranton.

But Tommy could never stand to be just another anything. The father and the son had that in common. They had a great deal in common. Start with the voice: gravelly, like a car trying to start on a cold morning. The father, of course, spends his life barking and regaling, never stopping; he's baseball's oral poet, an anti-Homer. It's a well-worn voice. Issuing from the son, a man so attractive that men tended to assume he was a woman, it was the most jarring of notes. One of his closest friends compared it to Linda Blair's in *The Exorcist* — the scenes in which she was possessed.

More significantly, the father's world was no less eccentric than the son's: The subset of baseball America found in locker rooms and banquet halls is filled with men who have, in large part, managed quite nicely to avoid the socialization processes of the rest of society.

Then, the most obvious similarity: Both men were so outrageous, so outsized and surreal in their chosen persona, that, when it came down to it, for all of one's skepticism about their sincerity, it was impossible not to like them — not to, finally, just give in and let their version of things wash over you, rather than resist. Both strutted an impossibly simplistic view of the world — the father with his gospel of fierce optimism and blind obeisance to a baseball mythology, and the son with a slavery to fashion that he carried to the point of religion.

But where the illusion left off and reality started, that was a place hidden to everyone but themselves. In trying to figure out what each had tucked down deep, we can only conjecture. "You'd be surprised what agonies people have," Dusty Baker, the former Dodger, reminds us, himself a good friend of both father and son, a solid citizen in a sport that could use a few more. "There's that old saying that we all have something that's hurting us."

In the case of the son, friends say the West Hollywood years were born of a Catch-22 kind of loneliness: The more bizarre the lengths to which he went to hone the illusion, the less accessible he became. In his last years, friends say, everything quieted down, markedly so. The flamboyant life gave way to a routine of health clubs and abstinence and sobriety and religion. But by then, of course, the excesses of the earlier years had taken their inexorable toll.

As for the father, there's no question about the nature of the demon he's been prey to for the past two years. Few in his locker room saw any evidence of sadness as his son's illness grew worse, but this should come as no surprise: Tom Lasorda has spent most of four decades in the same baseball uniform. Where else would he go to get away from the grief?

"Maybe," Baker says, "his ballpark was his sanctuary."

It's a plague town now, there's no way around it. At brunch at the French Quarter, men stop their conversations to lay out their pills on the tables, and take them one by one with sips of juice. A mile west is Rage, its name having taken on a new meaning. Two blocks away, on Santa Monica Boulevard, at A Different Light, atop the shelves given over to books on how to manage to stay alive for another few weeks, sit a dozen clear bottles, each filled with amber fluid and a rag — symbolic Molotovs, labeled with the name of a man or a woman or a government agency that is setting back the common cause, reinforcing the stereotypes, driving the social stigmata even deeper into West Hollywood's already weakened flesh.

But in the late seventies, it was a raucous, outrageous and joyous neighborhood, free of the pall that afflicted hetero Los Angeles, thronged as it was with people who'd lemminged their way out west until there was no more land, fugitives from back east.

In the late seventies and the early eighties, say his friends and his acquaintances and those who knew him and those who watched him, Tommy Lasorda was impossible to miss. They tell stories that careen from wild and touching to sordid and scary; some ring true, others fanciful. Collected, they paint a neon scar of a boy slashing across the town. They trace the path of a perfect, practiced, very lonely shooting star.

His haunt was the Rose Tattoo, a gay club with male strippers, long closed now. One night, he entered — no, he made an entrance — in a cape, with a pre-power ponytail and a cigarette holder: Garbo with a touch of Bowie and the sidelong glance of Veronica Lake. He caught the eye of an older man. They talked. In time, became friends. In the early eighties, they spent a lot of time together. Friends is all they were. They were very much alike.

"I'm one of those gentlemen who liked him," says the man. "I was his Oscar Wilde. He liked me because I was an older guy who'd tasted life. I was his Mame. I showed him life. Art. Theater. I made him a little more sophisticated. [Showed him] how to dress a little better."

They spent the days poolside at a private home up behind the perfect pink stucco of the Beverly Hills Hotel, Tommy lacquering himself with a tan that was the stuff of legend. The tan is de rigueur. The tan is all. It may not look like work, but it is; the work is to look as good as you can.

He occasionally held a job, never for long. Once, he got work at the Right Bank, a shoe store, to get discounts. His father bought him an antique-clothing store. He wearied of it. Tommy, says one friend, wanted to be like those women in soap operas who have their own businesses but never actually work at them.

Tommy's look was his work. If there were others who were young and lithe and handsome and androgynous, none were as outré as Tommy. Tommy never ate. A few sprouts, some fruit, a potato. Tommy spent hours at the makeup table. Tommy studied portraits of Dietrich and Garbo to see how the makeup was done. Tommy bleached his hair. On his head. On his legs. Tommy had all of his teeth capped. Tommy had a chemabrasion performed on his face, in which an acid bath removes four of the skin's six layers. Then the skin is scrubbed to remove yet another layer. It is generally used to erase scars or wrinkles. Tommy had two done.

But he smoked, and he drank. Champagne in a flute, cigarette in a long holder, graceful and vampish at the same time: This was Tommy at the Rose Tattoo. His friend also remembers how well Tommy and his father got along. His friend would drive Tommy to the Italian restaurant where he'd meet his father for Sunday dinners.

"He loved his father, you know. They got along perfectly well." His friend was never his lover. Only his friend. That was all. That was enough. "He was very lonely."

On occasion, the nighttime ramble led him far from the stilted elegance of Santa Monica Boulevard. In the punk clubs, amid the slam-dancing and the head-butting, Tommy parted the leathered seas, a chic foil for all the pierced flesh and fury, this man who didn't sweat. This man who crossed himself when someone swore in public.

Penelope Spheeris met him at Club Zero. She would go on to direct the punk documentary *The Decline of Western Civilization* and, years later, *Wayne's World*. They became friends. They met at punk clubs — the blond man in custom-made suits, the striking woman in black cocktail dresses and leather boots. In 1981, she interviewed Tommy for a short-lived underground paper called *No Mag*.

PENELOPE: Have you been interviewed very much before?

TOMMY: No, but I'm very . . . *oral*. . . .

PENELOPE: People who would see you around town, they would probably think you were gay.

TOMMY: *I don't care.*

PENELOPE: What do you do when you get that reaction from them?

TOMMY: I like all people. And it's better having comments, be it GOOD, BAD or WHATEVER. I don't mind at all, but I dress quite . . . well, I wouldn't say it's FLAMBOYANT because it's not intentional. *It's just intentionally ME*.

PENELOPE: O.K., but you understand, when somebody looks at a picture of you, they're going to say, *this guy's awfully feminine*.

TOMMY: I'm there for anyone to draw any conclusions.

PENELOPE: Are you?

TOMMY: Well, I mean, I've done different things . . . of course. . . . I have *no label on myself* because then I have restrictions. I would really hate to state anything like that.

PENELOPE: When you were young did your dad say, "Come on, Tommy, Jr., *let's go play baseball*"?

TOMMY: *Never.* They always allowed me to do exactly what I pleased. I don't know how they had the sense to be that way. As parents they're both so . . . well, very straitlaced and conservative. I don't know how I was allowed to just be ME, but I think it was because I was so strongly ME that I don't think they thought they could ever STOP IT. . . .

PENELOPE: Do you feel like you should be careful in the public eye?

TOMMY: *I feel like I should,* but I don't.

PENELOPE: Do you think the press would be mean to you if they had the chance?

TOMMY: I'm sure they would, but I'll take ANY PUBLICITY.

PENELOPE: Why?

TOMMY: Because that's what I want. . . . I do everything TO BE SEEN.

"I found him totally fascinating. He was astoundingly beautiful, more than most women," Spheeris says now. "I became interested in . . . the blatant contrast in lifestyles. Tommy Lasorda, Sr., was so involved in that macho sports world, and his son was the opposite. . . ."

She laughs.

"I was astounded at how many clothes he had. I remember walking into the closet. The closet was as big as my living room. Everything was organized perfectly. Beautiful designer clothes he looked great in."

Often in the early eighties, when fashion photographer Eugene Pinkowski's phone would ring, it would be Tommy. Tommy wanting to shop or Tommy wanting Eugene to photograph his new look.

When they went shopping, they would fly down Melrose in Tommy's Datsun 280Z, much, much too fast, Tommy leaning out of the driver's window, hair flying in the wind, like some Valley Girl gone weird, hurling gravelly insults ("Who did your hair? It looks awful") at the pedestrians diving out of the way.

He was a terrible driver. Once he hit a cat. He got out of the car, knelt on the street and cried. He rang doorbells up and down the street, trying to find the owner.

Tommy would call to tell Eugene he was going to buy him a gift. Then Tommy would spend all his money on himself. Then, the next day, Tommy would make up for it. He would hand him something. A pair of porcelain figures, babies, a boy and a girl, meant to be displayed on a grand piano — very difficult to find, very expensive.

Then the phone would ring. It'd be Eugene's mother, saying she just got a bracelet. From his friend Tommy.

"He was a character," Pinkowski says at breakfast in a Pasadena coffee shop. "He was a case. He was a complete and total case."

Then he looks away.

"He was really lonely," Pinkowski says. "He was sad."

When he was being photographed, Tommy was always trying to become different people.

Eugene captured them all. Tommy with long hair. With short hair. With the cigarette. Without it. With some of his exceptionally beautiful women friends. Tommy often had beautiful women around him, Pinkowski recalls — vaguely European, vaguely models. Sometimes Tommy had Pinkowski take pictures of them.

Mostly he took pictures of Tommy. Tommy with a stuffed fox. Lounging on the floor. In the piano. Sitting in a grocery cart.

In red. In green. In white. In blue. In black and gray.

His four toes. Tommy had four toes on his right foot, the fifth lost in a childhood accident. He posed the foot next to a gray boot on the gray carpet. Then he posed it next to a red shoe on the gray carpet. The red looked better.

Tommy and his foot were a regular subject of conversation, often led by Tommy.

"Tommy was a great storyteller, and he'd tell you stories of his dad in the minor leagues," Pinkowski says. "Everybody'd like him. He was very much like the old boy. He could really hold his own in a group of strangers. And he'd do anything to keep it going. To be the center of attention. He'd just suddenly take his shoe and sock off at dinner and say 'Did you know I was missing my toe?' "

One day, Tommy wanted to pose wrapped in a transparent shower curtain. Tommy was wearing white underwear. For forty-five minutes they tried to light the shot so that the underwear was concealed, to no avail. Tommy left, and returned in flesh-colored underwear.

There was nothing sexual about Tommy's fashion-posing. Tommy's fashion-posing was designed to get Tommy into fashion magazines. Tommy was forever bugging the editors of *Interview* to feature him, but they wouldn't.

"As beautiful as he was, as famous as his father was, he thought he should be in magazines," Pinkowski says now. "He was as hungry as Madonna. But Bowie and Grace [Jones] could do something. He couldn't do anything. He could never see any talent in himself."

The closest Tommy came was when he bought himself a full page in *Stuff* magazine, in 1982, for a picture of himself that Eugene took.

He would pay Eugene out of the house account his parents had set up for him. On occasion, Eugene would get a call from

Tommy's mother: We don't need any more pictures this year. Still, Tommy would have several of his favorites printed for his parents. One is from the blue period.

At the Duck Club, down behind the Whiskey, in 1985, Tommy sat in a corner drinking Blue Hawaiians. To match his blue waistcoat. Or his tailored blue Edwardian gabardine jacket. This was during his blue period. In his green period, he was known to wear a green lamé wrap and drink crème de menthe. But the blue period lasted longer. The good thing about the blue period was that on the nights he didn't want to dress up, he could wear denim and still match his drink. And, sometimes, his mood.

"He walked around with a big smile on his face, as if everything was great because he had everything around him to prove it was great," Spheeris says. "But I don't think it was. . . . When you're that sad, you have to cover up a lot of pain. But he didn't admit it."

The nature of the pain will forever be in debate. Few of his friends think it had to do with the relationship with his parents. "The parents — both of them — were incredibly gracious and kind to everyone in Tommy's life," says a close friend of the family's.

Alex Magno was an instructor at the Voight Fitness and Dance Center and became one of Tommy's best friends. Tommy was the godfather of his daughter. "We used to ask him, 'You're thirty-three, what kind of life is that — you have no responsibilities. Why don't you work?' " says Magno. "You lose your identity when you don't have to earn money, you know what I mean? Everything he owns, his parents gave him. I never heard him say 'I want to do my own thing.' When you get used to the easy life, it's hard to go out there. I don't think he appreciated what he had."

He loved the Dodgers. He attended many games each season. His father regularly called him from the road. In his office at Dodger Stadium, the father kept a photograph of Tommy on his desk.

Tommy loved the world of the Dodgers. He loved the players. To friends who were curious about his relationship with his fa-

ther's team — and all of them were — he said it was great. He
told Spheeris they were a turn-on.

"He was a good, sensitive kid," says Dusty Baker, now a coach
with the San Francisco Giants. "There was an article one time.
Tommy said I was his favorite player because we used to talk music all the time. He loved black female artists. He turned me on
to Linda Clifford. He loved Diana Ross. He loved Thelma Houston.

"Some of the guys kidded me. Not for long. Some of the guys
would say stuff — you know how guys are — but most were
pretty cool. That's America. Everybody's not going to be cool.
Most people aren't going to be. Until they have someone close to
them afflicted. Which I have."

Baker spent last Christmas Eve distributing turkey dinners
with the Shanti Foundation, an AIDS-education group in California.

"There are a lot of opinions about Tom junior, about how [his
father] handled his relationship with his son," says Steve Garvey,
who more than anyone was the onfield embodiment of Dodger
Blue. "Everyone should know that there is this Tom [senior] who
really loved his son and was always there for him. The two loving
parents tried to do as much for him as he chose to let them do.
. . . Junior chose a path in life, and that's his prerogative. That's
every individual's right."

Garvey attended the memorial service for Alan Wiggins, his
former teammate on the San Diego Padres, who died of an
AIDS-related illness last year, after a seven-year career in the
majors.

"He was a teammate, we always got along well, he gave me one
hundred percent effort, played right next to me. I think the least
you can do, when you go out and play in front of a million people
and sweat and pull muscles and bleed and do that as a living,
when that person passes away, is be there. It's the right thing to
do."

Garvey was the only major league baseball player at Wiggins's
service. I ask him if he was surprised that he was alone.

"Not too much surprises me in life anymore," Garvey says.

In the mid-1980s, Tommy's style of life changed. It may have
been because he learned that he had contracted the human im-

munodeficiency virus. According to Alex Magno, he knew he
was infected for years before his death. It may have been that he
simply grew weary of the scene. It may have been that he grew
up.

He entered a rehabilitation program. He became a regular at
the Voight gym, attending classes seven days a week. Henry Sie-
gel, the Voight's proprietor, was impressed by Tommy's self-
assurance and generosity. Tommy moved out of his West Hollywood place into a new condo in Santa Monica, on a quiet, neat
street a few blocks from the beach — an avenue of trimmed
lawns and stunning gardens displayed beneath the emerald can-
opies of old and stalwart trees. "T. L. Jʀ." reads the directory
outside the locked gate; beyond it, a half-dozen doorways open
onto a carefully tiled courtyard. The complex also features
Brooke Shields on its list of tenants.

He was a quiet tenant, a thoroughly pleasant man. He had a
new set of friends — whom he regaled, in his best raconteurial
fashion, with tales of the past.

"Tommy used to tell us incredible stuff about how he used to
be . . . everything he'd done — drugs, sleeping with women,
sleeping with men," says Magno.

"He went through the homosexual thing and came out of it,"
Magno continues. "Gay was the thing to be back when he first
came to L.A. Tommy used to tell his friends he had been gay. He
didn't pretend. He let people know he had been this wild, crazy
guy who had changed. He was cool in that. When you got to meet
him, you got to know everything about him."

Including that he slept with guys?

"Yes. But . . . he didn't want to admit he had AIDS because
people would say he was gay."

This apparent contradiction surfaces regularly in the tale of
Tommy Lasorda.

"I think he wanted to make his father happy," says his Oscar
Wilde. "But he didn't know how to. He wanted to be more macho
but didn't know how to. He wanted to please his dad. He wished
he could have liked girls. He tried."

No one who knew Tommy in the seventies and the early
eighties recalls him having a steady romantic relationship. Pinkowski remarks on the asexual nature of the masks his friend

kept donning — and about how his friend kept some sides of himself closed off. "He'd never talk about being gay. He'd never reveal himself that way. He'd never say anything about anybody that way."

"Of course he was gay," says Jeff Kleinman, the manager of a downtown restaurant who used to travel the same club circuit as Lasorda in the early eighties. "No, I never saw him with another guy as a couple. [But] just because a man doesn't have a date doesn't mean he isn't gay! To say he wasn't gay would be like saying Quentin Crisp isn't gay. How could you hide a butterfly that was so beautiful?"

"Please," says his Oscar Wilde. "He was gay. He was gay. He was gay."

"Gay," of course, is not a word that describes sexual habits. It speaks of a way of living. No one interviewed for this story thought that Tommy wasn't gay; reactions to his father's denial range from outrage and incredulity to laughter and a shake of the head. Former major league umpire Dave Pallone, who revealed his own homosexuality in an autobiography two years ago, knows the father well, and also knew his son.

"Tommy senior is, as far as I'm concerned, a tremendous man," says Pallone. "I consider him a friend. I have a lot of empathy for what he's going through. [But] as far as I'm concerned, I don't think he ever accepted the fact that his son was a gay man. I knew him to be a gay man, and I knew a lot of people who knew him as a gay man.

"We don't want to be sexual beings. We just want to be human beings."

"If nothing else, his father should be proud that he repented," Alex Magno says. "He'd come a long way — denying what he used to be, so happy with what he'd become."

I tell him his father denies the illness.

"He died of AIDS," Magno says. "There's no question. But what difference does it make? He was a good man. He was a great man. You shouldn't judge. He had had no sex for a long time. We didn't know how he could do that. I mean . . . but he was incredible. He gave up everything. That's what he said, and there was no reason not to believe him. He was totally like a normal man. He was still feminine — that gets in your system — but there was no lust after men."

In the last two years of his life, Tommy's illness took its toll on his looks. He was not ashamed, though. The surface self-assurance remained. One night, he made an entrance into Rage — thinner, not the old Tommy, but acting every bit the part. He still showed up at Dodger Stadium, too, with his companion, a woman named Cathy Smith, whom Tom senior said was Tommy's fiancée. When he did, he was as elegant and debonair as ever: wide-brimmed hats, tailored suits.

"Nobody in their right mind is going to say it's not difficult — I know how difficult it is for them to try and understand their son," Dave Pallone says. "And to accept the fact he's not with them and what the real reason is. But . . . here was a chance wasted. The way you get rid of a fear is by attacking it. . . . Can you imagine if the Dodgers, who are somewhat conservative, could stand up and say, 'We understand this is a problem that needs to be addressed. . . . We broke down the barriers from the beginning with Jackie Robinson. Why can't we break down the barriers with the AIDS epidemic?' "

A close friend who was with Tommy the day before his death vehemently disagrees.

"If his father has to accept his son's death right now in that way, let him do it," she says. "If he can't accept things yet, he may never be able to . . . but what good does it do? [Tom's] world is a different world. We should all do things to help, yes, but at the same time, this is a child who someone's lost. Some people have the fortitude, but they simply don't have the strength. . . . There comes a point, no matter how public they may be, [at which] we need to step back and let them be. You can't force people to face what they don't want to face without hurting them."

"There's something wrong with hiding the truth," Penelope Spheeris says. "It's just misplaced values. It is a major denial. People need to know these things. Let's get our values in the right place. That's all."

*

"I'm in a position where I can help people, so I help people,"
Tom Lasorda says. We are strolling through the night in Dodgertown, toward the fantasy-camp barbecue. "You don't realize
the enjoyment I got with those nuns in that convent. I can't describe how good that made me feel."

I ask him what his dad would say if he were alive.

"I think he'd have been so proud of me. My father was the
greatest man."

He tells me that his winters are so busy with appearances that
"you wouldn't believe it." I ask him why he doesn't slow down.

"I don't know," he says. "I like to help people. I like to give
something back."

On Valentine's Day, 1991, Eugene Pinkowski's phone rang. It
was Tommy. His voice was weak.

"He was typical Tommy. He was really noble about it. He was
weak, you could tell. I was so sad. He said, in that voice, 'I'm sure
you've read that I'm dying. Well, I am.'

"Then he said, 'Thank you for being so nice to me during my
lifetime.' He said, 'I want to thank you, because you made me
look good.'"

On June 3, 1991, with his parents and his sisters at his bedside,
in the apartment on the cool, flower-strewn street, Tommy Lasorda died.

His memorial service was attended by Frank Sinatra and Don
Rickles. Pia Zadora sang "The Way We Were," one of Tommy
junior's favorite songs.

Tom Lasorda asked that all donations go to the Association of
Professional Ball Players of America, a charity that helps former
ballplayers in need, one of two charities to which baseball players
in trouble can turn for help. It is a conservative group, known
for its refusal to offer assistance to ballplayers who fall into the
trap of substance abuse.

In the coffee shop in Pasadena, it is late morning, and Eugene
Pinkowski is lingering, remembering. His Tommy portfolio is
spread across the table. Tommy is smiling at us from a hundred
pictures.

I ask Eugene if Tommy would have wanted this story written.

"Are you kidding?" he says. "If there's any sort of afterlife, Tommy is looking down and cheering. This is something he wanted. To be remembered like this. He'd be in heaven."

OCTOBER 1992

PETER RICHMOND *is one of the most enthusiastic writers I have ever met. He could teach any apprentice a valuable lesson: either like the person or thing you're profiling or, if you can't, learn to care just as much for the telling of the story. I know Peter was torn by this excruciating piece, because he knew how much Tommy Lasorda hated him writing about his son, and it frustrated Peter terribly that he couldn't make Tommy understand that the story really is a tribute to both the son and the father. It is, Tommy; it is.* — F.D.

ROY BLOUNT, JR.

Blunder Road

FROM MEN'S JOURNAL

THE NORTHERN CALIFORNIA COUNTRYSIDE was a vibrant blur,
and my car and I were alone, moving together, vehhhhhhhn,
knowing each other, as I squeezed and feathered the brake —
chirp, my back Goodyears sang to me, chirp — with one side of
my right foot, blipped the gas — VUM — with the other side,
moved my left foot from the dead pedal to the clutch (not that
I was conscious of all this footwork, for it had become second
nature), slipped smoothly into third, checked the tach (holding steady at five grand) and swept round the blind downhill corner as if the pavement were packed snow and I were
lying back on a Flexible Flyer powered by 100 invisible horses,
vahhhhhhn....

That may be how you want this story to begin. It may be
how I would like it to begin, myself. But this is how it is going to
begin:

"Unless you're sure that the car is in neutral, Roy, I just can't
talk to you anymore," said Kelly Collins, one of the Skip Barber
Racing School's Three Day Competition Course instructors, as
he crouched down next to the Formula Ford racecar I found myself elaborately strapped into all by myself on the morning of the
first day.

Evidently the car had been in second, fourth or some other
forward gear when I coasted to a stop, feeling rather pleased
with my coasting. After Kelly crouched close by the car to in-
struct me, I had let my foot off the clutch and the car had
lurched, causing Kelly to jump and then give me a look.

"Because this wheel," he continued, pointing to the right rear one, "will run over me."

I looked at the wheel. Rather than being where it ought to be, under the car, it was way out on the side. And so were the other three. That much wasn't my fault: The car was designed that way. It was also designed so that I was lying down in it, and my ass was only three inches off the pavement.

Several other things, however, were my fault apparently, because Kelly went on to make several helpfully withering comments about the lap I had just driven around blind and S and hairpin and up- and downhill curves at speeds that struck me as already breakneck and that were going to be doubled by the end of the course. And I determined that this would be one of my goals: to make it through the three days of the course without running over any of my instructors, even Kelly.

But I was also up for some speed, for some whipping around corners. What I didn't reckon with was being expected to do these things *right*.

My instructors were professional racecar drivers. They had been racing motorcycles and snow boards and various other vehicles since childhood. With a diploma from the Skip Barber Competition Course you can actually drive in serious professional auto races. After hurtling some 250 miles over the Sears Point International Raceway track (one of the most technically demanding tracks in the world), in Sonoma, California, I have been awarded that diploma, on one condition: that I never even think about using it.

Fair enough. It's not as if I aspire to be the next Mario Andretti. But sometimes now on the road I remember that big round G-feeling, the force of a sweeping downhill curve pushing me and that little shell of a car away while I lean in and squeeze power through the arc I want — like a running back digging and torquing to turn a corner while a big linebacker tries to shove him out of bounds — and . . . and then I remember the time I determined to really show 'em some rotation on this turn, and I locked up the brakes and plowed way off the track, ninety degrees from the direction I was supposed to go, and I thought, "Well, I didn't quite nail that one," and I came around to be critiqued by Kelly, who said, "There's no excuse for that."

No excuse?

Maybe I should have worked my way up to the Competition Course by way of Advanced Driving and Introduction to Racing. The other seven guys in the course were an airline pilot, a professional skateboarder, an Olympic steeplechase rider, a graduate of Go Kart school, a carwash magnate whose lifetime dream was to drive a racecar, a graduate of another competition course in Europe and a professional golfer whose father used to be an official of the Indianapolis 500. All of whom spoke familiarly of Porsches, Alfa Romeos and Beemers.

Nothing against my classmates, who were unfailingly cordial when they might have felt justified in feeling infinitely superior to me, car-racing-wise. Nice people. Enjoyed their company. But generally speaking I do not hang out with people who say "Beemer."

For my part, for day-to-day road performance I look less to my engine, suspension and tranny than I do to my tape deck. My automotive pleasure is to move along briskly, with as much space as possible between me and everybody else on the road, in some low-maintenance vehicle that costs less than I paid for my first house, in 1966: $14,750. Lately I drive a Volkswagen Jetta. I like it. But I still have a soft spot in my heart for the Plymouth Horizon Miser I operated between 1981 and 1986, which got forty-two miles to the gallon and had enough headroom that I could wear a hat without getting a crick in my neck. That car could get way over the speed limit, even (if you planned ahead) uphill.

Which frankly I do not think disqualifies me as an American man. I have been making good time and passing people on the highway for thirty-five years. I have driven in forty-one states of the union — receiving tickets in seven — and in several foreign locales, including Senegal (where I got stuck in red sand), Paris, Iceland (where I got stuck in black sand) and London. I have driven a sleeping child through a blizzard, my ex-mother-in-law's Pontiac over the Rockies in an ice storm and a woman in a straw hat and a flowery dress down to Mexico. I have driven with a sick black cat wound around my neck like a steel coil.

Of course, when Mark Epperson, the pilot, told me, "In the navy I flew jets six hundred miles an hour at fifty feet, but this is more *connected*," I hated to come back with, "Well, one time in this little yellow Horizon I used to have, I was rushing the cat to the vet, and . . ."

"Maybe I have been depriving myself," I thought, as I sat there in class in my flameproof jumpsuit (with patches saying SKF BEARINGS, BOSCH SPARKPLUGS, KONI SOMETHINGS and also, I hoped not ominously, EASTERN AIRLINES), holding my sixteen-pound visored helmet in my lap. Maybe I drive the way people who read Sidney Sheldon read, the way people who eat Stove Top Stuffing eat, the way people who voted for George Bush vote. Maybe I am not getting what is to be got.

So I tried. I swear I tried. For three days, from eight till five, we'd sit in a classroom for an hour as our instructors drew everything from the pedals we had to heel-and-toe to the envelope one hoped to push, and then, *voom*, we were out in the cars, first driving through a short slalom course (somehow I managed to break my ignition key in that), and then after another lecture taking laps around the actual track, then another lecture and more laps, and after each lap I would pull up beside an instructor, feeling hopped up, and he'd say, "I don't mean to be hard on you, but . . ."

I had imagined the track would be an oval, which I could just sort of lock myself into and zoom. The Skip Barber School operates at more than twenty locations around the country, from Sebring to Seattle International, and of all those tracks, Sears Point is most like a bootlegger's escape route. It's beautiful country around Sonoma, wine country, mostly flat with hills jutting up like the tops of elephants' heads, but a lap around that two-and-a-half-mile track — shaped, from the air, like a highly irregular slingshot — is like a roller-coaster ride through a maze.

"I keep thinking," I told Kelly Collins, "that I'm going to come around a corner and find myself in the middle of traffic on the wrong side of the road with a siren behind me."

"I never heard that one before," he said.

I did in fact manage to get lost a couple of times. Not counting the time a wheel got off into loose gravel and I spun out, and *vwang*, rammed into the bank, which was a common enough error and kind of fun, at least after I sat there for a moment thinking, "Oh, well, this is it, I've torn it now, I'll probably go into shock, and they'll have to use the jaws of life to get me out of here or airlift me and the car together . . . ," and realized that I could just crank it again, back up and carry on.

But two or three times I accidentally got into the pit lane and found myself next to the Media Building, which fortunately did not contain any media representatives. And twice when I was supposed to wind up in the pits I bypassed the pit lane and had to sort of sneak back around to it as casually (not very) as possible. No one else did either of these things.

Although everybody had trouble (though not as much as I did) finding the optimum line around the track. Since the line was marked by orange cones, you might think it would have been easy to follow, but let me explain what the line is, and while I am at it I will answer the question people most often ask me, a vulgar and uninformed question: How fast were we going?

One of the first things we were told was "Any fool can go fast on a straightaway." Something I figured out for myself was, this track didn't have any straightaway to speak of. Just to get the speed over with: By the end of the course, when we were going at 5,000 rpm in fourth gear on what passed for straightaway, we were going about 100 miles an hour. But the car didn't even have a speedometer, so I will call it 400 miles an hour, which is what it felt like, and that was fun.

What the car did have was a tachometer, and our job was to keep the rpm up as close as we could to our assigned maximum (which was raised from 2,500 to 3,000 to 4,000 to 5,000 as the course went on) while running through four gears and negotiating twelve corners.

Negotiating these corners *correctly*.

What the orange traffic cones marked were the TP (turn-in point), the apex and the TO (track-out point) for each corner. The TP was where you swung to the outside edge of the track to begin the turn, the apex was where you just skirted the inside edge and started accelerating and unwinding the steering wheel, and the TO was where you came out of the turn back on the outside edge and started setting up for the next TP. You were supposed to come within six inches of each of these cones, meanwhile visualizing the cones ahead. Connect the dots — not mechanically, one cone at a time, but smoothly, sinuously tracing the ideal line, the line of least waste motion, the fastest line.

"You seem like an intelligent person," said Nick Kunewalder, another of our instructors, as he drove me around the track in a Beemer, on a special remedial point-by-point lap. He said it in a tone of genuine wonderment. "Don't you know the turns yet?"

The truth was, I didn't. But since this was probably the fifteenth time I had been through them, I said, "Yeah, sure, well . . ." The truth is, I've been known to make a wrong turn on a route I have been traveling daily for years.

"You get the line right once, but then the next lap, you're way off."

"Yes, well, I . . ."

"Think ahead. Turn your brain on and leave it on all the time."

I felt terrible. I felt like I felt a great deal of the time in adolescence and in the army. On the other hand, whoever said racecar drivers are hitting on all cylinders?

"You can't teach anybody how to make love or drive a racecar" was something Kelly said several times. Right. Nor can you get through to a racecar instructor the reasons you are racing impaired. But here they are, for those who care:

One: I Never Stayed Within the Lines in Coloring Books, Either. If it didn't sound so self-serving, I would give this point the subtitle You Seem Like an Intelligent Person, Mr. Edison. Why Can't You Match Up Your Socks? It wasn't that my brain wasn't turned on; far from it. I would let a TP slip up on me, which would force me to swerve over toward it and then swerve back in the direction of the apex and then say, the hell with the TO, because I was thinking: "It's because my mother taught me to drive. In a Studebaker. Well, forget the Studebaker angle — am I being sexist? No, the problem is not that my mother was a woman but that she didn't like to drive. She taught me how to read, too, and she liked to read. Of course, maybe I *read* in some kind of gender-tangled way — WHOOPS, missed another one. Damn! What's *wrong* with me? Kris [Wilson, an instructor] was saying in the classroom, 'It's not just a matter of who's got the biggest *huevos*. There's a lot of thought involved.' Maybe my problem is I've never been able to use my *huevos* and think at the same time.

"Or maybe I'm not screwed up, I'm rebelling. I was reading the other day that men's-movement thinkers see male fascination with cars as a symptom of puerility, real-human-relationship avoidance and loss of true organic manhood. Maybe I'm — WHOOPS, *damn*."

Two: It's Hard to Make Love When You Don't Fit In. The only point I scored during the entire three-day course was when Kris (who is not tall) said, "You don't see many tall drivers," and I said, "That's because tall people don't have to be racecar drivers to get the attention of women."

Naked heightism. All right. But in fact I can see that being six feet tall was a great disadvantage for me. With my arms bunched up around that slightly-larger-than-a-CD steering wheel and my legs banging against the side of the chassis (I had big bruises on my knees), I felt quite frequently the way I felt, years ago, when I lived in a trailer with a shower so small that once I got the water way too hot and kept twisting the knobs frantically and thought for a minute I was going to have to run outside *wearing* the shower. Of course, I am also about fifteen pounds overweight. And when they asked me in advance how much I weighed so they could have a car the right size for me, I may have lied slightly, because I figured I would lose a few pounds before I got there, which I didn't. My feeling when I finally got all five or six straps fastened over myself (oh, how I love to fumble with webbing) was that my entire body was in a shoe too tight for it.

Three: I Never Could Make Love With My Feet. Mine are size eleven and a half D, and if they are not entirely flat, they do have trouble staying on key. In racing, you see the cars roaring around, but you don't see all the little feet twinkling inside of them. They've *got* to be little feet. I'm telling you, Mario Andretti must have little elfin feet, only very wide in the right ball. Let me explain.

I was dismayed to learn that when I went squealing heavy footedly into a turn like Robert Mitchum in *Thunder Road*, I was met with disapproval. These cars had, as one instructor said, "superduperresponsive brakes," and we were supposed to learn "threshold braking" for maximum efficiency. I found it hard to accept how quickly you could stop that little hornet of a car and by how many delicately distinct degrees of modulation you could slow it. Scary as it got at high speeds, we didn't have to worry, rationally, about getting hurt, because the cars don't flip easily and the roll bar is strong. *Irrationally*, to be sure, I sometimes heard myself saying, "Help me, Jesus."

In racing you don't downshift to slow down into a curve, you downshift just before the curve so that you are in the right gear to come out of the curve at maximum speed. You go into the turn as fast as you can, and as you downshift, you squeeze the brakes down to just shy of lockup (when they lock up, they scream and you lose momentum, but when they are at the threshold, they chirp to you), and if you brake just right while turning you "get rotation": Your rear end swings around to where it pushes you straight through the turn.

Is that clear? It is to me, in principle, but in practice I found that it was like trying to play the flute with your feet. They call it heel-and-toeing, but actually it's not that simple. Your left foot stays to the left of the clutch, on the "dead pedal," until it's time to shift, and your right foot stays on *both the brake and the accelerator.* You have to articulate the ball of the right foot into two instruments ("modulated by the ankle," according to instruction). Going into a turn, you keep firm (but "feathering," or delicately adjusting) pressure on the brake with the left side of the ball of the right foot, and with the right side of the ball of the right foot you stand ready to "blip" the accelerator, rev it enough to get the engine speed up to wheel speed. (In non-racecars you don't have to blip, because their gears are synchronized.) While keeping your heel on the floor.

That, too, is clear to me in principle. In practice . . .

And here is the sequence you have to go through, to downshift from fourth to third:

BRAKE.

CLUTCH IN.

SHIFT TO NEUTRAL.

CLUTCH OUT.

BLIP.

CLUTCH IN.

DOWNSHIFT.

CLUTCH OUT.

EASE OFF BRAKE (unless you want to keep going down to second, in which case you have to go through the entire above sequence again).

No matter how deftly you danced through this little nine-step, the gears would grind somewhat: *ggrrrt*. I tended just to jam the damn thing into something. Occasionally, I would go from fourth to fourth. And meanwhile I would sometimes have forgotten to put my helmet-visor down, causing instructors to wave frantically at me (a bug could take out my eye). Every now and then I would weave through a sequence of turns like an otter down a waterfall and get a feeling of ooooo . . . , woooo . . . , woo-*hooo*. But unlike an otter (I assume), I kept wondering in the TO or the TP of my mind: "What am I probably doing, or just on the verge of doing, wrong and why, why, why?"

One lesson I hope I learned is this: The next time I'm with someone who is having a hard time picking up something I find easy (assuming there is such a thing), I will be sympathetic. Or burn in hell.

I did not learn to be a novice racecar driver. And everybody else in my class did. And they loved it. They also misshifted and spun out and knocked over cones, but toward the end they were saying, "I just grabbed my balls and went for it," and things like that. Some of them are thinking of going on to drive in races, finding their line while surrounded by other cars trying to find it and without the aid of cones. "My dad is getting into racing," said Roy Dillon, the professional skateboarder, "and he said, 'You're the perfect little dude to be the driver.' " Good luck to them.

Passing was allowed on our last six-lap run. My aversion to being overtaken was so drastically reduced that I gave a wave-by to everyone who hove into view, praying that I would pick up in my juddering rearviews all who hove. (Did I mention that behind my visor, which kept fogging up, I was wearing bifocals?) By the final lap I was in the clear, in a negative sort of way.

Suddenly I knew a certain peace. Linc Watkins, who runs a debt-syndication desk for a Japanese bank and seemed to be driving faster than anybody else, had told me part of his secret: "Just stay in third all the way around." So I tried this, and as I came through the gentle S curves and hit the longish barely curvy stretch toward the end, I pushed on up to 6,000 rpm, approaching the car's 120-mph capacity, and I finally felt like I wanted to feel — a fool going fast on the straightaway.

Of course, the instructors had stopped watching me by then.

But I want them to know this: The next time I drove my Jetta on the highway, I found that if I concentrated I could look farther up the road than usual and plot my course smoothly through a series of turns. Well, two turns. A turn and a half. At one point, as I swung all the way to the far edge of the right lane and unwound smoothly back toward the far edge of the left, I felt something. A fleeting connection with some Platonic vector matrix stretching from Detroit to heaven.

I like to think it was my apex.

MAY/JUNE 1992

Paul Gallico went into the ring (briefly) with Jack Dempsey in the 1920s, and lived to write about it. So, ever after, sports editors have loved nothing better than to put writers into the game to discover what it's really like. Among the stupider things I have done is wrestle a bear and play against the Harlem Globetrotters. As with Dave Barry's minor league story, I was prepared to hate this predictable piece — but ROY BLOUNT, JR., *always rises above his material as a writer, even when he's messing up the material himself as a subject of the writer.* — F.D.

The Year of Living Raucously

FROM GOLF DIGEST

IN FLORIDA, IN MARCH, in a period when his golf game was flat and his personal life was chaotic, John Daly played an exhibition match with three old pros, Raymond Floyd, Ian Baker-Finch and Jack Nicklaus. On a long par 5, Daly drove into an unreachable fairway bunker. Daly is endlessly surrounded by frenzy, and this mighty poke prompted even more frenzy: the unrealistic hope that he would let loose with the big stick again.

"Hey, John," somebody yelled out. "Show us how to hit a driver out of a bunker!"

Daly — performing under a tropical sun, his broad, blank face unprotected by hat or visor — strode eagerly to his bag. With a sudden yank that defied the steaminess of the day but matched exactly the frothing of his fans, he pulled out his massive metal driver. He flipped the head cover to his celebrity caddie, Greg Rita, with whom Curtis Strange won his two U.S. Opens, and jumped into the sand box. A cheer went up. A mighty swing ensued. The ball barely escaped the bunker. The long-whacking PGA champion had topped the shot. Daly went racing after his ball, eager to hit the next shot and quickly put the bad one behind him.

Later, in an interview in a locker room, you ask Daly about life values and he replies, "I just play for the fans." The answer doesn't appear to be relevant, but Daly isn't wholly focused on the question, so he gives one of his automatic responses. There are posters to sign. The shoeshine man is telling Daly to return Greg Norman's call. Company representatives are handing Daly

golf balls, gloves, invitations, sneakers, stuff in boxes. Everywhere there are boxes.

The reps know they have to seize this moment with him, before he splits for his mobile home. The reps know there will be
no lingering on the practice tee or on the practice putting green.
Daly, twenty-six, makes little time for practice and less time for
lingering. You feel a little nervous yourself, because you realize
that you are now part of the frenzy, part of the cacophony, part
of the dizziness that surrounds him endlessly. Earlier, Rita had
told you that if you want to talk to Daly you had better do it in
between tee and ball after a long drive in a practice round, *because those are the only sustained three minutes you are going to get with
him.* Now you're straddling the locker room bench, facing him.
His pockets are stuffed with business cards and little paper
scraps that people have handed him throughout his day. His skin
is red. His hair is yellow. His eyes are tired. His forearms look
like huge drumsticks. He's wearing a fancy lizard-skin belt, and
his stomach is hanging over it, just slightly.

He is trying to focus on you, trying to pay attention, but the
distractions are mounting. A message on his locker asks Daly to
call his agent. What could it be? An addendum to the Wilson
deal? An exhibition offer in Japan? A dinner invitation from the
vice president?

You ask him about last year's PGA Championship, whether
he had any premonition while driving there in a mad dash as
a twelfth-hour, we've-just-had-a-cancellation entrant, that he
might win the historic title. He's not a cynical person. It's doubt-
ful he's thinking, *Man, when is somebody gonna ask me an original
question?* He looks at you thoughtfully. He wants to make contact
with you. He's unlike many professional athletes: He enjoys his
public. He'd be happy to answer your question, but he doesn't
really have that much to say. He's not the premonition type, although he might get a good feeling about an Arkansas-Missouri
game from time to time. Besides, you sense that while you're asking him your stupid question about premonitions — trying to
make conversation with a kid who does not prize conversation, a
kid who could list his special interests as TV, sports bars and
hanging out — he's thinking, *What in the hell am I gonna do with all
these boxes?*

*

Since winning the PGA Championship at Crooked Stick last year without even a warm-up round, John Daly has been a regular on TV. An ad for his new friends at Wilson, in which Sam Snead speaks but Daly does not, appears regularly during golf telecasts. In the Skins Game, Daly pumped up his inflatable golf shoes as the cameras focused in tight on him. In an interview with ABC, he made a veiled physical threat, and also answered questions about drinking, gambling and random hotelroom destruction. He showed off his driving prowess on *Late Night with David Letterman,* almost as if he were a golfing carnival act. At the televised Bob Hope Classic, millions watched Daly play golf with Hope, Gerald Ford and Dan Quayle, en route to a missed cut. In an interview with USA Network, Daly used one of George Carlin's seven prohibited words, and the telecast producer made a short-lived threat to keep Daly off future telecasts. Through the winter, ESPN reported on Daly's disqualification for signing an incorrect scorecard at the World Championship, about his two-hour round of 80 strokes at the Players Championship, about his private meeting with tour commissioner Deane Beman, about his unusual road to matrimony. The kid's been on TV, as he might say, a whole lot.

But not often for playing good golf. So it was a relief to his legion of fans — they're starting to call him Johnny, as if he were a childhood pal — when he got some TV time for his play. After all, this is somebody who said recently, "Lee Trevino does his talking with his mouth; I do mine with my clubs." The clubs, after a long period of silence, finally began talking again in earnest at the Kemper Open, in late May, somewhere in that fast month between his marriage to the former Bettye Fulford (more on that later) and the birth of their daughter, Shynah Hale (a name Daly "just made up"). It was the first time since Crooked Stick that the bedlam caused by his fans was actually warranted by his play. He didn't win the tournament — he got greedy with his drive on the final hole and finished one shot back. But for those final nine holes, he was right where he wanted to be, and right where his fans wanted him to be, too: last group of the day, blowing drives past big-hitting Mark Calcavecchia, playing before *tens* of thousands of spectators, their necks craned, too many of them yelling, "You the . . ." Oh, hell, you know what they yell.

*

In the interest of sustained profitability, newly created celebrities often meet with media consultants to concoct winning catchphrases that, they hope, will work their way into TV interviews and newspaper and magazine stories. It appears that the media consultant at Reebok who coached Daly emphasized the appeal of the phrase, "I just play for the fans," because Daly has used that line dozens and dozens of times this year. It may be a programmed line, but it's a good one. It suggests selflessness and promotes the idea that the speaker does not put himself above others. Obviously the line is not wholly true. Professional sports are largely a selfish pursuit, and there is probably no professional sport more selfish than tournament golf. One of the nice benefits of being a professional athlete is that others may derive pleasure from watching your skill, but for no athlete imaginable is that the only motivation.

John Daly genuinely enjoys the adulation of his fans, but the fans, of course, are getting something out of the relationship, too. Into their life Daly brings *excitement*. Not since Arnold Palmer has there been a golfer who has won over so many fans so quickly.

Consider the case of Alfred J. Patenaude, a career cement-mixer until his recent Connecticut-to-Florida retirement. At the Honda Classic, in March, he was part of the stampede chasing after Daly. Against his chest, Alfred cradled a Ping putter.

Daly was having a first look at the Weston Hills Country Club, in Fort Lauderdale, two days before the start of the tournament, playing with Fuzzy Zoeller, who describes himself as Daly's best friend on tour, and Dan Marino, the Miami Dolphins quarterback. It was not a practice round; it was a show. Still, Alfred was worried about Daly's bad shots. Somebody asked if the putter Alfred cradled was special.

"Special?" Alfred replied. "Special? This putter'll be in a museum someday."

He explained, happily, that he had picked up the putter when working as a marshal at the New Haven Open, on the Ben Hogan Tour, in 1990. On the 14th, a par 4 of 365 yards, Daly nearly drove the green. He does that sort of thing. From the fringe, he took three shots. He does that sort of thing, too. As he came off the green, Daly heaved the putter far into the woods. "Plewwee," said Alfred, recreating the sounds of flight. "Sounded like a helicopter. So I go after it. I catch up to John with the putter and say, 'Hey, John, don't you want your putter back?' And he says, 'No way. You keep it.' "

Alfred recognized immediately the telltale signs of a golf legend in the making: the cavalier attitude toward material goods; the fantastic length; the incautiousness; the fiery temper that connotes internal competitiveness, and the willingness to make contact with another human being.

Eventually, Alfred managed to worm his way through the throng and found himself face-to-face with Daly, who listened while signing visors. "Damn," Daly said with mock amazement and a gentle twang. "I never expected to see this thing again."

In a neat and careful penmanship that seems so contrary to Daly's life as we know it, the PGA champion wrote these words on the putterface: "To Al, best wishes, John Daly." Before long, other people were tugging at Daly and Alfred was gone.

In every corner of American golf, there are Als. They seem not to care where Daly finishes in tournaments from week to week, for his appeal goes way beyond that. Daly does something we cannot do, yet he still remains approachable, one of us. In professional golf today, this combination is wholly uncommon. "Daly doesn't ignore us," Alfred says. "He makes us feel like we're part of his success."

Daly is great fun to watch, not only because of his length, but because of the speed of his play. In terms of pace, he is like no player in the game today, faster than Lee Trevino, Tom Watson or Ian Woosnam. The four of them could probably play a round of tournament golf in three hours. Daly seems to have an instinctive sense of exactly what he wants to do with a shot, without any analysis, almost like a savant who can count the number of matchsticks that have just fallen on the kitchen floor. At Doral, in March, while struggling to make the cut, he surprised his partners and spectators by playing a bunker shot to four feet, and tapping in, without lining up the putt or even wiping his ball clean of sand. He often does that sort of thing, too.

Daly enchanted millions of spectators with his heartfelt statements of idol worship for Nicklaus after he won the PGA Cham-

pionship. Even during the championship, people were comparing the two golfers, even though one is twice as old as the other.
It is true that the young Nicklaus and Daly bear some physical
resemblance to one another, from the neck down — the small-
ish sloping shoulders, the thick waist, the huge thighs. It is true
that both Nicklaus and Daly generate vast amounts of energy
through massive hip turns and a tremendous driving of the legs
through the ball. It is true each won a major title for his first professional victory: Nicklaus won the 1962 U.S. Open as a twenty-
two-year-old and Daly won the PGA Championship at age
twenty-five.

But there the comparisons must stop. Nicklaus has always led
a highly structured life, defined by his unyielding desire to win
major golf championships and his unabashed willingness to prepare for them. Daly is freewheeling. Although Nicklaus was a
golf star throughout his career, he was not a genuine celebrity.
Even in the mid-1980s, Nicklaus was doing American Express
ads in which he said, "Do you know me?"

Daly has come around in a different time. Since winning the
PGA Championship, the attention Daly has received, including
attention from Nicklaus, has been dizzying. He is a valuable commercial property, and he is aware of it. And even though he is
not obsessed with the trappings of his sudden success — his chief
pleasure in wealth seems to be in giving things to his friends and
his family — the trappings are trapping anyhow. If he is going
to last in the game, you get the idea that he is going to have to
find a way to stay focused. For everybody is coming at him, all
the time.

You see this in practice rounds. You see this on the practice tee.
You see this in the locker room. You see this at lunch. And when
you see him in these settings, you sense that he has not yet found
a way to handle the demands of fame.

Earlier this year, as he waited for a salad for lunch in a
crowded clubhouse dining room, Daly was tapping his thumbs,
drummer-style. His eyes were darting all about the packed room,
seemingly unaware that a couple of hundred pairs of eyes were
focused on him. Guys the size of small buildings, old men, kids,
middle-aged ladies, were coming up to Daly, grabbing the soft
muscle at the top of his shoulder, extending hands, patting his

forearm. "Hey, buddy," Daly would say. "Kay, bud." "Whassup?" "Howyoudoin?" "Catch you later." "Sign it for who?" "Sure, I remember."

He was asked if the burdens of fame are ever overwhelming.

"I wouldn't trade where I am now with where I was a year ago. What I've done is the dream of every young golfer in America," he says.

This is Daly on autopilot; he is answering a question posed to him routinely, and he always responds the same way. He signed a visor. Somebody asks, Do you ever think you'll change your style of play, maybe shorten your swing, maybe hit driver less frequently?

"I only play one way," he says, shoving a forkful of salad into his mouth. "Grip it and rip it."

He's on autopilot again. He doesn't even grin when he says it. He looks tired. Somebody asks, How important is winning golf tournaments to you? Is it a consuming interest for you?

Daly takes a crumpled napkin and tosses it on the table.

"I just play for the fans," he says.

It would be hard to imagine Daly's boyhood idol, Jack Nicklaus, ever making any comment like that at any point in his career. Earlier this year, Daly was taken out by Nicklaus for a quiet nine holes of golf, with Nicklaus hoping he and Daly would talk about golfing values. Daly asked about nothing, and that surprised Nicklaus.

"I kept hearing that he has all these things he wants to ask me, and we play nine holes and he doesn't ask me a thing," Nicklaus said last March. "He is immensely talented, but what he does with that talent is up to him. What kind of future does he have? I have no idea. He could have a great career and he could be great for golf, but he has to have focus."

Daly has two young agents, Bud Martin, thirty, and John Mascatello, thirty-two, who are the principles behind Cambridge Sports International, in Washington, D.C. Daly is not their only golfer — Scott Hoch, Roger Maltbie, John Huston, and fourteen others are with Cambridge. But as Daly's representatives, they have been propelled into an environment that is uncommon in the golf business. Daly is guaranteed to make at least $10 million in endorsements between now and 1996. That's if he does virtually nothing. If he wins more major tournaments, there is no saying how much he could make.

He has a five-year deal with Wilson and a three-year deal with Reebok. He has done a video called "Grip It and Rip It" and will have an instruction book coming out in December. He is a co-endorser, with Johnny Miller, of a product called Golf Tempo, a $300 device that measures swing speed. He is selling 950 lithographs, signed by himself and the artist, depicting a triumphant Daly at the 18th at Crooked Stick, for $599 each. Usually, art is sold in round numbers, but they are not catering to the traditional art-buying market. Meanwhile, a half-dozen other deals are in the works. John Daly golf gloves and John Daly clubs (both for Wilson), and a John Daly video game should be out before too long. "Major endorsements" are in the planning stages, says Mascatello.

But without ever making another deal, Daly has enough money to keep him rich for the rest of his life, provided he invests the money wisely. Daly's money is invested conservatively, says Mascatello, chiefly through the PGA Tour's account with Merrill Lynch. Daly does not live off an allowance sent to him by a money manager. He writes his own checks.

Martin first met Daly in 1989, and Mascatello in early 1990, when long-drive champion Mike Dunaway said to him, "This is a kid you need to watch." Soon after, Daly signed on with Cambridge.

Daly is not accustomed to playing par 5s as three-shotters, but what could he do at Kemper's 13th? He was in the rough, 260 yards from the flag, a tree blocking his line. But it was the last par 5, so he slashed at the ball with a long iron hoping for a mammoth slice.

The ball caught a bank a few yards short of the green and rolled down, practically into the stream that protects it. Daly climbed down, shaking his right hand, the one with the thick gold bracelet, to get some extra feel in his hand, until he disappeared. Seconds later, the ball magically appeared, rising softly out of the ditch and finishing eight feet from the hole. He made it. He was two shots off the lead again. His gallery went haywire.

This is how golf tournaments are won. When he birdied 14, a short par 4, to claw his way within a shot of the lead, his fans were almost out of control.

"Everybody was just so rowdy," Daly said later. "It was, 'You the man,' or, 'Bite baby bite,' or, 'C'mon John.' It was just the kind of thing we have been hearing, but I don't want it to ever stop."

Bettye Fulford Daly, nine months and two days pregnant, was screaming and yelling, too, in support of her husband of three weeks. It wasn't that long ago that her screaming and yelling had another purpose. But that was then. Now Bettye and John carry on as a sort of golfing version of Tom and Roseanne Arnold. Golf has never seen anything like them. After his final round at the Kemper, Daly sat on a small dais in a room jammed with reporters, Bettye sitting among them.

After asking a press official if it was O.K. to extinguish his cigarette in melted ice water intended to keep sodas cold (the answer was yes), Daly leaned into a microphone and asked, "Bettye, you walk all eighteen today?"

"Yes, I did," came a voice, with a soft twang.

"Amazing lady," said the press official.

"She's a diehard fan, I guess," Daly said. "Not too many pregnant ladies who are about to go into labor would be walking out here. She's a trooper." This public affirmation of their union was striking, given where they were just months earlier.

You may recall that at the conclusion of last year's PGA Championship, Bettye Fulford came shooting out of the gallery with a big hug for her triumphant fiancé. Daly described her then as a twenty-nine-year-old divorcée without children. Their plan was to marry last October, in Las Vegas, but they put the wedding off, Daly said at that time, because of the chaos attendant to his newly exalted status.

By Christmas, Daly had broken up with Fulford, after learning that she was ten years older than he had believed, that she was still married, that she had a child. Fulford responded by filing a palimony and paternity suit against her former fiancé. One set of papers was served upon Daly during a practice round before the Masters, in April.

"It's hard to believe that somebody could be that crooked, that mean," Daly told *USA Today* in January. "It makes me look stupid. Here I go with this girl for a year and a half, and I don't know how old she is or that she has a kid."

Regarding her pregnancy, Daly said that if the child was his, he would fight for custody because "I don't feel Bettye is capable of caring for it."

Bettye was eight months pregnant with their child when they married in Dardanelle, Arkansas, on May 8. It was a small wedding. John's parents, Jim and Lou, ran the barbecue, and John and his buddies went for a canoe trip before the ceremony. Bettye caught up with them upstream. She was in no condition for paddling. Daly now says he is happy to be married. They live in Memphis.

"I guess it's love and we're going to make it work the best we can," he said shortly after the wedding, at a press conference for this year's PGA. "I think it's going to be good for me. It's going to be good for Bettye, too. Hopefully we can live the rest of our lives together."

On the tee of the 15th hole at the Kemper, you could not tell where Daly was aimed. His clubhead seemed pointed into the right rough, and his feet seemed pointed into the left rough, yet the drive flew dead straight and forever. On a 467-yard hole, Daly had only a 9-iron into the green. After this mighty launch, Mark Calcavecchia actually looked a little amused, as if to say, "Who in his right mind swings that hard?" They said nothing to each other. When they walked out to their drives — Daly way ahead of the pack, of course — Daly saw that his ball was more than forty yards ahead of Calcavecchia's.

If Daly is impressed by his length, he never lets on. And if his fellow tour players are impressed, they never let on, either.

Some of Daly's colleagues speak negatively about him, but not publicly, not for attribution. One interview went as follows:

"Daly's a loose cannon."

"How so?"

"He's a drunk."

"How do you know?"

"Ask anybody."

"Have you seen him drunk?"

"I haven't, but others have."

"Do you think he'll stick around?"

"No. He's made so much, so fast, he thinks he doesn't have to work anymore. That doesn't cut it out here."

Some of Daly's colleagues believe that Daly has sullied the tour with his romantic problems, his scorecard-signing problems, his profane speech.

Most of the stories that swirl around Daly are undocumented and probably not true. Still, they become part of the baggage with which he must deal. As a result, Daly is increasingly distancing himself from his fellow tour players. When the rest of the tour flies to the next stop by plane, Daly travels in his elaborate motor home. Daly doesn't spend much time in the locker room, or on the practice grounds. If he hangs out in a lobby, he is mobbed by fans as other, more accomplished players walk by unnoticed.

"I'm sure there's some jealousy," Daly says, sitting in a locker room in a rare moment when nobody is hovering about. It is a brief moment of introspection in his chaotic life. "Not from the guys who were with me on the Hogan tour, they know me and they've been great, but from some of the others. I just try to be myself, and if they can't accept that, then that's their problem."

Daly says that while he does enjoy drinking beer, he states flatly that he "does not have a drinking problem." He says he used to be a whisky drinker — binges resulted in hospital visits several times — but that now he is not.

Part of the problem with Daly's colleagues is that they are not *fans*, they do not grasp the hoopla surrounding him. Their confusion is understandable, when you think about the things Daly is not. He is not good-looking, like Johnny Miller. He is not funny, like Trevino. He doesn't have the disinterested elegance of Fred Couples, or the analytic brilliance of Nicklaus, or the intensity of Watson, or the stylishness of Seve Ballesteros, or the worldly sophistication of Gary Player, or the physical presence of Greg Norman.

He is not a tour clone. He dresses like the kids you see shoving quarters into video machines in shopping mall pizza parlors. His pants have seams that go down the front, and his shirts are shades of green and blue and red usually found on the plumage of subtropical birds. His hairdo is a curious blend of rock-and-roll (over the collar in the back) and porridge-bowl mop in front. He has the wispy mustache of a teenager trying to get into a bar. He has a bloated face, and his body, although obviously strong and powerful, is largely devoid of definition.

He is not scholarly or introspective. He is not interested in politics ("I don't think of Dan Quayle as the vice president; I think of him as my friend, Dan"). He is not interested in books ("To be honest with you, I couldn't tell you the name of the last one I read straight through"). He is not well informed about current affairs ("I don't feel like I know enough to vote, you know what I mean?").

He is not fascinated by the shrines of golf ("I like the newer, longer courses, as long as they're not too tight.") Nor by the accomplishments of the players who came before him ("I'm more interested in the here and now"). He can be irresponsible at scoring tables (during the World Championship in December in Jamaica, he signed an incorrect scorecard, which disqualified him from a tournament in which it appeared he did not want to continue). He can be disingenuous with a microphone before him (for a while, he was plugging McDonald's at every chance, including during his appearance on *Letterman,* hoping for a fat endorsement, which never came. Now he's talking about Whoppers).

What his fans know is this:

He signs autographs tirelessly. He has managed to retain his former, pre-celebrity self, his former, pre-celebrity friends, and his former, pre-celebrity values. He is not bland. He is not boastful. He is unassuming. He is loyal. He is generous, to caddies, to waitresses, to bartenders, to small-town charities, to his family, and he was even before he could afford to be. He wants people to like him. An occasional phrase in his conversation is, "Please don't hate me."

Lou Hale met Jim Daly thirty-odd years ago when Jim ran a bar in Fort Smith, Arkansas. First they had a daughter, Julie, followed by two sons, Jamie and John. Today, Jim Daly works at a nuclear power plant in Arkansas and the Dalys have a driving range, called Wildcat Hollow, in the front yard of their home in Dardanelle, Arkansas.

John Daly's childhood was anything but usual. Before he was eighteen, Daly moved five times. He was born in California, moved to Arkansas, then to Virginia, over to Louisiana, then Missouri, before finally going back to Arkansas. For the last couple of his high school years, John and his brother were essentially living on their own for months at a time in Arkansas while their parents were in Kansas, where Jim Daly had work.

"That was probably a mistake," says John Daly. "I always made regular trips there," says Lou.

Father and son had a relationship that was based on sports. Jim, never an accomplished athlete himself, gave John a full set of Jack Nicklaus MacGregor irons when John was seven. They also played baseball and football together, and spent hours on end together practicing for Punt, Pass and Kick competitions, in which John excelled.

"I don't know where John got this need to win," Jim says. "He's the only one in the family who has it. As far as I know, I only gave him one piece of valuable advice. When we were in these Punt, Pass and Kick competitions, I would always say to him, 'Remember, this is your only chance to make this kick. It's now or never.' I think that helped him to try his hardest on every shot when he turned to golf. But it also made him lose his temper on bad shots, because he wanted every shot to be perfect. He's still learning that you can hit a bad shot and not have it ruin your entire round. He snapped some clubs as a kid."

"I can't say that he had a temper," says Lou Daly. "He was stubborn, and he still is stubborn. If you would tell John to do something, he would rebel. But if you asked him, he would respond. If you use reverse psychology on him, it will work."

Maybe that's how John and Bettye got back together. She filed a lawsuit against him, and a couple of months later they were married. Was that an example of reverse psychology? Lou Daly isn't saying.

"We were disappointed [when the lawsuit was filed] but we throw that in the past," Lou says. "If he can forgive her, then that's what's important. If they're happy, we're one hundred percent behind them. We all get along.

"John'll settle down now and start thinking about golf again," Lou said, just before the start of the Kemper Open. "And when he does, he'll start playing good golf again. It's been hard for him to think about golf this past year, he's had so much going on. He never had any spare time to practice, he was so busy with the outings and everything else, and there were a lot of complications in his personal life. But that's all in the past. I like to concentrate on the future. I think he'll win tournaments again very soon."

On 17 at Kemper, a downhill par 3 of 195 yards with water perilously close to the edge of the green, Daly had to wait about five minutes to play his tee shot. One wondered what the wait would do to his impatient swing. He took out a 7-iron and stiffed it: eight feet for birdie and a tie for the lead with Bill Glasson. Daly's putt was hit weakly and could have easily stayed out of the hole, but it caught the left lip and fell in. As it did, Daly thrust the putter into the gloomy sky, pressed the shaft against his lips, and pointed his nose heaven-bound. He could hear nothing. The din was deafening.

Finally, Daly was in the midst of some exciting golf, some of the most exciting golf a good golf year has produced.

On to 18, a 444-yard par 4. Birdie to win, par to tie, bogey to tie for second. Had Daly wanted to play for par, he might have hit a 1-iron. But Daly had his own idea: Hit a big driver, hit a wedge close, make a birdie, win the tournament, go to the Memorial. Daly pulled out the driver to hoots of approval. He tried to carry the bunker with a big draw. He swung extremely hard and extremely fast, even by his standards. He got up on his toes and hit an ugly toe-hook that would have gone O.B. were it not for the five-inch rough that kept it in play. His ball nestled deeply in it.

From there, he had 200 yards of rough and bunker to get home. The prudent play would have been to get back in the fairway and hope to hit a little pitch tight and make the par putt to force a playoff. Daly ain't prudent. He aimed at the pin, flailed at the ball mightily, and came up 50 yards short of the pin in the rough. This time his ball was virtually unseeable. He smashed a sand wedge as hard as he could. Grass and mud went flying; he left behind nothing but raw roots and exposed earth. The ball popped up and climbed up an embankment into the fringe. Now

Daly had to chip in for par and a playoff. His chip shot was dead on line, but a foot short. A bogey to finish. He played the final hole impatiently, and it cost him.

Glasson — who made a one-putt par on 18 after driving into the rough — was the winner. It was wonderful golf, and Daly's fans seemed not to mind that he did not win. The important thing was that he was there.

As Daly came off the final green, making his way to the press tent, *eight* security guards surrounded him, hugging every inch of his body to protect him from autograph seekers. All the while, Daly signed away. One woman, with an incredible show of pure physical will and ungraciousness, pushed herself up against Daly, shoving a pen in his face. This was too much even for Daly. "C'mon, lady," he said.

In the press tent, Daly explained his play on 18, how he had been driving the ball so well that he thought there was no reason not to hit a driver, how he felt good about his chances of making a birdie and winning the tournament. Somebody asked if he hit a driver because of fan pressure. "No," Daly said in a moment of total candor. "I hit the driver for me."

By his own admission, Daly has a lot to learn, about the game of golf, and the game of life, and it seems evident that he is learning. You get the idea that he wouldn't again hit his driver out of a bunker to please a fan, as he did in March, in Florida. You get the idea that he is again appreciating the value of practice, or dedication to his craft.

His new line is, "Endorsements are nice, but I want to make my living on the golf course." He says it often, but there's no reason to doubt his sincerity. When he played his final chip shot short, he hit himself in the head with his shaft. He was upset *for himself*. Any world-class athlete will tell you in a moment of truth that success and selfishness are inextricably linked.

What happened at Crooked Stick may never happen again. Kenny Knox, Daly's playing partner in the last round of last year's PGA, witnessed it. "You had to be there to really feel it," Knox says. "He didn't conduct himself like any other major championship winner I've ever seen. He actually allowed the spectators to come into his world, and that's something most professional golfers are afraid to do. He could feel that the people were behind him, and he was feeding off them and they were feeding off him. It got him higher and higher. It was like a flood stream, and he and the spectators were in it together. It was amazing."

In that one week of brilliant golf, Daly won over the public, probably forever. Now he is learning that one plays tournament golf for one's wife, one's progeny, one's checkbook and, ultimately, one's self.

AUGUST 1992

Unfortunately, more bad things befell John Daly after MICHAEL BAM-BERGER *wrote this most perceptive profile. In fact, having read this, you could almost expect that there'd be trouble ahead for Daly. Golf journalists, print and broadcast, tend to be the least critical of their sport and its heroes, and so this portrait of Daly is all the more striking for its forthrightness. (The sequel might be able to have a happy ending, though; Daly has gone on the wagon and he finished third at the '93 Masters.) —* F.D.

AMBY BURFOOT

White Men Can't Run

FROM RUNNER'S WORLD

THIS MONTH IN BARCELONA, for the first time in the history of the Olympic Games, runners of African heritage will win every men's running race. West Africans, including American blacks of West African descent, will sweep the gold medals at all distances up to and including the 400-meter hurdles. And East Africans and North Africans will win everything from the 800 meters through the marathon.

These results won't surprise any close observer of the international track scene. Ever since America's Eddie Tolan won the 100 meters at the 1932 Los Angeles Games, becoming the first black gold medalist in an Olympic track race, black runners have increasingly dominated Olympic and World competitions. An analysis of the three World Championships meets paints the clearest picture. In 1983, blacks won 14 of the 33 available medals in running races. In 1987, they won 19. Last September in Tokyo, they won 29.

What's more surprising is the lack of public dialogue on the phenomenon. The shroud of silence results, of course, from our societal taboo against discussing racial differences — a taboo that is growing stronger in these politically correct times.

A good example: *Sports Illustrated*'s changed approach to the subject. In early 1971, *Sports Illustrated* published a landmark story, "An Assessment of 'Black Is Best'" by Martin Kane, that explored various physical reasons for the obvious success of black athletes on the American sports scene. African-American sociologists, particularly Harry Edwards, wasted little time in blasting Kane's article. Wrote Edwards, famed for orchestrating black power demonstrations at the 1968 Olympics: "The argument that blacks are physically superior to whites is merely a racist ideology camouflaged to appeal to the ignorant, the unthinking and the unaware."

Edwards was right to question arguments attributing sports success primarily to physiology. American blacks fear that such an overemphasis on their physical skills may call into question their mental skills. Besides, sports success clearly demands more than just a great body. It also requires desire, hard work, family and social support, positive role models and, often, potential for financial reward.

For these reasons, the University of Texas's Bob Malina, Ph.D., the country's leading expert on physical and performance differences among ethnic groups, has long argued for what he calls a "biocultural approach." Nurture (the overall cultural environment) is just as important as biology (genetics).

Because Edwards and others attacked so stridently, mere discussion of the subject grew to be regarded, ipso facto, as a racist activity and hence something to be avoided at all cost. Last year, *Sports Illustrated* returned to the fertile subject of black athletes in American sports, devoting dozens of articles to the topic in a multi-issue series. Not one of these articles made even passing mention of physical differences between whites and blacks. Likewise, *USA Today* barely scratched the surface in its own four-day special report "Race & Sports: Myths & Realities."

When NBC-TV broadcast its brave "Black Athletes: Fact and Fiction" program in 1989, the network had trouble locating a scientist willing to discuss the subject in the studio. Instead, host Tom Brokaw had to patch through to two experts attending a conference in Brussels. In beginning my research for this story, I contacted one of America's most respected sports scientists. He didn't want to talk about the subject. "Go ahead and hang yourself," he said, "but you're not going to hang me with you."

Fear rules. Why? Because this is a story about inherited abilities, and Americans aren't ready for the genetics revolution that's already sweeping over us. In the next 10 years, scientists worldwide will devote $3 billion to the Human Genome Project. In the process, they will decipher all 100,000 human genes, cure certain inherited diseases (like cystic fibrosis, Tay-Sachs and sickle cell disease), and tell us more about ourselves than we are prepared to know. Including, in all likelihood, why some people run faster than others.

Many casual sports fans mistakenly believe that athletic competitions are fair. In fact, this is one reason so many people enjoy sports. Politics and corporate ladder-climbing may be rotten to the core, but sports at least provide a level playing field.

This simple notion of fairness doesn't go very far. Just ask any female athlete. Women excel in law school, medical practice, architectural design and the business world, but they never win at sports. They don't even want to compete side by side with men in sports (as they do in all other areas of social, cultural and economic life). Why not? Because sports success stems from certain physical strengths and abilities that women simply don't have. We all acknowledge this.

But we have more trouble understanding that what is true for women is also true for some male groups. In some sports, certain racial groups face overwhelming odds. Take the Japanese. The Japanese are passionate about sports and surely rank among the world's most-disciplined, hardest-working and highest-achieving peoples. These qualities have brought them great success in many areas and should produce the same in sports.

Yet the Japanese rarely succeed at sports. They fall short because, on average, they *are* short. Most big-time sports require size, speed and strength. A racial group lacking these qualities must struggle against great odds to excel.

Of course, a few sports, including marathoning, gymnastics and ice-skating, actually reward small stature. You've heard of Kristi Yamaguchi and Midori Ito, right? It's no mistake that the Japanese are better at ice-skating than, say, basketball. It's genetics.

A scientist interested in exploring physical and performance differences among different racial groups couldn't invent a better sport than running. First of all, it's a true worldwide sport, practiced and enjoyed in almost every country around the globe. Also, it doesn't require any special equipment, coaching or facilities. Abebe Bikila proved this dramatically in the 1960 Olympic Games when — shoeless, little coached and inexperienced — he won the marathon.

Given the universality of running, it's reasonable to expect that the best runners should come from a wide range of countries and racial groups. We should find that Europeans, Asians, Africans and North and South Americans all win about the same number of gold medals in running events.

This isn't, however, what happens. Nearly all the sprints are won by runners of West African descent. Nearly all the distance races are won, remarkably, by runners from just one small corner of one small African country — Kenya.

Track and field is the perfect laboratory sport for two more important reasons. First, two of the most exciting events — the 100 meters and the marathon — represent the far reaches of human physical ability. A sprinter must be the fastest, most explosive of humans. A marathoner must be the most enduring. Any researcher curious about physical differences between humans could look at runners who excel at these two events and expect to find a fair number of differences. If these differences then broke down along racial lines . . . well, so be it.

Second, since running requires so little technique and equipment, success results *directly* from the athlete's power, endurance or other purely physical attributes. This explains why drug-testing is so important in track. If a golfer, tennis player, gymnast or even basketball player were to take steroids or to blood dope, we'd be hard pressed to say that the drugs helped the athlete. In these sports, too much else — rackets, clubs, specialized moves — separate the athlete's physiology from his or her scoring potential.

Runners find, on the other hand, that if they improve the body (even illegally), the performance has to improve. Some scientists even acknowledge that a simple running race can measure certain physical traits better than any laboratory test. The results we observe in the Olympic Stadium are as valid as they get.

The evidence for a black genetic advantage in running falls into two categories: physique and physiology. The first refers to body size and proportions, the second to below-the-surface differences in the muscles, the enzymes, the cell structures and so on.

To appreciate the significance of either, you must first understand that very small differences between two racial groups can lead to very dramatic differences in sports performance. For example, two groups, A and B, can share 99 percent of the same human genes and characteristics. They can be virtually identical. Nevertheless, if the 1 percent of variation occurs in a characteristic that determines success at a certain sport, then group A might win 90 percent of the Olympic medals in that sport.

Over the years, numerous studies of physique have compared blacks of West African heritage with white Americans and consistently reached the same conclusions. Among these conclusions: Blacks have less body fat, narrower hips, thicker thighs, longer legs and lighter calves. From a biomechanical perspective, this is an impressive package. Narrow hips allow for efficient, straight-ahead running. Strong quadriceps muscles provide horsepower, and light calves reduce resistance.

Speaking a year ago at the American College of Sports Medicine's symposium on "Ethnic Variations in Human Performance," Lindsey Carter, Ph.D., observed: "It appears that the biomechanical demands of a particular sport limit the range of physiques that can satisfy these demands." Carter, a San Diego State University professor who has conducted a series of studies of Olympic athletes, concluded: "If all else is equal, can a difference in ethnicity confer advantages in physical performance? From a biomechanical point of view, the answer is yes."

A number of direct performance studies have also shown a distinct black superiority in simple physical tasks such as running and jumping. Often, the subjects in these studies were children (for example, fourth-graders in the Kansas City public schools), which tends to mute the criticism that blacks outrun and outjump whites because society channels black youngsters into sports.

A few studies have even looked beyond simple muscle performance. In one of the first, Robert L. Browne of Southwestern Louisiana Institute showed that black college students had a significantly faster patellar tendon reflex time (the familiar knee-jerk response) than white students. Reflex time is an important variable to study for two reasons. First, because many sports obviously require lightning reflexes. And, second, because classic biological theory holds that faster reflexes will tend to create stronger muscles, which will tend to create denser bones. All of these have been observed in blacks, whose denser bones may make it particularly hard for them to succeed in one major Olympic sport — swimming.

Since the study of black-white differences frightens off many U.S. scientists, it's no surprise that the best research on the subject comes from other laboratories around the world. In the last decade, scientists from Quebec City, Stockholm and Cape Town, South Africa, have been leading the way.

Claude Bouchard, Ph.D., of Laval University in Quebec City, is perhaps the world's leading sports geneticist, as well as a foremost expert in the genetics of obesity. When the *New England Journal of Medicine* published a Bouchard study on human obesity two years ago, it made headlines around the world for its finding that degree of fatness and locale of fat deposition (hips, waist, etc.) was largely determined by heredity.

Bouchard achieved these and many of his other remarkable results through carefully controlled studies of twins who live in and around Quebec City. From such experiments, he has determined the "hereditability" of many human traits, including some relating to athletic performance. Bouchard has shown, for example, that anaerobic power is from 44 to 92 percent inherited, while max VO_2 is only 25 percent inherited. From these findings, we might quickly conclude that sprinters are "born" but distance runners are "made," which, loosely, is what track observers have always thought about sprinters and distance runners.

What "makes" distance runners, of course, is their training, and Bouchard has also investigated "trainability." It's surprisingly easy to do. You simply gather a bunch of out-of-shape people, put them on the same training program and follow their progress according to certain key physiological measures. The results are astonishing. Some subjects don't improve at all or take a long time to improve; some improve almost instantly and by large amounts. This trainability trait, Bouchard has found, is about 75 percent inherited.

This means that potential for distance-running success may be just as genetically determined as potential for sprinting success.

Which is why many coaches and physiologists have been saying for years that the best way to improve your marathon time is to "choose your parents carefully."

Bouchard is now examining physiological differences between white French Canadians and black West Africans, both culled from the student population at Laval. In one study, the only one of its kind ever performed between these two groups, the researchers compared muscle-fiber percentages. The West Africans had significantly more fast-twitch fibers and anaerobic enzymes than the whites. Exercise physiologists have long believed that fast-twitch muscle fibers confer an advantage in explosive, short-duration power events such as sprinting.

Two Bouchard disciples, Pierre F. M. Ama and Jean-Aime Simoneau, next decided to test the two groups' actual power output in the lab. On a 90-second leg extension test (basically the same exercise we all do on our weight benches), the black and white subjects performed about equally for the first 30 seconds. Beyond 30 seconds, the whites were able to produce significantly more power than the blacks.

This experiment failed to show what the researchers expected — that West African blacks should be better sprinters. It may, on the other hand, have shown that these blacks generally wouldn't perform well in continuous events lasting several minutes or longer.

Of course, a leg extension test isn't the same thing as the real world of track and field. In particular, it can't account for any of the biomechanical running advantages that blacks may have. Which could explain the curious findings of David Hunter.

Two years before Ama and Simoneau published their study, Hunter completed his Ph.D. requirement in exercise physiology at Ohio State University by writing his thesis on "A Comparison of Anaerobic Power Between Black and White Adolescent Males." Hunter began by giving his subjects — high schoolers from Columbus — two laboratory tests that measure anaerobic power. These tests yielded no differences.

Then he decided to turn his subjects loose on the track. There the blacks sprinted and jumped much better than the whites. These results apparently disturbed Hunter, an African-American, whose dissertation concluded that the laboratory results (no differences) were more significant than the real-world results (big differences).

In attempting to balance his results, Hunter noted that a 1969 study in the journal *Ergonomics* found that blacks actually had *less* anaerobic power than whites. What he failed to point out, and perhaps even to recognize, was that the *Ergonomics* study compared a group of Italians with a group of *Kenyans*. Indeed, many of the Kenyan subjects came from the Nandi and Kikuyu tribes, famed for their distance running but scarcely noted for their sprinting (anaerobic power). From running results alone, we would expect these Kenyans to score low on any test of anaerobic power.

I mention this only because I believe it highlights an important point: The word "black" provides little information about anyone or any group. Of the 100,000 genes that determine human makeup, only one to six regulate skin color, so we should assume almost nothing about anyone based on skin color alone. West Africans and East Africans are both black, but in many physical ways they are *more unlike each other* than they are *different from most whites*.

When it comes to assumptions about Africans, we should make just one: The peoples of Africa, short and tall, thick and thin, fast and slow, white and black, represent the fullest and most spectacular variations of humankind to be found anywhere.

Tim Noakes, M.D., director of the Sport Science Centre at the University of Cape Town Medical School, has spent the last thirty years researching the limits of human endurance, largely because of his own, and indeed his whole country's, passion for the 54-mile Comrades Marathon. Noakes's book *Lore of Running* (Leisure Press, 1991) stands as the ultimate compilation of the history, physiology and training methods of long-distance running.

In recent years, Noakes has been trying to learn why South African blacks, who represent only twenty percent of their country's road-racing population, nevertheless take eighty percent of the top positions in South African races. (South African blacks are related to East Africans through their common Bushman ancestors. West African blacks, representing the Negroid race, stand apart.)

In one experiment, Noakes asked two groups of white and black marathoners to run a full marathon on the laboratory treadmill. The two groups were matched for ability and experience. While they weren't among South Africa's elite corps of distance runners, subjects from both groups were good marathoners with times under 2:45.

When the two groups ran on the treadmill at the same speed, the major difference was that the blacks were able to perform at a much higher percentage of their maximum oxygen capacity. The results, published in the *European Journal of Applied Physiology*, showed that the whites could only run at 81 percent of their max VO_2. The blacks could reach 89 percent.

This same characteristic has previously been noted in several great white marathoners including Derek Clayton and Frank Shorter. Clayton and Shorter didn't have a particularly high max VO_2, but they were able to run for long periods of time at a very high percentage of their max. This enabled them to beat other marathoners who actually had higher max VO_2 values.

Among white runners, a Clayton or Shorter is a physiologic rarity. Among black South Africans, however, such capacity may be commonplace. And even though the blacks in Noakes's lab were working very hard, their muscles produced little lactic acid and other products of muscle fatigue. How can they do this?

Noakes speculates that the blacks have a muscle fiber quality, as yet unnamed in scientific circles, that he calls "high fatigue resistance." It's pretty much the opposite of what the Canadian researchers found in their 90-second test of West Africans. Sweden's renowned exercise physiologist Bengt Saltin, Ph.D., director of the Karolinska Institute in Stockholm, has spent most of his professional career investigating the extraordinary endurance performances of nordic skiers, multiday bicyclists, orienteers and distance runners. Since all distance-running roads now lead to Kenya, Saltin decided to travel there two years ago to observe the phenomenon firsthand. He also took a half-dozen national-class Swedish runners with him. Later, he brought several groups of Kenyans back to Stockholm to test them in his lab.

In competitions in Kenya, at and near St. Patrick's high school, which has produced so many world-class runners, the Swedish 800-meter to 10,000-meter specialists were soundly beaten by hundreds of fifteen- to seventeen-year-old Kenyan boys. Indeed,

Saltin estimated that this small region of Kenya in the Rift Valley had at least 500 high schoolers who could outrace the Swedes at 2,000 meters.

Back in Stockholm, Saltin uncovered many small differences between the Kenyan and Swedish runners. The results, not yet published in any scientific journal, seemed most extraordinary in the quadriceps muscle area. Here, the Kenyans had more blood-carrying capillaries surrounding the muscle fibers and more mitochondria within the fibers (the mitochondria are the energy-producing "engine" of the muscle).

Saltin also noted that the Kenyans' muscle fibers were smaller than the Swedes. Not small enough to limit performance — except perhaps the high-power production needed for sprinting — but small enough to bring the mitochondria closer to the surrounding capillaries. This "closeness" presumably enhances oxygen diffusion from the densely packed capillaries into the mitochondria.

And when the oxygen gets there, it is burned with incredible efficiency. After hard workouts and races, Saltin noted, Kenyans show little ammonia buildup (from protein combustion) in the muscles — far less than Swedes and other runners. They seem to have more of the muscle enzymes that burn fat and "spare" glycogen and protein. Sparing glycogen, according to a classic tenet of work physiology, is one of the best ways to improve endurance performance. Added together, all these factors give the Kenyans something very close to Tim Noakes's high fatigue resistance.

Saltin believes Kenyan endurance may result from environmental forces. He told *Runner's World*'s "Fast Lane" columnist Owen Anderson, Ph.D., that the Kenyans' remarkable quadriceps muscles could develop from years of walking and running over hills at high altitude. Saltin has observed similar capillary densities among orienteers who train and race through hilly forests, and similar small muscle fibers among nordic skiers who train at altitude.

Of course, Peruvians and Tibetans and other peoples live at altitude and spend all their lives negotiating steep mountain slopes. Yet they don't seem to develop into great distance runners. Why the Kenyans?

The only plausible answer is that Kenyans from the Rift Valley, perhaps more so than any other peoples on Earth, bring together the perfect combination of genetic endowment with environmental and cultural influences. No one can doubt that many Kenyans are born with great natural talents. But much more is also at work. Consider a few of the following:

Boys and girls from west Kenya grow up in a high-altitude environment of surpassing beauty and good weather conditions. From an early age, they must walk and jog across hilly terrain to get anywhere. They are raised in a culture that emphasizes both stoicism (adolescent circumcision) and aggression (cattle raiding). Indeed, the British introduced track and field in Kenya as a way to channel tribal raiding parties into more appropriate behavior. Kip Keino and others since him have provided positive role models, and the society is so male-dominant that Kenyan men are quick to accept their superiority (an aspect of Kenyan society that makes things especially tough for Kenyan women). The financial rewards of modern-day track and road racing provide an income Kenyans can achieve in almost no other activity. In short, nearly everything about Kenyan life points to success (for men) in distance running.

Any close inspection of international track results yields one incontrovertible fact: Black-skinned athletes are winning most races. This phenomenon is likely to grow even more pronounced in the future. Many African athletes, and countries, have barely begun to show their potential.

Yet it would be incredibly myopic to conclude, simply, that blacks are faster than whites. A more accurate — albeit admittedly speculative — phrasing might go something like this: West African blacks seem to be faster sprinters than whites, who are better than East African blacks; and East Africans seem to have more endurance capacity than whites, who are better than West Africans.

Whites, always in the middle. Maybe this explains why whites have managed to hold on the longest in the middle-distance races, where Seb Coe still holds the world record for 800 meters and Steve Cram for the mile.

In the past, discussions of racial-group success in sports have largely involved the relative success of blacks in basketball, football and baseball and their relative failure in tennis, golf and swimming. The "country club" aspects of the latter three sports guaranteed that these discussions centered on social and economic status: Blacks weren't good at tennis, golf and swimming because they didn't belong to country clubs. Does an analysis of running add anything new to the discussion?

I think so. Where pure explosive power — that is, sprinting and jumping — are required for excellence in a sport, blacks of West African heritage will excel. The more a sport moves away from speed and toward technique and other prerequisites, like hand-eye coordination, the more other racial groups will find themselves on a level playing field.

The Kenyans and other East Africans, despite their amazing endurance, will hardly come to dominate world sports. As many of us distance runners have learned the hard way — from a lifetime of reality checks on playgrounds and various courts and fields — endurance counts for next to nothing in most big-time sports.

While sports aren't necessarily fair, we can still take heart in the many exceptions to the rule. The truly outstanding athlete always fights his way to the top, no matter what the odds, inspiring us with his courage and determination. In the movie *White Men Can't Jump,* the hero, Billy Hoyle, wins the big game with a slam-dunk shot that had previously eluded him. Billy's climactic shot stands as testimony to the ability of any man, of any race, to rise high, beat the odds and achieve his goal. The marvel of the human spirit is that it accepts no limits.

Of course, *Jump* is only a movie. The Olympic track races in Barcelona are for real.

AUGUST 1992

This conclusive treatment on the subject of race in athletics would be a significant one under any circumstances. It is all the more important — and even bold, too — because a taboo had grown up in sports journalism, all but prohibiting even the most intellectual and dispassionate observations about the obvious dominance that black athletes have exhibited in exercises of running and jumping. AMBY BURFOOT, *a past winner of the*

Boston Marathon, has been an editor at Runner's World *for fourteen years, and it is to both his credit and his magazine's that this subject that everybody whispers about was finally presented so diligently and thoughtfully. This serious analysis of the situation was nicely paired, too, by Ron Shelton's humorous movie about the same subject:* White Men Can't Jump. *So by the end of the year the subject was being aired much more candidly. Even* Sports Illustrated *wrote "White Guys Can't Run," about the near extinction of "the great white wideout" in football. All that's left to say for the moment is, white men can't write very imaginative headlines. — F.D.*

BEN JORAVSKY

A Simple Game

FROM THE CHICAGO READER

March 3, 1992

I can still see Terrell — whippet thin and all of seventeen years old — alone at the line, his team down by one, a few seconds on the clock, the whole season at stake.

His last shot, a jumper, had bounced off the rim, and he had been fouled in the fight for the rebound. If he hit his free throws, Roosevelt High would beat Prosser and move on to the next round of the Public League playoffs. If he missed, another season, his last, would end in disappointment. Either way Terrell Redmond would remember these free throws for the rest of his life.

The home crowd had been raucous, but now they hushed. It was an eerie, unnatural stillness that spread like a wave until it seemed that only Terrell was moving, and even he in a dreamy state of slow motion. A lesser man might have panicked. But not Terrell — this was his moment to be great.

For an instant he eyed the bench. His coach and teammates were standing, their expressions an odd mix of anguish and hope. Behind them stood a clump of fans — young blacks and older Jews — Pookie, Weiss, Arnie, Montrell . . . and me. I too was standing, my eyes half covered, almost afraid to look. I had been watching the team since tryouts, following them through injuries and illnesses, fights and fallouts, heartbreaking losses, disciplinary suspensions, and countless incredibly boneheaded teenage mistakes. And now, to tell you the truth, I was hooked, in love with the kids, their coach, the whole history of Roosevelt High.

I wanted Terrell to sink those shots because in twenty-three years of coaching Manny Weincord had never won a basketball title. Because Roosevelt was an average team in an awesome league. Because they played on slippery floors in dimly lit gyms before empty bleachers without cheerleaders, bands, or even parents present.

I wanted him to make those shots so that tomorrow's papers would *have* to cover them. Because the papers rarely cover them, and the scouts rarely watch them, and their last title was in 1952, when the school was Jewish and Manny was on an Army ship bound for Korea. I had this idea that if they won, Terrell would be a star, and the papers would quote Manny, and the school would hold a pep rally, and they'd bedeck the auditorium with bunting of blue and gold, and when the team hit the stage their classmates would cheer. My God, I wanted them to win.

Terrell bounced the ball once, then twice, then again and again and again before raising it and taking a breath. And now I really did close my eyes. It was funny. The season's so long. It stretches from November to March. There are so many games, so many practices, so many afternoons and evenings in a gym. When you're young and in high school, the days pass slowly. You're often bored and usually restless. You never think of endings. But this — this was different. Everything came down to this . . .

November 7, 1991

Twenty-one kids showed up for the first day of tryouts, though with all the whooping and hollering under the baskets it seemed like many more.

It was madness. Two half-court games going at once — a chaotic swirl of sneakers, shorts, socks, and columnar *House Party* haircuts. From the look of the kids I passed in the hallway on my way to the gym, Roosevelt was one of those schools principals like to call a little United Nations — its student body a rich, almost even blend of blacks, whites, Asians, Arabs, and Hispanics. But all the kids in the gym were black, except for a timid Filipino, two flabby whites, and a lanky Hispanic who could dribble between his legs and pass behind his back.

The best of the bunch was a spindly kid with jumping-jack legs. He held the ball high over his head, bounced it hard on the floor, caught it in midair, and then, twisting away from the basket, jammed it through the hoop. It took my breath to see that.

Manny Weincord was in his office, his ear to a black rotary phone, talking to some guy named Arnie.

"Look . . . Arnie," Manny stammered. "Arnie . . . For cry Pete, Arnie, you think I got time to make copies of song sheets?"

It was a small room behind the gym, with a sink in the back, takeout menus on the wall, and a big, paper-cluttered, coffee-stained desk clogging up the middle.

Manny couldn't get a word in edgewise. I could tell their conversation had a ways to go. So I walked back into the gym and sat at the end of the bleachers, under blue and gold banners honoring past triumphs of the Roosevelt Rough Riders. A slippery layer of dust coated the floor, and some of the ceiling lights hung dark. It wasn't a health club, but it was cleaner and brighter than most of the church and park gyms I had seen.

Two months had passed since my first visit to this gym. That was a lovely day in early September. I rode my bike to the school, dodging the kids who darted from the stoops of the old two-flats and walk-ups on either side of the street. The school consumed a full city block in the heart of Albany Park, at the corner of Kimball and Wilson, an enormous, rich-red brick building with tawny gold terra-cotta. Parapets and towers rose into the air, as though its designer wanted an air of ancient academia, a bit of Olde Oxford on the northwest side.

Manny met me in the front lobby and walked me to his office, through hallways and up stairs worn by thousands of feet.

I took a deep breath before I explained my business. I felt nervous, afraid he might say no. I told him that I loved basketball. Was a passionate and lifelong fan of the Bulls. I had always wanted to spend a season with a city high school team. I picked Roosevelt because . . .

Manny cut me off. "Fine."

"Fine?"

"Sure, why not? I'd love to have you. To tell you the truth, I could use the company."

"And I can sit on the bench?"

He grinned. "The *bench*? The bench is the first row of what you get when you pull out the bleachers. If you want to sit on the bench, sit on the bench. But you might be better off sitting behind the bench in the second row. Then you can hear me better."

"And have access to the locker room?"

"I've got no secrets. I only ask that every once in a while you laugh at my jokes."

Two months had dragged past since that moment, during which I wondered impatiently what I would find when the season finally began. And now — the Hispanic kid was knocking down threes, the jumping-jack kid was rattling the rim with turnaround dunks, and I was convinced that I had stumbled on the great undiscovered team of Chicago.

Manny stepped out of his office. He blew his whistle. The players lined up along the wall. He blew his whistle again. They sprinted up and down the court. The room reeked of sweat. Someone opened a window. I felt a chilly blast. Manny blew the whistle again. They gathered on the bleachers. The lanky Hispanic looked eager, like he wanted to run some more.

"Welcome to Roosevelt," Manny said. "I want to wish you all the luck in the world."

As he talked, he paced. He wore a green sweater, blue chinos, and black rubber-sole shoes. He had silver hair, bushy eyebrows, a long face, and big, soft eyes. He was short and lean, not even a touch of flab. His voice was gravelly. When he said *these,* it came out *dese.* The kids eyed him carefully. Only Manny spoke. As he saw it, he said, no one, not even the stars, had made the team. In fact there were no stars. Just players. Everyone gets treated the same. Play hard. Play smart. Hustle. And you'll make the team.

"I've been doing this for twenty-seven years, fellas. I've seen a lot. I've seen everything. There may be better coaches. There may be worse. But I'll tell you this — I'll give you one hundred percent. Maybe I will leave you with something in your head. And, fellas, that's important. 'Cause once it's in your head, no one can take it away."

Manny paused. "A few things about me. I'm not an Xs and Os guy. I don't call a lot of plays. How do you win? You score more points than the other team. How do you score? You get close and you put the ball in the basket. It's a simple game."

Some of the guys laughed, nervous laughter. Manny smiled.

"One more thing about me, fellas. I'm not a recruiter. I am what I am. You get what you see. Whoever walks through that door, I coach. And whoever walks through that door is coached by me."

With that he blew the whistle. The players divided into groups of five for a series of full-court scrimmages. I stood next to Manny on the sidelines at center court. He pointed out the players as they ran by. The jumping-jack guard was Terrell Redmond, the lanky Hispanic David Casas. Then there was Kenric, Carey, Ronnie White, Mario, Sylvester, Mace, Larry, Garner, Kevin, Schurz. The names came so fast I could barely keep up.

Some of the kids were too slow to make the team. Manny let them play anyway. After about an hour he blew his whistle one last time. "That's it. You're all invited back. We'll start making cuts next week." The players retreated to the bleachers. They dried their sweaty bodies with towels, lathered their armpits with deodorant, and put their clothes on over their shorts. The workout had been spirited. I could hear their good-natured bantering as I slipped out the door.

November 12

The roster had been trimmed to twelve. It wasn't hard. The slow guys got the message and quit on their own.

Practice began at 2:45, when the last class cleared from the gym. The players trickled in and started with lay-ups, followed by free throws and sprints. Then they formed two teams of five for an inbounding drill under the east basket. The offensive team wasn't trying to score. They didn't take a shot. They simply put the ball in play, as they would in a game after an opposing score, and tried to advance it across the half-court line; the defense pressured them, trying to force a turnover. They did the drill once. They did it again. And again. And again. Over and over. Manny watched, arms folded. He called out advice. Like: "Don't give your man the baseline."

And: "Don't dribble so much."

And: "Don't telegraph your passes."

And: "Don't turn into your man."

And: "Don't let your hands down — keep 'em up."

It went like this for at least an hour. Manny leavened his criticism with humor and praise. He good-naturedly called the players schmeckles, schmucks, putzes, and yutzes. They laughed.

They loved his Yinglish. They didn't care (or know) that he made most of it up.

Most of all they wanted to run full court. But they couldn't because the frosh-soph team practiced at the other end of the court. The carnival, that's what Manny called them. There were at least twenty of them. The exact number varied by the day. They ran around the gym. They shrieked. They hung from the rim. They wrestled. They were big on wrestling. They liked to roll around the floor. No one got hurt. It was all in fun. Their hormones were raging — it was that stage in life. "Hey, get off the rim — for cry Pete, they're brand new," Manny admonished. Other than that he ignored them. "I have enough to worry about," he said. "They'll learn the facts of life next year, when they move up to varsity."

Their coach, Hutch, was a good-natured, roly-poly drafting teacher. He tried his best. But they were usually out of control by the time he got to practice.

"Can't you kick 'em out?" asked senior guard Ronnie White. "I'm tired of their balls comin' on our side of the court."

"Some coach you'd make," Manny answered.

The high point of practice came at about 4:15, when Hutch exiled the frosh-soph to the hallway for sprints. Then the varsity got to run full court. No refs. No time-outs. No clocks. Just unrestricted play. An endless procession up and down the court. Every now and then someone dunked, or shot a three, or blocked a shot, or looked left and passed right. The others then roared their appreciation. They were young and strong and would run forever.

They dressed by the bleachers. They didn't use the locker room. "Why?" I asked Manny.

"Go see for yourself," he replied.

The locker room was in the basement, at the bottom of a winding stairwell that curled beneath the gym's northeast corner. It was like a jailhouse interrogation cell down there, with several rows of dented lockers illuminated by garish overhanging fluorescent lights. The urinals were stuffed with toilet paper. Smelly water ran on the floor. The shower water was cold. "There's no hot water," Manny said. "Now you know why no one takes a shower. Those showers will give you pneumonia. You'll have icicles hanging from your schmeckle."

Manny and I watched practice from the sidelines or under the basket. He with his whistle, I with my notebook. After practice we retired to his office. He entertained me with old stories and jokes.

"I had this kid ask me, 'Coach, how old are you?' I told him, 'Son, I'm the oldest man in the world.' He said, 'How old?' I said, 'I'm so old, I'm older than my mother.' Well, the kid looked at me, and then he walked away. Then he looked at me again, and then he talked it over with his friends. Then he comes back and says real serious, 'I'm sorry, Coach, but I just can't believe you're older than your mother.'"

I laughed and he told me about the kid who planned to drive from Chicago to Hawaii. "I told him, 'You'd better put a paddle on that car.' He says, 'Why?' I said, 'Don't take my word on it, but I think there's a little water between here and there.'"

We were the last to leave the gym. Manny killed the lights and locked the door. On the train home I thought about that kid driving to Hawaii and I laughed out loud. I told my wife and friends about Manny. I started saying "For cry Pete" — usually at my kids when they were doing something annoying. It bothered my wife. "It doesn't make sense," she said. In time, however, I caught her saying it herself.

November 13

Manny never introduced me to the team. But I heard one guy telling another that I was a reporter. Word spread and every now and then one of the players would sneak a look my way. Mostly they ignored me. They must have decided that whatever I was up to had nothing to do with them. I was there and that was that.

I drew up a roster — my own little trading cards — to keep track of the team. It read like this:

Terrell Redmond: Senior guard. Nickname: Red. Strong points: Jordan-like hang time. Awesome dunker. Quick hands. Weak points: Gets too nervous.

Kenric Mattox: Junior center. No nickname. Strong points: Six foot five. Strong — very strong. Clogs up the middle. Tough rebounder. Weak points: Got flabby over the summer. Misses too many lay-ups.

David Casas: Senior forward. No nickname. Strong points: Quick, long arms. Six foot six. Dunks, blocks shots, passes, dribbles — does it all. Wants to play like a guard. Weak points: Manny doesn't want him to play like a guard. Missed most of last season because of poor grades.

Herman Carey: Senior guard. Nickname: Mush. Strong points: Confident. Fast. Strong. Weak points: Dribbles too much. Talks too much. Prediction: his talking will drive Manny crazy.

Mario Ramos: Senior guard. Nickname: Rio. Strong points: Gorgeous rainbow jumper. Weak points: So quiet you forget he's there.

Maceo Tillman: Senior forward. Nickname: Mace. Strong points: Marble-slab biceps. Fearless. Great spirit. Weak points: No shooting touch — his shot's like a projectile.

Larry Wall: Junior center. No nickname. Strong points: Six foot five and growing. Weak points: Clumsy, just growing into his body. Can't shoot.

Kevin Lewis: Junior guard. Nickname: Cuz. Strong points: Superfast. Low-to-the-ground dribble. Weak points: Plays out of control.

Anthony Garner: Junior forward. Nickname: Orr. Strong points: Six foot six. Long arms. Weak points: Raw.

There were two others — senior guard Ronnie White and his good friend, senior forward Sylvester Turner. But there was something fleeting about them. They blended in. They didn't make an impression. At least not on me.

I shared my notes with Manny. He said I got it right. "Lots of potential on this team," he said.

"I'll go better than that. Manny, I think you may have one of the best teams in the city."

He smiled. "How much high school basketball have you seen?" he asked.

"Not much. I mainly follow the Bulls."

"Why did you pick us to follow?"

I reddened. "Well, I always wanted to spend a year with a team. And Roosevelt is so close to my home. And —"

"O.K., well, I won't lie to you. In my opinion, the world's best high school basketball is right here in the Public League. But there are sixty-four teams in the Public League. And those teams are divided into four regions: north, south, central, and west. And those regions are divided into Red and Blue divisions. Red is for the good teams and Blue is for the not-so-good teams.

We're in Blue North. Which, you might say, is the weakest division in the weakest region of the city. And we're not even the favorite in Blue North — Lane Tech is."

"But you have so many guys who can dunk!"

He laughed. "There's not a team in the city that doesn't have a guy who can dunk. That's nothin'. King High has two seven-footers. And they're only juniors."

I was silent. "Listen," Manny said, "if you want to back out of the story, I won't hold it against you."

"No, no — I wouldn't do that."

"See, 'cause I think we could have a pretty good year. Each year the winner of Blue flip-flops with the last place team in Red. I think we can beat Lane. I think we can move up to Red. That's my goal — to move up to Red."

November 14

I met Arnie Kamen today, but only briefly. He ran out as fast as he ran in. "Got another appointment," he said.

"Arnie and I graduated from Roosevelt together back in 1950," Manny explained. "Arnie's sort of a one-man booster club. He made his money tradin' commodities and now he spends a lot of his time raisin' money for the school. He paid for those backboards and he's buyin' us new uniforms. He's a wonderful man — he's a guy with a mission. He wants to teach all the kids the school song."

"The school song?"

"He's got the principal playin' it over the loudspeaker in the mornin'. He wants all the kids to sing it at a pep rally. That's why he wants those song sheets. He wants me to sing it with him — listen, I'll get up onstage with a grass skirt and a hula hoop if it means more money for the team."

I also met Sender and Weiss. Sender was a substitute teacher who called himself the assistant coach, although Manny had never officially appointed him to the position. He made himself useful by keeping track of rebounds, turnovers, and assists. He had a pointy face, perfect posture, and a puritanical outlook on things. To him, everything in life was a lesson. He was always telling the players to tuck in their jerseys and straighten their socks.

Weiss was big, round, and delightfully eccentric. He graduated from Roosevelt in the early sixties and now taught special ed. He wore a blue and gold Rough Riders sweatshirt, talked fast, distributed rock candy, and entertained the players by bantering with Manny in a thick Jewish accent.

Weiss: "So, Mista Veincord, how's your yutz?"

Manny: "Very vell, Mista Schmecklepuss; how's your putz?"

The kids thought stuff like this was hilarious.

Today Weiss introduced Manny to Efrain Cobos, a baby-faced, pear-shaped junior who wanted to be the team's manager.

Manny gave Efrain a serious look-over. "You'll have to fill the water bottles and keep score," Manny said.

Efrain nodded.

"We can't pay you anythin'," Manny added.

Efrain nodded again.

Manny smiled and patted Efrain's belly. "But after the season I'll buy you a corned-beef sandwich."

Efrain became one of the regulars who wandered in and out of the gym. There were others: big Montrell "Sin" Cochran, a tackle on the football team; tiny Tommie Redmond, who had a biting wit; Ramon "Pookie" Willis, who wore his Jheri-curled hair down to his shoulders; and dapper Ed — Eddie Kroger, who harbored hopes of one day making the team.

There was one other kid — a silent sort, with old, sad eyes. I'll call him Teddy. I asked Manny about him. "He was a great running back. Scored fourteen touchdowns when he was a freshman. A helluva basketball player, too. He'd be a senior if he was still in school."

"Why isn't he?"

Manny shook his head. "He got kicked out of school for throwing a garbage can out of the auditorium balcony. It hit a woman and hurt her pretty bad."

I snuck the kid another glance. "Why did he do it?"

Manny shot me a look of blank disbelief. *"Why?"* he repeated. "What possible reason could he have?"

November 15

Someone stole Manny's whistle. "Took it right off my desk," he said.

"Why would anyone steal a whistle?" I asked.

"Because it's there — it's the Mount Everest of whistles," he said. "Don't worry, I think they have one at Von Steuben [high school]. We'll work out a deal: I'll use it one day, they'll use it the next."

Practice was intense. A group of recent grads led by Tim Davis, last year's starting center, stopped by. Manny gave them a go at five randomly picked players. The alumni winded fast. They walked up the court for every two times they ran. They didn't have the energy to play defense. They lost 55 to 28.

While the graduates gasped for breath, Manny had the varsity run twenty sprints. Then he said, "You know, I'm not tired yet." They groaned. He laughed. They ran five more sprints.

Afterward he gathered them in a semicircle. He told them that he loved them. That he appreciated their hard work. That they could be as good as — or better than — any team he ever coached. "We got one week of practice before the opening of the season. Don't let down. Don't give up."

November 18

Only ten guys showed up for practice. Schurz hadn't been seen in days. Manny called his home. No one answered. He called around the system and discovered that Schurz was a recent transfer who had flunked out of his last school. As far as most of the kids knew, he had dropped out.

David wasn't at practice either. His grandfather had died, and David had flown to Mexico for the funeral. He'd be gone at least a week.

During warm-ups, Terrell left the court clutching his chest. Manny and Weiss rushed to his side. "It's my asthma," he told them.

"If it's your asthma, don't mess around," said Manny. "You should quit right away."

"Have you seen a doctor?" asked Weiss.

"No."

"Well, you should," said Manny. "Take time off from practice. Basketball means nothing if you don't have your health. First things first."

"Does it hurt when you breathe?" asked Weiss.

"Yes."

"Breathe," said Weiss, pressing his ear to Terrell's chest.

"Oh, he's stuffed," said Weiss.

"Look, son," said Manny, "have you ever taken Primatene?"

"No," said Terrell.

"All right. See a doctor, but also take this stuff."

"You can buy it off the shelf," said Weiss.

"Put it in your mouth and spray," said Manny.

"But don't spray more than once," said Weiss.

"O.K.," said Terrell.

" 'Cause it can open you up too much," said Weiss.

"That happened to me," said Manny. "I had a bad case of asthma and I went to the hospital. The guy asks me — *after* he gave me the shot — 'Did you take any medication?' I told him I took my daughter's medication. He says, 'You can die from this combination.' I said, 'Now you tell me — thanks a lot. I think I'll just lay down over there in the corner and die.' "

Weiss and I laughed. Terrell smiled.

"You know what you should really do?" Manny continued. "Take some chicken soup. I see my mother, today, she tells me, 'Manny, you don't look so good. Have some chicken soup.' I say, 'Ma, I'm almost sixty years old, for cry Pete.' "

Manny turned to me. "You know the story about the old lady who goes to her neighbor's funeral? She looks at the guy in the casket and goes up to the widow and says, 'Give him seventeen bowls of chicken soup.' "

"Oh, I know this joke," said Weiss.

Manny continued: " 'It won't help,' the widow says."

Weiss took the punch line: " 'Yeah, but it can't hurt!' "

Weiss, Manny, and I laughed. Terrell smiled. A few minutes later Manny called Terrell into his office, reminded him to see a doctor, and gave him $10 to buy himself some Primatene.

November 19

Six guys showed up ready to practice.

Terrell was still too sick to play, as was Sylvester, who had come down with the flu. Although he did show up, long enough to wheeze and cough on everyone else.

Two other guys were serving suspensions for getting into separate fights. "I saw the one fight," said Ronnie. "Our guy went after some freshman who was lippin' off. If you ask me, the kid deserved it."

"Great," said Manny, "that's comforting to hear."

November 20

During a half-court scrimmage, Kenric stumbled over Larry and fell to the floor. He was clutching his face and writhing in agony.

Manny hurried over. "Son, is it your nose?"

"No," Kenric moaned. "It's my ankle."

"Then why are you holding your face?"

Manny pressed and poked Kenric's ankle. "Mattox, I have bad news for you. I think you're gonna live."

Still, he had Kenric sit out the practice. Now they were down to five able bodies.

"Can you believe this?" Manny raged. "This is crazy."

At the end of the day he sat in his office behind his desk, which was covered with papers, and ran his hands through his hair. A season, he explained, is like a puzzle with hundreds of little pieces. You put it together one piece at a time. You don't just throw them the ball and let them run. You teach them the stall, the trap, the press, the inbounds plays, the four corners, working the ball to the big man in the middle, man-to-man defense, the zones. Through ceaseless repetition they master many different skills so that in the course of a game you call out a number and they respond with the right play.

But how could he teach them anything when they didn't have enough players for two three-man teams? Time was wasting. The season opener was a few days away. And aside from Kenric, David, and Terrell, Manny didn't even know who would start. "We're lost, damn it," he said. "And we had so much momentum."

November 21

On the last day of preseason practice, four guys showed up ready to play. The others were either injured, ill, in Mexico, or suspended.

We were one weekend away from the season-opening Taft Thanksgiving Tournament. It was a four-team tourney. Up first for Roosevelt was Taft, a Red North team, one of the best in the

city. Their star player was Kenny Pratt, a nimble forward capable
of scoring 25 or 30 points in a game. Manny wanted to talk to the
team about Pratt. He wanted to talk to them about a lot of things.
He wanted to tell them about fronting Pratt. About denying him
the ball. About all the good things that could come if they played
hard.

But who would he talk to? He poked his head out of his office
and saw Herman sitting in the bleachers, aimlessly watching
Mario and Larry play a lazy game of one-on-one. A sophomore
strolled by, eating french fries. "Hey man, give me some," said
Herman. He grabbed a bunch.

The freshmen and sophomores had been dismissed from
practice early. The gym was strangely silent without them, almost serene.

Manny sighed and returned to his office. So ended the final
practice before the start of the season.

Mandel "Manny" Weincord (born February 24, 1932)

Manny's father, Louis, was a conductor on the Ravenswood elevated line. His mother, Lillian, kept the house. They lived in Albany Park, which then was a predominantly Jewish working-class
neighborhood of walk-ups and courtyard apartment buildings.
They rented a two-and-a-half-room flat at 3546 W. Montrose.
Manny slept on a cot in the living room. "There was only one
entrance. In case of fire your best escape was to jump out the
window."

Manny was an only child — small, athletic, and fast like a bullet. He loved the Cubs, Sox, Bears, and Stags, an old professional
basketball team.

He attended Roosevelt, beginning in the fall of 1946. He
played lightweight basketball (for kids under five foot seven) and
was coached by Sam Edelcup. As a senior he finished second in
the citywide 100-yard dash. "I ran in argyle socks and baseball
shoes; I must have looked like a schmuck."

The center of his universe was the Max Strauss Community
Center, an old three-story brick building at Wilson and Lawn-
dale. The Jewish Federation operated it. "The gym was so small

you could install wall-to-wall carpeting at a reasonable price. The ceiling was so low we learned to shoot without an arc. I loved that place; I would have stayed there all night if they let me. I set the world record for the half-mile coming home from there every night. If I wasn't home at 9:30, my mother would call the cops."

He graduated in 1950, got drafted, and was sent to Korea. He had never been out of Chicago before that, had never really been out of Albany Park. He served in combat for more than a year, operating a howitzer cannon in the Forty-fifth Infantry Division. He shot and was shot at. He saw men killed. He lost most of the hearing in his right ear.

When he came home he got a job running the gym at Max Strauss. He took classes at night, earned a degree in physical education, got married, had three daughters, bought a house in the suburbs, and, in 1963, started working at Roosevelt. He taught gym and coached tennis, football, and track. On his own time he refereed basketball games, umped baseball games, and taught driver's ed. In 1969 Sam Edelcup retired and Manny became Roosevelt's head basketball coach. He was thirty-seven; he's been coaching there ever since.

Most of the Jews left Albany Park years ago, replaced by Koreans, Arabs, blacks, and Hispanics. The Strauss center was demolished to make way for a low-income housing complex. About fifteen years ago, some of the Slavic and Hispanic students asked Manny to start a soccer team. "All I knew about soccer was that there was a goalie and ten guys running around in short pants. Its strategy's not much different than basketball's: look for the open man, get back on defense, the ball gets there faster on the pass than the dribble. Besides, what counts in coaching is not the plays you run but the lessons you teach — teamwork, patience, responsibility. People ask me, 'They speak all those different languages, how do they understand you?' I say, 'They don't. That's how come they win.' Listen, if I can make them laugh, and have a little fun, I've succeeded."

His soccer teams won Public League championships in 1978 and 1990. After that last triumph, his players placed a sombrero on Manny's head, hoisted him on their shoulders, and paraded him around the field. "Instead of swearing at me in thirty different languages they praised me in thirty different languages. My father was dying of cancer. But as sick as he was, when I showed him that championship plaque, I could tell he was sharing my happiness."

A few weeks later, his father died. The whole team, Arab kids included, attended the memorial service. When Manny saw them there, dressed up in their best coats and ties, he started to cry. "I never had any problems with the Arab students. I tell the kids that this is America, not the Middle East. I can't resolve that conflict, I have enough troubles with the conflicts in my own life. I'm sure there's plenty of wrong on both sides."

The leading scorer on last year's basketball team was a Palestinian kid — Mohammed "Mo" Ghanimah. Just before the start of his senior season, Mo and several friends were arrested by police and charged with spray-painting "P.L.O." on a North Side synagogue.

"I called Mo into my office and told him that if he did what they said he did then he should be dragged through the streets like a dog. Not because I'm Jewish. That wasn't the point. But to me, a synagogue is like a church, a temple, or a mosque — a house of worship. What was done was the worst kind of desecration.

"Mo started crying and he looked at me and said, 'Coach, I swear, I didn't do it.'"

Some of Manny's friends and many older alumni wanted Mo kicked off the team. But Manny let him play. "Mo had never given me a day of trouble. I'm not judge and jury. He deserved the benefit of the doubt; if others don't like it, let them coach their own team."

Taylor Bell wrote about Mo and Manny in his *Sun-Times* high school sports column. But for the most part, Manny ran his bare-bones program in anonymity. The public school system was almost bankrupt, and each year the sports budget was cut. Manny was supposed to pay referees, rent buses, and buy equipment on about $350 a year. Most expenses came out of his (or Arnie Kamen's) pocket. He didn't have any assistants. He kept track of the water bottles. And the score book. And the basketballs, which he toted in a sack to road games for the pregame shoot-around.

The kids bought their own gym shoes. By season's end their soles were slippery, the leather torn. This year's uniforms were six seasons old. The shorts were short and tight. The players wanted the long baggy look popularized by Michael Jordan. Appearances don't matter, Manny told them. It's what's inside that counts. He once raced in argyles — remember?

But he saw their disappointment as they poked through the pile of torn, faded jerseys. He learned to live with such disappointments, just as he learned to live with the banged-up lockers, busted showers, dingy gyms, and, worst of all, the violence. There was more violence than his generation could have imagined. One of Manny's soccer players, Fabian Diaz, was shot dead by gangbangers who mistook him for a member of a rival gang.

Styles changed. As soon as Manny got used to earrings on boys, his starting point guard started wearing a ring in his nose. The game changed too. Manny came of age in the era of the two-handed set shot. In those days the best teams were almost all Jewish. The first all-black powerhouse was the DuSable High Panthers of 1954. Paxton Lumpkin, Sweet Charlie Brown, Reggie Henderson, coach Jim Brown — Manny still calls them the greatest team he ever saw. They revolutionized the game. They pressed. They ran the break. They dunked.

Nowadays every Public League team has a dunker and very few have any Jewish players. Blacks no longer are confined to one school or neighborhood (the North Side, once all white, has been transformed by three decades of peaceful demographic change). Even if they were, they can attend any high school they want, thanks to a 1978 desegregation accord. "We got kids from all over the city comin' to Roosevelt; half my team comes from the West Side."

Another thing that's changed: now there are fewer two-letter athletes. Kids play organized basketball spring, summer, and fall. Because the high schools are open to all, some coaches openly recruit the best players — luring them with promises of more playing time or new gym shoes — knowing that one superstar can remake a program and enhance a coach's reputation. If a player doesn't like his coach or if there's another coach he thinks he likes better or if he doesn't think he's playing enough, he changes schools. Nick Anderson, Mark Aguirre, Marcus Liberty — three city players who went on to star in college and the pros — they all changed high schools. Some kids transfer two or

three times, moving from one end of the city to the other and
even out to the suburbs.

Manny calls it a meat market and he wants no part of it. "It's
been forty years since Roosevelt won a city title and I'll let
another forty years pass if that's what it takes to win another.
How does it help a kid to go from school to school? Coaches
are just using kids. They're telling them that basketball is a
ticket to a future. But if you can't read, basketball is a ticket to
nowhere."

Manny warns his players that they need a C average to stay on
his team. He tells them the story of Charlie Taylor, the greatest
player he ever coached. Charlie practiced day and night, set a
Public League career scoring record, won a full basketball scholarship to Indiana State. But the competition was tough. He
didn't start. He got restless. He transferred. He dropped out. He
kicked around the city and wound up in the Marines. He caught
spinal meningitis and died at age twenty-four.

"I tell the kids that athletics is something they can lose in two
seconds — your knee goes out, bang, and it's gone. But they
don't listen."

Manny wishes they would drop the dream, but he knows they
can't. The game seeps into their veins. Look at him — sixty years
old and still hanging around the gym.

He wonders sometimes if he would have been better off doing
something else. When he was younger and might have been
spending more time with his wife and three daughters, he was
coaching and watching games instead. He works on the fringe of
a multibillion-dollar business, yet he's never made more than
$45,000 a year, and he has to coach two sports, teach gym, and
moonlight evenings and summers on the driver's-ed range just
to make that. His clothes are simple; he drives an old brown
Chevy; he never traveled around the world.

Other high school coaches, the slick ones, advanced through
the ranks, in some cases all the way to the pros. Manny would
have liked that. But no one ever offered him a college job and he
never asked for one. He stayed at Roosevelt. "The guy who's always here." Twenty-three seasons: 605 games, 375 wins, 230
losses. "Any coach can win with the best. But I never recruited. I
did the best with the horses I had."

His best team went twenty-four and two and made it to the semifinals of the Public League playoffs before he had to deliver another consolation speech.

He's the dean of city coaches, known and respected by coaches and refs as a classy competitor. He doesn't cheat. He doesn't run up the score. Modest in victory, gracious in defeat, he always remembers to congratulate a coach who beats him.

Every now and then some bucket-bellied guy with a boy at his side will come up and say, "Coach, you don't remember me, but I played against you. I'd like to introduce you to my son." And Manny will say: "Do I remember you? Of course I remember you! For cry Pete, you gave us fits." Then he'll turn to the little boy and say, "Son, your father was one helluva ball player. I hated playin' against him. He was one of the toughest competitors we faced."

Manny got a Christmas card from a former student teacher who went on to become an assistant basketball coach at a couple of major midwestern colleges. "I just wanted to say hello and Merry Christmas," the letter began. "I think about you all the time, I miss being around you. I never had a father who lived with my family — but if I did, I wish he could be like you. Take care. Our team is doing great. We're ranked twenty-fourth in the nation."

At times Manny thinks about retiring. But when tryouts come in November, his energy returns. He stands outside his office and watches another generation of players run up and down the court and he thinks: with a little luck, this might be the year we hang a new championship banner on the wall.

November 25

It took forty-five minutes in withering bumper-to-bumper holiday traffic to reach Taft High School. I drove a couple of the players, Sender took some in his car, and others took public transportation, having received detailed advice on routes and transfer points from Manny during a brief meeting in the gym. When we arrived, game one of the Thanksgiving tournament was under way: Wells versus Phillips.

The gym was nearly empty. I counted maybe fifty spectators, including several members of the Taft wrestling team taking a break from practice. The crowd was silent. There was no band. No cheerleaders. You could hear the basketball thumping, gym shoes scraping, and players grunting as they lunged for rebounds. The lighting was dim and there was little room along the baseline for players to maneuver without crashing into the walls. The scoreboard rattled and the three scorekeepers huddled around a rickety card table. They introduced starters and announced fouls and substitutions, but the loudspeaker's cackle swallowed their words.

The Taft team was on the sidelines. I recognized Kenny Pratt's hard, chiseled features and black bushy eyebrows from his pictures in the paper. The whole team looked lean and handsome in their blue warm-up suits and matching white and blue sneakers.

The Rough Riders, some wore black sneakers, others white. Some wore their socks low, others high. They looked awed when Taft began an orchestrated lay-up drill and seemed bewildered as to how they should line up for their own. This was the first full-team gathering in more than a week.

Manny and Frank Hood, Taft's coach, met at the scorer's table. They shook hands. It was then that they noticed that both teams were wearing blue.

"You should have worn home white," Hood told Manny.

"But we're the visitors," said Manny.

"No, you're the home team."

"But it's your gym."

"Yes, but this is a tournament game. And for this particular tournament game *you're* the home team. It was in the schedule."

Manny thought about this for a moment.

"I'm afraid you'll have to change into white," said Hood.

"But we didn't bring our white uniforms," said Manny.

Hood frowned. And his Eagles trudged back to the locker room, where they changed into their home whites, giving the Rough Riders another five minutes to practice their jump shots. Not a single one fell in.

"Oh boy, this is gonna be a long day," said Weiss. Manny clapped his hands and gathered the team around him. "We'll start with the zone," he said. "Front Pratt; deny him the ball. Don't let one guy beat you. O.K.?

"We're gonna go with David, Kenric, Terrell, Herman, and Maceo as the starters. Come on guys, we can beat this team."

The Rough Riders put their hands together and chanted: "One, two, three, win!"

It took a minute to prove Manny wrong. Taft pressed relentlessly — hands, arms, fingers in the face — and the Rough Riders collapsed. They couldn't advance the ball up the court. Manny tried everyone. He pulled players in and out every few minutes. Nothing worked. They traveled. They double-dribbled. They charged. They bounced the ball off their legs. In utter panic, they tossed the ball to a player from Taft. At one point Kenric abandoned his usual spot under the basket to lumber up-court with the ball. "Get back, get back," Manny roared — the whole point of his offense was to work it to the big man down low.

David started bringing the ball up. He was good at it too, a slicker ball handler than most of the guards. But he was six foot six (big for high school) and Manny wanted him down low next to Kenric.

"You're a forward, not a guard," Manny screamed at David during a time-out.

David nodded.

"You belong down low, not bringing up the ball!"

David nodded again. Two plays later David again brought up the ball. "Aw for cry Pete," Manny moaned, as he buried his head in his hands.

Somewhere in the onslaught Ronnie lost his pants. Or nearly did. He pulled them down so they hung from the hips, not the waist. He wanted the low, long-pants Jordan look. But he was almost exposing his crack. Manny turned red. "God damn it, White, pull up your pants!"

But Ronnie didn't hear him. "Mario," Manny yelled, "get in there for White." Mario, sprawled across two rows of bleachers, his mind lost in space, didn't hear Manny either. Manny got so angry he jumped up and down. "This is ridiculous. We look awful. Mario, get your ass on the bench. Come on — at least *look* like a team."

The players had apparently forgotten every lesson they had ever learned, or maybe they had never learned them at all. They exposed the ball to their defenders. They didn't guard the base-line. They dribbled inside the key. They did everything Manny had told them not to.

The slaughter continued even after Hood pulled his starters. David fouled out; Larry fouled out; finally even Arnie Kamen stopped cheering. Mercifully, the game ended. The final score: 83 to 35. "At least you didn't lose by fifty," I told Manny, vainly searching for some words of consolation.

Manny was not consoled. "This is the worst whippin' a Rough Rider team has ever suffered. And what do you expect from a team that can only get four guys to its practice?"

November 26

Ten people attended the game against Wells. The Rough Riders won, thanks to Sylvester Turner — skinny, gawky, freckle-faced Sylvester, one of the kids who made no impression on me during those first days of practice (which shows how much I know). Sylvester came off the bench, hit six straight points, ending up with 18, and brought the Rough Riders rooters (Montrell, Tommie, and Pookie, that is) to their feet. I'm still not sure how he did it. He had the strangest release — more like a shotputter's heave.

After the game I congratulated him. "That was some of the greatest shooting I've ever seen." Sylvester mumbled something and then looked at the ground. I walked over to Ronnie, Sylvester's best friend. "Where you guys been hidin' him?"

"Hey, man," said Ronnie, "Sylvester's been here all the time. You just didn't see him."

November 27

Sylvester kept up his hot shooting against Phillips, a South Side school, in game three of the tournament. He led the team with 16 points.

But Manny was mad at him anyway. He said Sylvester didn't play defense and he didn't box out under the boards.

So he pulled Sylvester and inserted long Anthony Garner, an all-arms-and-legs junior. Anthony had a great move to the basket, but he made a lot of mistakes. Manny kept yelling at him to stay under the basket, and still Anthony floated all over the court.

I don't think Anthony responded well to yelling. He was new to Roosevelt. He had transferred from Orr High School when his family moved to Albany Park. He didn't really know any of his teammates. He kept to himself, a quiet kid with big soulful eyes. His teammates nicknamed him Orr and said he looked like Scottie Pippen. He sort of winced when Manny yelled at him, absorbing the criticism like blows.

Manny replaced Anthony with Larry, another raw junior: tall, but clumsy. He always dribbled once before shooting a lay-up. At halftime Manny pulled him aside under the basket. "Larry, practice your lay-up. Stand on the right side. Lay it in. Catch it before it hits the ground and lay it in from the left. Now do it from the right. The point is to take the shot without dribbling."

Two minutes into the third quarter, Larry grabbed an offensive rebound. Instead of laying it right up, he dribbled once. A smaller opponent slapped the ball away. "I give up," Manny moaned.

His demeanor surprised me. At times he screamed so hard his neck veins bulged and his face turned purple. He called them gutless. He said they played like cowards and that he "could leave them in a gym for three weeks and they still wouldn't make a shot." When they hit a free throw, he clutched his heart and staggered, as though felled by disbelief. He cursed, he ranted, he threw his keys on the ground. After someone made a particularly boneheaded mistake, he rose from his seat and looked to replace him. The players on the bench pretended to be absorbed by the game. Manny paced before them, disgustedly eyeing them as if to say, "Look what I have to choose from." Finally he'd say something like, "Ronnie, go in for Redmond. And try not to do something stupid."

The players showed their dissatisfaction with Manny's yelling in little ways. They muttered or frowned or gave him the cold shoulder on their way to the bench. They sat far from him.

Superfans Tommie and Pookie were no help. If Manny called Sylvester a schmuck, they'd say: "Hey, Sylvester, Weincord called you a schmuck."

Near the end of the game Maceo missed a wide-open lay-up

and Manny pulled him. As he walked to the bench, Maceo said: "Damn, I missed that easy little shot."

"Damn straight, you did," said Tommie.

"Shut your mouth," said Maceo.

"Hey, Maceo," said Pookie. "You can cry on my shoulder for a dollar."

Roosevelt lost to Phillips, 72 to 64. After the game Kevin chased Tommie onto the court and tackled him. Both guys giggled as they wrestled on the floor — just like the frosh-soph team at practice.

I was almost out the door when Terrell ran up and asked if I would give him a lift back to Roosevelt. During the ride I tried to make small talk, but Terrell was distracted.

Finally, after about fifteen minutes in the car, he said: "He's in my head."

"Who?"

"Coach."

"Manny?"

"The guy be yelling all the time. I can't play my game."

We were a block from Terrell's house and I pulled over to let him out. He looked sad, almost anguished. "Look, Terrell, forget it. Tomorrow's Thanksgiving. Enjoy the holiday. You're a great player. The season's just starting." He shook his head. "I got to get him out of my head," he said. "I got to play my game."

December 2

By now I had my routine. I left home at two and rode the el to the end of the line at Kimball and Lawrence. From there I walked two blocks south to Wilson, passing a discount shoe store, a pawnshop, a seedy bar, a greasy spoon, a jewelry store, a Burger King, and a tide of students who all looked and sounded alike, regardless of race, as they came tumbling along the crumbling sidewalks, overjoyed to be done with school for the day. The boys cut their hair in some form of the Fade (long on top, short on the sides) and wore baggy pants, baseball caps, and jackets brightly blazoned with the names of their favorite sports teams.

I'd see some of the players killing time before practice at the Burger King — eating fries, drinking Cokes, nuzzling with the girls. Some would acknowledge me with a grunt. Some looked away, like they didn't see me. Herman, Ronnie, and Mario were the friendliest — always said hello.

Today before practice, on a whim, I told Herman, "Sink forty straight free throws and I'll give you a ticket to Friday's Bulls game."

"No problem," he said. He hit four, then missed.

"I can do it," he said.

"But you only made four," I said.

"Don't matter. Everythin's rhythm. I was just gettin' my rhythm."

"Herman, you're so conceited," said Sylvester.

"Hey, man, it ain't conceited if it's true."

I was becoming enough of a fixture in the gym that I could sneak up close to the bench at the start of practice, when the players were lacing up their sneakers, and overhear their conversations. They talked a lot about sex. (Bragged about it mostly. One player was a father. His girlfriend sometimes brought their baby to practice.) Sometimes they talked about the police. "Almost all of us been picked up at least once," said Ronnie. "You don't have to be doin' nothin'. They stop you for bein' young and black."

One player had been stopped over the weekend. "The cop sees my Roosevelt ID and says, 'Do you know Coach Weincord?' I said, 'Yes sir, I know Coach Weincord.' The cop says, 'I played against his team years ago.' Then he let me go."

Manny was a big thing in their lives. He had the power to bench them, play them, or kick them off the team. They all felt they deserved more playing time. But as Ronnie said many times, "The only vote that counts is Weincord's."

Over the weekend, Manny decided he had been too hard on the team and vowed to yell less.

"Believe it or not, I don't like yellin'," he said. "My own father once told me, 'The way you holler, if a kid had poked you in the nose, I would have shaken his hand.' He was right. No one should have to do anything out of fear. They might win, but they won't be winners in life. Some coaches smack a kid in the rear, and then the kid goes out in the world and can't do a thing unless someone smacks him."

At the start of practice today, Manny apologized for calling them gutless. "I have to admit that even after all these years, I still make mistakes. I like you guys — you might not believe that, but I do. I criticize you because I want you to be successful. This is an open door to college. There are scouts at these games. And they don't just watch the scorer. They look at guys who can pass and play defense. They're looking for a team man. And that means when a coach takes you out of a game you don't say, 'Coach, screw you.' Oh, you might not say that, but I can see what you're thinking by the look on your face."

And now he was off, he couldn't help himself, scowling, slouching, strutting — imitating a sullen player's angry exit from a game. He caught himself before he started yelling. "When I take you out, don't run to the end of the bench or talk with your friends in the stands. Sit next to me, I won't bite you."

Manny had them work on the four-corners offense: a man is posted in each corner and the center in the middle, and they work the ball around the perimeter until someone pops free. He reminded them of upcoming games: Schurz, Curie, and then the big one, the game that stood out on the schedule like an exclamation mark — Glenbrook North.

"Glenbrook's got Chris Collins. We all know about him. Doug Collins's kid," Manny said, referring to the former coach of the Bulls. "He's one helluva scorer. But one player can't beat a team. And that's what we are — a team."

"Right," said David. "A team."

"Now the game's gonna be at their place in Northbrook. We'll be takin' a bus. I hear a lot of old Roosevelt grads who live out there will be comin'. They aren't comin' for Collins — they're comin' for you."

A few of the players murmured.

"If you see a bunch of old guys with canes and walkers, you'll know those are Weincord's friends."

The players laughed. Manny looked relieved. "So O.K., guys, let's say the season starts today."

December 4

In the Schurz High School gym, chunks of paint fell from the walls and the floor needed a wash. At halftime a fat, oily centipede crawled across the court. The Rough Riders played their best game of the season, patiently working the four-corners offense. They found the open man and hit their open shots. At the half they led by twenty-two.

This time it was the other coach, Stu Menaker, who yelled. At one point he got so angry at his point guard that he turned to a kid sitting on the bench, grabbed him by the shirt, yanked him from his seat, and all but threw him into the game as a replacement.

The Rough Riders romped, 72 to 45. Efrain, the team manager, was particularly ecstatic. It was his first game keeping score (he had missed the Taft tournament), and he didn't make any mistakes. "I was really nervous, especially when I had to add everything up. I'm not very good at math."

Manny had high praise for the whole team. "You were brilliant," he said. "Really."

"Bring on Glenbrook North," said Herman.

December 6

One problem. The home opener against Curie came first. And Curie was fast, much better than expected. They raced to a ten-point lead, and the spectators started mocking the home team, as though they were watching their pesky little brothers screw up the fifth-grade play.

They howled when Ronnie double-dribbled and hooted when Terrell shot an air ball. If someone made an impressive move, they patronized. When Terrell scored off a rebound, Teddy, the kid who'd thrown the garbage can, said "That's my nigger."

There were about forty fans there, most of whom, like Teddy, were black. A lot of them laughed at his remark. Not me. Terrell was trying to elevate himself, and Teddy and the others were trying to knock him back down.

As a child, sledding with friends, I yelled out, "Last one down the hill's a nigger." I don't know why I said it. We didn't live near any blacks; I didn't know what the word meant. My father spanked me and I never used the word again. Years later I heard Lenny Bruce's routine in which he suggests that we drain the sting from the word by saying it again and again. But Lenny Bruce never sat in the stands at Roosevelt High and heard one black kid crack it like a whip to keep another black kid in his place.

I turned around to say something to Teddy about the evils of self-deprecation, but he looked me dead in the eye and I froze, pushed by his stare back behind the line that divides black from white. This is *our* word, he was saying, and I'll say what I want. Then another kid said it (in reference, this time, to Kenric), and I hunkered low, shamed by my silence, staring straight ahead, as if I had heard nothing, never so humiliated in my life.

At halftime the pom-pom squad — six girls, their names stitched in the bottoms of their blue and gold pajamalike sweat suits — turned on a silver boom box and boogied to some hip-hop beat.

"Shake yo' big black butt," one kid hollered. From the back of the bleachers came a long and loud orgasmic moan. Lots of kids laughed, including most of the players. The players didn't laugh, however, when the fans turned on them. "Sylvester, coach says you ain't no good," someone called. Maceo, sitting on the bench, whirled around and snarled: "Shut up."

"You gonna cry, Mace?"

Maceo looked like he wanted to wring the fellow's neck, but reluctantly he turned back to the game. "They don't stick by us, man," he complained. Manny called time. "Why is it that you put forty people into a gym and you get bothered?" he asked the team. "Don't listen to 'em. For cry Pete, ignore the crowd!"

But they couldn't, especially after he told them to. They ran from the ball, passing up the same sort of wide-open jumpers that they had eagerly accepted in the dim silence of Schurz.

With a minute or so left, Terrell accidentally bumped an opposing guard. The guard jammed his face against Terrell's and said something. Terrell said something back. The ref pulled them apart just as a dozen or so Roosevelt students streamed onto the court. The Curie players retreated to their bench, under a barrage of curses and threats, as Manny and Sender scooted across the court to lead the students back to their seats.

Curie won 74 to 68. "Coach," Manny said to Curie coach James McLaughlin, "I'm sorry. Really. This crowd, they have disgraced the school."

Long after the game, Manny sat in his office, feeling tired and blue. He wanted to go home, but there were so many things to do: phone the score into the City News Bureau, wait for the frosh-soph game to end, gather the balls, sweep the floor, collect receipts, lock the doors. He had been up early and now he would stay up late, stewing over the loss and the crowd's behavior. On top of that, they were off to Glenbrook North tomorrow.

December 7

The streets were quiet for a Saturday night, and we zipped right up to Northbrook in no time at all — the bus rattling with the happy shrieks of the players and a few of their friends. No one had to be told that this was a special night. Without any prompting from Manny, the players had dressed well for their trip to the suburbs, many wearing jackets and ties. We sliced through the city, cut along the expressway, and entered a world of shopping malls and subdivisions. Manny carried the warm-up basketballs in a sack.

Glenbrook North, rising out of the foggy night, looked like a pile of bricks stacked in a cornfield. The driver pulled into the front driveway and stopped.

"Where's the gym?" he asked.

"I'll find it," Manny sighed. He climbed off the bus, disappeared into the fog, and then reappeared with some good news. The gym was around the bend.

Actually it wasn't one gym but five (or six — I lost count), housed in a sprawling athletic complex. The Roosevelt players hushed as they entered. They tried not to gawk.

The floor was carpeted, the hallways lined with glass trophy cases. On the walls were photos of celebrated graduates: baseball players Scott Sanderson and Doug Rader, Olympic ice skaters Leah Poulos and Anne Henning. We passed security guards, janitors, ticket takers, and concession-stand operators. Someone handed me a one-page computer-printed letter written by Glenbrook North head coach Brian James. It was called "The View From the Bench." It featured up-to-date statistics on the Spartans.

From the main gym came the sound of basketballs bouncing. The Glenbrook frosh-soph squad was already well into warm-ups. They stopped shooting to watch our advance across the floor. It wasn't dusty. It wasn't slippery. It glistened. Our shoes squeaked. "Like walkin' on Velcro," I told Manny.

The walls were about fifteen feet from the baskets and cushioned by wrestling mats. There were about twenty rows of bleachers, a balcony, and a concrete plateau on which rested a line of television cameras. (The game would be aired on a local cable station.) A sound system blared Bachman-Turner Overdrive's hit "You Ain't Seen Nothin' Yet." You could hear every word.

They had a few minutes to kill, so the players wandered back into the lobby. It was like a museum, a sports hall of fame. The trophy cases were lit from within. The Rough Riders stopped at each case. They eyed the trophies. They read the inscriptions. They discussed what they saw. Then they moved on to the next case.

A security guard led them to the visitors' locker room — an enormous room, as wide and open as a soccer field. It was freshly scrubbed. No graffiti. No banged-in lockers. No broken lights. The players entered cautiously, afraid to disturb something. Then it dawned on them: this was theirs for the night. They got giddy as they undressed. They started bragging about who had the biggest muscles. Kevin flexed his biceps. "This is what the ladies want," he said.

"No, no, I'm the ladies' man," said Ronnie. To prove it he pulled from his wallet a condom, which he waved in the air.

"How 'bout this?" called Mario. He made his stomach shake and roll like a belly dancer's. His buddies laughed and begged him to do it again. So he did. And they laughed again. Then they began preparing for the game. Each had his ritual. Anthony lathered his legs with a creamy lotion. Herman adjusted his socks to look just right. Sylvester did pull-ups on a pipe that ran across the ceiling. Terrell jogged in place. David and Ronnie threw a basketball back and forth. Through the walls came the brassy sounds of a marching band playing old Chicago songs like "Colour My World" and "Make Me Smile."

Ronnie was particularly happy. He'd played error-free ball against Curie. After the game, Manny had told him that he'd start against Glenbrook North. The news had surprised Ronnie. He didn't think Manny liked him. He didn't think any of his teachers liked him; he thought they held grudges against him for things he said he never did. Now he was starting. In the big game. Against Chris Collins. Imagine that.

Kevin burst in from the bathroom, breathless with delight. "Guys," he loudly whispered. "Hurry up. Maceo's takin' a dump!"

Stifling giggles, holding their fingers to their lips, they crept on tiptoe to a stall in the bathroom. They pushed open the door to reveal Maceo — poor unsuspecting Maceo — pants to his ankles, toilet paper in hand.

Maceo looked sheepish. "Hey, what the hell?" was all he could offer. His teammates cracked up. They ran back into the locker room exchanging high-fives.

And now they were really loose. A bunch of them started passing the ball back and forth, chanting "Win, win, win." It was a special moment — a moment for thanks.

"Prayer," Terrell shouted. Maceo, having completed his business, gathered them in a semicircle. They dropped to their knees and rested their heads in their hands.

Maceo said: "God, we come to you as often as we know how. Lord, just give us strength, courage, and the power to go out and play the best possible game we can. And, you know, just carry us through the season injury free, Lord, and through any troubles that we have outside of the court. We should not bring our troubles onto the court with us, Lord. Lord, as I come to you, Lord, I thank you, Lord, for allowing us to be together one more time as a team. One more time, Lord. And I just want to say, amen."

In unison the others said amen. They rose, put their hands in the middle, and chanted: "One, two, three — hang 'em up!"

Meanwhile, out in the gym it was like homecoming, what with all the old Roosevelt alums wearing blue and gold sweatshirts on hand to cheer the team. There were at least forty of them, and the game was far from starting. They exchanged hugs and kisses, patted each other's bellies, joked about receding hairlines, boasted about summer homes in Michigan, consoled one another over divorces, deaths, and other such sorrows.

Mostly they reminisced. About Al Klein, the football coach, and Morrie's Hot Dog Stand, and sock hops, and old social clubs (the Senecas, the Ovikitahs), and the star players on the '52 championship team (Mortie Miller, Eddie Rothenberg, Roy Roe, Moose Malitz, Louie Landt, Mort Gellman). They laughed, sometimes so hard they had tears in their eyes. Those were the days. They hadn't had money. Or cars. They rode the trolleys and buses. They worked in their fathers' stores. They listened to George Burns and Gracie Allen on the radio. They were young.

"I'd take the starting five from the '52 champs over any of these teams any day," someone said.

"They couldn't jump like kids today, but they could hit the set shot."

"They were disciplined. They knew how to run an offense."

"And tough."

"Any kid make a crack about Jews, and Moose would flatten his face."

"God bless him."

Arnie Kamen was there, of course, collecting money for his Roosevelt athletic fund and leading his classmates in an off-tune rendition of the Roosevelt fight song. Someone put his arm around Manny and said, "Mandel, I envy you. I always wanted to be a coach."

At 7:15 Manny broke away and met with his players in the locker room. "O.K. guys, a couple of things," he said. "We're not going to press them early. Play Collins like you're playing anyone else. The idea is to deny him the ball. No one man can beat you, no one man is that good."

A security guard poked his head through the door and said, "It's time, coach."

Manny nodded. He turned back to his team. "I really, honestly enjoyed working with you guys over the last month. I enjoy you guys. Let's win."

They burst from the locker room and circled the gym floor, rhythmically clapping their hands as they ran. Awaiting them under the basket was Jack Sherman, Roosevelt's principal, a short, taciturn man with the steel-eyed stare of a skeptic who has heard every teenage excuse imaginable. He looked a little softer tonight, a little less rigid. He wore a Roosevelt sweatshirt and he shook the hand of each player as he ran past.

The air crackled with the hum of hundreds of conversations. The stands filled with high schoolers and parents, dozens of parents, wearing white turtlenecks and green sweaters; and children, lots of children, mostly little boys, fists clutching pencils, paper in their laps, ready to keep score.

The band kicked into the Glenbrook North fight song and the Spartans took the floor. They wore green and yellow satin warm-up suits, green and white sneakers, white anklets stenciled with the monogram GNS, and long, baggy, Jordanesque shorts. They had little American flags stitched to their jerseys. There was one black guy on the team, a seven-foot center.

Manny and coach James shook hands. Manny was wearing his best suit: gray, double-breasted, a little long in the pants. James wore a trim jacket, a skinny tie, pleated slacks, and dressy loafers. Except for his boyish face he looked like the host at a North Side *ristorante*.

The lights dimmed and the courtside announcer introduced the Roosevelt starters: Terrell, Anthony, David, Kenric, and Ronnie. He wasn't some kid, the announcer. He was an adult. And when the time came to introduce the Spartans, he jacked up his enthusiasm — just like the Bulls' courtside announcer at the Stadium. He said: "And now, the starting lineup for *your* Glenbrook North Spartans." A spotlight picked up the first Spartan as he ran between two rows of pompom girls and cheerleaders and through a paper hoop held at center court by the team mascot. The last player out was Collins. The crowd rose and their cheers swelled to the rafters as he jogged to center court.

"Please remain standing and honor America by singing the national anthem," the announcer continued. A deep-voiced man led the song and, yes, the crowd sang along, hands over their hearts, eyes glued to the flag hanging from the wall. In the last row of the bleachers was Doug Collins, the old Bulls coach himself, hand to his heart, looking proud to live in the land of the free.

The game was anticlimactic, the emotion of the evening having exhausted the Rough Riders. This wasn't five-on-five, skins against shirts. This was the main event, and I think they were overwhelmed. On his first drive to the basket, Terrell banged into Glenbrook's center. The foul could have gone either way, but the ref called Terrell for the charge. After that he avoided the lane and passed up open shots. You could almost see him thinking: don't take a stupid shot; don't make another foul. The fans at Glenbrook North would never see him slip along the baseline, they'd never see him soar to the basket. They'd never know what they were missing.

Collins was quietly brilliant. He dribbled up the court, drilled a shot if he had it, ran a play if not. That's it. Effortless, confident, flawless, deceptively quick. Never ruffled, never altered his shot. It was 9–0 before Roosevelt scored. At halftime the Spartans led 50 to 28. The cheerleaders danced, the band played, and the janitors swept the court. I couldn't take it. The kids from Glenbrook had so much. It wasn't right that they should also win the game.

I wandered through the lobby, packed with teenagers in jeans and designer jackets. The concession stand served hot dogs, potato chips, soda pop, and slices of pizza. By the time I tried to return to my seat, the second half had started. A security guard wouldn't let me in. He said: "You can't enter the floor once the game is going."

I had to climb the stairs and sit in the balcony, between Doug Collins and the TV cameras. Manny went with Herman at guard for the second half. I could see Ronnie on the bench, his head down. Manny's arms were waving, but I couldn't hear what he said. Most of the high schoolers around me had lost interest in the game. Obviously Roosevelt didn't pop out on *their* schedule like an exclamation point. They giggled and gossiped and tried to decide who would drive and which party to attend.

Five gawky teens wandered in. They wore White Sox baseball caps, torn blue jeans, and Michael Jordan gym shoes. They wore their hair short on the sides. A tall, thin blond-haired girl walked past. They squirmed self-consciously. She smiled and said "Hi, Joey."

Joey reddened. His buddies giggled.

"Fuck you," Joey said.

"Suck my dick," one of them shot back.

Joey pointed to his crotch. "Suck this, fag," he said.

"You're the fag."

"You."

"You."

"Hey, man, don't dis me."

I turned toward them. "Dis?" I said. "Where did you pick that up?"

"I dunno," said Joey.

"Well, what does it mean?"

"It's ghetto talk," said another one.

"Yeah, man," said Joey. "You know, *Boyz N the Hood.*"

That made them crack up and they turned their caps sideways and started walking with the exaggerated strut of the rappers they watched on TV.

The final was 80 to 63. Collins scored twenty-seven, even though he sat out the final quarter. I bumped into Arnie on the main floor. "Life's not fair," I said. He knew exactly what I meant. "Now do you understand?" he implored. "Now do you understand why I'm doing this? I want the kids at Roosevelt to have all of this too."

In the locker room, Sylvester sat with his head in his hands. Ronnie stared at his locker. Manny consoled the team. "Fellows, I'm proud of you. You could have died, but you hustled to the end. All these people who came — win or lose they still love you and they love your school. There's something special going on here. You're lucky you go to Roosevelt. There will always be people who love you. So don't get down."

"That's right," called Terrell. "We gotta take it one game at a time."

"O.K. fellas, no tears," said Manny. "Forget about it. No matter what happened today, tomorrow is still Sunday."

The Glenbrook Booster Club was sponsoring a postgame refreshment hour (coffee, soft drinks, and donuts) for players and their families. The Rough Riders weren't invited. (The Spartans didn't offer them so much as a cup of Coca-Cola.) The party was just starting as we boarded the bus for Chicago.

Manny was subdued on the way back. "I don't think I'll sleep much tonight. I'll be thinking about the game. Ah, the older you get the less you want to sleep anyway. It's because you're afraid that you might not wake up."

The bus started to turn on Kimball, two blocks from the school, when Herman bolted for the front door. "Let me off," he shouted. "I gotta get off." Apparently there was someone on the corner he needed to see. The driver, startled, screeched to a halt in the middle of the street, opening the door just in time to prevent Herman from plowing through it. Suddenly the whole team was rumbling down the aisles and out the door. Someone yelled "fight." I couldn't tell what was happening. The last I saw they were running down an alley. Manny shook his head. "What kind of sense is that — to jump off a moving bus in the middle of traffic?"

We rode the rest of the way to Roosevelt. Manny was still carrying that sack of basketballs as he headed for his car.

The team was gone by the time I returned to the intersection. The streets were empty. The stores were shuttered. The fog had lifted. A cold wind stirred bits of trash. On the corner stood one of the frosh-soph players, a gym bag slung across his back. He was waiting for the bus that would take him east to California Avenue, where he would have to wait for another bus that would take him home. It was almost eleven o'clock. With luck, he'd be home by midnight.

Terrell liked to slip beneath the turnstile and catch a train to Clark and Division, where he and his buddies would break dance on the corner for the nickels, dimes, and quarters pedestrians threw into their hats. Terrell loved break dancing. Most of all he loved the oohs and ahs of disbelief that he could elicit with a complicated turn or a backward flip from a standstill position.

Before long they'd have to flee, the cops on their trail, though they were too fast to get caught. Sneakers flying over pavement, they'd dart off into the night, back to the subway, back to the West Side. "My mama couldn't believe I was so good at break dancing. She would say, Is there anything you can't do?"

Terrell was also good at tagging — a "sport" he learned from the Puerto Rican kids he met soon after his parents divorced and his mom moved him and his sister to the North Side. "I had my own tag — Red. I tagged all over the North Side, West Side too. I know it's not right. But sometimes doin' wrong is a thrill. I can't explain it. I don't do it no more. I don't even miss it, 'cept maybe a little. I used to get a thrill knowin' that so many people could see my name."

He started with street-level signs and bus benches and worked his way up to the hard-to-reach viaducts and billboards. He'd slither up a pole, slap his tag, drop down, and run like the wind, his baseball cap on backward, his socks cut low, T-shirt flapping out of the side of his pants — setting a look that, in time, thousands of suburban kids would copy.

One day a cop caught him writing on a billboard. Terrell was handcuffed and taken to the station. "My mom bailed me out and she made me clean up the graffiti. She told me to stop. But I couldn't. I was livin' for that action."

He never thought he'd get caught — not if he was careful. There wasn't a cop fast enough to catch him. But a few months later he got careless again. He was at a North Side subway stop — no one on the platform but some bum dressed in rags. "I didn't pay him no mind. All of a sudden he yells, 'Freeze, you're under arrest.' He was an undercover cop."

Terrell ran to the end of the platform, jumped onto the tracks, and raced into the tunnel. To his surprise, the cop kept coming, huffing and puffing and cursing under his breath. Terrell ran faster, "Deep into the tunnel way under the ground. I lost that cop, I don't know what happened to him. But there was a train comin', gettin' louder. I'm not kiddin', man, I was scared. I saw this thing, like a cave in the wall. It's hard to describe. But I hid in it, and the train went by."

He was filthy and lost and could hear rats scurrying around him. "To this day I don't know how I got out, but I did. I walked around down there for an hour. Then I found this ladder that led to a pothole out on the street. I think that if I could escape that maybe I've been blessed. I walked over to this gas station and said, 'Are there any jobs I can do for a dollar so I can get a bus and go home?' The guy gave me a dollar and I went home. And that was it for me. No more taggin' after that."

In 1987 Terrell's family moved to a three-bedroom apartment in Albany Park, not far from Roosevelt.

"After I stopped taggin', I was looking for somethin' excitin' to do and a friend got me to try basketball. I had never done it before. I thought it was boring. But once I tried it I got so good so quick." In retrospect, it's remarkable that some coach hadn't already discovered him. Terrell's body was made for basketball — long, lean, and springy. Jumping came easy. He didn't really leap, he soared, hanging in the air while the others fell to the ground.

His long, quick arms were ideal for defense, as was his quick-start coordination. A guard moving to his right would see Terrell drifting to the left and lose track of him. Then bam, Terrell would double back, bat the ball away from the unsuspecting dribbler, and race for an uncontested lay-up.

He made the frosh-soph team at Roosevelt, but he was raw. He was still developing a jump shot, still learning the intricacies of zones and team defense.

He honed his skills in park and playground pickup games, where defense was a simple one-on-one. No zones. No double coverage. Your man picked you at the free-throw line. If you got past him, there was an open lane to the basket. Speed and quickness counted most. It was a finesse sport — like break dancing or tagging.

In his sophomore year he experienced a revelation. A friend who worked at the Chicago Stadium slipped him into a Bulls game. For the first time in his life Terrell saw Michael Jordan play. Everything Jordan did — taking the baseline, hanging in the air, playing rush-the-ball defense, jamming over seven-foot centers — invigorated Terrell. He started renting Jordan's videos and watching Bulls games, taping them if he wasn't home. He studied how Jordan stood on the sidelines, arms on hips, talking to the coach. How he entered a game, smacking chalk on his hands, how he left a game, always sitting at the far end of the bench (away from the coach). How he hung out his tongue, how he flashed that innocent, beguiling, aw-shucks smile. How he walked on the court in game five against Cleveland — three seconds left, Bulls down by one — his eyes burning, the whole world knowing the ball was going his way, him wanting it anyway.

All the kids imitated Jordan in one way or another — shaving their heads, wearing wristbands just below their knees, pulling their shorts down low. But for Terrell it was different. In some ways he had been waiting his whole life for Michael Jordan. In Michael Jordan Terrell saw a piece of himself. Michael Jordan didn't have to paint his name on a billboard. Somebody put it there for him, advertising the car he drove, the sneakers he wore, the hamburgers he ate. Michael Jordan was who Terrell wanted to be.

And there were times, moments of greatness, when Terrell almost made it. There were times when he spun past his man, slipped down the baseline, soared over the center, and jammed the ball through the hoop. They stopped practice after that. They had to. All the guys were high-fiving, yelling, pounding the floor and, yes, comparing him to Jordan. Terrell tried not to grandstand (Michael Jordan never did), but when that happened his heart raced with a higher high than tagging or break dancing had ever given him.

By his senior year Terrell was a big man at Roosevelt. There was so much he could do on and off the court. He was a good painter and steady with a razor, the best barber in the school. He cut hair for $2 or $3, carving designs and messages into the fellows' scalps. For Sylvester he cut a picture of two hands dunking a basketball; for Anthony he carved the letter X (as in Malcolm X); for Kevin, his nickname, "CUZ."

Terrell and his closest friends formed a social club, named the 49ers after their favorite football team. "We aren't a gang. We ain't into drugs. We just hang together is all."

One weekend they decided to throw a party at Terrell's. They charged $3 for admission, sold soda and potato chips, and charged fifty cents to check coats. They stationed Montrell at the door as a bouncer and Terrell behind the stereo. He played rap, hip-hop, house, every now and then slipping in a slow song from his mother's collection so the guys could dance a long, slow squeeze.

More than one hundred kids showed up for that party, and they danced until dawn. For weeks people asked him to throw another.

Things came easily to Terrell. Maybe that's why he was so easily frustrated on the basketball court. Organized ball was more grueling than the playgrounds. Defenders held, slapped, pushed, elbowed, even knocked him to the ground. They did whatever they could get away with, and to Terrell it seemed that the refs let them get away with too much. They upset him and he had to stop himself from stalking off the court or, worse, striking back.

On top of that there was Manny and his yelling. Terrell didn't like to be corrected in public. It made him second-guess what should have come as natural as walking. He'd start thinking instead of doing. Should I shoot? No. If I miss, he'll yell. Should I pass? No. Then he'll yell 'cause I turned down a shot. Sometimes, as a solution, Terrell would try to disappear from the game. Let the other guys take the shots, let the other guys run the ball, let Manny yell at someone else. But that didn't work. The team looked to him. Terrell was the igniter. If they were stalling, Manny blamed him. Why aren't you hustling? Why don't you shoot? Why don't you take the ball to the basket? Terrell was discovering the pressures that are bred by expectations. Do something once and they expect you to do it again. If you don't, they want to know why.

After each game Manny tried to say something nice. In order to boost Terrell's confidence, Manny named him cocaptain (along with Kenric). "You have the talent to be a late bloomer," Manny told Terrell. "You could score thirty points a game." In front of the whole team at a practice before the Glenbrook game, Manny said: "I think we have the guy who can stop Collins. And that guy is Redmond."

Terrell got shivers when he heard that. "I know Coach Weincord really wants to help me. He can be the sweetest man in the world. I don't mean to blame him for nothin'. I know I got it in me to be special. I just got to find it, that's all."

Terrell had big dreams — college, the pros, something more substantial than a playground sensation. He felt he could score on anyone. The opposing players were like that cop who chased him along the subway tracks through the tunnel. Terrell was too fast to get caught then, and he had too much talent to be stopped now.

December 9

On Monday the flu bug caught up with Manny. He missed school, but dragged himself out of bed for practice — his face was a yellowish green, his eyes glazed. He remembered to bring the sack of basketballs, which he carried on his back as he shuffled across the gym floor. He looked like Roosevelt's version of Willy Loman, burdened by the weight of the world.

"I feel like crap," he said. "I spent the day throwing up."

He sprawled across three rows of bleachers — his head tilted back, his arms stretched to the sides, his eyes closed.

Sender walked up. "You want me to lead the practice, coach?" he said.

Manny nodded.

"Can I have the whistle?"

Manny opened his eyes and stared at the ceiling. "There's no whistle," he said.

Sender was taken aback. "No whistle?"

Manny looked at Sender. "Coach, this is gonna be hard, but I gotta break you the news: the whistle's gone."

Sender said nothing, but he understood. He'd have to coach without the whistle. He turned back to the team, determined to carry on.

Manny rolled his eyes. "I'm dyin' and that putz wants to know about the whistle."

He lay motionless for a few minutes. There's no good time to get sick, but this time was worse than most. The Rough Riders were in the middle of their exhibition season. Tomorrow they'd play Senn, two days later it would be Steinmetz — both of them Red North rivals. "The Red teams aren't always better than the ones in Blue," Manny said. "We can beat Senn and Steinmetz. We gotta keep workin' on the four corners in practice."

But they'd have to do it without him. After laying sprawled over the bleachers for a while, Manny sighed. "That's it. I give up. I'm goin' home. If I stay any longer, I'll only throw up."

He left as he came, with his head down. Not once did he glance at the players.

But they sure glanced at him. When he had left, when they could no longer hear his footsteps, they rejoiced. Herman needled Kevin and Kevin needled back. A playful slapping match broke out. Stop, Sender demanded. They laughed. Sender pursed his lips. Where was that whistle when you needed it?

"Come on, guys," David pleaded. And they stopped. Sender gathered them under the basket. "Men, in Coach Weincord's absence, I'm in charge," he began. As he talked Kevin stood behind him and made goofy faces. A few players giggled. When Sender turned to look, Kevin abruptly stopped and adopted a solemn expression, as though he were listening intently. Sender turned back and Kevin started making goofy faces again.

The defiance surprised me. The players always had been so well behaved, calling Manny coach and never, ever, questioning his authority. At least to his face. But this looked like mutiny. The teacher was gone and they were alone with the substitute. Party time!

Sender divided them into two teams (with David sitting out) and announced that they would practice the shuffle.

The shuffle was a complicated weave play that Sender admired and Manny resisted. "I like to keep things simple," Manny had said. "We've got enough trouble running the easy plays."

But Manny was gone and Sender was in charge, so today they would run the shuffle.

"What's the point?" asked Maceo. "Coach Weincord's never gonna let us run it in a game."

"Men!" said Sender.

"But it's true," said Herman.

"That's enough," said Sender.

"Yes sir, yes sir," said Kevin, sarcastically saluting Sender.

"Coach Weincord told us to play differently," said Ronnie.

Sender smiled. "Coach Weincord and I agree on some things and disagree on others. He left me in charge, so do it."

"But that don't make sense," said Ronnie.

"That's it, White," Sender said. "Get out. Go to the sidelines. David, come in."

David rose from the bleachers.

Maceo scowled. "That's bullshit."

Ronnie was upset. "Man, you can't do that," he said. "We had teams."

Kevin and Herman joined the chorus of complaints. "Come on Sender," said Herman, "let us play."

Emboldened by their support, Ronnie turned defiant. "I'm not leavin'."

David, who had walked onto the court, raised his hands in exasperation and returned to the bleachers.

"Casas," said Sender. "I told you to get in the game."

"Man, you guys figure this out," said David.

The standoff finally ended when Ronnie, muttering, left the court.

"What's that you say?" Sender demanded.

"Come on, coach," yelled Terrell. "Why hold up practice for one guy? You have all the rest of us sitting out here."

Reluctantly Sender turned back to the practice. And the team kind of shuffled through the shuffle. No one hustled. And Kevin continued to make funny faces.

"This stinks," said Ronnie, watching from the sidelines. "Coach Weincord's never gonna run this. Why waste our time? We got two big games this week. Two big ones. We got a game tomorrow and we're running this stuff. I tell you what. Say what you want about Weincord. But he's been gone only twenty-five minutes and I already miss him."

December 10

Manny, still sick, missed the game against Senn. In his absence the players continued their insurrection, violating all of his prohibitions: David brought the ball up-court. Herman (head down and oblivious to teammates) recklessly drove for the hoop. Terrell fired up threes. Kenric, frustrated that no one attempted to get him the ball, left his post under the basket and tried an outside shot. Not once did they run anything remotely resembling a play. Despite a few clutch steals and baskets by Mario, the Rough Riders lost 68 to 56, and their record fell to 2–5.

Poor Sender. The players rolled their eyes at his pep talks, ignored his instructions, and then blamed him for the loss.

December 11

Only eight guys showed up for practice. They didn't practice free throws or run sprints, and their raggedy 45-minute practice ended after Sender dismissed Sylvester for insubordination. I didn't even hear what it was that he said.

Not knowing what else to do, I joined Ronnie on the bench and watched Maceo and Herman flex their biceps to see whose was bigger. Maceo won, only Herman said he cheated.

"Jesus, Maceo," I said, "your arms are like marble slabs."

Maceo beamed. "I'm a football player first," he said. "I plan to play in college and, eventually, the NFL. That's my dream. I'm six foot two and I weigh two hundred pounds, and I plan to put on at least twenty more pounds of muscle."

"Why bother with basketball at all?"

" 'Cause I love the game and my teammates. I love these guys with all my heart, although they upset me and frustrate me."

"Do you love Manny?"

"Yes, I do. I love Manny as a coach and a person. I'm gonna miss that man when I leave here. Out of all the people at Roosevelt, I'll miss him the most. I respect him as a person. He doesn't hold anything back. He's not two-faced. He'll tell you how he feels, and he'll tell you it to your face. But then, when the chips are down, he'll be on your side."

Herman yawned loudly. "Hey, man," he said to me, cutting Maceo off. "I wanna tell you what's wrong with the team."

"O.K.," I said.

He didn't say anything. "Well?" I said.

"Aren't you gonna take notes?" he asked.

"Oh yeah," I said, opening my notebook. "Sorry, I forgot."

"O.K. Well, first thing is, we're good. This same bunch of guys won twenty-four games two years ago as the frosh-soph team. Now, you can't do that unless you're good."

"So what's that prove?"

"That Sender can't coach."

"Sender? He's only been your acting coach for a week."

"Well, I got problems with Weincord, too. He don't substitute enough. He's playin' guys too long. You gotta keep guys fresh. Michael Jordan don't even play a whole game. I should coach this team."

"Aw, Herman," said Maceo, "you just want to play more."

"That ain't it, man. That ain't it at all. I would be sayin' the same thing if I was playin' the whole thirty-two minutes, like David or Terrell."

"Aw, Herman," said Maceo, "you can't coach."

"I could. Man, I should be doin' it. We'd be five and two — at least."

One by one the guys left, until it was just me and Ronnie.

"Wanna go to Burger King?" I asked.

He shrugged. "Sure."

We took a shortcut, through a side exit and across the barren baseball diamond. It was bitter cold. Ronnie wore no hat, scarf, or gloves, just tucked his hands deep into his pockets. At Burger King he bought a soda and fries. We talked a little about a lot of things, including literature.

"The last book I read was a biography of Elijah Muhammad," Ronnie said.

"Did you like it?"

"It was O.K., as far as I got. I haven't finished the whole thing yet, to tell you the truth."

"Are you a Muslim?"

"No, but I respect them. They don't take no shit."

"Have you read *The Autobiography of Malcolm X*?"

"I was plannin' to. Then I saw that Spike Lee was makin' the movie. So I decided to see the movie first."

I asked him how Kevin Lewis, the junior guard, got his nickname, "Cuz."

"It's 'cause Kevin knows everyone — everyone's his cousin. You be sittin' with him in a restaurant or somethin' and some guy comes up and says, 'Hey, Kev.' And you say, 'Hey man, who's that?' And Cuz'll say, 'Him? Oh, he's my cousin.'"

I laughed. Then we fell silent. Just sat there, eating french fries and whiling away the time that ought to have been practice.

December 12

Manny returned for the home game against Steinmetz, his energy sapped by the flu. He was pale and hoarse. He tried not to yell because yelling made him cough. But it was tough; so many little things infuriated him. In the middle of the second quarter the scoreboard died and play had to stop. Sender jiggled the cord and the scoreboard flickered back on. But no one really knew why it had stopped or why it had started or whether it would go out again. "That damn thing's gonna cost us a game sometime," said Manny.

With thirty seconds left and his team ahead by one, David got the ball about fifteen feet from the basket. He faked left and drove right, spinning past his man and forcing Steinmetz's center to leave his position to cover him. In one smooth move he fired a bullet pass to Maceo, who was wide open near the basket and laid the ball in. It was David at his best, a splendid display of on-court vision and coordination. But it was Maceo who impressed me. It was a pressure shot, and he hadn't panicked. Roosevelt went on to win 57 to 49 as Terrell scored twice in the final seconds.

After the game, players and fans rushed onto the court and embraced Maceo. "Yes, yes, yes," Maceo bellowed. "I live for this."

December 19

Manny opened practice with another team talk. "Guys, I know you're happy you beat Steinmetz. But you made a lot of mistakes in that game. Some of the same mistakes you were makin' two weeks ago. And then when I yell, you look at me with this hurt look on your face. Well guys, what do you want me to do, hug and kiss you? You say coach gets too angry, well, you bet I'm angry. This is your chance to play basketball and get a free college tuition. And you're screwing it up."

He paused, and as he stopped speaking his anger faded and his voice softened. "Is it somethin' I've done? Is it somethin' I've said? Tell me."

Silence. Manny's voice got even softer. He was almost pleading. "Come on — we're like family here." Finally Sylvester spoke, slowly and quietly — his words almost choking him as they came out.

"It's just that, uh, coach, you, uh, your yellin' takes us out of our game."

Unfortunately, Manny didn't understand exactly what Sylvester had said. I think he thought Sylvester was complaining about playing out of position — in this specific case, that Sylvester would rather play forward than guard.

"Is that it, Sylvester?" said Manny. "You guys don't want to play out of position. I see. O.K., I learned something."

I thought about speaking up and explaining what Sylvester had really meant. But I kept quiet. It wasn't my place. No one said anything, all heads looked down. The frosh-soph ruckus took over the gym. Manny shrugged. "O.K., guys, the Luther North Christmas tournament's next. There's a lot of good teams in that tournament. We can show what we've got. Let's act like this was the first day of practice." The team formed a lay-up line and Manny watched from center court. "When I talk to these guys, I talk from my heart," he said sadly. "They think I'm blowing out of my ass."

December 23

A basketball junkie's fix — that was the Christmas tournament at Luther North, a private school on the city's far-northwest side. Sixteen teams, public and private, from city and suburbs. Each team playing four games over six days, with the action going almost around the clock. Roosevelt's first opponent, Saint Rita, a perennial football powerhouse, ran a cautious offense and played rugged defense. It was a plodding, defensive struggle. At the half, Saint Rita led 21 to 20.

"They're stymied, baby," Manny said, as the team gathered in the locker room. "They thought they'd be beating you by ten, and you've got them scared. Your defense is tremendous. I'm proud of you. I love you. Give yourself a hand. We didn't come here to play — we came here to win!"

But what a frustrating fight for the Rough Riders: lay-ups clanked off the backboard; open jumpers rattled off the rim; and free throws — they missed them all. Or so it seemed. It had to be psychological. The Rough Riders were too good, too smart, to shoot so poorly. Manny, Sender, every coach they'd ever known had told them the same thing about free throws: find your style and keep it. The great free-throw shooters never wavered; they all had their almost mindless routines. But few Rough Riders shot the same way twice. Nor did they take a moment before shooting to relax and collect their thoughts. At one point the team missed eight free throws in a row (including four "one and ones" — you don't get a second free throw unless you make the first).

Desperately searching for a combination that could score some points, Manny benched several starters at the start of the fourth quarter for Kevin, Ronnie, Sylvester, and Larry. But the subs were nervous and cold. At one point Ronnie was surrounded by defenders, arms in his face, panic in his eyes, Manny's voice in his ears screeching, "Pass, pass, pass." He finally lofted a pass, or maybe it was a shot. It fell shy of the basket and bounced out of bounds.

"God damn it, White," bellowed Manny.

Saint Rita won 49 to 33. It wasn't going to be a very merry Christmas.

December 26

With no games on Christmas Eve or Christmas Day, Manny had two days to stew on the loss, and on the headline in the *Sun-Times,* which just made it worse: "St. Rita crunches Roosevelt."

"We weren't crunched," said Manny. "I've seen crunchings. That was no crunching. That game was close until the end."

It was about 11 A.M., an hour before the game against Luther North. Manny sat in the host school's cafeteria sipping coffee. He watched his players file in, heading for the downstairs locker room.

"Yesterday we got the upstairs locker room," Manny said. "One loss and they put you in the dungeon."

He was in a sour mood. "I'm beginning to take this personally," he said. "I think they've stopped playing for me."

"Come on, Manny," I said.

"No, seriously, these shots that they're missing. These mistakes. I could understand it if they were bad. But they're too good for that."

Maceo walked into the cafeteria and Manny called him over. "Mace, I'm startin' to wonder: have the players stopped playin' for me?"

Maceo squirmed. He'd been up late with his teammates at a Christmas-night rap party. His mind was fuzzy. Now this. "We don't have our heads in the game, coach," he said. The answer didn't satisfy Manny. "You see what he said?" Manny said after Maceo left. "Nothin'. And he's one of the guys I get along with best. He could have said, 'Coach, we're behind you.' But he didn't say nothin'. Well the hell with that." Suddenly Manny was up and heading toward the back door. I scampered after him. "Manny, what are you doin'?"

He bustled down the stairs. "I tried to be nice. I tried to understand. It got me nowhere. Sometimes people mistake niceness for weakness. They take advantage of you. They think they can get away with anything they want. They're just gonna show up when they want to and do what they want to. I can't let them get away with that."

He headed down a basement hallway. "They think they can just go through life doing what they please. Show up when they want. Do what they want. Don't follow directions. They'll see — the world's not like that."

He marched into the locker room, without a hello or how are you to his players, most of them in their jockstraps or underwear. Manny cleared his throat. "Guys, I'm beginning to take this personally, like you're not playin' for me. You don't want to play, you can turn in your jerseys right now. Because, I'll be honest with you, you're not showing me anythin'. You don't care. You don't play with pride. You shoot free throws like first-graders. You just go up there and fling away. You don't set, you don't take your time. I tell you one hundred times how to do things and you still don't do them.

"See, now maybe some of you don't think I'm a good coach. Well that's bullshit. 'Cause if you don't want to play for me, you can just turn in your uniforms. I'll outlast you all. I'm not leavin' till I'm ready. And your not wantin' to play for me only makes me want to stay longer. See. I may stay another ten years. I'll be walkin' down the halls with a cane — old man Weincord. But I'll be here."

With that he left. The players were stunned, their mouths agape. They were hung over. Tired. It wasn't even noon. They had a game in an hour. And already he was yelling.

"Man, what the hell got into *him*?" said Herman.

The game against Luther North featured more of the same: more botched shots, more missed free throws, more yelling. At halftime Manny ordered them to practice free throws. "You do it like this," he said. He planted his feet at the free-throw line, bounced the ball five times, and threw up a shot. It swished through the net. Manny tried not to show his surprise. "If an old man can do it," he said, "you can too."

Midway through the second quarter, Saul Lutwig walked in. Manny had told me about him. Saul was a seventy-year-old retired milkman who had known Manny since the 1950s, when they both worked at the Strauss Center. He rarely missed a soccer or basketball game, but for the last few weeks he'd been laid up, recuperating from knee surgery.

It took him five minutes to cross the gym. He walked on crutches. Tough old codger. He looked a lot like Bill Veeck, with his big baggy ears and a jowly face. Manny hugged him.

"Saul, it's good to see you."

"Hey, Manny, I saw in the *Times* you guys got crunched."

Manny shook his head. "Saul, it's nice to see you too."

Saul took a seat behind the bench and kept a patter up for most of the game.

"Geez, Manny, is that Mattox?"

"Yeah. Who do you think it is, Mr. Magoo?"

"He got fat."

"Yeah."

"What?"

"I said, 'Yeah.' "

Roosevelt won 52 to 44. But Manny wasn't satisfied. Neither was Saul. "Missed too many free throws," he told Manny. "Especially down the stretch. Shouldn't have been so close."

Manny shook his head. "Saul, you're a wonderful man."

December 27

Back they came for game three. Manny was edgy, the team tense. It seemed like he had been mad at them for weeks. Resentment festered in the locker room. The players didn't laugh. Or crack jokes. Arnie wasn't there (he was on vacation) to break the tension with his upbeat chatter.

"We won, what does he want?" said Ronnie.

"With him, we can't do nothin' right," Terrell complained.

Maceo sang a mournful dirge: "Nobody knows the troubles I've seen."

"Jesus, Maceo," cracked Weiss, "you aren't on a chain gang."

Their opponents for game three were the Ridgewood Rebels, a slow and cumbersome team from the suburbs. Ridgewood played hard defense — stabbing for the ball, hoping to steal, usually fouling, not caring if they did. They managed to stay close, but Mario sank a clutch three-pointer and Herman hit two free throws; with a minute left, Manny looked relieved.

"Not a bad effort," he told the players on the bench. "When the clock hits thirty seconds stand up and give the guys a hand."

Just then a husky guard named Bob Amelio slammed into Terrell. Amelio was going for a steal, and he missed. Terrell should have shrugged it off. Ordinarily he would have. But he'd been shrugging them off through the whole tournament and now he was tired. Tired of being hacked, tired of being held, tired of the shellacking he routinely received from his slower, more cumbersome opponents. And most of all, tired of not getting the calls.

He lost control. He elbowed Amelio. Hit him hard in the back, just above the kidney. Amelio collapsed and for a split second no one moved. Then a student from Roosevelt (whose name I never learned) leaped from the stands and stood above Amelio, taunting him, saying that Terrell had kicked his butt.

Up in the stands a woman in a green Ridgewood windbreaker began screaming: "He's laughing at my boy."

The Rebels and the Rough Riders rushed from the benches. One team was black, the other team white. We were heading for a nasty confrontation. The coaches — Manny and Ridgewood's Ron Kalina — quickly intervened. They corralled their players. Sender pulled the taunter back to the stands. Terrell was ejected from the game, banished from the gym. The two teams were ready to take the floor. And still Amelio didn't get up.

He was having convulsions; his moans were muffled because his cheek was flat against the floor. Kalina applied an ice pack to his back.

The crowd hushed. Someone called for an ambulance. Two paramedics arrived. They unfolded a wheelchair.

"Who's got his clothes?" Kalina asked. A skinny kid from the Ridgewood team held up a green and white satchel. Gingerly, Amelio rose to his knees. The paramedics eased him into the wheelchair. They wheeled him out the door and drove him to a hospital.

The game continued. Someone hit some free throws, someone scored a three. The thirty-second mark came and went; no one stood. No one cheered. Roosevelt won 50 to 41. Terrell, fully dressed, waited in the stairwell leading to the lockers.

"Terrell," I asked, "what happened?"

"I don't know. It happened so fast. I didn't want to hurt anyone. I feel awful, man, I feel terrible."

He tried to apologize to Kalina, but the coach refused to shake his hand. Manny, meanwhile, followed Kalina downstairs and stood with him outside the Ridgewood locker room.

"Really, coach, I'm really sorry, very sorry," he said. "I make no alibis. If there's anything I can do, I'll do it." Kalina lit a cigarette. He took a long drag. "Forget it, Manny. It wasn't your fault." I was sort of hoping Manny would give it up after that. Go home for the night. Not Manny. Not yet.

He stormed back to the locker room and kicked open the door. Once again the players stood before him in their underwear and jockstraps. They looked angry and hurt. The whole damn tournament had been nothing but torment and humiliation. I remembered what Manny's father had told him about getting punched in the face. I figured this was it: how much more could the team take? I wondered who would take the first swing. If there was a fight, Manny didn't stand a chance. He didn't have many friends in the room.

But Manny was fearless. He stood in that cramped, stinky locker room, amid a dozen sweaty young men a third his age and twice his size. This little man, almost sixty years old. His gray hair falling over his forehead. His face contorted. His body trembling. His neck veins bursting. And he called them a bunch of gutless cowards. He said that what they did was far worse than losing. He said that they had tarnished their reputations and disgraced their school. He said that the next player who threw a punch would be banished from the team.

He told them: "I'll start a team of girls and freshmen before I put up with any bullshit like this." And then he stopped, his mouth quivering, almost daring them to say something in response. They said nothing. No one moved. He waited a moment, pivoted, and left as furiously as he had entered, the door banging hard behind him.

Arnold "Arnie" Kamen (born April 21, 1933)

Time wasted was opportunity lost — a lesson Arnie Kamen learned long ago. Which is why he always moved fast, his eye on the clock, his day organized around the setting of goals and the completion of tasks.

He grew up in Albany Park, in an apartment at the corner of

Hamlin and Montrose — about six blocks from Roosevelt High School and just down the street from his classmate Mandel "Manny" Weincord, who went on to become coach of Roosevelt's basketball and soccer teams. Arnie's father, Harry, was a wholesale liquor salesman. His mother, Belle, ran the house. By the time he was twenty-nine, Arnie had graduated from Roosevelt, spent two years in the army, graduated college, married, had one child (the first of seven), bought a house in the suburbs, and started a business on the Chicago Mercantile Exchange.

"I was always good with numbers, always had a head for quick calculations. We traded butter and egg futures. You didn't have to know the product. You have guys trading soybeans, most of them have never even seen a soybean. You have to be quick on your feet."

Within a few years he was operating his own clearing company, which meant customers could trade directly through his firm. Eventually he owned seats on five exchanges, including the New York Coffee and Sugar Exchange and the New York Cotton Exchange, and operated offices in eleven cities. He bought a bigger house, put his kids through college, traveled around the world, made shrewd investments, built his own little fortune, and became one of Roosevelt High School's many rags-to-riches success stories.

There were a lot of them, particularly in Arnie's class, the class of 1950. At reunions they told and retold their triumphs. One graduate, Howard Lazar, conducted an informal survey of their achievements. According to Lazar, the class contains seventy-two millionaires, fifteen lawyers, fourteen doctorates, seven authors, six doctors, five certified public accountants, five aerospace engineers, three judges, two newspaper columnists, one entertainer, and a rabbi.

"Considering that there were only 280 of us to start with, I'd say we have done well!" Lazar wrote in an article for the Jewish United Fund *News.* "We were born at the height of the Depression. Our parents were foreign born or first-generation Americans. We grew up during World War II, a period of unrest, turbulence, and change. We were hungry for all America had to offer. Hungry for the security that wealth and position could bring. So we marched down the hall on Wilson Avenue, got our diplomas, and went out to conquer the world."

In their hunger, their rush to conquer the world, most left Roosevelt and Albany Park far behind. But there are still some ties. The school's principal, Jack Sherman, and several teachers (including Manny Weincord and Don Weiss) are Roosevelt graduates. There's an alumni association. Regular reunions. Old-timer basketball games.

And a newsletter, the *Roosevelt Alumni News,* published by Al Klein, the school's former football coach. It consists of bubbly blurbs, melancholy reminiscences, and cheery updates extracted from the hundreds of letters sent to Klein from Roosevelt graduates across the country.

In one issue, Tom Sigrist, a dentist from the class of '65, wrote that he and his wife had spent two years "serving our Lord as missionaries in the jungles of Peru."

Irwin Schulman (class of '59) wrote: "Had a great time at the All School Reunion. Hope you have forgiven me for going offsides against Englewood down at the five-yard line at Soldier Field."

Benton Curtis (class of '27) wrote: "I am eighty years old and my memory fails in many ways, but I will never forget moving from then Hibbard High School (a temporary school while Roosevelt was being built). We actually carried the chemistry lab on our laps while being driven to the new school. It's too bad that the person who could have written about that period is long gone. That was Nelson Algren (known as Nelson Abraham in school), writer of *The Man with the Golden Arm.* Basketball being our only major sport, it drove us wild when our lightweight team won the city championship. That was possibly one of the greatest years of our lives. As seniors in the new building we were floating on air — the school was not completely finished and we stumbled over boards and bags but it was ours. We felt close to the other students and thought a great deal of our teachers. Even with my bad memory, I still remember them all, even most of their names."

Arnie Kamen was one of Roosevelt's sentimental alums. He subscribed to Al Klein's newsletter and attended the old-timer basketball games and reunions. And yet as the years rode by he came to the realization that reminiscing about the old days wasn't enough. After every reunion, he — like the others — returned to the suburbs, went back to his office, went on with his life. Arnie decided he wanted to do more. Much more was needed. He owed it to the school — he owed it to the kids.

He wandered through the old building and he felt something was wrong. The halls were clean. The school was safe. Order was kept. But some essential spirit was missing. He was determined to bring it back.

It was all part of a larger effort to change his own life, to spend his time "doing something more important." He left the Merc. He rented his seats. He spent more time with his family and more time at Roosevelt.

"I walked down the halls and when I saw those kids I saw myself forty years ago. I started thinking about where I was and where I had been and all the time that had passed. As I got older I realized that I was lucky. I've had a good life and it all started at Roosevelt."

As Arnie saw it, he and his classmates had prospered because they were confident about their future. They believed that Roosevelt was preparing them for success. They saw Roosevelt as their gateway to a greater world outside of Albany Park.

The school nurtured them. Gave them spirit and pride. He remembered the great games against Von Steuben. What a rivalry. Von was just a few blocks away from Roosevelt. They were as close as any two high schools in the city. Two Jewish schools at a time when basketball was still a very Jewish game. The gym filled with noisy, partisan students, parents, and neighborhood kids — grade-schoolers — who idolized the players, knew their names and numbers by heart.

Arnie never saw kids at the games anymore. Rarely saw parents either. The games started at 3:15 P.M., when many parents were working. Even if the school system could afford to open the gyms at night, it wouldn't — for fear of crime.

"My generation didn't have money, we didn't have connections, but we had pride in ourselves and pride in our school. You'd go to a game and you'd see the people in the stands and you'd hear their cheers and you'd sing the school song and you'd swell with pride and feel part of a larger tradition. You shared the spirit. It gave you self-confidence. That's what it's all about. Self-confidence. That's what gets people motivated to go out there and conquer the world!"

Arnie could see that the Roosevelt students of today lacked

that confidence. They didn't have the edge his generation had. They weren't basking in the glow of a U.S. victory in a world war. Roosevelt was still a gateway to life, but the future didn't glow as bright as it had for the class of 1950. The world looked elsewhere — to the suburbs — for the next generation of leaders.

So Arnie decided that, if nothing else, he would lead the cheers. He would be a one-man bridge linking the Roosevelt of yesteryear with the Roosevelt of today.

"We were the fortunate generation. We grew up in a world where we were happy, and then our generation screwed up the world. Most of us said we will give to our children all the things that we did *not* have. So we gave them the cars and TV sets and the trips to Europe. And yet we forgot to give them the one thing we did have: happiness. That's what I want these kids at Roosevelt to have more of. I want to give these kids pride in their school that they might transfer to themselves."

Arnie launched his campaign at a Roosevelt basketball game in the 1990–91 season. He climbed to the top of the bleachers, where he couldn't be avoided, and asked all those around him — all six or seven students — to join him in the school song.

"What song?" one kid asked.

"What song!" Arnie exclaimed. "Why it's only the greatest school song for the greatest school in the whole world. Jerry Bressler wrote it, and he was a Roosevelt graduate who went on to have a big career in Hollywood. He did music for *The Jackie Gleason Show*."

Some kids giggled. Others stared wide-eyed in amazement, as though Arnie were from Mars. And, indeed, he might as well have been trying to bridge an interplanetary generation gap. They didn't know from Jackie Gleason, let alone Jerry Bressler.

"I told them, 'If you won't join me, fine, I'll sing it myself.' "

And so he did, unabashedly loud and slightly off key.

"Go on you Rough Riders go, go Roosevelt, go / Wave, wave your banners high / For V-i-c-t-o-r-y! / So go you Rough Riders go, go Roosevelt, go / We all are true to the gold and blue / So go Rough Riders, go / The gold and blue shall wave forever high / Our Alma Mater, shout it to the sky / Rough Riders show our spirit, / All shall fear it, go, go / Go Roosevelt, go / We all are true, to the gold and blue, / So go Rough Riders, go!"

He sang that song at every game he attended, sometimes accompanying himself with a recording he played on a cheap plastic tape recorder he'd borrowed from his son. Sometimes he'd cajole Manny or Jack Sherman into joining him.

"After I had been doing this for a while, I noticed that the kids were sitting on the other side of the gym. I walked over there and said, 'Oh no, you guys can't get rid of me that fast.' "

And he sang the song again — louder.

It was an odd sight to behold — a lone middle-aged Jewish guy singing in a crowd of black teenagers. But race wasn't an issue. It was rarely mentioned. Once Arnie saw Mario Ramos, a senior guard on the basketball team, reading a copy of *The Final Call*, Minister Louis Farrakhan's newspaper. "How can you admire Farrakhan?" Arnie implored.

Mario stood firm. "He's a great leader."

"But he's anti-Semitic."

"No, no. That's got nothing to do with what he's all about."

Eventually they pretty much agreed to disagree. There were no racial or religious slurs — then or ever. Maybe the kids didn't understand Arnie's mission. Or his message. Or the world from which he came. Or why he was there. But they weren't rude. They treated him a little like they treated me: without curiosity. They accepted his presence, no questions asked.

Arnie became a regular at the basketball games (girls' and boys' teams) as well as at soccer, track, swimming, softball, and baseball events. He wore his blue and gold Rough Riders sweatshirt and cheered until his voice was hoarse, his cheeks were flushed, and his sandy bangs flopped over his sweaty brow. Aside from one or two scouts, he was usually the only adult in the stands.

At the start of the 1991–92 school year he went to Jack Sherman with a plan. He was going to initiate a mass mailing to raise as much as $100,000 for a Roosevelt athletic fund.

Great, said the principal.

With the money to be used for equipment, uniforms, and fees for summer training camps and tournaments.

Wonderful. And now there's one small thing I need from you.
Oh?

I want these kids to learn the school song. I want it taught to them in music class. I want a recording made and then played

over the loudspeakers at least once a day, maybe during home-
room — I'll leave the details to you. I want song sheets distributed to every student. And I want to have a mandatory pep
rally — maybe before the Lane game. I'll bring some alumni and
together we and the students will sing the song.

Sherman was skeptical. He wanted to be polite. He wanted to
be appreciative. But it was a lot of extra work. As if running a
public high school wasn't demanding enough. "I love his spirit,
but times have changed," said Sherman. "This is a different day
and age, and songs don't matter so much."

One day Manny raised the issue while they were watching
practice. "Listen, Arnie, this business about the song. It's not like
when we went to school. You can't press it."

"What, are these kids stupid?" snapped Arnie.

"It's not that."

"Did we learn the song?"

"Yes."

"Then they can learn the song."

So the conversation ended. Arnie wouldn't budge. He had a
goal. Don't tell him it couldn't be done. He had no tolerance for
delay. He was used to the pace of the traders' pit, where a second
of indecision could cost millions.

There was so much to do. Phone calls to make. Letters to mail.
Money to raise. Pep rallies to plan. And so little time to do it. He
called the school two, three, sometimes four times a day. He visited at least once a week. He could be a persistent pain in the
neck. He knew that, but he didn't care. He badgered Sherman
into piping the song into the classrooms once a day. "It's a start,"
Arnie said. "But the music's not loud enough."

He taught the school song to his wife, children, and friends.
He enlisted Marvin Levin, an old classmate, to go with him door-
to-door, seeking contributions from local merchants. He solic-
ited funds from friends and classmates he hadn't seen in years.
He reminded them of the school motto: "You can if you will for
Roosevelt." By the start of the 1991–92 school year, he had
raised about $4,000, enough to buy new backboards, uniforms,
and a video camera. He put a plaque on the gym wall, thanking
and naming the alumni whose donations had paid for the backboards.

"It's a token of appreciation. We didn't build a hospital. You start small, you work your way up. You've got to give *kovid* [honor] to people. You've got to make them feel good."

He was as busy as he'd ever been. He'd rush into the gym having been out and about all day, juggling three or four different deals at once, and head straight for the phone in Manny's office.

"Who you callin'?" I asked him one day.

"Melamed."

"Leo Melamed — the guy who used to run the Merc?"

"Yeah, what about it?"

"You're gonna call *him*? Why would some rich guy like that care about Roosevelt?"

He gave me a look of impatient disgust. "Because he went here, silly. Class of '50. I've known him since our freshman year. He was one of us then and he still is."

Melamed donated $100 to the athletic fund. "I asked for one hundred dollars and that's what he gave. He did it for Roosevelt. You can if you will for Roosevelt. You're never too good to lend someone a hand. Those kids in the suburbs — you don't think anyone ever helps them?"

January 6

After the debacle at the Luther North tournament, the team had a week off for Christmas. Manny stayed away from the school — he didn't see his players and they didn't see him.

The players slept late. They partied. They worked. Most of them had part-time jobs. Herman Carey and Kevin Lewis worked at one Burger King, Maceo Tillman at another; David Casas, the long senior forward, worked at a sub shop and Larry Wall at a Taco Bell; Ronnie White worked at a shoe store, Mario Ramos at a copy shop.

They came back refreshed. "Great to see you, coach," said Kevin as he charged into the gym.

"Great to see you, Cuz," Manny said.

The casual camaraderie perplexed me. I wondered what happened to all of that hostility from the last week of December. Things were so strained between Manny and his team, I feared that one of the kids was going to deck him.

But they all seemed to have forgotten about it. "What, I'm

gonna hold a grudge?" said Manny. Things had worked out reasonably well. After the ugly incident against Ridgewood, the
Rough Riders closed the tournament with a victory over Morton.
They were 6–6. Bob Amelio, the Ridgewood kid who'd been laid
out by Terrell Redmond's elbow, wasn't hurt: he had checked
out of the hospital a few hours after the game. Now Manny was
upbeat. "On Wednesday Arnie's got his pep rally and we have
the big game against Lane — the start of the Blue North season," Manny said. "Think of today as the first practice of a new
year."

Then Herman burst into the gym. Talking a mile a minute.
Something about David Casas. A fight. Sociology class. "The
boy's crazy, coach, he's crazy."

Manny didn't know what Herman was talking about.

It became apparent soon enough, however, when the sociology teacher stopped by to give his account: David and Herman
had been quarreling over something having to do with the team,
which led to a crude and loud exchange of obscenities, with Herman making a crack or two about Hispanics.

"Aw, geez," said Manny.

"I had to send Herman to the office, coach. I don't want to
complain. But it got out of hand."

Manny sighed. "Listen, don't apologize. You did the right
thing. I apologize. Really. There's no excuse for that kind of behavior."

After the teacher left, Manny ordered the team into the basement locker room for a meeting — a special meeting.

They clumped down the stairs and lined up on a bench while
Manny slowly paced back and forth before them, his shoes
squeaking on the shiny white marble-tile floor.

"Well, well, well," he began. "So I hear we had a fight. And
geez, well, I guess I was under a misconception. I guess I thought
we were family. I guess I thought we were friends."

He stopped pacing and faced them directly, his voice tough-
ening. "I don't want to do it, but fellas, if I have to, I'll pull one
of you aside and say, 'You're hurtin' the team, hand in your jersey.' See. What I'm sayin', fellas, is that this has got to stop."

He looked at Herman, whose account of the argument had
differed substantially from the sociology teacher's. "And another

thing. Don't try to bullshit the old coach. O.K.? You can't bullshit a bullshitter. You may aggravate me. But you won't fool me."

He started pacing again. "Now I also hear there were some ethnic remarks. I don't like that. You know, a few years back people said, 'Coach, your school is ninety-eight percent white, how come your team is black?' I said, 'They are?' See, I don't see race. I see people. When it comes to minorities, I belong to the oldest minority in the world — the Jews. I don't appreciate ethnic remarks, 'cause I know what it's like to hear them.

"Another thing. Your choice of language. You guys are basketball players. People look up to you. How would you like to hear that in front of your sister or mother?"

He stopped pacing. "I'm in the twilight years of coachin'. It's been a long time. You know, when I started I was six feet tall and three hundred pounds."

He paused for laughter. A few guys grunted.

"Now, fellas, I don't have to tell you that we got a big game comin' up against Lane. Their coach, John Lewis, I've known him for years. They got a great scorer in that guard, David Kaplan. The experts say we can't beat them, but I know we can. Except we can't beat them if we're fightin' ourselves. So O.K., fellas, look, kiss and make up. You have to think like a team. Let's go out and make it a good, happy, worthwhile season."

Afterward David refused to accept Herman's apologies. "I'll never play with him again," David said. "Never."

"This looks serious," I told Manny.

Manny scoffed. "Aah, these are high school kids. They'll forget about it by tomorrow."

January 8

At Arnie's urging, seven graduates from the class of '50 showed up for the pep rally and the big game: Howard Lazar, Jerry Wolf, Bruce Mertz, Howard Rudy, Sid Retsky, Al Zelinsky, and Gene Helfand.

They arrived at the school about an hour before tip-off, each in his own way looking a little gray, stoop-shouldered, and lost. Arnie greeted them outside the front office and escorted them to the gym. He showed them the new backboards and the plaque with their names. He introduced them to the players. He walked them to the auditorium for the mandatory assembly where about three hundred juniors and seniors were waiting.

The alumni sat in metal folding chairs on the stage and watched while Eldevon Malcolm, the print shop teacher, called on Manny and the team. When the team took the stage, the crowd roared. It was hard to tell if the roar was facetious, but onstage, under the lights, with the cheers cascading down, it didn't much matter. Their first pep rally — you could wait a lifetime for a moment like this. The players wore their uniforms. They were loose and giggly. They tickled each other. They waved to friends.

"Thank you for your support; we need support," said Manny. "We can't stay long because we've got to practice. We've got Lane waiting for us in the gym. It's a big game, a real big game. If you can make it, we'd love to have you."

Manny introduced each player by name. They stepped forward, took a bow, then dashed from the stage, down the hallway and toward the gym.

Then it was Arnie's turn. He asked his classmates to rise. "We graduated in June 1950," he said. "We must be smart because we're still here."

He paused. "We're here for one reason and one reason alone. We love you guys. We're committed to Roosevelt. And we want to help you in any way we can."

He led his friends off the stage. They walked up the aisles and shook hands with the students, who looked startled to see them up close. Coach Jerry Taylor and the girls' basketball team took a bow. Former football coach Al Klein offered a brief history of the school song. "You should be proud of this song," he said. "It belonged to me, and it belonged to them [the graduates], and it belongs to you because it's the Roosevelt song, and you're part of Roosevelt and that makes you special."

Music teacher Harriet Moore and the beginning girls' choir assembled onstage. Arnie took the mike. He stood before a sea of faces: gum chewing, giggling, yawning, chattering, snickering, and scowling. All races, all ethnic groups. He'd been preparing for this moment for months.

He nodded to the choir and they started to sing: "Go on you Rough Riders go, go Roosevelt, go . . . ."

I'd heard Arnie sing that song countless times — on the phone, in the gym, in front of the local school council — but never had I heard him sing it with such emotion and pride. Some of the class clowns in the front rows giggled and made faces. Arnie didn't pay them any attention. He reached down to the mushy part of his heart and sang so tears came to his eyes.

A lot of the kids joined in. They didn't know the words, but they had Arnie's song sheets. As he sang, they sang. Soon almost everyone onstage was singing: the print shop teacher, the music teacher, the graduates, Coach Klein, Jack Sherman.

After that the assembly ended and at least one hundred students (whites, Hispanics, and Asians as well as blacks) made their way to the gym. They filled the bleachers, the largest crowd of the year. They inspired the Rough Riders, who climaxed their lay-up drills with a series of crowd-pleasing dunks.

Sherman dug up an old hand-held microphone and Manny found an extension cord and Arnie introduced the starters, identifying them by streets in Albany Park: "From Central Park and Sunnyside, David Casas; from Kimball and Leland, Anthony Garner . . ."

The players laughed and clapped and they gathered around Manny. Herman turned to Terrell Redmond, the cocaptain and star senior guard. "Whatever you do, stay in Kaplan's face. Don't give him no room and he can't hurt you with that shot."

"I believe in you," Manny told the team. "I believe in you." They scored the first two baskets. Terrell led the way. He drove the baseline. He nailed his jumper. He blocked a shot. He made a steal.

Lane's big shooter, David Kaplan, turned out to be a stocky redhead with a buzz cut. He wasn't fast. He couldn't shake Terrell. After one quarter Kaplan was scoreless and Roosevelt led 17 to 8 .

They broke huddle for the second quarter with confidence. "Come on, guys," screamed David, "it's showtime."

And then the scoreboard died. Play stopped. The players sat on the bench or on the floor or stood to the side with their hands on their hips. Sender, the assistant coach, and Hutch, the frosh-soph coach, and Herman and Eddie Kroger and Jack Sherman — they all took their turns jiggling the wires and poking at the computer keyboard that fed the scoreboard. Nothing worked. Sherman blamed the plug; Herman blamed the wiring; Manny blamed his old friend Saul Lutwig, a retired milkman who rarely missed a game.

"Damnit, Saul, quit steppin' on the cord," Manny snapped.

"I didn't step on nothin'," Saul retorted. "Honest, Manny."

After a ten-minute delay, the scoreboard went back on. Like magic — no one knew how or why. Play resumed, but the Rough Riders had lost their momentum. Particularly Terrell. He forced a shot and got called for charging. He turned tentative. He forgot to front Kaplan, who suddenly scored back-to-back threes.

"I told you, man, you gotta stick that guy," Herman screamed from the bench. "He's too smart. You can't give him any room."

Kaplan's buckets keyed an eleven-point run and Lane took the lead.

Then the scoreboard stopped again. The refs, Lane coach John Lewis, Efrain, the Roosevelt team manager — now they tried wiggling the cord. Nothing worked.

"I think Arnie staged this," Gene Helfand wisecracked.

"Hey, Arnie, are you gonna hit us up for a new scoreboard?" added Howard Lazar.

The gym filled with the murmur of time-killing chatter. The graduates sat in an even line in the second row (behind Manny). Kevin, Terrell, and David sat on the floor. Ronnie entertained everyone with his imitation of Manny. Herman laughed so hard he almost fell off the bench. Amthal Fakhoury, a frosh-soph guard, read his English assignment — until Eddie Kroger nabbed his book.

"Hmm, big book for a little boy," said Eddie as he held up Amthal's copy of *The Scarlet Letter*.

"Hey, man, gimme that book back," Amthal insisted.

"Boy, you can have it. I read that book last year. The moral is that women ain't no good."

"You didn't read it."

"Did too. The minister did it."

Fifteen minutes passed and still the scoreboard didn't work. Manny, Coach Lewis, and the referees caucused at center court. They decided that maybe the keyboard was broken. Someone said that there was another keyboard just like it at Immaculate

Heart of Mary, a girls' Catholic school not too far away. An assistant coach from Lane offered to drive over there and borrow the keyboard. Manny and Lewis agreed to finish the half without a scoreboard.

So the game continued with Sender standing at half court, a stopwatch in his hand. After a basket everyone asked everyone else for the score. Or how much time was left. Players on both teams kept calling out to Sender, "Hey man, how much time?"

At the half, Roosevelt led by one. Manny took them into the hallway for a pep talk. "Play hard, play tough," he said. "Play like this is the most important half of your life."

And they did. Both teams played ferociously. They drove to the basket. They skidded on their knees across the floor. They pushed and shoved and grunted and groaned. The lead bounced back and forth, neither side dominating, until a chubby kid with jet-black hair slipped off a screen, caught a Kaplan pass, and snapped the net with a high-arcing three.

"Who's that?" I asked the scorekeeper.

"Rivera — Victor Rivera. He's a senior guard."

I'd never heard of him. But in the next four or five minutes Rivera looked like the best pure three-point shooter I'd seen all year, Chris Collins included. He hit four threes in succession — each shot a perfect rainbow arc — building Lane's lead to ten. Smelling victory, Coach Lewis unleashed the full-court press.

Manny countered with Kevin — Cuz, the slashing guard. Body low, dribble quick, slicing through the press, dishing to the big men — Anthony, Larry, Kenric Mattox — the crowd chanting "Cuz, Cuz, Cuz." But no matter how daringly Kevin drove, Lane held the lead. Roosevelt's shots weren't falling, not even the lay-ups. And they missed free throws, too.

With 1:38 remaining Lane scored to build their lead to twelve, 66 to 54.

"Game's over," said Eddie Kroger. I turned to him. "Not yet," I said.

Eddie shook his head. "Is so. Damn. And we had 'em, too."

No one seemed to notice Sylvester Turner, up off the bench for the final two minutes. He got the ball and took a shot. A desperation three. Just sort of heaved it — out of anger and frustration — still mad at Manny for not playing him more. It went in. Then Herman stole the ball — slapped it away from Kaplan. He fed Sylvester, who nailed another three. It was 66 to 60 and in the stands we were roaring. Herman fouled a baby-faced forward, sending him to the line for a one and one. The noise was deafening — we stomped, shrieked, yodeled, whistled, rattled our keys. The kid's shot bounced off the rim. Larry rebounded and passed to Kevin, who dribbled up-court and passed to Sylvester, who was wide open in the corner just behind the three-point line. Sylvester's shot slipped through the net. 66–63. Utter pandemonium. In the bleachers students were jumping up and down. The old-timers were hugging one another. I was pounding Eddie Kroger on the back.

"I told you, I told you."

"O.K., O.K. I believe."

Back came Lane and once again Roosevelt fouled. And once again the baby-faced kid had to face the din. He looked terrified, standing alone on the line. As he bounced the ball the crowd noise grew louder — a steady roar, rattling the backboards, vibrating the walls. The shot clanked off the rim. Kenric rebounded, passed to Herman, who passed it to, yes, Sylvester, wide open once again, who launched a three.

From where I stood, it looked perfect: rising, arcing, falling gently — falling from the ceiling, heading for the net. I felt happy for Sylvester. How many times had he dreamed about taking this, the last-second shot? And now he was going to tie the game at 66 . . .

Oh well. It spun round the rim and fell out. I couldn't believe it didn't go in. Lane rebounded and the game ran its course. Kaplan went to the line. Gritty little senior. *He* hit his free throws — damn the noise.

The final was 70 to 63.

Suddenly everyone had to leave. The crowd was clotted trying to squeeze through the door. The game had gone on for almost two hours, what with all the scoreboard delays. Everyone had other things to do. Soon it was just me, Saul, and Manny, alone in Manny's office. Manny, the phone cradled against his neck, on hold with City News, was going over the score book.

"Saul," Manny said, "these numbers don't add up."

"Don't blame me, Manny, your scorer added 'em up. I know how to add. I went to Crane, I didn't go to Roosevelt."

Saul looked at me and winked. Manny grunted. I said: "You would have beat 'em, Manny, if not for that scoreboard."

He nodded: "When it went off, we lost our momentum."

A few seconds passed. "What the hell, they gave it their best," Manny said. "That's high school basketball. Sooner or later, it's gonna break your heart."

He was still on hold with City News when I left the room a few minutes later.

At home, in bed, I thought about the day for hours: Arnie. The song. The alumni. The players, gooey-eyed and giggly as they stood under the lights. The big game, a great game, epitomizing everything magical about basketball. Thirty-two minutes of heart-pounding action — everything happening so fast, faster almost than the clock itself — building to one last shot. Sylvester's shot. And it rolled out. I couldn't believe it. I could still see it, too: a rainbow jumper, falling from the ceiling. I lay awake wondering what might have happened had it gone in.

January 10

The gym at Von Steuben was so small, the bleachers extended onto the playing floor; players going up and down the court had to dodge the feet of their teammates sitting on the bench.

This was supposed to be a big game — a 1990s enactment of a venerable rivalry between two high schools only a few blocks apart. I counted about seventy fans crowded into the four rows of bleachers that ran along the wall across from the Roosevelt bench. Their cheers and chants reverberated off the marble walls. It was like playing basketball in a tin can.

The Rough Riders were taller, stronger, and faster than Von, but the loss to Lane had bled them of energy and smarts. Von (three and ten coming into the game) scored first, and with each basket their confidence rose. Kenric didn't play (sore foot). Terrell bombed away futilely. Anthony got a two-shot technical for hanging on the rim. David fouled out. At one point Roosevelt failed to advance the ball across halfcourt in five consecutive tries. Manny screamed.

The gym heated up as the game wore on. I took off my sweater and rolled up my sleeves. Von's lead hit thirty and their fans were ecstatic — stomping, hooting, howling — raising a racket that pounded against my brain. Across the gym, a few girls from Von and a few boys from Roosevelt exchanged obscenities. Nothing serious. Just a little "suck this" and "lick that." I would see them fraternizing in the hallway after the game.

Roosevelt lost 80 to 53. Manny drifted through the locker room too disappointed and demoralized to yell. The Rough Riders dressed alongside a bunch of skinny white boys, members of Von's swimming team. One Roosevelt student, his baseball cap tilted to the side, menacingly glared at the swimmers. "Hey, Weincord," he said. "Want me to kick their ass?"

Great judgment, I thought. Just what we need — a locker room brawl between whites and blacks. Manny didn't hear him. Just as well. He muttered some platitudes to his players, but his heart wasn't in it. No one was listening. No one seemed to care.

January 14

Arnie's new uniforms arrived today and lifted everyone's spirits. As the senior cocaptain, Terrell got first crack at them. For a moment he stared at the pile of new shirts and shorts on Manny's desk. They seemed to glitter — so clean and fresh, every stitch in place, the gold lettering bright, the shorts Michael Jordan long.

"Stylin' clothes," said Terrell.

Manny leaned back in his chair. "Maybe they'll help our free throws. Nothin' else works."

Terrell sifted through the pile. He was searching for number 23 — Jordan's number. He found it and picked it up.

"Look at Terrell," snickered Kevin. "He wanna be like Mike."

Terrell put the jersey down. Kevin's smile faded. "Hey man, I didn't mean nothin'."

Terrell rummaged through the pile, coming back to 23. He scooped it up and darted from the room. On his way out, Kevin slapped him a high-five. One by one each of them picked through the pile. "Whatever you do, guys, try not to wear the shirts all the time, O.K.?" Manny cracked. "Some of you guys probably wanna wear them to bed."

The guys laughed. Then they gathered along the bleachers to argue about who looked the best in the new duds.

"Manny, you're amazing," I said. "Where do you get your energy to put up with this stuff, even after that Von game?"

He smiled. "I'm like the Old Man in the Sea. You keep fightin', or you drown."

"But after the way they played against Von, why reward them with new uniforms?"

He bristled. "What, I should send the uniforms back and kick them off the team for losing a game? Whether they're 24 and 4, or 4 and 24, I'm still the coach and they're still my team. See. Everyone always wants to know about the winners. Oh sure, the papers wanna give all the headlines to the winners. But what about the kids who don't win? What, they don't matter?

"So maybe I should be Bobby Knight — Mr. Hardass. I should kick them off for missin' a practice. Then what? They wander around the halls. They drop out. Wonderful solution. Look, these aren't bad kids. O.K., they do somethin' stupid sometimes. They screw up. Sometimes I have to yell, sometimes I have to stroke their backs. Half the time I'm not even sure I know what I'm doin'. Then ten years later some guy comes up and says, 'Hey, coach, remember me? I'm a cop. You helped straighten me out.' I think, geez, he was the world's biggest jagoff. I helped him? I coulda swore he never heard a word I said."

January 15

The Rough Riders beat Amundsen 75–56. David shut down Amundsen's star center — a six-foot-eight Yugoslavian immigrant named Haris Mujezinovic — even blocking a few of his shots.

Terrell scored 26 points, twice slipping past his man for baseline dunks. In the stands was a freelance talent scout for several junior colleges. "All the scouts know about King High School," he said. "My clients want to know about the guys playing for Roosevelt or Amundsen."

"So which Roosevelt kid impressed you the most?" I asked, certain he would name Terrell.

"Well, I knew about Kenric already, so he wasn't a surprise. I'd say Wall, your backup center."

"Larry?"

"Yeah, Larry Wall."

"But he hardly played."

"I know, but he's six foot six. Coaches like tall guys. They're closer to the basket."

"But, but, but . . . David."

"Oh, I like Casas. What's he, six foot five? He'll play somewhere next year."

"And Terrell?"

He shrugged. "What's he, six-two? I don't know. He's gotta bulk up and work on his defense."

"But did you see the way he drove the baseline?"

"Hey, in college all the guards can do that. You have to ask yourself what's he gonna do when he turns that corner and finds himself face-to-face with a six-foot-eight leaper?"

I felt a burst of sympathy for Terrell. By the time I was seventeen, I had long dropped any delusions of a career in sports; I was too slow, soft, and small for that. But Terrell was strong and fast enough to be part of the mad, desperate scramble — a million black kids trying to run, jump, and shoot their way to the top. Watching from the sidelines and tracking with almost sadistic fascination which ones made it and which did not were guys like this scout and me. "It's kind of sad what we've done with these kids in the Public League," the scout was saying. "They haven't been prepared for a realistic future. They think there's a future for them playing basketball. A guy like Terrell, you have to ask yourself, does he have what it takes to spend hours in a gym, shooting jumpers and lifting weights? And even if he does all that, even then he probably won't make it."

On the other side of the gym, Terrell sat in the bleachers with his friends, watching the frosh-soph game. The scout shrugged. "Then again, who knows? Maybe Terrell's gonna grow six inches over the summer. Stranger things have happened. He may be that one in a billion — the next Michael Jordan. Then you can watch him on TV and tell your friends that you knew he was gonna be a star all along."

January 17

Manny started Sylvester at forward against Clemente. But on the first shot of the game, Sylvester's man grabbed an offensive rebound. Manny leaped from the bench. "That's it," he screamed.

"I'm sick of this guy not blockin' out. Larry, get in the game for Turner."

A few seconds later the substitution buzzer sounded and the players looked up in bewilderment, no doubt wondering who was getting yanked so early. Larry, pointing at Sylvester, lumbered onto the court. Sylvester's mouth dropped in disbelief.

"Me?" he mouthed.

"Yeah, man," Larry whispered. "Who are you coverin'?" Sylvester didn't respond. He stood alone for a second or two and then slowly headed toward the sidelines, his eyes misting over. He sat on the far end of the bench and buried his head in his hands.

Mercifully, the guys in the bleachers held their tongues. The game continued. It was no contest. Clemente was fast, but small. Kenric dominated the boards. Terrell scored twenty-three points. David blocked a bunch of shots. Roosevelt won 69 to 55. Sylvester missed it all; he didn't look up once.

January 18

Tonight the Rough Riders had a Saturday-night exhibition game, a benefit for a homeless shelter against Niles West, a public school in Skokie. Arnie and Jack Sherman brought their wives to the game. "My wife won't sit with me," Arnie told Manny before the game. "She says I yell too much for an old guy."

"You're not old, Arnie," said Manny. "You look around thirty. Like you've been around thirty twice."

"Hey, Weincord. *Kish in tuchus.*"

David was awesome, blocking shots, stealing the ball, making behind-the-back passes. The Rough Riders won 66 to 52. They never trailed. Manny got mad only once and it had nothing to do with the game. Poor Efrain, the team manager, forgot to list Larry Wall on the official roster of players.

"Why didn't you put Larry's name down?" Manny asked.

"Well, 'cause. He was in the bathroom when I was takin' down the names," Efrain explained.

Manny paused. He looked at Efrain. He looked at me. He looked back at Efrain. "Son, what did you think? He drove up here to take a crap?"

Efrain reddened.

"Did you think he was gonna sit on the toilet for three hours, wipe himself, and go home?"

"No."

"Son, I wouldn't yell. But if you don't list him and he plays we get called for a technical. And . . . aw, forget it."

After the game, Terrell, Herman, and Larry asked me for a ride back home. It was a bitter-cold night, and my car windows were caked with frost. I got lost in a tangle of subdivisions, missed the turnoff for the expressway, and wound up taking the long way home, driving south on Crawford, past an endless string of two-flats and darkened storefronts, from Skokie to the far West Side. I dropped Larry off first and it was nearly midnight by the time we reached Herman's house. A few tough-looking characters, their baseball caps tilted to the side, congregated on the sidewalk.

"Will you be all right?" I asked Herman.

"Don't worry," he said. "Those guys love me."

"You sure?"

"Yeah, man, no problem. They think I'm a star. Hey, it's O.K. This is where I live."

After Herman got out, Terrell and I headed north.

"Do you think I should have heard from the colleges yet?" Terrell asked.

"I don't know."

" 'Cause I haven't heard from none and I was just wonderin'. Most guys have picked their colleges by now. I see it in the papers."

"What will you do next year?"

He shrugged. "I don't know. I guess junior college. But I haven't talked to none of them and no one's called me. I don't know what more I can do. Do you know what it is that they're lookin' for in a player?"

I remembered my talk with the scout. "Defense. Hustle. Grow six inches."

Terrell smiled. We drove in silence for a while.

"Listen, Terrell, you don't *have* to play basketball. I mean, you're so talented, there's a hundred other things you could do — like cutting hair. My wife's a hairstylist and I'll give her your number and she can tell you about the good haircutting schools you can go to and how to get a haircutting license."

He nodded, but I don't think he heard a word I said. "I think the key is recognition," he said. "If I could get my picture in the paper, you know, a little recognition, then the colleges will know about me. And things will be all right."

Kelvyn Park had the smallest, darkest gym I'd ever seen — two-thirds the size of a normal court. It was like playing in a shoebox.

It was a pathetic contest, winless Kelvyn Park being one of the city's smallest and slowest teams. Roosevelt outscored them 27 to 4 in the first quarter. Terrell hit almost every shot he took, scoring 31 points. "That ought to get you mentioned in the paper," I told him.

By the fourth quarter, Manny's main concern was playing time for Eddie Kroger, who had been invited to join the team only last week. "Why not?" said Manny. "Eddie's quite a leaper. And I have an extra uniform."

With Roosevelt up by 40 and five minutes left on the clock, Manny turned to Eddie. "O.K., kid, here's your chance." Eddie gulped. "O.K., coach." He was so nervous he accidentally took off his jersey with his warm-up shirt.

"Eddie, I told you to go into the game," said Manny. "I didn't tell you to strip."

The team started chanting: "Ed-die, Ed-die, Ed-die." His first shot, a lay-up, rolled around the rim and out.

The players on the bench groaned.

"He's nervous," said Weiss.

"How can he be nervous when his team is winning by fifty?" asked Hutch, the frosh-soph coach.

"You try it," said Ronnie. "You see what it's like." With a few seconds left in the game, Herman stole a pass and drove toward the basket. He was in the clear, but instead of shooting himself he flipped the ball to Eddie, who laid it in as the buzzer sounded. The bench exploded into cheers. "Unbelievable," Manny said, "he should retire right now."

On the day of Roosevelt's game at Lake View, the *Sun-Times* published its midseason prep basketball review. Cited as outstanding Blue North players were David and Kenric; Terrell wasn't mentioned. The oversight hit him hard. He had averaged twenty-four points over the last four games. He was playing as well as anyone on the North Side. Herman tried to console him during warm-ups. "They robbed you, man." Terrell shook his head. "What do I have to do to get mentioned?"

It was a spiritless game played in Lake View's bright red gym, where the running track hung over the court, blocking any shot from the corner. Terrell was in a funk. He stood apart from the team during time-outs and barely looked at Manny when the coach talked to him.

Manny turned to the guys on the bench. "What's the matter with Terrell?" he asked.

No one said a word.

Terrell launched a three-point bomb that bounced out of bounds.

"Hey, Terrell," Manny bellowed, "what kind of shot is that?"

"I'm tired," Terrell called back.

"He's tired," said Manny. "Whenever he misses, he's tired."

Suddenly Terrell was walking off the court.

Manny was speechless.

"It's my chest," Terrell gasped. "My chest."

"Is it your asthma?" asked Manny.

"Yeah," said Terrell.

"Well geez, why didn't you say so? Sit down."

"Hey, coach," Herman called out, "we only got four guys in the game."

"Oh geez," said Manny. "Sylvester, get in the game."

"I can't just walk in," said Sylvester.

"Call time-out," Manny yelled.

"But hey, man, Terrell's on the court."

Sure enough, Terrell, as if in a daze, had drifted off the bench and back into the game.

"What the hell's goin' on?" Manny exclaimed.

Referee Vince Mancini blew his whistle and approached the bench. "Manny, a player can't leave the court and then reenter without checking with the scorer."

Mancini was a thirty-four-year-old Chicago cop who had played basketball for Sullivan High School. He had played against Manny's teams and had known him for almost twenty years.

"I know," said Manny.

Mancini winced. "I hate to do this, Manny, but I'm gonna have to call a technical."

"Vince, call it, I'm not gonna yell at you."

A few minutes later, Manny asked Terrell if he wanted to return to the game, but Terrell declined, on account of his asthma. Herman and Ronnie traded knowing looks. Roosevelt won 66 to 44, but no one celebrated. "If that had been me walkin' off the court, Weincord wouldn't ask me if I wanted to play," said Herman. "I ain't playin' as it is. I'm hustlin' my ass off in practice and in games and Weincord, he ain't even watchin'."

January 27

The frosh-soph team had the day off, so the varsity, acting on their own and without Manny's permission, skipped warm-ups and started practice with a full-court game.

It was a raggedy, bombs-away game. Maceo and David were disgusted. They kept looking at Manny — everyone was. They were breaking the rules and they knew it. They were waiting for him to intervene.

But Manny sat in the corner of the gym and didn't say a word. "I want to see how far they'll go," he told me.

Kevin and Sylvester grappled for a loose ball and fell on the floor giggling.

Manny snorted. "As long as they're having fun, nothin' matters."

During a break I asked Terrell why he had walked off the floor against Lake View. "I was frustrated, man," he said. "I just got tired of playin'. I play hard; I'm scorin' more than any other guard in Blue North, and the paper doesn't even list my name. How am I gonna get into college if I don't get the recognition?"

"Was your asthma bothering you?"

He shrugged. "A little."

After practice, Manny was still angry at Terrell. "What really bugs me is that people are gonna think that I play kids when they're sick. And that's not true. You know that. How many times have I told Terrell, 'Don't play if you're sick!'?

"I tell all the guys: your health comes first. But this guy, every time I ask him about his asthma he says, 'It's fine, coach.' What am I supposed to do — read his mind? I've tried. I've really tried. But with some kids, it's not 'What can I do for you, coach?' but 'What can you do for me?'

"I've been too nice. Sometimes people mistake niceness for weakness."

January 28

Manny called the team into his office and let them have it.

"In all my years I've never had a player walk off the floor. And it ain't gonna happen again. If you don't want to play here, leave. You're a bunch of babies. You don't do anything unless I tell you and even then I gotta tell you it a million times. I watched you yesterday. You didn't shoot your free throws. You didn't do your lay-ups. You played a scrimmage that was disgraceful. You wanna play like that — go play in a park!"

In his anger, Manny accidentally knocked over a can of Sprite; the soda dripped off his desk and onto the floor. No one snickered. They crowded around the desk, silent and motionless, eyes on the floor.

After practice, Manny pulled Herman aside. "Son, I want to tell you that I appreciate what you're doing. I know one thing. I put you in, you're gonna give one hundred and fifty percent."

Herman was overwhelmed. He opened his mouth and then shut it. Usually so loquacious, he didn't know what to say.

January 29

Against Benito Juarez — a bunch of small but scrappy Mexican kids — Manny benched Terrell and started Herman. Terrell took it well. He cheered his teammates and hustled when he finally got to play. I think he was relieved that the ordeal was over.

Roosevelt won 98 to 41, as the hapless kids from Juarez flailed for rebounds but rarely jumped higher than Kenric or David's chest. Next was the big rematch — at Lane. "I got a good feeling about that game," Manny said.

So did I. The tongue-lashing had sparked the team. Manny hadn't berated them like that since Luther North. In a strange way, they missed it. Like Herman, they all needed to know someone was watching.

Ronnie White (born September 11, 1974)

In the early eighties, when Ronnie was growing up in Edgewater, his best friends were a Puerto Rican kid and a Cuban kid — call them Robbie and Ozzie. They played baseball together, starting in early spring, as soon as the snow melted; it was their passion.

"I knew Robbie since I was six. I used to sleep at his house. Robbie was the best hitter I ever saw. He could hit the ball three hundred and fifty feet — and that was when he was twelve. Ozzie pitched. He could throw some heat — seventy-five miles an hour. He lives in Puerto Rico now. He went down there to get away from the gangs."

Ronnie played the outfield and led off, like his idol Rickey Henderson, and passionately followed the Eastern Division title march of the '84 Cubs. "I tacked their pictures on my wall and listened to their games on the radio. I even stayed up late to catch the West Coast games.

"How's that? Me, loving baseball. Ronnie White, all-American kid."

Ronnie attended Roosevelt because it offered computer courses. Robbie went there too. But they stopped being friends. Blacks and Puerto Ricans weren't supposed to hang together in high school.

"Robbie started hangin' with his gang and I started hangin' with mine. If I saw him in the hall, it wasn't, 'Hey, Robbie, man, how ya' doin'?' It would be cool, real cool, like: 'What's up, man?' I wouldn't even say his name.

"Let me say this — I hung with gangbangers, but I didn't join a gang. O.K.? I wasn't a banger. There's a difference. I might stand on the corner with them, but I didn't gangbang. I didn't hassle people. But you see, once people see who you're hangin' with, they think they know you. You fit the nice little category they got laid out for you in their mind. I became Ronnie White, gangbanger. They didn't see me as an ordinary kid."

And Robbie?

"Robbie's dead. He got shot. The way I heard it, he and another gangbanger were sittin' on the front of Our Lady of Mercy School and a car drove up and someone shot him. I think he was sixteen when it happened. Left his woman pregnant, too."

As time wore on, Ronnie started having his own troubles. He was always in and out of the principal's office, always on the verge of expulsion. "You go look at my folder in the central office and it's thick with all sorts of write-ups. Cuttin' class — that sort of thing. I got suspended for cuttin' into the lunchroom line. Isn't that horrible? I got suspended for using the teachers' washroom. I had to go, man — bad stomach.

"Mr. Sherman called me in his office and said I do one more thing and I'm getting kicked out. I was labeled an outcast."

He had a bad habit of being in the wrong place at the wrong time. He said he was playing basketball in River Park the night Fabian Diaz, Manny's soccer player, was shot.

"We'd be playin' basketball while Fabian and them be playin' soccer until three in the morning. This one night, I heard a pow, pow. And I saw everyone scatter. We saw two guys runnin' with trench coats and hats over their faces. It was a Friday night about ten. Bein' it so dark and they had a dark coat, you couldn't see their faces. I don't know why they would shoot him. Fabian wasn't in no gang."

Ronnie says he also saw the fabled incident in which a Roosevelt football player threw a garbage can over the auditorium balcony and hit a woman standing below.

"There were five of us sittin' up there. And someone said, 'Let's make some noise.' And the only thing Teddy [not his real name] saw was this garbage can. He got ready to do it and I said, 'Don't do it, man.' He didn't mean to hit anyone. He just threw it. And then we ran. He hit a lady and she went out on a stretcher. She was the parent of an eighth-grader in for orientation. I bet her kid didn't come here.

"Teddy was the best football player I'd ever seen. They kicked him out of school and told him he was lucky he wasn't in jail. Sender took him over to Triton College to talk to the coach. They said if he passes his GED he can come. But I don't know. The man ain't stayin' in shape. Saddest damn thing, the way a guy's life can change just like that."

Ronnie learned something from Teddy's fate: sometimes you do things without really knowing why. You may think you're in control, but you're not. You're just following the pack. Doing things not because you want to, but because it's what others expect of you.

Ronnie stopped playing baseball. "I had no particular reason. I didn't, you know, say, 'That's it, I don't like this, I quit.' I don't think the coach liked me — that was part of it. And I guess I was hangin' with the wrong crowd. Maybe it's a race thing. Baseball ain't somethin' that blacks are supposed to do."

Ronnie might have studied more after he quit playing baseball. He was one of the smartest kids on the team — a philosophizing wiseass wit who read the paper every day.

He was also funny. He could tell a joke and do impersonations. He had Manny cold, right down to the movement of his hands. "I'd like to do a stand-up routine in a comedy club, just once. Just to see what it's like. Maybe I will."

Instead, he spent most of his free time playing basketball. That's what his friends did, and he liked being with his friends. He was the shortest kid on the team, but he hustled, never missed practice, and played team defense.

His parents were divorced and his mom moved to the suburbs. Ronnie chose to stay at Roosevelt with his friends, so he moved into a basement apartment in his grandmother's flat on the West Side. His own bachelor's pad: waterbed, VCR, stereo, big-screen TV. He got a job selling shoes at a store on Maxwell Street. He saved enough money to buy a '78 Impala. "Just like Michael Jordan says in the commercials. 'When I drive, I drive a Chevy.' "

He drove his teammates to school and to games. "I love my teammates. We might have our fights, but we stick together in a jam. You know why we ran off that bus after the Glenbrook game? 'Cause some Puerto Rican gangbangers were lookin' like they might mess with Herman. You shoulda seen their faces when they saw us come chargin' off that bus. We chased them into the alley and got in a few good hits. Nothin' serious. Just a few whacks. But I'll tell you what, they're gonna think twice about messin' with Herman again."

Despite his run-ins with other teachers, Ronnie got along with Manny. "I went up to Manny before the season started and I said, 'Coach, I want to thank you for givin' me the chance to play.' I meant it, too. I don't say nothin' I don't mean. I wasn't tryin' to suck up. He was givin' me a break. I don't get many breaks."

Ronnie thought Manny was hilarious. "One time I was sittin' with him in the gym and Manny said: 'I've been going with the same woman for thirty years.' I said, 'Really, coach?' And he says, 'I hope my wife doesn't find out.' I cracked up. It was the way he set it up, with the pause before the punch line. The man knows how to tell a joke.

"I like to sit behind him during the games. That's the best seat in the house. He'll stand up and shout, 'Sylvester's been shootin' forty-eight times and he ain't hit the front of the rim.' Or he'll say, 'For cry Pete, would you tell me what kind of defense that is?' One time he got really mad at Maceo and yelled: 'Maceo shoots like his balls weigh eighty pounds apiece.' It happened to be really quiet in the gym at the time and everyone heard him."

In the season's first few games, Ronnie played a lot as Manny tested different lineups. "After the Curie game, Manny told me, 'Ron, you don't make many mistakes. You ran the offense.' He said I don't have a lot of talent like the other guys, but I do my best. It pumped me up. I thought about that a lot. Manny doesn't realize how much we listen to what he says.

"It was the high point of my career when Manny let me start against Glenbrook. When Sherman shook my hand during warm-ups, I could have passed out. He said, 'Ronnie, good luck. Take it easy. Play a good game and have some fun.' That was the first nice thing he ever said to me. I think maybe he liked me then.

"I made one mistake in that game and Weincord pulled me out. I said, 'O.K., I'll get my chance in the second half.' But he didn't start me in the third quarter. When I finally got in, I got a steal from Collins and I hit a jumper. But all of a sudden I see Kevin comin' in for me. It was back to the bench. I don't know why he pulled me. I could have cried, I felt so awful."

Ronnie didn't have the basketball confidence of, say, David or Herman. He didn't feel about basketball the way he had about baseball. The game didn't come naturally to him. When he knelt at the scorer's table, waiting to enter a game, his palms sweated and his stomach churned. "You don't know what it's like, waitin' at the table. You hear Manny yellin' and you're sayin' to yourself, 'Please, don't make any mistakes.' "

Sometimes he tried to hide his anxieties by strutting defiantly to the scorer's table, wearing a cold look of indifference. But that didn't impress Manny. "Look at White," Manny would say, "he looks like he doesn't care." In reality, he cared very much.

Ronnie didn't see himself as a mop-up player. He felt he had a greater contribution to make. "People make judgments about you. They put you in a little box and they say, 'This is who you are and this is what you can do.' But they don't know what I got inside me. They don't know what I can do.

"All I need is a little extra playin' time, a little boost of confidence. Then things will come together. Then people will see me for what I am."

Ronnie thought about the paths he might take after high school. "I might go to college and get a degree in physical education. I'd love to coach. I'd be good at it too; I'd be a little like Weincord — I'd crack a lot of jokes. I might do a nightclub thing. I'm young. There's more to life than high school."

As for the rest of the season, Ronnie's main goals were to play hard, help his teammates, and graduate. "I've done a lot just to get this far. No one thought I'd ever graduate. But I will. I'm gonna surprise the hell out of everybody. The main reason I stay on is that I wanna prove 'em all wrong. When I walk across that stage on graduation day, none of them are gonna believe it. I used to think that I'd walk up to Sherman and say, 'Sherman, kiss my butt.' But now I think I'll just say thanks.

"I don't know if I'll go out for the baseball team. I still can play. Maybe not as good as I used to. Me, Ozzie, and Robbie — we could have gone anywhere in the city and played varsity. I was good and I just let it go. I could have played in the minor leagues. I think about that every night before I go to sleep."

February 5

A large, spirited crowd turned out at Lane, and they went wild when the home team took the floor, chanting: "Seniors, seniors, seniors."

Victor Rivera, the three-point wonder who'd iced the first game for Lane, was missing. "He's out for the season," the scorekeeper told me. "Academically ineligible."

I was disappointed; I wanted to see his shot again.

Kenric played strong, shoving his man out of position, grabbing rebounds. Unfortunately, his teammates were cold — they could barely hit a lay-up. After one quarter they trailed by one, Kevin had three fouls, and Herman was itching to play. He sat next to Manny, rocking with restless energy, saying things like: "I'm ready, coach." Or "Need me yet?"

One minute into the second quarter, Manny turned to Herman and said: "Go in for Kevin."

They were magic words. Herman looked to the ceiling; I swear he offered a silent prayer.

They were down by eight when Herman took the floor, 23 to 15. But he stripped the ball from Lane's star Kaplan and drove for a lay-up. Then he harassed Kaplan into making a crummy pass, which Terrell intercepted, setting off a three-on-one fast break. Terrell threw it to Herman who threw it to David (who once said he'd never play with Herman again). David buried a three: 23 to 20. Lane's coach called time. The crowd was silenced. Roosevelt was back in the game. Herman fell to his knees. He banged the floor with his hands. He looked up, offering more thanks, and bellowed: "Yes, yes, yes." His teammates (David included) rushed onto the court and embraced him.

At halftime, still down by three, Manny gathered the team in the stairwell that led to the locker room. "Kenric, you're magnificent," Manny said. "Herman, I can't say enough; I'm so proud of you. For cry Pete, we can do it."

Herman started the third quarter. He drove past Kaplan and fed Kenric for a lay-up that cut Lane's lead to one. On defense he swarmed over Kaplan, picking him up at the half-court line, taking away his drive, forcing him to make foolish passes. He took charge. The game came down to whether Kaplan or Herman would get the better of their match.

But with five minutes left in the fourth quarter and Lane up by two, Manny pulled Herman and inserted Kevin. It was a hunch. "I think Herman's tired," Manny said.

It was a mistake. Herman's hustle was carrying the team. Kevin was out of sync and indecisive. Worried that Kaplan might drive past him, he backed up, giving Kaplan too much room. Kaplan dribbled to the three-point stripe and boom, the quick release. A three-pointer. All net. Lane led 49 to 44.

David hit a jumper, but back came Kaplan. He dribbled to the three-point line, then stepped back, his eyes not even on the basket, like he was going to pass. Kevin relaxed. Again the quick release. Again all net: 52–46.

"Herman," Manny yelled, "get back in the game."

The crowd was going berserk. They chanted: "Hey, seniors, what's your number? 92, 92 — 9, 9, 9, 92."

The Rough Riders cut the lead to three with just over a minute left. Kaplan dribbled up-court. Herman hawked him, wouldn't let him go. Kaplan went left, right, Herman stayed with him. His eyes locked in on Kaplan's; he talked to him, too. He made him give up the dribble. He pressured him into making a stupid pass, which Terrell picked off, driving for a lay-up that cut the lead to 52–51. Larry, Eddie, Ronnie, all the guys on the bench jumped with excitement. Thirty seconds remained; Kaplan had the ball. "Foul him," Manny yelled. To hell if Kaplan made the free throw. The point was to kill the clock and get the ball back.

But the team didn't hear. The clock ticked down to ten seconds and still no one fouled Kaplan. "Goddamn it, foul him!" Manny yelled. I thought he was going to run out on the court and do it himself.

Maceo took charge. He marched across the floor, grabbed Kaplan by the wrist, and yanked him, good and hard. Too hard. The ref blew his whistle and called a flagrant foul. That meant Kaplan would shoot two, and Lane would get the ball. Maceo looked stunned by the call.

Manny jumped up and down. He threw his keys on the floor. He kicked his chair. He kicked his keys. His neck veins bulged. "What the hell kinda foul is that?" he screamed at Maceo.

"But I barely touched him, coach," said Maceo, still wearing a wide-eyed look of incredulity.

"Barely touched him!" Manny roared. "You practically pulled his goddamn arm out of its goddamn socket!"

Kaplan hit both shots and Lane went on to win 55 to 51 as the crowd broke into a chorus of: "Nah, nah, nah, nah / Hey, hey, hey / Good-bye." Herman and Kaplan met at center court. They shook hands and then embraced.

Manny and Coach Lewis met at the scorer's table. Veteran coaches: one white, one black. Old friends. They embraced.

"Coach, I wanna congratulate you," Manny said. "Your guys played one helluva game."

Lewis put his arm around Manny. "It could have gone either way, Manny. You know that."

Manny paused. "Well, John," he said, "it looks like you'll be division champs. You'll be movin' up to Red. I guess we won't be playin' you next year."

"No way. As long as I'm coachin' Lane and you're at Roosevelt, there will *always* be a game between these schools. It may be a December exhibition, but we'll figure somethin' out."

They embraced again. Manny walked down to the locker room. He was pale. I'd never seen him so down. "I blew this one," he said. "I can't blame anyone else. I never should have taken Herman out."

The impact of the loss was just hitting him. They had a league record of five and three — three games behind Lane. They weren't going to win the Blue North. Or move up to Red. Or hang a divisional banner on the wall.

February 6

Another cold, gray, miserable day. I waited fifteen minutes for a train. The sidewalks along Kedzie were crumbling. A group of Asian kids stood on the corner calling each other muddahfukahs. I didn't want to go to practice. I don't think anyone did.

There wasn't any practice. The girls had the gym for their game against Von. I sat with Sylvester and Ronnie in the bleachers and watched. They were also miserable, particularly Sylvester. "Weincord never gave me a chance," he said. "He just pulled me out of that Clemente game like I was a dog."

"He wouldn't have done that to Terrell," said Ronnie.

Sylvester nodded. "Or David. Or Kenric. That man plays favorites. He never did like me. I started on the frosh-soph team that won twenty-four games. Then I come to varsity and the man don't even give me a chance. I'm sick of it. He calls me a schmuck. I ain't no schmuck."

We watched the girls shuffle up and down the court. Then I heard one freshman boy tell a freshman girl, "Bitch, suck . . ." Well, you get the idea.

I got up. The kid saw me rise and started to apologize. "Hey man, sorry. I didn't see you there."

"Hey, if you have to apologize to me, you shouldn't have said it to her."

As soon as I said it, I felt old. I'd been feeling older and older for some time now. Everywhere I went — Von, Lane, Glen-brook, Taft — I heard kids telling each other to suck this or lick that and I wasn't taking it well. I was turning into the kind of reactionary old crank who constantly harps on how things *used* to be even though he knows they really weren't that way at all. I was sick of teenagers, tired of their excuses, sick of their whining. Tired of watching well-intentioned grown-ups lose their compo-sure in a vain effort to pound some sense through those thick teenage skulls. I felt for the teachers. I couldn't do what they did. I wouldn't survive one year in a high school. I'd be one of those burnout cases, the kind of teacher who winds up selling real es-tate. I had no idea how Manny had lasted so long.

Speaking of Manny, he too looked miserable, sitting all alone in a folding chair outside his office, still down on himself for yes-terday's loss, still upset for having taken out Herman.

I wandered over to where he sat and, trying to make conver-sation, inquired after the unofficial assistant coach. "Where's Sender?" I asked. "I haven't seen him in weeks."

"How do I know? The guy just stopped comin'. Look, people come and people go. I don't ask questions. I guess he had some-thin' better to do. What am I, his babysitter?"

So much for him cheering me up. We didn't say another word for the rest of the game. He looked as sour as I felt. His asthma was bothering him. It was keeping him up at night. Winter was wearing him down. The season was long. I looked at my pocket schedule. Six regular-season games remained — six games against some of the worst teams in the city. How in the world would we ever make it to the end?

February 7

Arnie led a second pep rally before the Von Steuben game. He brought in several other old graduates, including Jerry Wolf, Mickey Rottman, Freddy Rosen, and Louie Landt (the great Louie Landt, one of the leading scorers on the '52 championship team).

Arnie introduced the girls' team. They were section champs. And still a bunch of boys in the front rows booed. "It's too much for them," said Manny, "cheerin' for girls."

Al Klein said a few words about believing in your dreams. Herman, going along on a dare, joined Arnie at center stage to sing the school song. The kids in the audience mostly hooted. Then thirty or so showed up for the game.

Roosevelt creamed Von, leading from start to finish. Larry played a big game, his best of the season. He grabbed 14 rebounds and scored 12 points.

Right in the middle of the game — while Manny berated Anthony for some kind of defensive lapse — a kid walked into the gym. His cheeks were flushed; he was fresh from the outside. He took his time, walking toward the Roosevelt side of the gym. Past the Von bench. Past the scoring table. Right up to Manny. He stood there — a foot or two from play — waiting for Manny to stop yelling at Anthony.

I said: "Uh, Manny."

Manny looked at me, and then followed my eyes to the kid.

The kid said there was a car blocking the driver's-ed range.

Manny didn't say a word, he just stared at the kid, and I thought uh-oh, we're on the edge of an explosion. But the interruption seemed to soothe Manny. It gave him some perspective. It reminded him of where he was.

"What kind of car?" he asked.

"Cadillac."

Manny nodded. He walked over to where Jerry Wolf was sitting. "Hey, Jerry," he said, "your car's blockin' the lane."

Jerry left and Manny returned to his seat. A few minutes later he was interrupted again, this time by Weiss, who was taping the game with the video camera Arnie had purchased for the school. The camera was stuck on pause. Manny fiddled with it for a while and finally got it working.

"Thanks," said Weiss.

"No problem," said Manny. "Come to me anytime. Really. For anything. I've got nothin' else to do — I'm only coachin'."

February 10

I bumped into Efrain outside the school. He was waiting for a bus.

"I had to quit as manager," he said. "I got a job."

"Congratulations. But we'll miss you."

"I'll really miss the team. And Coach Weincord. You know what? I think next year I'm gonna go out for the team."

I'd seen him play Manny in H-O-R-S-E. Manny always won.

"That's great, Efrain."

"It's somethin' I've always dreamed about. Coach Weincord always said never give up our dreams."

February 11

They played at Amundsen — the skinniest gym in the league. Almost every player was in a funk. Each had his own reason, mostly to do with not enough playing time.

At halftime, Manny didn't take the team to the locker room. He didn't give them a pep talk or a tongue-lashing. No instructions. They just sat silently on the bench.

"Manny, aren't you gonna talk to them or somethin'?" I asked.

"What's there to say that I haven't said a hundred times? If they don't know what to do by now, they'll never know."

They won 56–52. Mario was outstanding. He scored two crucial fourth-quarter baskets and made a rally-ending steal. Everyone was happy for him. "If Mario gets goin', you'll go far in the playoffs," Arnie told Manny.

For the first time in days, Manny's mood brightened. "You gotta love Mario," he said. "He's a great kid. And he's a good player. Sometimes the solution is right under your nose."

February 13

The *Sun-Times* ran a picture of Terrell playing tough, hands-in-the-face defense against Amundsen (the photographer had shown up to take a shot of Haris Mujezinovic, the six-foot-eight center). The fellows were delighted and the gym rang with laughter, as though some curse had been lifted. "That picture may be the tonic Terrell needs to get goin'," said Manny. "I've always said he could carry this team."

They also got a new manager, Hersey Jackson, a fifteen-year-old sophomore with big brown eyes and baby-round cheeks. He spent about an hour a day on buses and trains to reach Roosevelt from his home on the far South Side. "There were too many gangs at my neighborhood high school," he said.

"Can you figure out averages for each player if I give you the score book?" I asked him.

Hersey looked insulted. "Sure."

He worked out the averages in about twenty minutes and didn't make one mistake.

"Geez, Hersey, you're a wizard."

"I need to know math 'cause I plan to be an architect."

During the scrimmage, Manny was his old self. "Did I tell you about the film of the Von game? Mr. Weiss is a beautiful man, but keep him away from a camera. He got excited and started cheerin' and the camera started goin' up and down. We got more pictures of the ceilin' than the game. I got seasick watchin' it. God bless him. At least he's out here helpin' the kids."

Aisha Walls, the starting forward on the girls' basketball team, wandered into the gym. She sat next to Manny.

"You want me to tell you what's wrong with the team?" she asked Manny.

"Certainly."

"O.K., we'll start with Kenric — he's too fat."

"Wait, I'll take it down in shorthand," Manny said. "Look, one hand's shorter than the other."

On the court, the scrimmage had stopped. Larry stood alone under the basket while the others walked away, holding their noses.

"Dang, Larry, a rat crawl up your ass and die?" said Kenric.

"What's going on, fellas?" Manny called out.

The players looked embarrassed. Finally, Kenric spoke. "Larry — farted."

Manny didn't hear him. "What?"

"I said Larry — passed gas."

"Oh, he passed gas. Well, catch it and put it in the basket and it will be his first assist of the season."

A couple of plays later, Larry banged Kenric on the head. "Look at Larry," said Manny. "First he farts, then he fouls. What a day."

The scrimmage went on for another few minutes. Then Kevin left for work. Manny brought in a freshman who had been watching on the side. His first pass sailed over Herman's head and flew out the open door.

"That's it," Manny said. "Practice is over. Let's clear out before someone gets hurt."

He laughed when he said it, and I started to think that maybe the worst of the season was over.

February 14

They killed Clemente. On Clemente's home court, too. And Clemente wasn't bad (11–8 coming into the game). A hell of a lot better than, say, Kelvyn or Juarez.

Sylvester hit two threes and made some quick moves to the basket. At the half, Manny patted him on the shoulder. "You think I've got something against you when I yell. But I like you, Syl. I want you to do well."

Terrell was brilliant. He made one midair move, switching the ball from his left hand to his right, that brought the crowd to its feet. After the game a skinny, wide-eyed freshman girl nervously approached him.

"Excuse me," she said, "can I have your autograph?"

Terrell smiled and obliged her. Didn't faze him a bit, like it happened all the time.

February 19

Herman didn't suit up for Kelvyn Park (another blowout for Roosevelt). "Sherman suspended me from the team," he told me. "They said I was harassin' a teacher. That's a lie. I never did it. I swear."

The suspension caught Manny off guard. "Herman never gave me any trouble," said Manny. "He's cocky, but he's always polite to me. He should be suspended for doin' what he did, but I can only judge him on what I see."

Manny thought about things for a while and then shook his head. "Ah geez, what luck. I figured somethin' was bound to go wrong cause things were finally startin' to look good."

February 21

After the Lake View game (Roosevelt won, 76 to 62) I sat in the bleachers with Herman while the frosh-soph team played. Ronnie wandered over and we listened to Herman's side of the story.

"There's this teacher, man, she's always harassin' me. Over my earrings, over anything. Supposedly what happened is this. She called me a dog. And she said I said, 'Give me some hoochie, and I'll show you what a dog is.' "

"Did you say it?"

"No, man. I swear. They called this big meeting. Me, my mama, Sherman, four lady teachers, and a security guard. They talked about my attitude. They made me admit to sayin' it. I was cryin', man. My eyes were bloodshot red. They're not only takin' a sport from me, they're takin' away my future. I begged them: 'Let me play.' They made it seem like I was a bad influence on the team. Man, how can that be? I'm almost the youngest senior on the team. How am I gonna be tellin' someone what to do? The counselor said, 'We keep givin' Herman chances.' Like I'm a murderer or somethin'. Man, I'm seventeen years old.

"I don't think I'm insensitive to teachers. I'm tryin' to get what they got. A job, a little security. And they're tryin' to take it all away."

He stopped talking, and we watched a tiny guard for Lake View dribble up-court.

"Herman, I can't believe this," I said. "If you didn't say these things, why would these teachers make it up?"

"They're black females," he said.

"So?"

"Man, don't you know what black females are about?"

"That's right," said Ronnie.

"They don't know how much power they've got," said Herman. "They just want to drag down us males."

"Come on, Herman. It doesn't make sense. Why would they lie?"

"I don't know. But they do."

"Look at what happened to Mike Tyson," said Ronnie.

"They're draggin' him to jail," said Herman.

"That was the bullshittiest trial I've ever seen," said Ronnie. "Ain't no million-dollar man gonna rape anyone. But whatever a woman says goes, especially when it's about a black man. Now what trips me out, they're doin' nothing against that Kennedy kid."

I didn't know what to say. On the court, the Rough Riders were in the midst of a six-point run.

"I just feel bad for my teammates," Herman continued. "I love them all, every last one. Through thick and thin, I'm with them. I feel like I let them down."

February 24

The gym rumbled with rumors about a locker room fight between Lake View and Roosevelt students after Friday's frosh-soph game. In the ruckus, a Lake View player's jacket had been stolen. Now the frosh-soph team faced an ultimatum from Jack Sherman: return the jacket by February 25 or forfeit the rest of the season. Coach Hutch assembled ten members of his team for a conference outside Manny's office.

"I know you know who took the jacket," Hutch said. "I can't believe you'd risk your season to save him."

"But Hutch, man, this ain't got nothin' to do with us," one stocky kid said.

"That's right," another kid said. "None of us took it."

Manny watched. Then he cleared his throat. "Coach, I'd like to say a few words."

"Go ahead, coach," Hutch said.

Manny started talking quietly, but he quickly raised his voice. "I tell you what, fellas. I don't know if any of you took that jacket. But I do know that you know who took it, and if you don't get him to give it back, then you ain't playin' for me. You hear that? You either return that jacket or you don't play for me next year. None of you. And I'll tell you somethin' else. I was thinkin' of retirin'. But this gives me a reason to come back. See. Because I've been watchin' you guys all season, and, to tell you the truth, you're nothin' but a bunch of jagoffs. I hate usin' that word, but how else can I call it? Really. It's like Romper Room down here. And now with this, I don't want none of you playin' for me. I'll take my chances with any kid walkin' down that hall. I'll go zero and twenty if I have to. That's the way it's gonna be."

With that Manny and Hutch walked into the office, leaving me and the frosh-soph players alone by the bleachers. I hadn't paid them much attention lately, but now it seemed to me that they had changed in the last few weeks. They had grown. They had hair on their faces. Their voices didn't squeak quite so much.

They didn't know what to say. They had heard all the stories about Manny, but this was their first face-to-face confrontation.

"He's bullshittin', man," the stocky kid said. "Figure it out. There's seven seniors on this team: Mario, Redmond, Herman, Mace, Ronnie, Sylvester, and Casas. He needs us more than we need him. How the hell he gonna field a team without us?"

The others weren't so sure. "You heard him say he could do it," said another.

"Right, what's he gonna do — play a bunch of girls? Man, you guys are chumps."

"Yeah, well, what if he kicks us off? What are we supposed to do? Transfer? Man, I plan to play basketball in college."

They were silent. You could almost see their minds wrestling with the two sides of the argument.

"Better get that jacket," one kid said.

"Hell with him," the stocky kid said. "I don't need him. I got football anyway."

Manny sat at his desk staring out the window. "Is it my imagination or do these kids keep gettin' younger?" he said as I walked in.

"Nah, we're just gettin' older," I said.

He nodded and pointed to a bouquet of colorful balloons. "Today's my birthday. My daughters sent me these balloons."

"Oh, geez, Manny. Happy birthday. Which one is it?"

"Number sixty."

"Damn, Manny. I'm sorry, I should have at least sent you a card."

"Forget it. I don't need a lot of attention. It only makes me feel older. Christ, I feel old enough as it is. My mother threw a party for me this weekend. My aunts and relatives were there. People who knew me when I was just a baby. Birthdays never really meant much to me. But hittin' sixty was somehow, I don't know, different. I feel, where did the years go? You see these kids come and go. I coached guys who are grandfathers now. And I still remember being a young man."

"How are you going to celebrate your birthday?"

"Oh, I've got big plans. I'm gonna help my mother buy her groceries."

As we walked out the door, I called to the players, "Hey, fellas, did you know that it's coach's birthday today?"

A few of them waved. Mario came over and shook Manny's hand. "How old are you, coach?" he asked.

Manny pointed to one of the balloons. "Like it says, I'm over the hill."

Mario laughed and put his arm around Manny. "Not yet, coach," he said. "You're still climbin' that hill."

February 26

They chartered a bus for the game at Benito Juarez, and the frosh-soph got to go: somehow, someone had found and returned the missing jacket. It was the last game of the regular season.

The Juarez coach, an upbeat black man named Curtis Danzy, had his own player problems. He had suspended the starting center for insubordination.

"When I kicked him off he said: 'I was wondering when you would do this,' " Danzy told Manny. "Isn't that something?"

At the half the Rough Riders led 42 to 16.

"I'll take off the press," Manny told Danzy.

Danzy shook his head. "Keep it on. They need to learn pressure. Tomorrow's the playoffs — a whole new season."

In the fourth quarter, Manny brought in Ronnie, Eddie, Sylvester, and Maceo. Juarez countered with a full-court press; the second unit, unable to advance the ball, was outscored by eleven points in three minutes.

Manny was furious. How could he claim his team had progressed? This comedy of errors revived memories of game one against Taft. If I had been coach I would have called a time-out, gathered the guys around me, patted them on the back, and, you know, settled them down.

Of course I wouldn't last one season as coach, let alone twenty-three. Manny certainly hadn't survived by coddling teenagers. Like Maceo said, he told you how he felt. So the season ended the way it started: Manny's neck veins bulging, his face purplish red. He yanked Maceo, Ronnie, and Eddie ("You don't want to play, fine. I'll play someone who does") and brought back three starters.

What a miserable end to a disappointing season — getting yanked from a blowout against one of the city's weakest teams. Maceo and Ronnie took it hard. Maceo kicked the bench, then sat well behind the team in the bleachers. "I'm sick of this bullshit," he roared. "I give my heart and soul to this school. And they don't do nothin'. Nothin'! They don't have no school spirit. Nothin'."

Ronnie was near tears. "Man, these starters ain't doin' so great. They ain't impressin' me with no Georgetown offense. What am I supposed to be, Isiah Thomas? To hell with this. This don't mean a thing. I'm still goin' to college. I can play; I know I can play. I'll show 'em, man. I'll show 'em."

Finally he ran out of energy and, like Maceo, watched in angry silence as the regular season ticked to a close. Throughout their outburst Manny stared straight ahead, chin in hand, engrossed in the game. Like he didn't hear them. Good strategy. One thing he had learned in all his years of coaching was when to let the players blow off steam.

Roosevelt won 85 to 57, though you wouldn't know it from watching the players shuffle morosely to the bus. "I saw some good things out there today," said Manny, trying his best to cheer them up. "The important thing is we won the game. We won our last six — not bad, not bad. A season is like a puzzle, gotta put all the pieces together. I think we're comin' together just in time for the playoffs."

I wasn't sure they believed him or even if he believed himself. It didn't really matter. One thing about Manny, he's loyal. And win or lose, good or bad — they were still his team.

David Casas (born February 12, 1974)

In the middle of his junior year, David flunked English and got kicked off the team.

"Manny had no choice — my grade-point average fell below C. Coach told me that if I studied hard and brought my grades up, I could come back and play senior year. But man, I was too down to think about that."

In retrospect, David realized that he was going through a restless, rebellious stage: ignoring his homework, watching too much TV, bickering with his father, buckling under the pressure of being the Hispanic kid on the team.

"My teammates welcomed me, but other students didn't. Some

people said, 'Hey man, basketball isn't a Hispanic sport.' And some of my Hispanic friends would say, 'Hey man, are you trying to be black?' That stuff doesn't bother me now. It's a challenge to be the only Hispanic on the team, and I like a challenge. But then, it did get to me."

His parents didn't know what to do with him. His mother, Juanita, worked in a factory. His father, Jesus, drove a cab. They were Mexican immigrants who worked hard to support David and his two brothers. Jesus Casas told David that if he was going to sit around moping — if he wasn't even playing basketball — he should at least get a job and develop a usable skill. David snapped back: "Don't tell me what to do. I'm not a kid anymore. I'm seventeen. Almost a man.

"I had a real bad attitude, but what happened is that I went to visit some relatives in Mexico and I played basketball and I realized how good I was. I saw how much talent I had. And I realized that this was something I shouldn't waste."

Over the summer before his senior year, he grew to six foot six, taller than anyone in his family. He started lifting weights. He would jog home from his girlfriend's house, a five-mile run, his gym bag strapped to his back, dodging traffic, skipping over potholes. As he ran, he imagined himself under the lights, bringing up the ball, seconds ticking down, the crowd on its feet. Sometimes he'd hit the game-winning jumper, other times he'd set up a teammate with a no-look, behind-the-back pass.

In July, he, Kenric, Terrell, Maceo, and Sylvester took a trip downstate for the Morris Shootout, a tournament for some of the state's finest high school teams. Sender drove them. They weren't scheduled to compete, they were just going to watch. But one team didn't show up, and Sender asked the ref if his boys could play. The next thing you know they were beating a good team, Joliet West, by eleven or twelve points. They wilted in the heat, blew the lead, and wound up losing by one. But that tiny taste of big-time basketball — the uniforms, the crowds, the big-name coaches who were watching, including Notre Dame's John MacLeod and Duke's Mike Krzyzewski — thrilled David. "That one game made me realize how much I love playing basketball. How much I get fired up when the crowd is cheering or booing. I don't mind that — that only makes me play harder. I love it when my opponent talks trash. I'll say, 'Hey, babe, let's go.' Once we get started, I'm on. Just give me the ball. Most of the things I do it's to embarrass people. Not off the court. Off the court my opponent can be my friend. But on the court, it's showtime. Me against them. 'Come on, guy, show me what you can do.'

"I like to watch tapes of Jordan, Magic, and Bird. I play their moves over in my mind. I love when Magic does one of his passes, when Michael takes it to the hoop, or when Larry hits his shot. It makes me tingle. I want to play like them. I want to play in the pros."

He was transformed. His confidence soared; he made peace with his father. (In fact Jesus Casas was a regular at the games — one of the few parents in the crowd.) He was upbeat, almost bubbly, the friendliest, most outgoing guy on the team. "Mr. Personality" is what Manny called him. "One of the nicest kids I've ever coached."

At time-outs or after great plays, David led the cheers, pumping and twirling his arms and yelling "showtime!"

He was determined to remain academically eligible. When necessary, he stayed up late, fighting off sleep and battling boredom as he struggled with his books. Math wasn't too bad, but literature was torture. "Especially Shakespeare, I hate that guy. It's all thou this and thou that. Hey man, why can't they talk English?"

Sometimes late at night his mind would detour into a fantasy in which he imagined himself studying medicine at Northwestern University. He wasn't sure why he had picked Northwestern (or, for that matter, medicine); it just sounded like a classy school. "First thing I'd do if I was a doctor is that I'd take the money I'd made and buy my parents a nice house. Then I'd do somethin' for the community, 'cause, like, I wouldn't be one of those guys who walks away from his people."

As the school year wore on, David saw basketball as his ticket to the larger world outside Roosevelt High. He became obsessed about improving his game. "I have certain disadvantages because I started playin' later than a lot of these guys. My aunt was the one who suggested that I try it. And my junior-high gym teacher was the one who taught me how to dribble and shoot."

He said he didn't care if Manny yelled at him. "That's how I learn, when he tells me things. If he says it loud, so what."

When Manny called his name, David came running, saying,

"Yes, coach." Some of his teammates snickered and called him coach's pet.

"I don't care what they say. To tell you the truth, I think a lot of them complain too much. Some of them are always cuttin' corners. They keep talkin' about the frosh-soph team winnin' all of those games. I was on the frosh-soph team and we were good. But our competition wasn't that great. The best freshmen and sophomores go straight to varsity, they don't even play on the frosh-soph level. And a lot of the other guys got bigger and stronger. You remember that skinny little guard you dunked over? Well, guess what, he grew over the summer and now he's knockin' your stuff down. You see, it's not good enough just to be good, you got to keep gettin' better just to stay even with everyone else."

There was a fire in David, an almost grim determination, as though every practice sprint — every shot, steal, pass, and rebound — was a tiny step toward some distant goal.

At practice he kept to himself, rarely joining the banter about parties, girls, or movies. The one player he admired most was Mario. Now there was a guy with his head on right: good grades, tough courses, high score on the college exams. Mario was going to Northern Illinois University, going to get away from Chicago, with all of its fights and gangs and hassles.

"That's what you got to do — you got to get away. You can't just hang around the neighborhood and expect to get anywhere. You got to go to get out. Look at any of the old Roosevelt guys, like Arnie, all of them left the neighborhood and then they came back. I like that. I want to be like Arnie. I want to come back, and when I do, I want to come back with somethin' to show."

A few college scouts came to watch David play — one small college in Wisconsin even talked about a scholarship — and they all said the same thing: lots of promise, little polish. "David is talented, but he's raw," Manny said. "The year off hurt. He doesn't always know the defenses, he's not sure about his place in a zone. Sometimes he tries to do too much. I tell him, 'David, you don't have to block every shot. You don't have to score every point.' Then on the next play, you'll see him knocking over his man, gettin' called for the charge."

He was an Hispanic kid playing a black kid's game. He had

started late and he had missed a lot. Now he was rushing to catch up.

February 27

As the second-place team in Blue North, Roosevelt's first playoff opponent was Mather, the second-to-last-place team in Red North.

"It's so much more intense in the playoffs," said Manny. "You lose the game and the season's over. Last year we opened with two playoff wins. Then we played Marshall — the best team out of the West Side — and took a lead in the first quarter."

"And?"

"They blew us out."

Manny still didn't know who would start with Kenric, Terrell, David, and Kevin. Herman was out, as was Anthony (injured ankle). He asked Kenric and Terrell; they recommended Mario. "I guess it's Mario," Manny said. "He hustles and he can shoot. I could do a lot worse."

"You gonna tell him?" I asked.

"Not today. He'd think about it too much and wouldn't get any sleep. I'll break it to him tomorrow." The team scrimmaged for forty-five minutes, then Manny gathered them in the bleachers.

"Fellas, a few years ago I had a soccer team finish the regular season with a losing record. No one gave us a chance in the playoffs. Well, see that banner on the wall? They won the city title. There's no reason you can't do the same. I'm 250 years old, fellas. I've seen a lot. I've seen teams go on a roll when it was least expected. Let's not be satisfied with one, or two — let's win five."

He let his eyes roll over them. "Everythin' is in your favor. We didn't practice all this year to lose. We came to win. The only thing that can beat us is if we beat ourselves."

February 28

Five minutes before game time, Terrell broke the word to Mario: "You're startin'."

Mario thought Terrell was kidding, until Manny made it official. He was so nervous his fingers trembled and he couldn't remove his gold chain.

The centers were lining up for the jump and Mario was still fiddling with his chain. He asked me for help, but what did I know about necklaces? Herman rescued us. Cool and calm. He snapped the chain off in two quick moves.

Mario hit his first two shots — both of them threes. He grabbed a rebound and fed David for a basket, then stole the ball and hit Terrell with a perfect bounce pass on the fly. "Mario, Mario," some of the fans were chanting his name.

The Rough Riders led by thirteen at the half and then blew Mather away in the third quarter. Kenric grabbed nine rebounds and Terrell had seven steals. Five guys scored in double figures. They won 79 to 49. Afterward they were ecstatic.

"Prosser's next," I told Maceo.

"I don't care who we play," said Maceo. "When we're on, we can beat anyone."

"Even King?"

"Anyone!"

Manny was all smiles. "Don't be satisfied with one," he told the fellows. "Let's make it two. Let's keep on going."

Mario, in particular, played brilliantly, racking up sixteen points, three rebounds, and five assists.

I handed him back his gold chain and he slipped it around his neck. Friends patted his back; Manny shook his hand. He wore a giant grin. All of them were happy. Every one of them believed they could go all the way.

March 3

They played Prosser at home, and at the half Roosevelt was leading by fifteen. As Manny took the team down to the locker room, there wasn't one of them who didn't think they were going to win.

"This is like a chess game," Manny told the team at halftime. "Every move they make, we make two."

"They can't do nothin'," said Herman. "All they can do is wish. Damn, I wish I could play."

They put their hands together and chanted: "One, two, three, win," and then trotted up the stairs, through the darkness of the stairwell toward the light of the gym. The stands were filling up; there were even a few students in the balcony. Where they came from I don't know. Word must have spread that the Rough Riders were about to win. The crowd roared when they took the floor.

"I bet if Roosevelt wins there's gonna be a big pep rally," I told Herman.

He nodded. "The whole school's gonna get into it. *Damn,* I wish I could play!"

Maceo and the five starters knelt in a circle at center court. They held hands. Maceo led them in prayer.

The crowd started clapping; Arnie led five members of the girls' team in the school song.

The Rough Riders started the second half like they had ended the first: finding the open man, hitting the open shot, scrapping for loose balls. "The game is so easy," said Manny. "You work it to the open man and put the ball in." They led 57 to 40 with two minutes left in the third.

Then Prosser's coach, Lynn Mister, called for the press. Kevin, who had been flawless, lost control of the ball. Prosser scored. They stole the inbounds pass and scored again. Roosevelt missed a shot. Prosser rebounded and scored again. Six straight points. Now *their* players were cheering. Prosser pressed harder. Hands in the face. Kevin lost his dribble. Sandwiched between two men, he made one of the oldest mistakes: he turned toward a defender. The defender pried loose the ball and then accidentally stepped out of bounds. His foot was at least six inches over the line.

But the ref didn't blow his whistle. The guard dribbled in for an uncontested lay-up. Manny started screaming: "He was outta bounds!"

The ref said: "Your man pushed him."

"Then the basket shouldn't count."

The ref just ran the other way. At the end of the quarter, Prosser had cut Roosevelt's lead to eight.

"Stay cool, guys," Manny urged. "Help each other out."

Prosser scored to start the fourth, then stole the ball and scored again. There was 6:40 left. The lead was four.

"I can't look," said Montrell. "I can't take it."

"We can't lose this lead," I said. "It's impossible."

On the inbounds, Mario stumbled. The ref called traveling.

Manny put his head in his hands. "This is where we miss Herman's ball handling," he said.

David blocked a shot. The ref called a foul. It was David's fourth. One more and he was out. He looked at Manny. Manny waved him back into the game. "There's no tomorrow. Keep playin'."

Prosser hit a three. The lead was one. David rushed the ball up-court. "Slow down," Manny called. David lunged toward the basket. A Prosser player stepped forward. They collided and David crashed into the wall.

The ref called a foul on Prosser, but David was too shaken to shoot the free throws. Herman helped him from the floor and over to the bench. Saul massaged David's neck. Manny brought in Sylvester to shoot the free throws. Sylvester hadn't played all day. He missed both shots.

Prosser scored. The impossible had happened. The lead was lost. With about four minutes left, Prosser led by one.

After that the lead bounced back and forth, changing hands on almost every possession. Kenric fouled out, but others rose to the moment. David, back in the game, hit a turn-around jumper. Mario blocked a shot and dove into the wall trying to keep the ball from going out of bounds. Kevin sliced through the press, the ball zipping from hand to hand. At one point Manny called time and the players, sucking on the water bottle and gasping for breath, gathered at the bench. "Get the ball to Red," Manny pleaded. "And Red, take it to your man. The only way they can stop you, Red, is to foul you." Sure enough, Terrell was fouled on the drive, then hit both free throws. Just like that. Mr. Clutch.

With twenty-eight seconds left, Roosevelt led 69 to 66 and Prosser had the ball. The crowd rose to its feet.

"We're gonna win," screamed Herman.

"Don't say that," I said.

"Don't jinx us," said Montrell.

"Can't jinx us," said Herman. "We're gonna do it."

The ball went to Eddie Washington, Prosser's six-foot-eight sophomore center. He was standing way out. Beyond the three-point line. He held the ball for a moment, looking for someone to pass to. Then, with no one open, he turned toward the basket and shot.

It was one of those low-percentage heaves that drive coaches crazy. But it went in. Swish. All net. Big Eddie had hit a shot he should never have taken. A three-pointer that tied the game. Overtime.

In the stands, we didn't say a word. Not me, not Montrell, not Herman, not Arnie — no one. We just stood there, dumbstruck. Never again, not in a million years, does that guy hit that shot.

Maceo, playing for Kenric, won the overtime jump. Things happened fast. We missed. They scored. We scored. The ball rolled out of bounds. Prosser's ball, the referee said. The crowd moaned. From the din I could make out Arnie screaming, his voice a raspy gasp, "Press, press, press." I realized he'd been screaming for several minutes straight.

David fouled out on a blocking call. He slumped to his knees, his hands behind his head. He looked up to the ceiling. His eyes misted with tears. "I didn't touch him," he cried. "I didn't touch him."

Larry came in. The seconds ticked down. Prosser led by one. "Get it to Red," Manny bellowed, "get it to Red." Terrell drove to the basket. His shot bounced off the rim. In the fight for the rebound, he was fouled . . .

So there he stood, on the line — seventeen years old and whippet thin. Where I will forever see him in my mind. Bouncing the ball. The crowd's stillness spreading. Me, afraid to look. My stomach aching. I couldn't believe that I cared so much about this game. I hadn't meant to get emotionally involved. I had planned to remain disinterested. But there was something infectious about this team. Maybe it was knowing how far Terrell and the others had come or how much farther they had to go. Or maybe it was seeing Manny nervously pulling at his hair or hearing Arnie destroy his voice or watching the boys in the stands, jaded no more, their fists clenched in hopeful desperation, wanting, praying for their team, their *high school* team, to win the big game.

No, I hadn't meant to root for the Rough Riders, but what can I say? Some guys play, other guys follow. Give them credit, Manny and his Rough Riders brought out the rooter in me.

"Down, down," pleaded Hersey, the scorekeeper, on his tiptoes, straining to see above the crowd.

I silently pleaded for Terrell to make these shots. I couldn't bear to see the season end this way. They had spent too much time in this gym to end the season by blowing a seventeen-point lead against an 11–13 team. They were better than this. They were better than mediocre. They had to beat Prosser and advance to the next round and maybe the round after that. They had to get their shot at mighty King.

I closed my eyes.

The crowd roared. His first shot had gone in. Game tied.

I watched Terrell shoot the second one. It rattled out. Another overtime. I blamed myself; I never should have watched him shoot that second free throw.

I don't want to think about the second overtime. It's still too painful to remember. They scored. We scored. They scored again. With forty-six seconds left Roosevelt had the ball, down by two. Manny called time.

"Bring in Sylvester," I pleaded. "We need the three."

Manny looked surprised. It was my first coaching recommendation all year.

"A three is too much of a long shot," he said.

"I know. But still. If the play breaks down it's good to know Sylvester's in the corner."

Manny shrugged. What the hell. In twenty-three years of coaching he'd done dumber things than listen to me. Sylvester came into the game.

The teams lined up. Terrell stood at the half-court line. The ref handed him the ball. The players broke. Terrell looked left. He looked right. No one open. He had two seconds to inbound. "Pass the goddamn ball," Manny yelled.

It was more of a lob. To no one in particular. It bounced once, then twice. For an instant I had a vague memory of a similar play months before. Now a Prosser player retrieved the ball. Terrell intentionally fouled him, trying to stop the clock. The guy made one of two free throws and big Eddie Washington grabbed the miss. Terrell intentionally fouled him. His fifth. He sat on the bench between Kenric and David. That's when it hit me: we weren't going to win. We never had a chance. Like Manny said, there are winners and there is everyone else. I'd been deluding myself just like the rest of them.

Prosser won 82 to 77. For the record, Mario, Kevin, Larry,

Sylvester, and Maceo were on the court when the season ended.

Prosser's jubilant players swarmed over their coach.

"I feel sick," Arnie said. He did look a little green.

"We had a seventeen-point lead," I said.

"I can't believe we lost," said Montrell.

"What a horrible way to end a season," I said.

Arnie whirled around. "Hey, listen you," he said to me. "You can't give up. It's not about winning or losing. It's about the kids. You gotta come back next season. You gotta hang in there for the long haul."

David lay on the floor, looking at the ceiling. Mario sat on the bench holding his head in his hands. Kenric sat next to him and stared into space. His girlfriend tried to comfort him. Kevin, his T-shirt drenched with sweat, congratulated Prosser's players.

Boom — Maceo kicked the bench. "My last game."

Boom — he kicked the bench again. "I can't believe this is my last game!"

Then he collapsed against the wall.

"It ain't gonna be my last game," said Ronnie defiantly. "No way. Unh-uh. I'm playin' in college. You'll see."

They sat on the bench for about ten minutes. Eventually they peeled off their jerseys, wiped their sweat with towels, lathered their armpits with deodorant, slipped their clothes over their shorts, and headed for the door. Nine of them in a row (a few had already departed), leaving the way they came — the Rough Riders of Roosevelt High.

I called out their names, shook their hands, and wished them well. Even promised to stay in touch. They looked so sad. They had worked so hard. They had endured so much. They deserved so much more. They had lost every big game they played (from Taft to Glenbrook to Lane to Prosser), but I didn't feel too sorry for them. They didn't realize how lucky they were. At least they were good enough to play on the team. Some guys, well, we would have given up a lot just to sit on the bench.

There would be a new bunch of bodies wearing the blue and gold next year (including some of the knuckleheads from the frosh-soph team; thank goodness they turned in that jacket). In a few years the 1991–92 basketball season at Roosevelt High would mean nothing. Except to them. And me. I tried to imagine where they would be or what they would be like in ten or fifteen years. I couldn't do it; it wasn't fair. "You never know what a guy's got in him." Ronnie taught me that.

Within twenty minutes the gym was empty, except for two Hispanic kids playing one-on-one at the far east end of the court. I walked into Manny's office. He had the phone to his ear, on hold with City News. Saul sat at the other end of the desk, flipping through a newspaper, having just totaled up the score book. The slogan on his T-shirt read: "Old age and treachery will always prevail over youth and skill."

"For cry Pete, Saul, you made a mistake in your math," said Manny. "You gave us too many points."

Saul shrugged. "Only tryin' to give you a break."

Saul chuckled and looked at me. "Did I tell you my joke?"

"No."

"O.K., this old lady shocked her family on her eighty-eighth birthday by sayin' she lives with three men."

"Yeah?"

"Yeah. She wakes up with Will Power. Plays tootsie with Art Ritis. And goes to bed with Ben-Gay."

I laughed. Manny groaned. Coach Mister from Prosser walked into the room. He was glowing.

Manny rose and extended his hand. "Coach, I want to congratulate you. Your kids played a helluva game."

They shook hands.

"What did you tell them at halftime?" I asked.

"I threatened them," Mister said. And then he laughed, deep and from the heart.

Manny smiled. "Well listen, coach. I wanna wish you all the best luck in the world. I hope you do well. I really do."

Mister left. We sat in silence. Then I spoke. "Remember that play back in the third quarter, Manny? The one where their guy stole the ball from Kevin? The ref blew the call, Manny. The kid was out of bounds — I saw it."

Manny shrugged.

"If that ref calls that guy out of bounds, they don't score and you win the game," I said.

Manny nodded. "Isn't that somethin' — a whole season comes down to one play. What can you do? I realized long ago that there are things in life a whole lot worse than losin' a game."

After that we were quiet. Saul read the *Sun-Times*. Manny, still on hold, looked out the window. I picked up the basketball sitting on Manny's desk.

I'd hardly touched a ball all season. I felt a little self-conscious around so many good players. I didn't want to be embarrassed. But with no one around to watch, I slipped back into the gym.

My first shot fell short. The second bounced in. I went under the basket and practiced lay-ups. Easy shots, just to get the feel. Shooting from one side and then the other, grabbing the ball before it hit the floor. Like Manny taught Larry.

I had a ton of restless energy, pent-up frustration over the game. I started shooting long-range. Knocked down three in a row. I stepped back and tried a three. In my mind I was Sylvester, with the clock ticking down, taking that last shot against Lane. The net snapped — perfect. I'd been away from the game for too long. It felt great to be back. Maybe I could hook up with some of the old-timers down at the Y.

Manny ushered me and the kids out of the gym and turned out the lights. He had finally got through to City News.

November 5, 1992

Twenty-one kids showed up for tryouts, including Kenric, Kevin, Eddie Kroger, and Larry. They had grown over the summer, especially Kenric. Manny said he looked like two guys roped together.

Hersey, the mathematical wizard, was also there, scampering amid the big men, the smallest guy trying out — it was that hopeful time of year.

Arnie had planned to attend, but stayed home nursing a cold. His dedication to Roosevelt, however, had not wavered: he's organizing an April 2 fundraiser in honor of Manny. ("Have people call me at 708-432-2773 if they want information; also, put a plug in the paper for the December 5 game against Glenbrook North.")

Last year's seniors were elsewhere, of course. David, an inch or two taller and bulked up by weights, is playing small forward at Triton College this year. Maceo enrolled at Illinois Benedictine and Mario at Northern Illinois. Herman and Ronnie joined the navy. Sylvester works as a messenger for a local bank. Terrell is a sales clerk at Montgomery Ward and plays in a Park District basketball league, scoring twenty points a game, still rattling the rims. He plans to attend Wright College in January.

Manny was back, smiling in the face of the school system's fiscal troubles. The Board of Education, confronted with a $300 million budget deficit, had halved the high school athletic budget; the principals were going to cut the basketball season altogether until a consortium of business leaders raised close to $2 million to keep it going. This year Manny will receive $300 with which to run the basketball program. Anything over that will come out of his own pocket. He let the hopefuls scrimmage awhile and then gathered them on the bleachers. Unlike last year, he didn't pace, he sat in a chair. "Fellas, this is my twenty-eighth year, but every year I look forward to more than the year before. I'm asked, 'When are you gonna quit?' I always say, 'When I don't think I'm any good, I'll quit.' Some of the guys last year, they came up to me and said, "What's wrong coach? You're not shoutin'.' Well, I learn from you. I can see that with some guys shoutin' doesn't work. So this year I will suggest instead of criticize. And when I tell you, fellas, how important it is to study, I mean that from the bottom of my heart. I have guys who come back twenty years later and say, 'Coach, I wish I had listened to you. I wish I had studied.' I tell them, 'It's never too late. You're never too old.' Look at me — I didn't go back to college until I was twenty-six.

"I wanna tell you somethin' else, fellas — you guys mean a lot to me. I love all my players. I remember their names. I can remember the faces of guys who played for me twenty-eight years ago. It was a pleasure coachin' them. I hope I gave them somethin' they could use. The only thing I ask is that every now and then after you graduate you come back and say, 'Hey coach, how ya' doin'?' Really. That's all I ask."

Manny sat silently for a moment and then rose from his seat. "My goal, fellas, is to win the section. Then a year from now you can say, 'Hey, we boosted Roosevelt to Red.' " He had them form two lines facing the basket. "We'll practice some lay-ups. Don't be nervous. If you miss a lay-up, don't worry. I've seen the Bulls miss lay-ups."

Manny clapped his hands, and another season began.

NOVEMBER 22, 1992–DECEMBER 4, 1992

Team diaries are not uncommon — going back at least thirty years to Jim Brosnan's The Long Season. *But* BEN JORAVSKY's *year with a high school basketball team is original and special of the genre. He has managed to blend these boys we've never heard of before in with their coach and their school and their city (Chicago). It is so easy, in stories about inner-city athletics, to dwell only on the terrors and the abuses, but Joravsky manages to keep it all in balance — basketball and growing up and the terrors and the abuses. —* F.D.

ROGER ANGELL

Early Innings

FROM THE NEW YORKER

I WAS BORN in 1920, and became an addicted reader at a precocious age. Peeling back the leaves of memory, I discover a peculiar mulch of names. Steerforth, Tuan Jim, Moon Mullins, Colonel Sebastian Moran. Sunny Jim Bottomley, Dazzy Vance, Goose Goslin. Bob La Follette, Carter Glass, Rexford Guy Tugwell. Robert Benchley, A. E. Housman, Erich Maria Remarque. Hack Wilson, Riggs Stephenson. Senator Pat Harrison and Representative Sol Bloom. Pie Traynor and Harry Hopkins. Kenesaw Mountain Landis and Benjamin Cardozo. Pepper Martin. George F. Babbitt. The Scottsboro Boys. Franklin Delano Roosevelt. Babe Ruth. In my early teens, I knew the Detroit Tigers' batting order and FDR's first cabinet, both by heart. Mel Ott's swing, Jimmy Foxx's upper arms, and Senator Borah's eyebrows were clear in my mind's eye. Baseball, which was late in its first golden age, meant a lot to me, but it didn't come first, because I seem to have been a fan of everything at that age — a born pain in the neck. A city kid, I read John Kieran, Walter Lippmann, Richards Vidmer, Heywood Broun, and Dan Daniel just about every day, and what I read stuck. By the time I'd turned twelve, my favorite authors included Conan Doyle, Charles Dickens, Will James on cowboys, Joseph A. Altsheler on Indians, and Dr. Raymond L. Ditmars on reptiles. Another batting order I could have run off for you would have presented some prime species among the Elapidae — a family that includes cobras, coral snakes, kraits, and mambas, and is cousin to the deadly sea snakes of the China Sea.

Back then, baseball and politics were not the strange mix that they would appear to be today, because they were both plainly where the action lay. I grew up in New York and attended Lincoln School of Teachers College (*old* Lincoln, in Manhattan parlance), a font of progressive education where we were encouraged to follow our interests with avidity; no Lincoln parent was ever known to have said, "Shut up, kid." My own parents were divorced, and I lived with my father, a lawyer of liberal proclivities who voted for Norman Thomas, the Socialist candidate, in the Presidential election of 1932 and again in 1936. He started me in baseball. He had grown up in Cleveland in the Nap Lajoie–Addie Joss era, but he was too smart to try to interpose his passion for the Indians on his son's idolatrous attachment to the Yankees and the Giants, any more than he would have allowed himself to smile at the four or five Roosevelt-Garner buttons I kept affixed to my windbreaker (above my knickers) in the weeks before Election Day in 1932.

The early to mid-1930s were tough times in the United States, but palmy days for a boy-Democrat baseball fan in New York. Carl Hubbell, gravely bowing twice from the waist before each delivery, was throwing his magical screwball for the Giants, and Joe DiMaggio, arriving from San Francisco in '36 amid vast heraldings, took up his spread-legged stance at the Stadium, and batted .323 and .346 in his first two years in the Bronx. He was the first celebrated rookie to come up to either team after I had attained full baseball awareness: *my* Joe DiMaggio. My other team, the New Deal, also kept winning. Every week in 1933, it seemed, the White House gave birth to another progressive, society-shaking national agency (the AAA, the NRA, the CCC, the TVA), which Congress would enact into law by a huge majority. In my city, Fiorello LaGuardia led the Fusion Party, routed the forces of Tammany Hall, and, as mayor, cleared slums, wrote a new city charter, and turned up at five-alarmers wearing a fire chief's helmet. (I interviewed the Little Flower for my high-school paper later in the decade, after sitting for seven hours in his waiting room. I can't remember anything he said, but I can still see his feet, under the mayoral swivel chair, not quite touching the floor.) Terrible things were going on in Ethiopia and Spain and Germany, to be sure, but at home almost everything I

wanted to happen seemed to come to pass within a few weeks or
months — most of all in baseball. The Yankees and the Giants
between them captured eight pennants in the thirties, and even
played against each other in a subway series in 1936 (hello, am-
bivalence) and again in 1937. The Yankees won both times; indeed, they captured all five of their World Series engagements in
the decade, losing only three games in the process. Their 12–1
October won-lost totals against the Giants, Cubs, and Reds in '37,
'38, and '39 made me sense at last that winning wasn't everything
it was cracked up to be; my later defection to the Red Sox and
toward the pain-pleasure principle had begun.

There are more holes than fabric in my earliest baseball recollec-
tions. My father began taking me and my four-years-older sister
to games at some point in the latter twenties, but no first-ever
view of Babe Ruth or of the green barn of the Polo Grounds remains in mind. We must have attended with some regularity, because I'm sure I saw the Babe and Lou Gehrig hit back-to-back
home runs on more than one occasion. Mel Ott's stumpy, cow-
tail swing is still before me, and so are Gehrig's thick calves and
Ruth's debutante ankles. Baseball caps were different back then:
smaller and flatter than today's constructions — more like the
workmen's caps that one saw on every street. Some of the visiting
players — the Cardinals, for instance — wore their caps cheer-
fully askew or tipped back on their heads, but never the Yankees.
Gloves were much smaller, too, and the outfielders left theirs on
the grass, in the shallow parts of the field, when their side came
in to bat; I wondered why a batted ball wouldn't strike them on
the fly or on the bounce someday, but it never happened. John
McGraw, for one, wouldn't have permitted such a thing. He was
managing the Giants, with his arms folded across his vest (he
wore a suit some days and a uniform on others), and kept his
tough, thick chin aimed at the umpires. I would look for him —
along with Ott and Bill Terry and Travis Jackson — the minute
we arrived at our seats in the Polo Grounds.

   I liked it best when we came into the place from up top, rather
than through the gates down at the foot of the lower-right-field
stand. You reached the upper-deck turnstiles by walking down a
steep, short ramp from the Speedway, the broad avenue that

swept down from Coogan's Bluff and along the Harlem River, and once you got inside, the long field within the horseshoe of decked stands seemed to stretch away forever below you, toward the bleachers and the clubhouse pavilion in center. My father made me notice how often Terry, a terrific straightaway slugger, would launch an extra-base hit into that bottomless countryside ("a homer in any other park" was the accompanying refrain), and, sure enough, now and then Terry would reaffirm the parable by hammering still another triple into the pigeoned distance. Everything about the Polo Grounds was special, right down to the looped iron chains that separated each sector of box seats from its neighbor and could burn your bare arm on a summer afternoon if you weren't careful. Far along each outfield wall, a sloping mini-roof projected outward, imparting a thin wedge of shadow for the bullpen crews sitting there: they looked like cows sheltering beside a pasture shed in August.

Across the river, the view when you arrived was different but equally delectable: a panorama of svelte infield and steep, filigree-topped inner battlements that was offered and then snatched away as one's straw-seat IRT train rumbled into the elevated station at 161st Street. If the Polo Grounds felt pastoral, Yankee Stadium was Metropole, the big city personified. For some reason, we always walked around it along the right-field side, never the other way, and each time I would wonder about the oddly arrayed ticket kiosks (General Admission fifty-five cents; Reserved Grandstand a dollar ten) that stood off at such a distance from the gates. Something about security, I decided; one of these days, they'll demand to see passports there. Inside, up the pleasing ramps, I would stop and bend over, peering through the horizontal slot between the dark, overhanging mezzanine and the descending sweep of grandstand seats which led one's entranced eye to the sunlit green of the field and the players on it. Then I'd look for the Babe. The first Yankee manager I can remember in residence was Bob Shawkey, which means 1930. I was nine years old.

I can't seem to put my hand on any one particular game I went to with my father back then; it's strange. But I went often, and soon came to know the difference between intimate afternoon games at the Stadium (play started at 3:15 P.M.), when a handful

of boys and night workers and layabouts and late-arriving busi-
nessmen (with vests and straw hats) would cluster together in the
stands close to home plate or down in the lower rows of the
bleachers, and sold-out, roaring, seventy-thousand-plus Sunday
doubleheaders against the Tigers or the Indians or the Senators
(the famous rivalry with the Bosox is missing in memory), when
I would eat, cheer, and groan my way grandly toward the distant
horizon of evening, while the Yankees, most of the time, would
win and then win again. The handsome Wes Ferrell always
started the first Sunday game for the Indians, and proved a
tough nut to crack. But why, I wonder, do I think of Bill Dickey's
ears? In any case, I know I was in the Stadium on Monday, May
5, 1930, when Lefty Gomez, a twitchy rookie southpaw, pitched
his very first game for the Yankees, and beat Red Faber and the
White Sox, 4–1, striking out his first three batters in succession.
I talked about the day and the game with Gomez many years
later, and he told me that he had looked up in the stands before
the first inning and realized that the ticket-holders there easily
outnumbered the population of his home town, Rodeo, California, and perhaps his home county as well.

I attended the Gomez inaugural not with my father but with a
pink-cheeked lady named Mrs. Baker, who was — well, she was
my governess. Groans and derisive laughter are all very well, but
Mrs. Baker (who had a very brief tenure, alas) was a companion
any boy would cherish. She had proposed the trip to Yankee Stadium, and she was the one who first noticed a new name out on
the mound that afternoon, and made me see how hard the kid
was throwing and what he might mean for the Yanks in the future. "Remember the day," she said, and I did. Within another
year, I was too old for such baby-sitting but still in need of late-
afternoon companionship before my father got home from his
Wall Street office (my sister was away at school by now); he solved
the matter by hiring a Columbia undergraduate named Tex
Goldschmidt, who proved to be such a genius at the job that he
soon moved in with us to stay. Tex knew less about big-league
ball than Mrs. Baker, but we caught him up in a hurry.

Baseball memories are seductive, tempting us always toward
sweetness and undercomplexity. It should not be inferred (I re-

mind myself) that the game was a unique bond between my father and me, or always near the top of my own distracted interests. If forced to rank the preoccupying family passions in my home at that time, I would put reading at the top of the list, closely followed by conversation and opinions, politics, loneliness (my father had not yet remarried, and I missed my mother), friends, jokes, exercises and active sports, animals (see below), theatre and the movies, professional and college sports, museums, and a very large Misc. Even before my teens, I thought of myself as a full participant, and my fair-minded old man did not patronize me at the dinner table or elsewhere. He supported my naturalist bent, for instance, which meant that a census taken on any given day at our narrow brownstone on East Ninety-third Street might have included a monkey (a Javanese macaque who was an inveterate biter); three or four snakes (including a five-foot king snake, the Mona Lisa of my collection, that sometimes lived for a day or two at a time behind the books in the library); assorted horned toads, salamanders, and tropical fish; white mice (dinner for the snakes); a wheezy Boston terrier; and two or three cats, with occasional kittens.

Baseball (to get back on track here) had the longest run each year, but other sports also got my full attention. September meant Forest Hills, with Tilden and Vines, Don Budge and Fred Perry. Ivy League football still mattered in those times, and I saw Harvard's immortal Barry Wood and Yale's ditto Albie Booth go at each other more than once; we also caught Chick Meehan's NYU Violets, and even some City College games, up at Lewisohn Stadium. Winter brought the thrilling Rangers (Frank Boucher, Ching Johnson, and the Cook brothers) and the bespangled old Americans; there was wire netting atop the boards, instead of Plexiglas, and Madison Square Garden was blue with cigarette and cigar smoke above the painted ice. I went there on weekends, never on school nights, usually in company with my mother and stepfather, who were red-hot hockey fans. Twice a year, they took me to the six-day bicycle races at the Garden (Reggie McNamara, Alfred Letourner, Franco Georgetti, Torchy Peden), and, in midwinter, to track events there, with Glenn Cunningham and Gene Venzke trying and again failing to break the four-minute mile at the Millrose Games. Looking back, I wonder how I got through school at all. My mother, I should explain, had been a Red Sox fan while growing up in Boston, but her attachment to the game did not revive until the mid-1940s, when she fetched up at Presbyterian Hospital for a minor surgical procedure; a fellow patient across the hall at Harkness Pavilion was Walker Cooper, the incumbent Giants catcher, drydocked for knee repairs, who kept in touch by listening to the Giants-game broadcasts every day. My mother turned her radio on, too, and was hooked.

Sports were different in my youth — a series of events to look forward to and then to turn over in memory, rather than a huge, omnipresent industry, with its own economics and politics and crushing public relations. How it felt to be a young baseball fan in the thirties can be appreciated only if I can bring back this lighter and fresher atmosphere. Attending a game meant a lot, to adults as well as to a boy, because it was the only way you could encounter athletes and watch what they did. There was no television, no instant replay, no evening highlights. We saw the players' faces in newspaper photographs, or in the pages of *Baseball,* an engrossing monthly with an invariable red cover, to which I subscribed, and here and there in an advertisement. (I think Lou Gehrig plugged Fleischmann's Yeast, a health remedy said to be good for the complexion.) We never heard athletes' voices or became aware of their "image." Bo Jackson and Joe Montana and Michael Jordan were light-years away. Baseball by radio was a rarity, confined for the most part to the World Series; the three New York teams, in fact, banned radio coverage of their regular-season games between 1934 and 1938, on the theory that daily broadcasts would damage attendance. Following baseball always required a visit to the players' place of business, and, once there, you watched them with attention, undistracted by Diamond Vision or rock music or game promotions. Seeing the players in action on the field, always at a little distance, gave them a heroic tinge. (The only player I can remember encountering on the street, one day on the West Side, was the Babe, in retirement by then, swathed in his familiar camel-hair coat with matching cap.)

We kept up by reading baseball. Four daily newspapers arrived at my house every day — the *Times* and the *Herald Tribune* by breakfast time, and the *Sun* and the *World-Telegram* folded under my father's arm when he got home from the office. The games were played by daylight, and, with all sixteen teams situated inside two time zones, we never went to bed without knowledge of that day's baseball. Line scores were on the front page of the afternoon dailies, scrupulously updated edition by edition, with black squares off to the right indicating latter innings, as yet unplayed, in Wrigley Field or Sportsman's Park. I soon came to know all the bylines — John Drebinger, James P. Dawson, and Roscoe McGowen in the *Times* (John Kieran was the columnist); Rud Rennie and Richards Vidmer in the *Trib;* Dan Daniel, Joe Williams, and Tom Meany in the *World-Telly* (along with Willard Mullin's vigorous sports cartoons); Frank Graham in the *Sun;* and, now and then, Bill Corum in the *Sunday American,* a paper I sometimes acquired for its terrific comics.

Richards Vidmer, if memory is to be trusted, was my favorite scribe, but before that, back when I was nine or ten years old, what I loved best in the sports pages were box scores and, above all, names. I knew the names of a few dozen friends and teachers at school, of course, and of family members and family friends, but only in baseball could I encounter anyone like Mel Ott. One of the Yankee pitchers was named George Pipgras, and Earle Combs played center. Connie Mack, a skinny gent, managed the Athletics and was in fact Cornelius McGillicuddy. Jimmy Foxx was his prime slugger. I had a double letter in my name, too, but it didn't match up to a Foxx or an Ott. Or to Joe Stripp. I read on, day after day, and found rafts of names that prickled or sang in one's mind. Eppa Rixey, Goose Goslin, Firpo Marberry, Jack Rothrock, Eldon Auker, Luke Appling, Mule Haas, Adolfo Luque (for years I thought it was pronounced "Lyoo-kyoo") — Dickens couldn't have done better. Paul Derringer was exciting: a man named for a pistol! I lingered over Heinie Manush (sort of like sitting on a cereal) and Van Lingle Mungo, the Dodger ace. When I exchanged baseball celebrities with pals at school, we used last names, to show a suave familiarity, but no one ever just said "Mungo," or even "Van Mungo." When he came up in conversation, it was obligatory to roll out the full name, as if it were a royal title, and everyone in the group would join in at the end, in chorus: "Van Lin-gle MUN-*go!*"

Nicknames and sobriquets came along, too, attaching them-

selves like pilot fish: Lon Warneke, the Arkansas Hummingbird;
Travis (Stonewall) Jackson; Deacon Danny MacFayden (in
sportswriterese, he was always "*bespectacled* Deacon Danny Mac-
Fayden"); Tony (Poosh 'Em Up) Lazzeri (what he pooshed
up, whether fly balls or base runners, I never did learn). And then,
once and always, Babe Ruth — the Bambino, the Sultan of Swat.

By every measure, this was a bewitching time for a kid to discover baseball. The rabbit ball had got loose in both leagues in
1930 (I wasn't aware of it) — a season in which Bill Terry batted
.401 and the Giants batted .319 as a team. I can't say for sure that
I knew about Hack Wilson's astounding 190 RBIs for the Cubs,
but Babe Herman's .393 for the Dodgers must have made an
impression. (The *lowly* Dodgers. As I should have said before,
the Dodgers — or Robins, as they were called in tabloid headlines — were just another team in the National League to me
back then; I don't think I set foot in Ebbets Field until the 1941
World Series. But they became the enemy in 1934, when they
knocked the Giants out of a pennant in September.) The batters
in both leagues were reined in a bit after 1930, but the game
didn't exactly become dull. Lefty Grove had a 31–4 season for
the A's in 1931, and Dizzy Dean's 30–7 helped win a pennant for
the Gas House Gang Cardinals in 1934. That was Babe Ruth's
last summer in the Bronx, but I think I was paying more attention to Gehrig just then, what with his triple-crown .363, 49
homers, and 165 runs batted in. I became more aware of other
teams as the thirties (and my teens) wore along, and eventually
came to think of them as personalities — sixteen different but
familiar faces ranged around a large dinner table, as it were. To
this day, I still feel a little stir of fear inside me when I think
about the Tigers, because of the mighty Detroit teams of 1934
and 1935, which two years running shouldered the Yankees out
of a pennant. I hated Charlie Gehringer's pale face and deadly
stroke. One day in '34, I read that a Yankee bench player had
taunted Gehringer, only to be silenced by Yankee manager Joe
McCarthy. "Shut up," Marse Joe said. "He's hitting .360 — get
him mad and he'll bat .500." Gehringer played second in the
same infield with Hank Greenberg, Billy Rogell, and Marv
Owen; that summer, the four of them drove in 462 runs.

The World Series got my attention early. I don't think I read about Connie Mack's Ehmke strategem in 1929 (I had just turned nine), but I heard about it somehow. Probably it was my father who explained how the wily Philadelphia skipper had wheeled out the veteran righty as a surprise starter in the opening game against the Cubs, even though Howard Ehmke hadn't pitched an inning of ball since August; he went the distance in a winning 3–1 performance, and struck out thirteen batters along the way. But I was living in the sports pages by 1932, when the mighty Yankees blew away the Cubs in a four-game series, blasting eight home runs. It troubled me in later years that I seemed to have no clear recollection of what came to be that Series' most famous moment, when Babe Ruth did or did not call his home run against Charlie Root in the fifth inning of the third game, out at Wrigley Field. What *I* remembered about that game was that Ruth and Gehrig had each smacked two homers. A recent investigation of the microfilm files of the *Times* seems to have cleared up the mystery, inasmuch as John Drebinger's story for that date makes no mention of the Ruthian feat in its lead, or, indeed, until the thirty-fourth paragraph, when he hints that Ruth did gesture toward the bleachers ("in no mistaken motions the Babe notified the crowd that the nature of his retaliation would be a wallop right out the confines of the park"), after taking some guff from the hometown rooters as he stepped up to the plate, but then Drebinger seems to veer toward the other interpretation, which is that Ruth's gesture was simply to show that he knew the count ("Ruth signaled with his fingers after each pitch to let the spectators know exactly how the situation stood. Then the mightiest blow of all fell"). The *next*-mightiest blow came on the ensuing pitch, by the way: a home run by Lou Gehrig.

I remember 1933 even better. Tex Goldschmidt and I were in the lower stands behind third base at the Stadium on Saturday, April 29, when the Yankees lost a game to the ominous Senators on a play I have never seen duplicated — lost, as Drebinger put it, "to the utter consternation of a crowd of 36,000." With the Yanks trailing by 6–2 in the ninth, Ruth and then Gehrig singled, and Sammy Byrd (a pinch-runner for the portly Ruth) came home on a single by Dixie Walker. Tony Lazzeri now launched a

drive to deep right center. Gehrig hesitated at second base, but
Walker, at first, did not, and when the ball went over Goslin's
head the two runners came around third in tandem, separated
by a single stride. The relay — Goslin to Joe Cronin to catcher
Luke Sewell — arrived at the same instant with the onrushing
Gehrig, and Sewell, whirling in the dust, tagged out both runners with one sweeping gesture, each on a different side of the
plate. I was aghast — and remembered the wound all summer,
as the Senators went on to win the A.L. pennant, beating out the
Yanks by seven games.

Startling things happened in baseball that season. The first
All-Star game was played, out at Comiskey Park, to a full-house
audience; Babe Ruth won it with a two-run homer and Lefty
Gomez garnered the win. On August 3, Lefty Grove shut out the
Yankees, terminating a string (sorry: a skein) of 308 consecutive
games, going back almost exactly two years, in which the
Bombers had never once been held scoreless. The record stands,
unbeaten and unthreatened, to this day. Later that month,
Jimmy Foxx batted in nine runs in a single game, a league record
at the time; and, later still, Gehrig played in his 1,308th consecutive game, thereby eclipsing the old mark established by a Yankee teammate, Everett Scott, in 1925. *That* story in the *Times,* by
James P. Dawson, mentions the new record in a terse, two-graf
lead, and brusquely fills in the details down at the bottom of the
column, recounting how action was halted after the first inning
for a brief ceremony at home plate, when league president Will
Harridge presented Gehrig with a silver statuette "suitably inscribed." Then they got back to baseball: "This simple ceremony
over, the Yankees went out almost immediately and played like a
winning team, but only for a short time." There was no mooning
over records in those days.

It's always useful to have two teams to care about, as I had already learned. My other sweethearts, the Giants, moved into first
place in their league on June 13 and were never dislodged. On
the weekend of the Fourth of July, they gave us something to
remember. I was just back from an auto trip to the Century of
Progress World's Fair, in Chicago, taken in the company of three
schoolmates and a science teacher, all of us crammed into an ancient Packard, and of course I had no ticket for the big double-

header against the Cardinals at the Polo Grounds. I'm positive I read John Drebinger the next morning, though — and then read him again: "Pitching of a superman variety that dazzled a crowd of 50,000 and bewildered the Cardinals gave the Giants two throbbing victories at the Polo Grounds yesterday over a stretch of six hours. Carl Hubbell, master lefthander of Bill Terry's amazing hurling corps, blazed the trail by firing away for eighteen scoreless innings to win the opening game from the Cards, 1 to 0. . . . Then the broad-shouldered Roy Parmelee strode to the mound and through semi-darkness and finally a drizzling rain, blanked the St. Louisans in a nine-inning nightcap, 1 to 0. A homer in the fourth inning by Johnny Vergez decided this battle."

Trumpet arias at this glorious level require no footnotes, and I would add only that Tex Carleton, the Cardinal starter in the first game, threw sixteen scoreless innings himself before giving way to a reliever. He was pitching on two days' rest, and Dizzy Dean, the starter and eventual loser of the afterpiece, on one. The first game got its eighteen innings over within four hours and three minutes, by the way, and the nightcap was done in an hour and twenty-five.

The Giants went the distance in 1933, as I have said, and took the World Series as well, beating the Senators by four games to one. Hubbell, who had wound up the regular season with an earned-run average of 1.66 (he was voted Most Valuable Player in his league), won two games, and Ott drove in the winning runs in the opener with a home run, and wrapped matters up with a tenth-inning shot in the finale. I had pleaded with my father to get us some seats for one of the games at the Polo Grounds, but he didn't come through. I imagine now that he didn't want to spend the money; times were tough just then. I attended the games by a different means — radio. Five different New York stations carried the Series that year, and I'm pretty sure I listened either to Ted Husing, on WABC, or to the old NBC warhorse, Graham McNamee, over at WEAF or WJZ. (Whoever it was, I recall repeated references to the "boy managers" — Bill Terry and the Senators' Joe Cronin, who had each lately taken the helm at the old franchises.) I knew how to keep score by this time, and I rushed home from school — for the four weekday games, that is — turned on the big Stromberg-Carlson (with its glowing Bakelite dial), and kept track, inning by inning, on scorecards I drew on one of my father's yellow legal pads. When my father got home, I sat him down and ran through it all, almost pitch by pitch, telling him the baseball.

I was playing ball myself all this time — or trying to, despite the handicaps of living in the city and of my modestly muscled physique. But I kept my mitt in top shape with neat's-foot oil, and possessed a couple of Louisville Slugger bats and three or four baseballs, one so heavily wrapped in friction tape that making contact with it with a bat felt like hitting a frying pan. (One of the bats, as I recall, bore lifelong scars as the result of a game of one-o'-cat played with a rock.) Neat's-foot oil was a magical yellow elixir made from cattle bones and skin — and also a password, unknown to girls. "What's a *neat?*" every true American boy must have asked himself at some point or other, imagining some frightful amputation made necessary by the demands of the pastime.

What skills I owned had been coached by my father from an early age. Yes, reader: we threw the old pill around, and although it did not provide me with an instant ticket to the major leagues, as I must have expected at one time, it was endlessly pleasurable. I imagined myself a pitcher, and my old man and I put in long hours of pitch and catch, with a rickety shed (magically known as the Bull Pen) as backstop; this was at a little summer colony on the west bank of the Hudson, where we rented. My father had several gloves of his own, including an antique catcher's mitt that resembled a hatbox or a round dictionary. Wearing this, he would squat down again and again, putting up a target, and then fire the ball back (or fetch it from the weeds somewhere), gravely snapping the ball from behind his ear like Mickey Cochrane. Once in a while, there would be a satisfying pop as the ball hit the pocket, and he would nod silently and then flip the pill back again. His pitching lexicon was from his own boyhood: "inshoot," "hook," "hard one," and "drop." My own drop dropped to earth so often that I hated the pitch and began to shake him off.

I kept at it, in season and out, and, when I finally began to get

some growth, developed a pleasing roundhouse curve that sometimes sailed over a corner of the plate (or a cap or newspaper), to
the amazement of my school friends. Encouraged, I began to
work on a screwball, and eventually could throw something that
infinitesimally broke the wrong way, although always too high to
invite a swing; I began walking around school corridors with my
pitching hand turned palm outward, like Carl Hubbell's, but nobody noticed. Working on the screwball one cold March afternoon (I was thirteen, I think), on a covered but windy rooftop
playground at Lincoln, I ruined my arm for good. I continued
pitching on into high school (mine was a boarding school in
northern Connecticut), but I didn't make the big team; by that
time, the batters I faced were smarter and did frightful things to
my trusty roundhouse. I fanned a batter here and there, but took
up smoking and irony in self-defense. A short career.

When I began writing this brief memoir, I was surprised to find
how often its trail circled back to my father. If I continue now
with his baseball story, instead of my own, it's because the two are
so different yet feel intertwined and continuous. He was born in
1889, and lost his father at the age of eight, in a maritime disaster. He had no brothers, and I think he concluded early on that
it was incumbent on him to learn and excel at every sport, all on
his own. Such a plan requires courage and energy, and he had
both in large supply. A slim, tall, bald, brown-eyed man, of handsome demeanor (there is some Seneca Indian blood on his side
of the family), he pursued all sports except golf, and avidly kept
at them his whole life. He was a fierce swimmer, mountain
climber, canoeist, tennis player, fly fisherman, tap dancer, figure
skater, and ballplayer; he was still downhill skiing in his middle
seventies, when a stern family meeting was required to pry him
from the slopes, for his own good. He was not a great natural
athlete, but his spirit made him a tough adversary. My Oedipal
struggles with him on the tennis court went on almost into my
thirties, but we stayed cheerful; somewhere along the line, a family doctor took me aside and said, "Don't try to keep up with him.
Nobody's ever going to do that."

Baseball meant a great deal to my father, and he was lucky
enough to grow up in a time when there were diamonds and

pickup nines in every hamlet in America. He played first base
and pitched, and in his late teens joined a village team, the Tamworth Tigers, that played in the White Mountain valleys of New
Hampshire, where he and his mother and sister went on their
vacations. Years later, he told me about the time he and some of
the other Tamworth stars — Ned Johnson, Paul Twitchell, Lincoln and Dana Steele — formed a team of their own and took a
train up into Canada, where they played in a regional tournament; he pitched the only game they got to play, against a much
better club (semipros, he suspected), and got his ears knocked
off. The trip back (he said, still smiling at the pain) was a long
one. Many years after this, on a car trip when he was in his seventies, my father found himself near the mountains he knew so
well and made a swing over to Chocorua and Tamworth to check
out the scenes of his youth. He found the Remick Bros. General
Store still in business, and when he went in, the man at the
counter, behind the postcards and the little birchbark canoes,
was Wadsworth Remick, who had played with him on the Tigers
long ago. Waddy Remick. There were no signs of recognition,
however, and my old man, perhaps uncomfortable in the role of
visiting big-city slicker, didn't press the matter. He bought a pack
of gum or something, and was just going out the door when he
heard, "Played any first base lately, Ernest?"

I think people gave up with reluctance in olden days. My father sailed through Harvard in three years, making Phi Beta
Kappa, but he didn't make the varsity in baseball, and had to settle for playing on a class team. Most men would call it a day after
that, but not my father. He went to law school, got married, went
off to the war in France, came back and moved from Cleveland
to New York and joined a law firm — and played ball. I think my
very first recollection of him — I was a small child — is of standing beside him in a little downstairs bathroom of our summer
place while he washed dirt off his face and arms after a ballgame.
Rivers of brown earth ran into the sink. Later that same summer,
I was with my mother on the sidelines when my father, pitching
for some Rockland County nine, conked a batter on the top of
his head with an errant fastball. The man fell over backward and
lay still for a moment or two, and my mother said, "Oh, God —
he's done it!" The batter recovered, he and my father shook

hands, and the game went on, but the moment, like its predeces-
sor, stayed with me. Jung would envy such tableaux.

Years passed. In the summer of 1937, I worked on a small
combined ranch and farm in northern Missouri, owned by a relative who was raising purebred white-faced Herefords. I drove
cattle to their water holes on horseback, cleaned chicken coops,
and shot marauding evening jackrabbits in the vegetable garden.
It was a drought year, and the temperature would go well over a
hundred degrees every afternoon; white dust lay on the trees. I
was sixteen. Both the Giants and the Yankees were rushing
toward another pennant in New York (it was the DiMaggio, Hen-
rich, Rolfe, Crosetti Yankees by now), but I had a hard time finding news of them in the austere, photoless columns of the Kansas
City *Star*. All I could pick up on the radio was Franc Laux doing
Cardinals games over KMOX.

My father arrived for a visit, and soon discovered that there
would be a local ballgame the next Sunday, with some of the
hands on the ranch representing our nearby town. Somehow, he
cajoled his way onto the team (he was close to fifty but looked
much younger); he played first base, and got a single in a losing
cause. Late in the game, I was sent up to pinch-hit for somebody.
The pitcher, a large and unpleasant-looking young man, must
have felt distaste at the sight of a scared sixteen-year-old dude
standing in, because he dismissed me with two fiery fastballs and
then a curve that I waved at without hope, without a chance. I sat
down again. My father said nothing at the time, but later on in
the day, perhaps riding back to supper, he murmured, "What'd
he throw you — two hard ones and a hook?" I nodded, my ears
burning. There was a pause, and Father said, "The curveball
away can be very tough." It was late afternoon, but the view from
my side of the car suddenly grew brighter.

It is hard to hear stories like this now without an accompanying inner smirk. We are wary of sentiment and obsessively knowing, and we feel obliged to put a spin of psychology or economic
determinism or bored contempt on all clear-color memories. I
suppose someone could say that my father was a privileged
Wasp, who was able to pursue some adolescent, rustic yearnings
far too late in life. But that would miss the point. My father was
knowing, too; he was a New York sophisticate who spurned cyn-

icism. He had only limited financial success as a Wall Street lawyer, but that work allowed him to put in great amounts of time with the American Civil Liberties Union, which he served as a long-term chairman of its national board. Most of his life, I heard him talk about the latest issues or cases involving censorship, Jim Crow laws, voting rights, freedom of speech, racial and sexual discrimination, and threats to the Constitution; these struggles continue to this day, God knows, but the difference back then was that men and women like my father always sounded as if such battles would be won in the end. The news was always harsh, and fresh threats to freedom immediate, but every problem was capable of solution somewhere down the line. We don't hold such ideas anymore — about our freedoms or about anything else. My father looked on baseball the same way; he would never be a big-league player, or even a college player, but whenever he found a game he jumped at the chance to play and to win.

If this sounds like a romantic or foolish impulse to us today, it is because most of American life, including baseball, no longer feels feasible. We know everything about the game now, thanks to instant replay and computerized stats, and what we seem to have concluded is that almost none of us are good enough to play it. Thanks to television and sports journalism, we also know everything about the skills and financial worth and private lives of the enormous young men we have hired to play baseball for us, but we don't seem to know how to keep their salaries or their personalities within human proportions. We don't like them as much as we once did, and we don't like ourselves as much, either. Baseball becomes feasible from time to time, not much more, and we fans must make prodigious efforts to rearrange our profoundly ironic contemporary psyches in order to allow its old pleasures to reach us. My father wasn't naïve; he was lucky.

One more thing. American men don't think about baseball as much as they used to, but such thoughts once went deep. In my middle thirties, I still followed the Yankees and the Giants in the standings, but my own playing days were long forgotten; I had not yet tried writing about the sport. I was living in the suburbs, and one night I had a vivid dream, in which I arose from my bed (it was almost a movie dream), went downstairs, and walked outdoors in the dark. I continued down our little patch of lawn and crossed the tiny bridge at the foot of our property, and there, within a tangle of underbrush, discovered a single gravestone. I leaned forward (I absolutely guarantee all this) and found my own name inscribed there and, below it, the dates of my birth and of the present year, the dream time: "1920–1955." The dream scared me, needless to say, but providentially I was making periodic visits to a shrink at the time. I took the dream to our next session like a trophy but, having recounted it, had no idea what it might mean.

"What does it suggest to you?" the goodly man said, in predictable fashion.

"It's sort of like those monuments out by the flagpole in deep center field at the Stadium," I said. Then I stopped and cried, "Oh . . . *Oh*," because of course it had suddenly come clear. My dreams of becoming a major league ballplayer had died at last.

FEBRUARY 24, 1992

Well, I'll be honest. I picked up this article with my most critical face on. Baseball nostalgia. Baseball fathers and sons. Please, if you must torture me, the bamboo shoots will be easier to take. But, as I discovered by about the second paragraph, even when the hacks have turned a subject to drivel, one wonderful writer can restore faith in the genre. Sorry I doubted you, ROGER ANGELL. — F.D.

JENNIFER BRIGGS

My Life in the Locker Room

FROM THE DALLAS OBSERVER

I WAS TWENTY-TWO YEARS OLD and the first woman ever to cover sports for the *Fort Worth Star-Telegram*. Up until then, my assignments had been small-time: high school games and features on father-daughter doubles teams and Hacky Sack demonstrations. But now it was late September, and my editor wanted me to interview Mr. October about what it was like not to make the playoffs.

I'd heard the stories: the tales of women who felt forced to make a stand at the clubhouse door; of the way you're supposed to never look down at your notepad, or a player might think you're snagging a glimpse at his crotch; about how you've always got to be prepared with a one-liner, even if it means worrying more about snappy comebacks than snappy stories.

Dressed in a pair of virgin white flats, I trudged through the Arlington Stadium tunnel — a conglomeration of dirt and spit and sunflower seeds, caked to the walkway like 10,000-year-old bat guano at Carlsbad Caverns — dreading the task before me. It would be the last day ever for those white shoes — and my first of many covering professional sports.

And there I was at the big red clubhouse door, dented and bashed in anger so many times it conjured up an image of stone-washed hemoglobin. I pushed open the door and gazed into the visitors' locker room, a big square chamber with locker cubicles lining its perimeter and tables and chairs scattered around the center. I walked over to the only Angel who didn't yet have on some form of clothing. Mr. October, known to be Mr. Horse's

Heinie on occasion, was watching a college football game in a
chair in the middle of it all — naked. I remember being scared
because I hadn't known how the locker room was going to look
or smell or who or what I would have to wade through — literally and figuratively — to find this man.

It was mostly worn, ectoplasm-green indoor-outdoor carpeting — and stares. But on top of it being my first foray behind the
red door, I was scared because of *who* I was interviewing: a superstar with a surly streak. I fully expected trouble. This was
baptism by back draft, not fire.

But I couldn't back out. In many ways, I had made a career
choice when I walked through that locker room door.

"May I talk to you?" I asked Reggie, as everyone watched and
listened.

He did not answer.

"Can I talk to you for a minute," I said. Or at least that's what
I thought I said. I might have actually said, "Can we talk about
how your face looks like one of those ear-shaped potato chips
that the lady from the Lay's factory brings on *The Tonight Show*
once a year?"

Because his reaction to my question was to begin raising his
voice to say, "There's no time."

He still didn't answer my question directly.

"Are you going to talk to me or not?" I asked.

A simple no would have sufficed. But instead, the man who is
an idol to thousands of children launched into a verbal tirade,
loudly insulting my intelligence and shouting for someone to remove me from the clubhouse.

Here I was in my white flats, some fresh-out-of-college madras
plaid skirt, one of those ridiculous spiked hairdos with tails we all
wore back then, and probably enough add-a-beads to shame any
Alpha Chi.

And there was Reggie, in nothing but sanitary socks.

His voice was growing louder. Mine, firmer.

Now almost everyone had stopped watching football and was
watching me and Reggie. "Is she *supposed* to be here?" he demanded. "You can't be in here now."

"Are you going to talk to me or not?" I asked one more time,
interrupting.

He wouldn't answer.

"All right, *heck* with it then," I said. I spun around and walked out — past the staring faces, through the red door, down the 10,000-year-old bat-guano tunnel — and emerged into the dugout and the light of the real world, where I was nothing but a kid reporter who didn't get the story. It was the last time I would ever try to interview Reggie. And it was my first failure covering sports. But it wouldn't be my last.

Long before I was allowed to eat fish with bones, could go all night without peeing in my bed, or understood *Gilligan's Island* wasn't real, I loved baseball. It's the reason I'm a sportswriter, and I learned it from my dad. Back then, almost thirty years ago, passion for the national pastime was an heirloom fathers passed to their sons. But a little girl with blond pin curls somehow slipped into the line of succession. I don't have a radio talk show yet, but I now make my living writing about sports — at the moment, mostly the Texas Rangers. Covering major league baseball full time is my goal.

Career ladders are never cushy for anybody, man or woman, unless of course your dad is president of GM or GE or whatever NationsBank is called this week. My dad was a buyer for Better Monkey Grip Rubber Company, and I'm not complaining. But the road has been anything but smooth. Family trips in an eggshell-white Impala to see the cousins in Plainview took fewer rough turns.

I've wanted to write stories about baseball since I was ten years old — to write words so good that people would read them twice. I used to write Dallas Cowboys columns in blue Crayola on a Big Chief tablet in the part of my sister's walk-in closet I had designated as the press box. Bell bottoms hung over my head as I berated Tom Landry for not getting rid of Mike Clark or praised Roger Staubach the way little kids now get all slobbery over Nolan Ryan.

I never told my friends. I always won the big awards in elementary school, went to football games, and performed in talent shows. What kind of a goob would they take me for if they knew? But after getting home from school, I'd quickly skip back to the sports section of the evening *Star-Telegram* to compare my work to that of the pros. Sometimes I'd turn the sound down on the TV and try to do baseball play-by-play, too. I can look back now and see I was sunk early, my heart hopelessly immersed in a severely codependent relationship with a kids' game played by grown-ups.

It began when I was three and my daddy took me to Turnpike Stadium — now Arlington Stadium — to see the old minor league Spurs. We lived in Arlington, about five miles from the ball park. He carried me to the back of the outfield wall and climbed the slatted boards with his right arm and clutched me in his left. Then he held my head over the top of the wall in center. And there, not 1,000 days after I had emerged from the darkness of the womb, hundreds of bright light bulbs made me squint as I watched the first half-inning of my life, the last three outs of a Spurs game.

All I remember is green and light and the security of my daddy's arms.

We were a middle-class family of four with one kid just a few years from college and another a few years from kindergarten. We never wanted for anything we really needed, but my parents, raised in the Depression, were cautious about spending.

Buying ball tickets to as many games as my dad and I wanted to see was out of the question, so we climbed the wall in the late innings or sat in those free grassy spots behind the Cyclone fence.

There were nights in the stands, too, where, just so I could enjoy the game more, my daddy patiently tried to teach the basics of scoring to a child not yet versed in addition.

One night in the stands, I had my Helen-Keller-at-the-well experience. Suddenly it all made sense: the way the numbers went across in a line on a scoreboard, what the three numbers at the end of the nine meant, even why the shortstop didn't have a bag. "He just doesn't" was suddenly sufficient and I knew a grown-up secret, like writing checks, making babies, or reading words.

My daddy and I saw our first major league game together on Opening Night here in 1972. Some summers we went to twenty games; others we went to about fifty-six.

Sometimes we'd just watch any game on the TV. Other summer nights we sat on the back porch and listened to the Rangers on the radio. If my mom made us go to Wyatt's for supper, my father would wear his primitive Walkman through the serving line, once scaring the meat lady by hollering, "Dadgum Toby Harrah!" when she asked if he'd like brown gravy or cream.

He'd pull me out of school at lunch once a year to go to the spring baseball luncheon and take me to games early so I could collect autographs. The balls with the signatures still sit on my mantel, most reading like the tombstones of major league also-rans.

When I was fourteen, I heard from a friend that the Rangers would soon be hiring ball girls. The rumor was bogus, but it planted an idea. I began a one-kid campaign to institute ball girls at Arlington Stadium — as well as to become the first.

I wrote management — repeatedly. The executive types weren't too hot on the idea. So when I was about sixteen, I wrote every major league club with ball girls and asked about the pros and cons. I sent copies of their responses to the Rangers' front office. I corresponded with them for another two years before the call finally came.

They were trying ball girls.

They picked three — Cindy, because she was a perky cheerleader at the University of Texas at Arlington; Jamie, because she had modeling experience; and me, because I was a pest.

We shagged foul balls, but in retrospect, I guess we were more decorative than functional. They used to have us dance to the "Cotton-Eyed Joe" in the seventh inning, and for a while we shook pom-poms during rallies — acts I now, as a baseball purist, consider heresy. But hey, I was the center of attention on a baseball field; I could sell out for that.

The next year, I was booted because I couldn't do backflips.

But by then I had gotten to know the sportswriters and broadcasters, and the *Star-Telegram* offered me a job — in sports — typing in scores and answering the phone.

I dropped my plans to go to the University of Texas and study broadcasting. I had enough natural talent, I felt certain, that with one high heel in the door, I could work my way into a writer's job — maybe even someday cover baseball.

The realities of the corporate world and the attitudes of Texas high school and college coaches quickly clouded my idealistic vi-

sion of a quick ascent from eighteen-year-old ball girl phenom to
big-league ace baseball writer.

You see, folks in the world of sports weren't used to working
with a "fee-male." And you know, they all say that word so well.

I started out in the office, taking scores on the phone and taking heat from the guys. Writing this the other night, tears filled
my eyes, and I got that precry phlegm in my throat. I was surprised to realize that some of the wounds still hurt.

It wasn't Reggie or pro-locker-room banter.

It was an area high school coach who routinely tried to get me
to drop by his house when his wife was out of town; when I refused for the third time, he refused to provide any more than
perfunctory answers to my story questions.

It was when all the guys were inside doing interviews, and I
was standing in the rain, makeup peeling, outside the high
school locker room at Fort Worth's Farrington Field, waiting beneath the six-foot-long "No Women" sign for the players to come
to the doorway. It was walking into the football locker room at
the University of Texas in Austin and having a large man with
burnt-orange pants and dark white face pick me up by my un-
derarms and deposit me outside the door.

God, I hate making a scene.

I have complained little through the years because the last
thing I ever wanted to do was to single myself out from the guys.
I didn't want to be branded as some woman on a crusade. I've
never been on any campaign to debunk the myth that testicles
are somehow inherent to a full understanding of balls.

I just wanted to cover sports.

But much of the early abuse came from the place I least expected it — my own paper.

Like a lot of kids starting out, I'd do office work all week and
help cover games on the weekends — anything for a chance to
prove my worth as a sportswriter. During my first four years at
the *Star-Telegram* I took one day off to model at an auto show and
five days off to get married. Those years were perhaps the most
trying. There was a sports editor who would stop by every time
he saw me eating, stare at me, and say in all seriousness, "Jenn, if
you get fat, we won't love you no more." I could see my worth
resided within the confines of a B cup and size six jeans. I wanted
to cry each time he said that.

The guys screamed at me and demanded to know if I was "on the rag" when I was surly; yet they could scream and be surly at me all they wanted.

One editor in the chain of sports command kept trying to get me to check into the Worthington Hotel with him after work. Another superior had his assistant let me off early so he could be waiting for me in the parking lot.

He said he wanted to talk. I got in the car.

"Jenn," he asked, "do you want to be treated like an eighteen-year-old kid or a woman?"

At first, I thought he meant on the job. He meant on the bed.

I never went near a bedroom with any of them, but I told him "a woman" because I didn't know how answering "eighteen" to this loaded question would affect my precarious career.

I was quite confused. My most innocent comments were greeted with sexual innuendo. I'm no wimp; I can take a lot. I know people make sexual comments to one another, and they are not always inappropriate. But this was something else.

All the culprits are either long gone or have actually apologized, saying they just didn't know better at the time.

But how was I supposed to do my job with all that crap going on? I had to think as much about how to handle the next unwanted advance or suggestive quip as I did trying to figure the Mavericks' averages.

Some readers had similar problems accepting a woman. I can't remember the number of times I've picked up the phone in the sports department, answered some trivia question, and, when the answer didn't win the guy a bar bet, had the caller demand, "Put a man on this phone." Some simply called me a "stupid bitch" and hung up.

I know they don't know what they're talking about. But the remarks still hurt.

For years I was hopelessly mired in phone answering and score taking, watching as others in similar positions moved up and on. Once, after they'd let me try my hand at writing for a year or so, editors told me I'd never make a writer. I was creative and funny, but I just couldn't write, they'd concluded. So I didn't write. For eight months, the editors refused to assign me any stories.

I was close to giving up. I seriously considered taking a job as a researcher for a law firm.

But one thing kept me in sports: I got a Rangers media pass every year. It was the lonely thread that tied me to my game.

In the arbitrary world of newspaper politics, the arrival of a new sports editor breathed life into my career. I began investigating the pay-for-play scandals of the Southwest Conference. I broke several stories, one of which won a national award for investigative sports reporting.

I remember hiding in a tree outside a North Dallas bank waiting for an SMU running back because we had heard this was where he picked up his money. Then there was the time we had a story about an SWC coach paying players, and I appeared one morning at the school where he was an assistant. Tipped off to my presence, the coach broke into a near run when I headed towards him in the hall. He ran into a dark office where I found him hiding under the desk.

Hey, this is pretty cool, I thought. When you've got dirt on them, all the condescending good-ol'-boy stuff goes out the window.

I was actually in charge.

An SMU booster threatened to have my legs broken — and I was delighted. That's something he'd say to anyone, I realized.

While all this was going on, I began helping out with Dallas Cowboys sidebar articles and weekend coverage of the Rangers. I helped cover the team for the Associated Press.

And I was entering the peak of a seven-year stint as the masked wrestling columnist Betty Ann Stout — Fort Worth's equivalent of Joe Bob Briggs — whose unofficial duties included opening appliance stores, riding elephants when the circus came to town, and acting as rodeo Grand Marshal on the backs of large, hoofed animals.

Oh sure, little stuff happened, like the time one of the Oakland A's made a big point of standing next to me naked in the middle of the clubhouse or one of the Los Angeles Raiders chucked a set of shoulder pads at my butt.

Then there was the occasion Rangers manager Doug Rader

spat corn on me after I asked a dumb question. Of course, Rader would have spat corn at anybody.

By then, I had become accustomed to the nudity and byplay of the locker room. I've always considered the real hurdle of all this to be players' perception of me, not suppressing my thoughts. Before a team got used to me, there might be some giggling each time someone made a smart remark or cursed loud enough to get you kicked out of the Watauga Dairy Queen.

The players didn't know I'd grown up with games or that my best friends had usually been crude guys or that I could open a beer bottle with my incisors or that I liked to fish as much as they did. They didn't know, and it made me feel awkward that they didn't know that this stuff really didn't bother me outside of the fact that I felt obligated to respond with a remark, which took away from my ability to do my job.

I was nervous the first time I entered the Rangers locker room, about seven years ago. Not about naked bodies or about crude remarks but about how they would *think* I felt — and how I intended to respond with confidence, no matter what happened.

So I stepped down the tunnel from the dugout to the clubhouse and peered around the open door.

The first thing I saw was four guys in a big shower.

Because of my vantage point, it appeared I would have to walk through the shower, through the four wet, naked men, to get to the actual locker-room area. I retreated back behind the door before anyone could see me.

God, I can't believe someone didn't *warn* me, I thought. And what if someone saw me in this state of trepidation? It was critical no one smelled fear or I'd lose respect from the get-go.

Maybe I didn't belong here. Maybe I'd never fit in. Maybe I should write news or features because I'll never have the fortitude it takes to stay on your toes with one-liners and be tough enough to handle this.

Maybe McDonald's was hiring.

But I had a deadline. I had to go in.

I wasn't afraid of naked men. I was afraid of the unknown.

A few feet in, I realized a hall ran in front of the showers. You take a right turn before you have to walk straight into the naked men and the soap.

The first Ranger I interviewed was drying his stomach with a towel. Before I could utter a word, he said, "Wait, let me rub it, it will get hard."

That seemed like such a dumb thing to say. I mean, I know how penises work. And I know how smartass remarks work, too. The latter are supposed to be more humorous than the former, though adulthood has taught me different.

I'll always remember that no one else laughed, for whatever reason, and that made me feel good.

So I went about my business. I asked my question; he answered.

I should have told him how sad it was that he had to rub his own.

Nudity rarely bothered me, but I prefer never to see Nolan Ryan in anything but Ranger white or blue jeans. I have no idea why, except that Nolan Ryan and my daddy are my heroes, and I just have no need of seeing either one of their white heinies.

About 1986, there was a college football convention in Dallas. There were reporters all around the lobby of the downtown Hyatt, waiting for coaches to arrive after a golf game. I was leaning against a post, waiting for Grant Teaff, holding a notepad. That's when a security guard came up to me to ask why I was there. I told him. He told me I had to leave unless I was staying at the hotel. He could not allow me to bother the guests.

I explained again that I was a sports writer waiting for Grant Teaff and pointed out other reporters, all men, around the lobby. He said I was loitering. I refused to leave. He said he would have me thrown out physically.

"Do you think I am a prostitute?" I asked.

"That's possible," he replied. "I don't have any idea what you're up to."

Mortified, I pondered my attire (a baggy smock top and pants). We both approached the front desk, where the clerk sided with the guard, saying I could remain for ten more minutes, but only if I stayed out of the central lobby and remained "mobile." No sitting or leaning. Each time I stopped pacing, the clerk and guard started towards me. I'd had enough. Once I stopped and they looked up, so I started spinning around in circles.

That did it; now they were ready to call the police. I went

home and called my sports editor. He got an apology from the Hyatt; I got suspected of prostitution while waiting in a hotel lobby for Grant Teaff.

About 1987, I got crossways with the sports editor. I ended up covering minor events full time, even doing the dreaded office score-taking work again. At the same time, my marriage began taking ugly, unspeakable turns. I began to wonder, what had I done with the last seven years of my life? Had all that I'd put up with just been for nothing?

When the coveted Rangers beat came open, I was passed over. My dream of covering professional baseball seemed further away than ever. And I didn't want to go back — to putting up full-time with condescending high school and college coaches and jerks guarding locker room doors.

I began experiencing panic attacks and became practically addicted to the antianxiety drug Xanax, buying it from bartenders and acquaintances when my prescriptions ran dry. My face broke out. And I gained forty pounds.

Good God, all I had wanted to do was cover sports. The bouncing, wide-eyed ball girl who wanted to write about baseball more than anything was gone, abandoned in increments on football fields, at locker-room doors, in editors' offices, and on barstools. I had become a sweating mass of raw nerve endings.

I felt like a cancer victim who was finally ready to give up the fight because it meant giving up the pain and humiliation.

The dream was dead.

I went to features.

They gave me all the weird stories. They knew I could write even the most boring stuff into something of interest. But I learned to do news as well. I wrote about civil rights issues and roamed through abandoned warehouses alone in search of skinheads.

Yet all the time I was still dreaming up stories to get me to the ball park. A feature on the woman who washes the Rangers' clothes was not out of the question. A three-part series on Ruth Ryan, spouse of Nolan, turned into a delightful three-week chore that included stops at the Ryans' ranch in Alvin and the stadium.

I had started wandering longingly over to the sports depart-

ment, just to talk about baseball. More than two years ago, I told
the sports editor I wanted to return to sports. And I wanted to
cover the Rangers someday.

I concluded my sports hiatus last year with a stint on a special-
projects news team, collaborating with another reporter on a series about Fort Worth's high infant-mortality rate. We won some
awards, and I gained some confidence and perspective. When
you've interviewed a seventeen-year-old mother whose daughter
was stillborn for lack of prenatal care, how tough can it be to talk
to a young pitcher who's lost to the Angels for lack of run support?

It was time to go back to the dream. I asked for — and received — a transfer back to sports.

In my three years away, I'd shed a husband, a house, a lot of
weight, and a collection of unhealthy habits. I began bicycling
and training for a marathon. Fueled by my own version of a life-
affirming experience, I felt as though I was taking back ten years
of my life.

I was ready once again to be the greatest sportswriter who ever
lived.

I was in the visiting clubhouse waiting to interview one of the
Oakland A's this year when one of the players called, "Here,
pussy" — as though he were calling a cat. But of course, he
hadn't lost Fluffy; he'd found a woman in his locker room.

It doesn't make me angry anymore; it just seems silly and ab-
surd. But some paranoia lingers. Sometimes I'm kind of quiet in
a group interview, and I have this feeling other reporters will
think it's because I'm a dumb ol' girl.

I'm a general-assignment sports reporter now, which means I
do whatever they ask of me. My aim as a writer is to make the
people I cover seem human to the readers. You can't do this
without asking about their dogs and their mom and what bugs
them even worse than dropping the soap in the shower. It seems
logical to me. I mean, we know a guy is probably happy to be a
number-one draft choice, but what makes him real is how he is
like or unlike us. It's the way we measure all people, the *Homo
sapiens* equivalent of sniffing butts by the fire hydrant.

But I don't think it seems very logical to some of the other reporters. Sometimes I will request an interview at someone's house, and my peers act as though it's weird. But how can you really profile a guy if you haven't seen his coffee table or the junk stuck to his fridge?

Sometimes before the game when everyone is milling about, I go sit around the corner in equipment manager Joe Macko's office and visit for a while just so I don't wear out my welcome in the room o' nakedness. Some nights I walk out the back door where all the wives are waiting, and they stare at me strangely, as though they think I'm the woman *Cosmo* warned them about or something.

After a long game, while standing in the middle of the clubhouse waiting for someone to appear, I sometimes gaze off in one direction, the way you stare when you're bored and become transfixed on an object until your eyes cross and you snap back into the reality of car payments and cellulite. I was doing that one recent day when a wet, naked body walked into my trance. It might as well have been a water cooler. I had to remind myself that I should probably look away.

That's another thing that has changed. I really want to be as unobtrusive as possible, so I will turn away from someone who is dressing or, if I have the time, wait until he has put his shorts on before I approach. I've been around long enough now that if they see me turn away, they probably know it isn't because I'm scared or intimidated. I like to think I've earned a little respect.

The Mavericks pose an entirely different set of problems. I'd actually never been in an NBA locker room until last winter. Then, just as I walked in the door, it struck me that I was five feet, three inches tall — about the height of an NBA crotch.

Point guards became my instant favorites for those early post-shower interviews. It is one thing not to look at your notepad, but another not to be able to look straight ahead without a big clothesline of boy parts.

James Donaldson was the very tallest, and I almost always waited until he had some small piece of fabric on before I walked back there. If necessity of deadlines or getting to someone before another reporter called for it, sure, I'd talk to Oral Roberts's 900-foot Jesus naked, no matter where the crotch fell.

But you try to walk a fine line.

The Mavericks were a delight to be around even when pissed off. The Rangers treat me like anyone else who wanders in.

Oh sure, they may actually think I'm an idiot. But there's a strange sort of comfort in feeling that if they think I'm an idiot, it's probably not because I'm a woman but because I'm just acting like an idiot.

The most puzzled responses to my job come from the friends and acquaintances in my personal life. Kids at the tanning salon want to know if I date the players. Friends at Bible study ask if the players are mean to me. And then there's the guy — almost any guy in any bar in town — who subjects me to a sports-trivia quiz during the usual getting-acquainted foreplay.

It usually goes about like this:

Leaking testosterone and reeking of beer, a Jethro Bodin-esque character sidles up and asks what I do.

"A sports writer, huh? So do you know about sports?" (I'm serious, they really ask this.)

"Hey, if you know so much about sports," he continues, "let's see if you can answer this question: Who was the last NFL running back to also play quarterback in an even-numbered Super Bowl?"

I falter, and he complains, "Hey, I thought you said you knew sports."

Lately I've just started saying I'm a secretary at Wolfe's Nursery. But unfortunately, in north Arlington, this seems to be an enviable attribute on a par with big Dallas hair and coaching shorts as after-five wear.

And of course, women everywhere want to know about that great walled fortress of wet boy flesh, the locker room.

We're sitting around the salon one day making bets on when the rest of the country will catch on that Ross Perot is a weasel when someone says he finished ahead of Bush and Clinton in another poll. Cindy, who is dabbing brown goop on my roots, figures this is like when the seniors get all reactionary and vote in the ugliest girl for homecoming queen, and it just might happen on a bigger scale.

Donna doesn't like politics, so she asks what it is I do for the paper again. Donna doesn't like newspapers either. Donna is a good argument for euthanasia.

The immediate response is curiosity: Do I get to go in the locker room?

Well, yeah.

So you've been in the Mavericks locker room? Yeah.

And you won't believe this, and I swear it's true: the immediate response of three women who don't even like sports outside of bungee jumping at Baja is, "You've seen Ro Blackman *naked?*"

Well, I guess I had; I wasn't sure.

I'm sure he's been naked in the room where I was at some time. But the point is that you don't even think much about people being naked after a while, and unless you have some peculiar reason for remembering, you don't know who you have seen naked because they all kind of waltz in and out of the shower naked, just one wet butt covered with soap film after another.

I tried to explain that it is probably a lot like being a male gynecologist: the daily procession of personal parts becomes so routine that it ceases to be of anything but professional interest.

Yet I wonder. When men gather at bars and golf courses and any of the other traditional salt licks for male bonding, do they ask the gynecologist what Mrs. Holcombe's hooters look like? Do they want to know if it's hard for him to keep his professionalism with his hand inserted in some babe's bodily cavity — and whether it's scary?

I doubt it.

Donna persists.

"I can't believe you are not in love with these men," she says, biting her cuticle. I try to explain, which is difficult because Donna and I are on different sexual wavelengths. But then Donna likes the men she meets at Baja.

If I did ever fall hopelessly head over heels for one of these men, it would not be because I had noticed a pterodactyl-size penis, but for the same reasons I'd fall for anyone else.

Like many people, Donna, who should have been named Brittany, just can't accept this.

"O.K., you mean you've *talked* to Troy Aikman, and you didn't notice what a hunk he is?"

"Well, I have talked to Troy Aikman," I say, and one woman

bites down hard on her blow-dryer and rolls her eyes as though she's just gotten the high school quarterback in spin-the-bottle.

Actually, I tell them, one of the most peculiar side effects of my job is that it seems to run off men in personal relationships. Oh sure, at first they think it's pretty cool that you're the only person at a party who can remember Neil Lomax's name or that you can name all the Rangers managers in eighteen seconds — with a shot in your mouth.

But that's while they are still trying to maneuver you quickly into bed. During this phase of courtship, most men would be reassuring Lassie that her role as a dog star doesn't matter, that they just like her nice, shiny coat.

For most of the guys that hang around for more than three dates, my job suddenly becomes a problem. Apparently a guy has to be awfully secure not to be intimidated by my frequent trips into locker rooms (as though I'm doing comparative shopping) or by my knowing a good bit about sports.

I can't tell you the bizarre arguments I've had with a few of these creeps who keep suggesting I become a teacher. Or go back to feature writing. Or maybe into public relations. One even said, "You know you don't have to do this work," in a tone that sounded like Sting telling Roxanne she didn't have to put on the red light.

The dirty little secret I've discovered is how little men know about sports, since this is what men are supposed to know more about than women. Most of the men I've dated certainly don't know about the social fraying of America or why it might be at all amusing that a guy named Fujimori is in charge of Peru, so you'd certainly hope they knew some inane facts about NFL rushers. All most know how to do is bitch about the Cowboys and Mavericks and Rangers — about their (a) record, (b) salaries, (c) coach or manager — and praise the "kick-butt" barbecue they make before watching eighteen hours of football on Sundays. That's before they tell me I don't have any business in the locker room.

I have assimilated to a large degree but probably never will completely.

I can't understand the idiots who call the sports department and want to talk to a man on the phone instead of me — or some guy who goes out of his way to spit Niblets on me. But I can understand the athletes being naturally uncertain what to make of women, of me.

Many of the women they're around — other than the reasonably stable ones like their wives and mothers — are groupies. I understand that uniforms — unless they say, "Eb, your man who wears the star" on the lapel — are a great aphrodisiac in contemporary culture. I admit, some days even the UPS guy looks awful good.

Yet anyone who gets self-worth through random sex with a professional athlete is not exactly MENSA material. So you've got all these big-haired babes who think the electoral college is a beauty school, ready to hoist their miniskirts for the first athlete who comes along. And then you've got this woman who comes in to interview them, maybe with big hair and a short skirt too, depending on the humidity and what's off at the cleaners that day.

So why are they going to think the reporter is any different at first? Logic says they might not. So I remain cautious, probably overly cautious, about appearances.

For instance, there are things I might say to a friend or even a casual coworker that I wouldn't think a thing about, but I stop short of saying such things to the players. Like the other night when I was interviewing Kenny Rogers after the game, and I just happened to notice he had really healthy-looking hair. The hamster in my mental Wonderwheel never seems to stop running, so my mind keeps a lot of thoughts going at once. So while I'm asking him about his family's strawberry farm, I'm wondering if eggs have given him this nice, shiny coat or if he uses his wife's conditioner, and if so, what is it?

I almost said matter-of-factly, "You know, Kenny, you've got a fine head of hair." I stopped myself because he might not take it right. He might not understand that I meant its thickness and shine were enviable.

There are a lot of times I want to compliment a player or make a personal observation, just because it's my nature, but my nature has to change for a moment because I don't want anyone to get the wrong impression about my intentions.

If I ever dread talking to players now, it is not because I feel that *I* don't belong there. It is because it doesn't seem that *any* reporter should be there.

One of the most sickening feelings I get is when I have to go interview some pitcher who's been shelled or some guy who is struggling at the free-throw line or a coach who is on the verge of not being a coach. I hate to invade their pain and their anger and sometimes even their happiness. What does it really matter if the rest of the world knows? I think about what it would be like to have them asking me every day, "Well, how about that really thrown-together graph there at the top?" or "You wrote a good piece, Jenn, but then your headline writers let you down at the end; what does that feel like?" or "You haven't written any good stories in the last month. Can the slump be permanent?"

Man, I'd hate them.

No less than two or three times a home stand, the feeling hits again — almost always as I walk down that tunnel from the upper deck that spits you out in back of home plate. It's just before batting practice, about 4:30 P.M. The TCBY people are pouring half gallons of yogurt stuff into the soft-serve machines; a guy is sweeping up peanuts in three-quarter time. I think how cool it is to watch a stadium yawn to life. Last night's trash still blows, even though people are sweeping all over the place. It reminds me of a debutante waking up in last night's party dress, reeking of beer.

About two yards down, I see legs behind the batting cage. Someone has come out early for batting practice. In a few more feet, the torsos appear and the warm breeze melts around my face. Near the field, I can see it is Al Newman and somebody. Always Al Newman, and he's always smiling because he's kind of happy to be here too.

The grass spreads out in the shape of a precious gem, and there are fans here and there who have come to see batting practice just because it's relaxing. Then it hits me: My job means I get to be around this game and write about it. And it's O.K. to spit your sunflower seed hulls on the floor. I head down the steps, past the seats where I couldn't even afford to sit when I was a kid, open heaven's gate, and walk onto the field.

Sometimes I take a seat in the dugout, where a few of the guys are filtering in, grabbing bats and bubble gum. For a minute, before I start to work, I smell the bubble gum in the breeze and look at the kids leaning over the dugout and the boys of summer in it.

And every once in a while I think about slatted billboards and a daddy's arms.

The other night, there were two girls in the clubhouse after the game. They were reporters and looked young enough to remind me of my old days — except they weren't wearing white flats.

No one did or said anything off-color. But there were a few giggles. And a few guys maybe flounced around a little more just for brief amusement. Quite normal, nothing harmful.

I mentioned this to someone later.

I noted being in the middle of the room when a player came out of the shower, spotted me, and turned around and went back in. A few minutes later he came back out wearing a towel.

By now I wouldn't really notice if he'd worn a towel or hadn't. But it struck me that something had changed: that my presence was no longer cause for flouncing; that I'd somehow earned this strange sign of courtesy and respect.

"Jenn," my friend told me, "I guess you rate a towel now."

JUNE 4, 1992

Many female sports writers have poured themselves out on the subject of their vocation long before JENNIFER BRIGGS *wrote this account, and their painful confessions have overflowed with as much despair and frustration. But a special tone of candor and blessed determination to this narrative shone through. I wanted this piece to run in tandem with Roger Angell's recollection, because, all else aside, they're ultimately just two stories about a couple of kids who grew up loving baseball.* — F.D.

CORY JOHNSON

Free Fallin'

FROM THE VILLAGE VOICE

WHILE HE AWAITED TRIAL, Mark "Gator" Anthony's cell in the San Diego County Jail lay at the foot of a hill in Vista, California. At the very top of that hill, four-and-a-half miles up from the jail, was the rundown skateboard park where Gator had his last ride, MacGill's Skatepark. There, a handful of teenagers skated the ramps, rolling in and out, doing flips, handstands, board slides, ollies . . . and every once in a while, some daring kid would attempt a "lean 360." It's a notoriously difficult move, in which the skater tries to get enough momentum and height to fly vertically out of the bowl with his body almost perpendicular to the ground, spin around once completely, and then land where he'd taken off, inside the bowl, but this time rolling backward toward the bottom.

That move was called the "Gait-air," named for its originator, the man who sat in the jail at the bottom of the hill. For years Gator was skateboarding's biggest star. When he first started skating, fifteen years ago, his moves were so creative, so aggressive, so — there's no other word for it — *radical*, that he was able to turn pro at the tender age of fourteen. By the time he was seventeen, he was making $100,000 a year.

To skateboarders everywhere, he was a hero. He boasted of being a roving ambassador, telling skating magazines how he was going to turn the whole nonskating world on to the sport. He and his beautiful live-in girlfriend, Brandi McClain, were *the* skateboarding couple: they starred in skating videos together, they worked as models together, they even appeared together in a Tom Petty video. Gator gave tips to beginners in *Sports Illustrated for Kids.* There was a Gator clothing line, Gator skateboards, Gator videos. "I had it all," he says today, sitting in his prison cell. "I had different cars, a big house on an estate, even girls — I had the prettiest, most popular, hah, most voluptuous, most unscrupulous girls. I say that I 'had a girl.' I once considered girls a possession. That's crazy."

Crazy or sick. Because despite all he had, on March 20, 1991, Gator beat twenty-one-year-old Jessica Bergsten over the head with a steering-wheel lock called the Club and raped her for nearly three hours. Then he strangled her in a surfboard bag and buried her naked in the desert one hundred miles away.

There were no witnesses, no one heard her screams, and the murder weapon was never found. Yet something drove Gator to confess his crime.

This is the story of the rise and fall of Mark "Gator" Anthony.

Skateboarding, like other California phenomena such as surfing and savings-and-loan scams, had a tremendous surge in popularity in the 1980s. Skateboard parks were erected across the planet. Skateboard manufacturers became multimillion-dollar companies branching out into clothing, sneakers, even movies. Crude videos were slapped together featuring the latest moves by top skaters, and they sold by the thousands. The National Skateboarding Association was sponsoring contests all over North America, Europe, and Japan, and first-prize money reached $5,000 to $7,000 per event.

All this was fueled by a handful of San Diego County teenagers who had become the sport's superstars, and Gator was one of them. Born Mark Anthony Rogowski in Brooklyn, he moved with his mother and older brother to San Diego at age three, following his parents' divorce. They ended up in Escondido, a sun-baked, middle-class suburb in northern San Diego County. Classic Reagan country, with surfers, malls, churches, and loads of disaffected middle-class youth, it was there that Gator, at age seven, discovered skating.

"I grew up without a father from day one," Gator told *Thrasher* magazine interviewer M.Fo in 1987, "and my brother kinda filled that gap. He was a bitchin' influence on me. He made me a good baseball player and an athlete in general. What was cool was that he was stoked that I was skating, too. Skating was somewhat deviant."

By 1977, Gator, ten, was skating regularly, but because he didn't have as much money as his friends he didn't quite fit in. "I was a social outcast back then," he told *Thrasher*. "My fellow skater friends were all hyped on the surf thing — who had what board, the newest O.P.'s, and who had a Hang Ten shirt. Then there I was, running around in Toughskins, y'know. . . . They were all wrapped up in the fashion and those types of superficial interests, they ended up fading out and I fucking lasted."

Gator got his chops down at a local skatepark's half-pipes, moguls, and pool in the shape of a bra dubbed "the 42D Bowl." And he found a new set of skating friends. "These guys were so into it, having such a good time, sweatin' and laughin' and crackin' jokes and just snakin' each other. It was a full soul session, everybody was just shralpin' it up. When they went into the bowl, their expressions changed to a 'going into battle' expression, going for it, no holds barred. When they popped out of the bowl, they'd get a smile on their faces and yelp and chime. It was hot."

An obvious talent, young Gator was picked up by the skatepark team and began winning local contests. Bigger sponsors followed, and in 1982 he won the Canadian Amateur Skateboarding Championships in Vancouver, his first major title. With his green eyes and dark, lean good looks, charming personality, and aggressively physical skating style, he rose to the top rank of the sport.

Tony Hawk and Christian Hosoi rounded out the triumvirate of 1980s skating superstars. "That was a great time for us," says Hawk, who has been called the Wayne Gretzky of skating. "We were making a ton of money, we flew all over the world, there were skating groupies at every stop. It was pretty cool to see a bunch of guys from San Diego County at the center of this huge thing. No doubt, we were stoked."

The primary vehicle for the wealth of pro skaters was skateboard sales, and Gator was one of the hottest tickets in that market too. A Gator skate "deck" — the board (decorated with his nickname rendered in an op art vortex or pastel quasi-African design), sans wheels and suspension system — would sell for up to $50, of which Gator would receive $2. At their peak, monthly sales of the Gator board reached seven thousand, earning him an easy $14,000. But the cash didn't end there; he also had his contest winnings and lent his name to a slew of products made by Vision Sport, a skateboard merchandising company. There were Gator shirts, berets, hip packs, videos, stickers, posters — it seemed kids couldn't get enough of him.

"Gator, Gator, Gator . . . every issue of *Thrasher* had Gator doing something," says Perry Gladstone, who owns FL (formerly Fishlips), a skateboarding company near San Diego. "He was always a part of everything. There were Gator stories, Gator spreads, full-page Gator ads — he was a hero to us. We'd read about their parties, the girls . . . you've gotta understand, top skaters were like rock stars, traveling all over the world, living the life . . . and Gator was the wildest of them all."

Wild for sure, as Gator himself indicated in the '87 *Thrasher* interview, when he talked about the rush he got from riding walls at 90 degrees, and "on the left side of the picture there's a bum with a bottle or a junkie with a needle hangin' out of his arm," and on the right side there's a skater "sweatin' it out and cussin' at the wall and — Bam! — fucking forging reality, pushing his body up the wall." One of the benefits of this, said Gator, was that "it's a real productive way of venting some way harsh aggressions. Instead of breaking a bottle and slashing somebody's face, you're throwing yourself at a wall with sweat dripping in your eyes."

Gator boasted to friends that while touring the South he would walk into liquor stores and 7-Elevens stark naked, rob them, then get drunk in the cornfields while police helicopters searched for him overhead.

On another of those wild tour dates, in Scottsdale, Arizona, in 1987, Gator, then twenty-one, met two beautiful seventeen-year-old blonds from rich families, Jessica Bergsten and Brandi McClain. Brandi and Gator partied that entire weekend, which wasn't unusual considering the groupies who awaited him in every town. But Brandi was different. Soon he was flying her to San Diego to visit him, and a few months later, she left Tucson for good and moved in with Gator.

He had bought a ranch in the mountains near Tony Hawk's

new ranch, which he'd equipped with a whole series of wooden skating ramps. But Brandi became bored with the ranch and a few months later Gator sold it. They moved to a condominium in the upscale beachside community of Carlsbad, one block away from the ocean.

Gator and Brandi were inseparable. They caroused all night in Carlsbad bars, made the scene at all the San Diego parties. They were the hottest couple on the beach. "We would get high every night," says Brandi. "We wouldn't do coke every night, but we'd do bong hits, we'd go to the Sand Bar at the end of his street, and get *fucked up*. Then we'd hang out in his Jacuzzi, get drunk off our asses, and go in and have wild sex all night."

Gator spared no expense on Brandi. So that she could join him at competitions, "he flew her to Brazil and Europe," says Gator's brother Matt Rogowski. "He bought her two cars. She was a gold-digger, but when they were together, they were absolutely in love and you could see it." The couple did modeling jobs together. Brandi appeared in Gator's videos, and when he appeared in Tom Petty's "Free Fallin' " video, she was in it too.

If he was a celebrity in southern California, in Carlsbad, the unofficial skateboarding capital of the world, he was a megastar. Surfboard shops would just give him all the equipment he wanted, skaters would ask for his autograph or Gator stickers to put on their boards. Despite his ardor for Brandi, when he was alone he'd walk up to beautiful women on the beach, say, "Hi. I'm Gator," and instantly have their undivided attention. With his looks, youth, and arrogance born of money and fame, in the holy land of skateboarding, Gator was his own god.

But while Gator was getting fat and happy cashing in on his skateboarding fame, by the late eighties a new, hipper type of skateboarding was challenging the dominance of his genre. It was called street skating, where skaters opted for urban obstacles like curbs, garbage cans, and stairways over the traditional skate-board parks. Street skaters wore their pants around the knees, eschewed protective pads and helmets and counted on frequent run-ins with the police. Characterized by the sound of boards smacking against the pavement, it was louder, more dangerous, decidedly anti-establishment and, therefore, more appealing to the kids. Vertical ramp skating techniques, of which Gator was the master, were rapidly becoming obsolete. Vision, the company that sponsored Gator and dozens of other top skaters, was about to file Chapter Eleven.

"He was really worried about becoming a dinosaur," says Perry Gladstone, to whom Gator confided. "This was an entirely new type of skating. It was rad, more amped, and all the kids wanted to be a part of it. But except for Tony Hawk, none of the old pros could really skate both vert and street, and Gator was stressed out about it." Gator himself once told M.Fo just how stressed out he would get if he had to quit skating. "I'd probably have some suicidal tendencies. I'd feel low, cheap. I'd feel like nothing. I couldn't exist . . . no way, I'd kill myself. Lose my spirit, I'd float away and my carcass would get buried."

Gator was still trying to milk vert skating for all he could. He talked to his family about marrying Brandi and settling down. Then, in October 1989, after a competition in West Germany, the party animal in Gator reared up and bit him. In typical Gator fashion, he spent the night getting sloshed, wandering from party to party. The accident that ensued is a skateboarding legend — a drunken Gator, partying with a bunch of other skaters, leapt out of a second-story window, convinced that he could fly.

Although Gator himself doesn't remember what happened, some of his friends say that he was actually trying to sneak back into his hotel after hours by crawling up a terrace. Whatever the cause, the result nearly killed him. He landed on a wrought-iron fence, impaling his neck, face, and thumb. He survived and was patched up in Germany, but upon returning home he spent months in San Diego with plastic surgeons trying to save his modeling career.

The Gator who emerged from the San Diego hospital shocked his friends and admirers. He looked the same, but he sounded completely different. "Jesus Christ spoke to me through that accident," said Gator. "I was a blind dude, but now I can see." Gator had been born again.

Augie Constantino takes the credit for Gator's metamorphosis. A skateboarder and former professional surfer who lived just two blocks from Gator and Brandi, Constantino had suffered an accident similar to Gator's four years earlier. "I was in Hawaii out drinking with some other pro surfers," says Constantino. "After leaving the party, me and a friend of mine were playing chicken when he hit me head on, doing 45 miles per hour. I guess I lost." The quadriceps in his right leg were severed, ending his pro surfing career. But Constantino decided that it was a message from God, and that he should devote his life to Christ.

Thus was born the man known as "the skateboard minister." In his stonewashed jeans, cowboy boots, and bolero jacket, he stands out from his fellow Calvary Chapel parishioners. He's built like a fireplug, wears a goatee, and has one eye slightly askew — a result of his accident. "I met Mark just before he left for Germany," says Constantino from the office he keeps in the back of the church. He's vague about his official role at the church, where, he says, he is "a lay minister" who runs a youth hotline, but he adds that officially he is a church custodian.

"I introduced Mark to a personal God, a God the father," says Constantino. "Mark never had a father to speak of. I showed Christ to him and as the Bible says, He's our own true father. So of course that appealed to Mark." It was around this time that Gator started calling himself Mark Anthony instead of Mark Anthony Rogowski, because, as he later said, "I didn't want to be associated with my father at all."

When Gator's wounds healed, he joined Constantino. He started covering his boards with religious symbols and preaching to skaters, surfers, and anyone else who would listen about his "secret friend," Jesus. Witt Rowlett, owner of Witt's Carlsbad Pipelines, the premier surf shop in Carlsbad, says that everyone was amazed. "I believe in the Lord, don't get me wrong," says Rowlett. "But Mark was just fanatic. Everything he said was 'Jesus this, the Bible that.' He was *way* into it."

Others, however, dismissed it as typical behavior from Gator. "Yeah, he was fanatic, but that's just it, he was fanatic about *everything*," says Gladstone. "That was just Gator."

But Brandi would have none of it. Gator dragged her along to Calvary Chapel a few times, but she wasn't ready for the party to end. "We literally had sex five times a day, we were so in love," says Brandi. "Then he met Augie and started saying, 'We can't have sex anymore unless we get married.' And I'm like, 'Wait a minute. We've been going out for four years, having *mad* sex for

four years, and we can't have sex anymore? I can't deal with this.
Later.' "

Brandi moved in with her mother and stepfather, who had recently moved to San Diego.

"Mark was devastated," says Constantino. "I think that it upset
him even more than his accident in Germany. Look, here's an
exact explanation of what happened to her." He reaches for his
"sword" — a well-thumbed, red Bible on his bookshelf.

"First Peter, Chapter 4, Verse 3. 'Then, you lived in licence and
debauchery, drunkenness, revelry, and tippling, and the forbidden worship of idols. Now, when you no longer plunge with
them into all this reckless dissipation, they cannot understand it.' "
He shuts the Bible with a thump. "There. You see? Brandi just
didn't get it. Mark had found a new life in Christ."

Despite his newfound devotion to Jesus, Gator's response to
Brandi's leaving was decidedly un-Christian, particularly after
she started seeing one of the guys she surfed with. Gator started
calling her mother's house, leaving messages on the answering
machine. "Mark was crazy," says Brandi. "He was calling me up
leaving all these freaky messages. He'd growl. 'You bitch! You
cunt! You're gonna fry in hell from your toes!' Weird shit like
that."

One night, Brandi came home to find that someone had broken into her house through her window, taking everything that
Gator had ever given her. Brandi and the police suspected Gator.

"He took it all back, including the car," says Terry Jensen, an
investigator from the San Diego County district attorney's office,
to whom Brandi later recounted the story. "It's kind of like a typical young teenage stunt. That's what you do when you're fifteen,
sixteen years old and you lose your first girlfriend. You want all
your money back, every necklace, every ring. You know, 'Give
me my high school jacket and my class ring because we're not
going steady anymore.' Well, that's what he did."

Brandi still hoped they might reconcile. On one such attempt,
she invited Gator to take her out to dinner. But they started arguing as soon as they pulled out of her parents' driveway. "He
was still so mad about the guy I was seeing," says Brandi. "He's

the one that told me to go out and find one of my surfer friends to party with. So I did! I found this hot little blond surfer guy, six-one.

"And Mark was furious. He was driving out in the middle of this nowhere road out where my parents live when he turned to me with this really scary, serious look in his eye. His voice got all deep and, you know, he sounded like the devil. He says, 'You know what? I should take you out to the desert right now. I should drive you out right in the middle of the night and beat the shit out of you and leave you there. And I would get away with it, because everybody would know that you deserved it.'

"I started crying and begging him to take me home right now. I'm like, 'My mother knows where I am.' And he took me back."

Brandi was scared enough to flee to New York, not telling anyone but her family where she was going. She didn't even tell her best friend Jessica in Tucson about the incident, so when Jessica showed up in San Diego a few weeks later, she called Gator asking him to show her the sights.

"Everything that I hated about Brandi, I hated about Jessica," Gator would later tell the police. "She was of the same mold that Brandi was made of." He told the police that he blamed Jessica for his breakup. Jessica, of course, had no idea about any of this.

Like Brandi, Jessica was tall, blond, and beautiful, and her friends remember her as tough, savvy, and adventurous. "She was an incredibly intelligent, free-spirited girl," recalls Brandi. "She wanted to have fun and nothing else mattered. We would go to Mexico together, and she would, say, get so drunk that she would leave me there. If I couldn't get into bars — because we were under age and had fake IDs — she would leave me outside for three hours waiting while she drank.

"But we were best friends. We were very much alive. It was, like, quick, we're going to have the very best lives, and we're going to have them now."

On Wednesday, March 20, Jessica and Gator had lunch at an Italian restaurant in La Jolla, then returned to his condo with some movies and a few bottles of wine. As she was getting ready to leave, Gator went to his car, ostensibly to see if his driver's license was there.

Waiting in his living room, Jessica looked at the picture on his mantel, where Gator proudly displayed his favorite picture — a shot of him skydiving, facing the camera, screaming at the top of his lungs while plummeting to earth. As she stared at the picture, Gator snuck up behind her, hitting her two or three times in the head and face with the metal steering-wheel lock. She fell to the floor, blood gushing from her head, so much so that it soaked right through the carpet. He handcuffed her and carried her upstairs to his bedroom. There, he shackled her onto the bed, cut her clothes off with scissors, and raped her for two or three hours.

Jessica, still conscious, begged him to stop, occasionally screaming. In an attempt to shut her up, he pulled a surfboard bag from his closet and stuffed her inside it. She screamed that she couldn't breathe. He clasped his hands around her neck and strangled her.

Gator flipped over his mattress to hide the blood that was there, then put Jessica's body, her cut-up clothing, the bag, the handcuffs, and the club in the trunk of his car. He drove for two hours into the desert, pulled off the highway at a desolate place called Shell Canyon, and buried her naked body in a shallow grave. As he drove back to Carlsbad, he tossed her bloodstained clothes, his sheets, and the club out the window. On his way back to the condo, he rented a carpet steamer, and cleaned out every spot of blood he could from the rug. When police came to question him about her disappearance a couple of weeks later, there was no evidence to be found.

Jessica's father, Stephen Bergsten, a Tucson lawyer, had enough to worry about without his daughter disappearing. One of his clients was under investigation by an Arizona drug task force, while rumors were rife that he himself was being investigated for money laundering. But when his daughter stopped calling soon after leaving for southern California, the panicked father, unsatisfied by efforts of the San Diego police, flew to San Diego to find her himself.

He plastered the entire county with posters that read MISSING PERSON with a picture of a grinning Jessica, her vital statistics (five-eight, 115 pounds, blond hair, blue eyes, fair complexion), and the telephone numbers for the San Diego police department. He talked to her friends, he even met with Gator to ask about her whereabouts. Gator shook his hand and told him, No, he didn't know where Jessica was. Bergsten's efforts were to no avail. There were no other witnesses to her disappearance. Two months went by without any leads.

But one of the posters stayed plastered up next to a phone booth at a 7-Eleven two blocks from Gator's condo. Next to the beach, with a pizza shop next door, the convenience store is a favorite hangout for young Carlsbad surfers and skateboarders. It was also a favorite place for Constantino and Gator to preach their message of Christianity to young kids hanging out. For Constantino, he was terrific bait for young skaters willing to listen to just about anything to meet Gator.

"One night at the 7-Eleven," remembers Constantino, "Gator and I were witnessing and I saw this young girl with what they call a miniskirt — I call them towels. I said to her, 'Go and put some clothes on and when you come back, I'd like to talk to you about Christ." And she said, 'I've got nothing to worry about, I've got no problems.' I pointed to the poster. 'What about that girl?' I said. 'She had nothing to worry about. But where is she now? She could have been involved in drugs, pornography. Maybe she's dead.' The girl just ignored us and jumped into a car. But I got a strange reaction out of Mark. He was just kind of blank, silent."

Seeing the picture of Jessica, and seeing it in the presence of Constantino, was too much for Gator. One night, after a Bible study at Constantino's house, Gator returned to the house with tears streaming down his face. "I was getting ready for bed when I answered the door," recalls Constantino. "He was crying and said he was Judas Iscariot. We both sat and cried. We prayed for about an hour, asking God what we should do. About a week later he came to me and said, 'Remember that girl in the poster? She was the one I killed!'"

Constantino remembers what he told Gator as he drove him to the police department in the early morning of May 5. "I said to him, 'Mark, you don't need a lawyer. You don't need innocent-until-proven-guilty. What do you need a lawyer for, if you answer to a higher power? If a person is accountable to God, then he's accountable to society — the Bible says that.'"

Constantino scoffs at the idea that perhaps his legal advice wasn't the best. Nor does he think it was unethical for him, as a minister, to turn in someone confessing to him. "Mark didn't come to me as a minister, he came to me as a friend. Anyway, I'm not an ordained minister. He knew exactly what was going to happen."

The police were astonished that someone was turning himself in for a murder that they didn't even know had happened. Jessica's body had been found in the desert by some campers on April 10, but the body was so badly decomposed that it could not be identified. The next morning Gator led detectives to where he'd buried the body. Uncuffed, standing under the hot desert sun, Gator watched as they dug around for more evidence, photographed the site, and talked to the local police.

When the police announced Gator's confession, the press jumped all over it. It was the lead story in the local papers, local television ran nightly updates as the case unfolded, and on national TV, *Hard Copy* did a "dramatic reenactment" of the rape, murder, and subsequent confession. The initial reaction of the skateboarding world's street wing was best expressed by Koby Newell, a fifteen-year-old who skated with Anthony at Carlsbad. "He was getting old," Newell told the *San Diego Union*, "but he was keeping up with the moves."

Skating's more established wing reacted with a bit more shock. Perry Gladstone had just signed Gator to endorse a new line of skateboards for Fishlips, which ironically featured a takeoff on the 7-Eleven logo. "I came home the night he confessed to find eighty-seven messages on my answering machine. They were all reporters wanting me to talk about Gator. My wife and I were with him two or three days every week for months setting this deal up. He was such a great guy, I just couldn't believe it."

The violent, anti-authority image of skateboarding — symbolized in *Thrasher* magazine's old motto "Skate or Die" — combined with the sex and bondage aspects of the murder, fed the press's sensationalist treatment of the story. One of the many videos Gator did with Brandi was called *Psycho Skate,* which fed the frenzy even more. Skateboarders felt that the coverage was turning into an indictment of their sport, not just Gator. "It's likely the skateboarding world will be placed under a microscope in the media," warned *Thrasher*. "Let's just hope that we can all remain strong."

He became a cause célèbre in San Diego County. Kids decorated their jeans jackets with the phrase *Free Mark Anthony*. But there were also bumper stickers that read *Skateboarding Is Not a Crime — Murder Is. Mark Anthony Should Die*. Skateboarders who talked to the press about it were ostracized. "It was a terrible event for skateboarding," says Gladstone. "Skating's no more inherently violent than heavy metal is inherently satanic. But people in the media tried to make it seem as if skating is a threat to the youth of America. I think you'll find that most skaters won't even talk about Gator."

The police continued to compile evidence in case Gator decided to plead not guilty to a murder charge. They found the bloodstains under Gator's carpet, and a carpet-cleaner receipt (Gator's accountant had instructed him to save all his receipts). Gator was charged with "special circumstances," committing a murder during rape, which under California law can warrant the death penalty or life imprisonment without possibility of parole.

Unable to get a lawyer, he was appointed a public defender, self-described "glory seeker" John Jimenez, a short, stocky former PTA president who drives a Harley-Davidson. After taking the case, Jimenez immediately challenged the validity of the confession, saying that Gator's minister had no right to turn him in. Jimenez appealed the rape charge, insisting that the decomposed body could show no signs of forcible rape. Although he never denied that Gator had killed Jessica, he suggested that it was her own fault. He told a reporter that Jessica was a "slut," claiming to have a long list of people with whom she'd had sadomasochistic sex, including the entire University of Arizona basketball team and a handful of pros — their names, however, were off the record. "Hey," says Jimenez, "it's like Sam Kinison said, some girls just turn Mr. Hand into Mr. Fist."

At the time these remarks were made, the San Diego Metropolitan Homicide Task Force was investigating the murders of forty-four women whose bodies had been dumped in isolated places around the county since 1985.

*

Eventually, when the higher court refused to toss out the rape charge, on Jimenez's advice Gator pleaded guilty to first-degree murder and rape, thus avoiding the death penalty or life without chance of parole. At the January 1992 hearing in which he entered his plea, Gator submitted a remarkable four-page written statement that hinted at the struggle going on in his mind before his crime, during its commission, and afterward. In the statement he admitted that although his original confession "was directed by the Lord," in the subsequent eight months he had been "tempted to dodge responsibility, deceiving myself as well as others." But now, at last, "I've been led to a full, true repentance, having nothing to hide. Thank God."

Finally able to express "my regret and my sorrow over our loss of Jessica," Gator tried to explain why he'd done what he did. "Two months prior to the incident," he wrote, "I found myself in the midst of some surprisingly strange and almost uncontrollable feelings. All at once the plague of vile visions and wicked imaginations and the daily battle to suppress them was overwhelming. It's no exaggeration to say I became completely enslaved to these devious mental images and unescapable thoughts. . . .

"Essentially, I became a victim first, because I turned my back on God in several ways, thinking I could get through it on my own power."

Slave, victim, but still expressing regret and "without deferring the blame for my actions," Gator targeted three things that influenced his state of mind:

"Firstly, sex outside of marriage, i.e. promiscuity, premarital sex and cohabitation, the disease of jealousy, and the unhealthy obsession that so often attaches to these.

"Secondly, pornography and its addictive character. Ranging from risqué public advertising, all the way to hardcore S&M, this dehumanizing of women and men and its dulling of the senses occurs at all levels. Porn is a consuming beast. . . .

"Thirdly, closing the ears and heart to God's counsel, including partial or nonrepentance and disobeying and ignoring the Bible. . . . So people, we must realize, without reduction, the gripping strength and deceptive subtlety of sin! What will it take for us to examine ourselves and listen? The tragedy of an innocent young woman's death? The fall of your favorite celebrity?

O.K., perhaps the imprisonment of your best friend or relative?...

"I know the Lord forgave me two thousand years ago on the cross at Calvary. And although I attempt to forgive myself daily," wrote Gator, the struggle over his ultimate culpability still raging in his head, "I haven't quite been able and may never be able to do so."

Gator's sentencing took place on March 6. It was quite a spectacle for a suburban courtroom. Five uniformed bailiffs used a hand-held metal detector to screen each observer. They had received information that Stephen Bergsten, who would attend the hearing with his wife, Kay, was going to try to harm Gator. Eight months earlier Bergsten had been indicted, along with forty-four others, as part of a nationwide drug ring. With his property in two states seized by the government and his daughter brutally murdered, there was speculation that he had nothing left to lose by killing Gator.

With the bailiffs standing between Bergsten and Gator, the skater offered a solemn apology to Jessica's family, asking them to forgive him. "God has changed me, and it was no typical jailhouse conversion," pleaded Gator. "I sincerely hope that they can accept my apology for my carelessness."

"Carelessness?" Bergsten shouted. "He is a child-murderer and child-rapist. He is evil incarnate." Gator, along with many others in the courtroom, cried as Bergsten continued in an angry twenty-minute monologue. "Cowards die a thousand times and he will die a thousand deaths," Bergsten shouted, his voice breaking. "He raped her and raped her and raped her and then thought, 'Let's kill her.' We couldn't say goodbye to Jessica because that filth left her with nothing but a piece of skin, left her for the coyotes and the goddamned birds to eat her." He glared directly at Gator and said in a firm voice. "I told you — and you remember, Rogowski — what would happen if anyone hurt my daughter. He says he's undergone a religious conversion. Judge, you must have heard that same story one hundred times. If he underwent a religious conversion, it was to evil, degradation, filth, and satanism."

Shortly thereafter, Superior Court Judge Thomas J. Whelan sentenced Gator to consecutive terms of six years for forcible rape and twenty-five years to life for first-degree murder. Gator will not be eligible for parole until 2010 at the earliest.

Jimenez says that Gator "took some shit" when he was first put in the San Diego County Jail. But one night soon after he was incarcerated, inmates crowded around a television to hear Gator's story on *Hard Copy*. "After that," says Jimenez, "I guess they thought he was a heavy dude, because the rest of the population has kept their distance ever since."

Gator is trying to surround himself with other born-again Christians in jail. He is appealing his sentence, and has been placed in a medical facility (for manic depression).

Augie Constantino is continuing his studies to be a minister, while cleaning up the Calvary Chapel. He still preaches to surfers and skaters in the San Diego area working with a group called Skaters for Christ.

Stephen Bergsten's money-laundering charges were dismissed two months ago in Tucson.

Brandi lives in a penthouse apartment on the Upper East Side, working as a flower arranger.

Jessica's remains were buried in a family plot in Georgia.

Those who visit Gator in prison are struck at first by how truly repentant he seems, sitting in his cell in a loose-fitting navy-blue jumpsuit with SD JAIL stamped on the back, his once wild long hair now shorn and carefully combed, as he talks about his fall from grace.

"I had been exposed to pornography since I was a little boy, three years old," he says. "In what form? In the form of sex, *actual sex* with people. I'm not going to say who, but with people in my childhood. First let me say that it wasn't only incest. I don't want to mention family members, of course, because I want to protect them. But let me put more emphasis on the fact that it was babysitters and older neighborhood kids."

Has it occurred to him that if he was the victim of sexual crime as a child, he might have a propensity to carry out such crimes as an adult? "If you believe that it was a revenge killing and that it was prompted by Brandi, I would say yes," he replies, and suddenly you're listening to a dramatically different Gator than the one at whose sentencing a Catholic priest testified, "Never before have I encountered a person so clearly open about his responsibility." You're listening to a man skating away from the idea that the murder was really his fault.

"I did lay upon her with a steering lock at one point, but that was part of the S&M," he says. "The fact is that it wasn't rape. It was more like an involuntary manslaughter. If it weren't for my submission to her wiles and the temptation of having such sex with her. . ."

Gator takes a deep breath, sighs, then continues. "I don't want to defame Jessica at all. I'm very, *very* sorry about what happened to her. I just want to make it known that I was led into a sexual situation that I didn't want to have anything to do with.

"I wouldn't have submitted if I didn't have some weakness, some background desire. You can go down the street to Coronet bookstore in Oceanside and buy a vast array of S&M bondage magazines, pictorials, descriptive pictorials, paperbacks that are step by step about how to lynch somebody sexually. It's pretty sick. I got a lot of ideas.

"That night, I didn't realize what kind of a purring feline she was. It's really hard for me to say these things about Jessica; we lost her and I don't feel good about that. I just want to make it known that I was led into a sexual situation that I didn't want to have anything to do with. I was scared I'd be discovered with this wayward woman.

"There were a lot of kids in my neighborhood, my protégés in skateboarding who would have Bible studies with me. I was being an example to these impressionable kids. For them to see me with this woman and all that had been going on — the wine bottles, the cigarettes upstairs — it would have been devastating. In my attempt to quiet her, in her intoxicated and belligerent state, I had put my hand over her mouth to quiet her for a second so I could hear the voices and the footsteps coming up my walkway. She must have suffocated or had a seizure or a stroke or something. The next thing I knew, I look down and she's not breathing and not moving."

Mark "Gator" Anthony, who has finally broken up and out of the half-pipe of his guilt, will be forty-three years old before he is eligible for parole. He says he doesn't think he'll ever ride a skateboard again, but hopes that someday he'll be free so he can learn to fly a kite.

This is one of those sagas where you are obliged to say, is it really a sports story? Sometimes we do stretch the category, just as kids who get in trouble are often identified as "football players" even if they barely made the team. The awful conclusion to CORY JOHNSON'S *piece is that now, in America, you don't have to be a basketball first-round choice to get messed up by idolotry. Our society will ruin you with deification merely for your being an adolescent skateboarder. So, this is a horror story more than it is a murder mystery. And it is definitely a sports story. — F.D.*

E. M. SWIFT

Not Your Average Ice Queen

FROM SPORTS ILLUSTRATED

LORD KNOWS SHE'S TRYING. Problem is, when life has been dealing you cards from the bottom of the deck for most of your twenty-one years, the aces and jacks all start to look marked, and it's kind of hard to trust the dealer. Even after winning a couple of hands.

But Tonya Harding, the reigning U.S. women's figure skating champion, is trying. Trying to save her twenty-two-month marriage despite the reservations, both implied and spoken, of nearly everyone who cares for her — father, mother, coach, manager, best friend. Trying to gain a measure of stability at home that has eluded her all her life. Trying to look at the bright side of a world that has shown her its underbelly with unseemly meticulousness. Trying to fulfill a preposterous childhood dream in which a hardscrabble, dispossessed kid from Portland, Oregon, hoists herself above a troubled past and wins the most refined gold medal of the Olympic Games — the women's figure skating title — propelling her toward a happily-ever-after she has never known.

It could happen, and wouldn't it be rich if it did? An ice princess who has her own pool cue — Harding's the name, nine ball's the game — an interloper in the realm of pixies and queens who's as at home doing a brake job as she is performing an arabesque. Aspirant to the throne of some of the most elegant women in the sport — Peggy Fleming, Dorothy Hamill, Katarina Witt — who can curse like a sailor, bench-presses more than her weight, and drag races in the summer for kicks.

Harding shatters all stereotypes of the pampered and shel-tered figure skater who has spent his or her youth bottled in an ice rink, training. At twenty-one, she has seen a lot of life, and she is unapologetic if the experience has left her just a little rough around the edges. "I don't regret anything that I had to go through," she says. "The way I am today must be the way God wanted it."

God moves in a mysterious way / His wonders to perform. . . . If so, then He must be a figure skating fan, for Harding's skating tal-ent is real.

That became apparent last February, when after years of dis-appointment and ill luck, Harding sent shock waves through the figure skating community with an upset victory in the nationals in Minneapolis against one of the strongest fields in memory. The shock waves were emitted when Harding, in the free skating portion of the event, became just the second woman to land a triple Axel in competition (Japan's Midori Ito was the first). She repeated that feat in March at the world championships in Mun-ich, where she finished second to U.S. teammate Kristi Yamagu-chi in an unprecedented 1-2-3 American sweep. Ito was fourth. If form holds, one of those women will win the gold medal at Albertville. But if the prize were awarded on the size of the ob-stacles that had to be overcome to get there, the five-one, 96-pound Harding would win in a walk. "She's a tough cookie," says her coach, Dody Teachman. "And she's had to be."

For all practical purposes, Harding was an only child. Her mother, LaVona, had had four children from previous mar-riages (Al Harding was her fifth husband). One died in infancy; the other three were much older than Tonya.

Money was tight. LaVona worked as a waitress and made most of Tonya's clothes. This became a source of friction between them as Tonya grew older. "They were pure polyester blends, and the other kids made fun of them," Harding recalls. "My first day of high school my mother made me wear these forest-green pants with white polka dots. We had a big fight over that, and she won."

The Hardings moved around a lot. Tonya can remember liv-ing in eight different homes in six communities before she was eighteen years old. "We'd rent places," she says, "and they'd raise

the rent, and we'd have to move. Or we'd move in with relatives
or friends. I changed schools just about every year, so I didn't
have friends hardly at all. I was basically a loner."

Al Harding, who is now fifty-eight, worked variously for the
Huntington Rubber Corp. or driving trucks for nonunion wages
or managing an apartment building. He seldom earned much
more than $5 an hour, and he was unemployed for long
stretches of time after he hurt his back while lifting. "Four times
in my life I bought a new car," Al says. "And all four times I got
laid off within two weeks. I ain't going to buy no more new ones."

Tonya's happiest hours as a child were spent with her dad. Al
may not have been the world's greatest provider, but he is a
teddy bear of a man, likable and almost cuddly. Al remembers
taking his daughter deer hunting when she was only three years
old. He told her how important it was to walk quietly. As they
tiptoed through the woods, every time he stepped on a twig his
young daughter would put her finger to her lips and say, "Shhh."
That day she followed him a mile and a half. Oh, she was a pistol,
that girl.

A year later, Al and LaVona took their daughter elk hunting.
Heck, they took her everywhere. The only time she had a babysitter was once when her parents had to appear together in
traffic court. The day of the elk hunt, they left Tonya in the truck
and trekked down the hillside in search of game. "She was a
pretty good trooper," says Al. "Most kids would scream and cry
when they saw Mom and Dad go walking down the mountain."

Al bought Tonya a .22 when she was five, cutting down the
stock so it would fit her. They would go behind the house and set
pop cans on their sides, and Tonya would aim at the tops from
75 feet away. She got to be quite a shot. "I was a better shot than
he was," she says, grinning, her competitiveness bubbling out. Al
bought her a .243 deer rifle when she was nine, and she killed
her first deer while hunting with him when she was thirteen.

They would fish together too. Al used to take her to the Columbia River at the Bonneville Dam, where he would cast for
sturgeon. Tonya would roam the shoreline at low tide, looking
for the ten-ounce sinkers fishermen had lost; they were sometimes attached to lines that had wrapped around pieces of brush
and had broken off. The sinkers cost a buck and a half new, and

her dad would give her a quarter apiece for them. Once, when she was seven, Al heard Tonya screaming, and he left his rod in the holder and came running, fearing she had fallen into the river. He found her hauling in a sturgeon that was almost as long as she was — 41 inches. She had found a sinker on a snag, and as she unwound it, she discovered that the sturgeon was still on the hook. "The kid even beat you fishing when she didn't have a pole," Al says, beaming. It's easy to believe it when he says that he has watched the tape of Tonya winning the national championship at least fifty times, not once with a dry eye.

She helped him work on his car, learning to adjust the valves every 10,000 miles. Today she can replace a transmission, rebuild an engine and do a brake job. After Al hurt his back, Tonya would split and stack the wood he had cut with a chain saw. "I was happy with my dad," she says. "We did everything together. But I wasn't very happy as a child. I was lonely. I never went to Disneyland or Knott's Berry Farm or any place like that when I was young. Skating was the only thing I did that really gave me confidence."

It was a small miracle she ever started, tight as the money was at home. It began when she was three and a half years old. Her parents were shopping one day at Portland's Lloyd Center, a mall with an ice rink, and when Tonya saw other kids skating, she wanted to join in. "My dad said O.K., and my mother said no," says Harding. "So I cried, and finally she agreed. The first thing I did was make a pile of shavings on the ice and start to eat them. My mother told me I had to skate like the others, or we'd leave. So I skated."

Her parents gave her a pair of second-hand skates for Christmas, and Tonya began taking group lessons. She quickly outgrew the program, and one of the teachers suggested to her mother that Tonya take private lessons from Diane Schatz — now Diane Rawlinson — in nearby Jantzen Beach. Rawlinson's initial reaction, when the Hardings drove out to see her, was that she didn't coach skaters that young. "My mom told me to go out and pester her," says Harding, "so I skated around her in circles and drove her nuts until Diane agreed to a six-month trial."

That trial ended up lasting almost fourteen years. And at times it was a trial for all involved. LaVona used the money she got in tips to pay for Tonya's lessons — $25 a week at first — while Al's wages went toward household expenses. As Tonya progressed, the costs mounted. When Al was laid off from work, Rawlinson would donate her coaching time. She also bought Tonya new skates and raised money from friends and area businesses to offset travel and training expenses. LaVona made Tonya's competition outfits. Grooming a world-class skater is an expensive proposition, eventually costing as much as $25,000 to $30,000 a year. "Diane was really good to her," says Al. "It cost $400 to $500 for a new pair of skates. We never had that kind of money. Tonya had to do more with less coaching than any of the girls she skates against."

But the talent was there. Harding is a terrific natural jumper, and she's fiercely competitive. She landed her first triple loop at nine, after another skater had bet that she couldn't do it. Nothing frightened her. One stark difference between most boy and girl skaters, according to those who coach them, is that when challenged to try a new move, most boys will shrug and give it a go. Most girls protest that they are being asked to attempt the impossible, and have to be coaxed.

Harding tried new things at the drop of a hat. She loved that aspect of skating, and of life. She still does. When she was fourteen, she began landing imperfect triple Axels in practice at a time when no woman in the world was attempting that three-and-a-half-revolution jump in competition. More recently, she has been working on quadruple-revolution Salchows and loops.

But she had something else besides talent. "Tonya's got this burning desire inside," says David Webber, fifty, a Portland taxi driver who got to know Tonya when he was the manager of a fast-food restaurant. "Her mother told me she never had to wake Tonya up to go practice. That was all Tonya's doing."

Webber and Harding have become so close since they met in January 1985, when Harding went to his restaurant for coffee, that Harding now refers to Webber and his wife, Ruth, as Mom and Dad. She calls the three Webber kids — Mark, Brent and Stephanie — her brothers and sister. "If I ever had a family, they're it," says Harding. "They basically adopted me into their family. You don't need papers to be adopted into a family."

"She kind of adopted us," says Ruth Webber. "And we don't

mind at all that she calls us Mom and Dad. Not at all. I don't think Tonya got a lot of love as a child growing up."

Whatever affection Harding once held for her mother was altered by the rancor that developed between the two during Tonya's teenage years, when mother and daughter found themselves increasingly at odds over any number of issues, big and small. All the elements for domestic disaster were in place. The Hardings' marriage was falling apart. Tonya was a stubborn and independent-minded young woman. Al was unemployed, and LaVona was working late hours as a waitress.

There were other problems too. The most terrible night came when Tonya was fifteen. She was at home alone, preparing for her first date with Jeff Gillooly, the man she would later marry. Tonya's half brother, Chris Davison, came home inebriated. He was twenty-six at the time. When he found that the Hardings weren't home, he approached Tonya and tried to kiss her. This had happened once before, and Tonya had stopped him by slapping his face. This time she threatened to burn him with her curling iron, and when he kept coming, Tonya made good her threat and burned him on the neck. Terrified, she ran upstairs and locked herself in the bathroom. Davison followed her, and when she wouldn't open the door, he broke it down. She was able to get away from him and dialed 911.

"He told me, 'If you say something's wrong, I'll kill you,' " she remembers. "So when the operator asked me if everything was O.K., I said yes. But she must have known something was wrong, because she called right back and asked, 'Are you sure everything's O.K. there? It's not, is it?' I just said, 'Yup.' "

Davison wouldn't leave, and when he came after her again, Tonya hit him with a hockey stick and ran across the street to the neighbors. Again she called the police. After Davison took off in his car, Tonya went back to her house, locked all the doors and windows, and waited. It seemed forever before anybody came. Finally she heard a car pull up, and she ran to the window. It was Davison. She couldn't believe this was happening. He was screaming at her, "I'm gonna get you!" and trying to get in the house. She heard someone pounding on the door, and the pounding continued and continued, until finally she understood what was being shouted: "Just open the door. It's the police."

Shaking and in tears, she let them in. Her half brother was at the bottom of the stairs, in handcuffs. The police hauled him off to jail, and when Al visited him the next day, Davison didn't remember the visit.

"That night I tried to tell my mom and dad what happened," Harding says. "My dad didn't want to believe it, and my mother slapped me and told me to get in my room. To this day she doesn't believe me."

"He did have a problem with drinking," admits LaVona. "I wouldn't put it past Chris to try and get a kiss. Tonya has a vivid imagination. She has a tendency to tell tall tales."

"After Chris got out of jail, he told me, 'If I ever catch you alone, you won't be around anymore,'" says Harding.

Davison was struck and killed by a hit-and-run driver three years ago in Portland. "I wouldn't go to his funeral," says Harding. "I know it sounds terrible. My mom tried to make me, but I wouldn't."

Harding talks about these things with a steady voice and dry eyes. She talks about them because she is asked, not because she feels it is time to share her troubles with the world. She has never spoken of these things publicly before. *She's a tough cookie, and she's had to be.*

LaVona left Al and Tonya later that same year. Tonya came home one day to find her mother gone and all the furniture removed from the house. Six cords of wood she had split and stacked with her dad were also gone. "I stayed with Dad," Tonya says. "Mom didn't want anything to do with me. I remember she told me I was the only reason my parents had stayed together. That didn't make me feel good at all."

For the next six or seven months Harding lived with her father, but when Al got a job offer in an arms-and-tackle store in Boise, he accepted it and moved to Idaho. Tonya moved back in with her mother, who had married for the sixth time, in December 1987, and was now Mrs. James Golden. The mother-daughter relationship continued to be strained. Tonya stayed with the Goldens until she was eighteen. "Then my mother and her husband basically kicked me out," she says. "If I was to live under their roof, I had to live under their rules. They wanted me to pay rent or move out. I couldn't handle it."

Her mother denies ever asking Tonya to pay rent or leave and feels she was a good mother. "When I wasn't home, I was working. I did try," says LaVona. "She couldn't wait to turn eighteen so she could be with Jeff."

Harding moved in with Gillooly, her boyfriend of three years, who is three years her senior and works in distribution at the Oregon Liquor Control Commission.

Naturally, Harding's skating was affected by the turbulence in her personal life. Skating was her anchor, but it is difficult to excel in anything when you're unhappy. She had dropped out of high school in the middle of her sophomore year, and her sense of self-esteem was largely dependent on how she performed on the ice. In her first senior nationals, in 1986, Harding finished sixth. She moved up to fifth in 1987 and remained fifth in 1988, an Olympic year.

Her working relationship with her coach, Rawlinson, was growing increasingly strained as Harding began to rebel against all forms of authority. Rawlinson, like most figure skating coaches, was more than just a coach to her skater. She was a fundraiser, taskmaster, mentor and conscience. The coach was involved in all facets of Harding's life.

At the 1989 nationals in Baltimore, the first held after Debi Thomas and Caryn Kadavy had retired from amateur skating, Harding finished a strong third, so strong that many observers thought she deserved to be placed in the top two. Unfortunately, only two U.S. women were invited to the 1989 world championships in Paris. That left Harding as the team's first alternate. "I thought I could have won at the worlds that year," she says.

She cut back on her training, and Rawlinson decided that after working together for nearly fourteen years, they both needed a change. "The bottom line is, it wasn't working," Rawlinson says. "Tonya wasn't training, and wasn't meeting the goals she had set for herself. So I delegated her to Dody."

Teachman had been one of Rawlinson's first pupils, way back in 1970, and at Rawlinson's behest had worked with Harding on her compulsory figures and endurance since 1988. "Tonya and Diane are both pretty stubborn," says Teachman, "and they didn't get along very well by the time I got involved. They had spent a lot of years together. The older Tonya got, the more she wanted to do things her own way. My philosophy was to remember what I was like at that age. I knew Tonya had a rough exterior, and I'd heard all these horror stories, but I also felt that inside there was this nice little girl trying to get out."

Says Harding, "Dody was more like a big sister or a friend than a coach. All I wanted to do was be happy, and I wasn't happy skating for Diane. Nothing was ever good enough for her. She tried to control everything: Everything. Who I'd talk to. How I'd talk to them. How I wore my hair. She basically tried to be my mother."

Rawlinson says she never tried any such thing, but she doesn't want to get into a war of words with her former pupil. She still cares deeply about Harding. "My whole association with Tonya has been like being on an adventure," says Rawlinson, who sounds like a grateful survivor. "I wanted to be a wonderful, positive role model for her, and I feel very proud of what I did for Tonya and Dody both."

As disappointed as Harding was after finishing third in the 1989 nationals, the next year's nationals in Salt Lake City were worse. Standing second after the compulsories and the short program, which together accounted for 50 percent of the scoring, Harding was poised to break through to the top, or at least the top three, which would have meant an invitation to the worlds that year in Halifax, Nova Scotia, and would have increased her financial aid from the U.S. Figure Skating Association (USFSA). But the night before the free skate program, Harding, who'd been ill all week, came down with pneumonia. She has had asthma since she was eight years old, which aggravated the illness. She stayed awake all night coughing and in the morning had a 103-degree temperature. Against her doctor's orders, Harding competed. "I'd have had to be on my death bed not to," she says.

Guts and obstinacy can take one only so far. Completing just three of her seven planned triples, Harding was marked tenth in the free skate, which dropped her to seventh overall. Al Harding was in the stands. "She was so humiliated from skating poorly," he remembers. "But she told me, 'At least I didn't quit.'"

Nope. No quit in this kid. After that experience, many thought Harding would finally give up the sport. And few were weeping at the prospect. The other skaters, who knew little about her family or her past, generally considered Harding standoffish and unfriendly. "People like her because she's a great skater, not because she's Tonya," says David Webber, whose daughter, Stephanie, is Tonya's best friend. "She has an air about her that puts people off, an air of, If you don't like it, tough luck — that's me. That's a hard way to make friends. You and I give a little and bend a little to make friendships and to keep them. Tonya doesn't. She has no security."

And small wonder. Why would she? The only person who seemed always to be there for her was Gillooly. So in March 1990, at nineteen, she married him. "I never liked you," Al told Gillooly at the wedding party. "But welcome to the family."

"I tried to talk them out of getting married," says LaVona. "I knew Jeff had a violent streak. Once when Tonya was living with me and my new husband, he tried to break down the door because he thought she had gone out with another boy. It turned out it was her brother she'd been with."

Harding later said that one of the reasons she got married then was so she could be covered under Gillooly's health insurance policy. Because, after a pep talk from Teachman and having pondered the troubling question of what she should do with her life, Harding had decided to stick with skating for one more year.

So it was that last February, after all those lousy breaks and all those troubled times, life up and dealt Tonya Harding a full house. Jammed. On a bitter-cold day in Minneapolis, with the national championship at stake, Harding skated the performance of her life. It was a rousing, full-throttle four-minute show in which she landed seven triples six different ways, including her historic triple Axel. The crowd stood and cheered for forty-five seconds, and the judges could not and did not deny her. Harding, in the spotlight at last, put a glow on the entire event.

It would be nice to be able to write that that championship changed her life and marked the end of Harding's trials. But real life doesn't work that way, and Harding is up to her elbows in real life. In early April, less than a month after finishing second in her first world championships — a remarkable achievement in itself — Harding announced she was leaving Teachman and would coach herself in the future, getting occasional input from Rawlinson. "I was real hurt," Teachman says. "We'd had a couple of rocky phone calls, and she told me she couldn't work with me right now."

The rift concerned the distribution of USFSA funds and whether Harding had or had not given her coach permission to sign her name when submitting expense receipts. "I had a lot of input from Jeff when I decided to leave Dody," Harding later admitted. After seven weeks, she saw she had overreacted. "I went back and said, 'Dody, I need you.' It was miscommunication, because everything was fine. I learned you have to talk things out."

On June 17, shortly after reuniting with Teachman, Harding filed for divorce from Gillooly, citing irreconcilable differences. As is usually the case in such instances, those closest to Harding weren't surprised. "We were never in a competition where they weren't in a fight before we left," Teachman says. Stephanie Webber, maid of honor at Harding's wedding, had disapproved of the union from the start. Stephanie had expressed her opinion so many times that she finally developed a code, holding up four fingers every time she heard about Tonya's marital difficulties. Translation: I told you so. Al, recently resettled in Portland, blames himself for the whole thing. "I feel like I deserted Tonya when I went to Boise," he says. "I don't think she'd have married Jeff if I hadn't gone."

The couple had been married fifteen months. Two days after filing for divorce, Harding petitioned for, and was granted, a restraining order to prevent Gillooly from entering any skating rinks or her apartment. "He wrenched my arm and wrist and he pulled my hair and shoved me," she wrote in the petition. Harding further stated, "I recently found out he bought a shotgun, and I am scared for my safety."

A hearing on the distribution of property and the finalization of the divorce was scheduled for November. Harding and Stephanie got an apartment together over the summer, and during her separation from Gillooly, Tonya seemed happy to be on her own. She taught Stephanie how to play pool. Twice Harding went drag racing at the Portland International Raceway — once in a friend's car, once in her Jeep CJ-7. But she gave racing up when her automobile insurance company got wind of it and threatened to cancel her policy. She came in second in a celebrity roller-blading event in Orlando, Florida, that was put on for television — Elizabeth Manley and Bonnie Blair were among the contestants. Harding had roller-bladed only four times before the competition. "She got back and said, 'I wasn't going to let all those girls get in front of me,'" recalls Teachman. "She should be on the front line of a football team."

By early fall, Harding's training was going well and her weight was down to a lithe 96 pounds — four pounds less than she weighed when she won at the nationals. "This year I've just been thinner," Harding said. "I think that comes from being happy, too." Three times a week she worked out in a gym, bench-pressing 110 pounds. Harding believes it is her upper-body strength, first acquired while splitting wood for her father, that enables her to land her triple Axel.

"She jumps like a male skater," said Brian Boitano, the men's 1988 Olympic champion, after watching Harding win the prestigious Skate America competition in Oakland in September. "There's an incredible strength and control in her jumping." Among the contestants Harding defeated at Skate America was Yamaguchi, the defending world champion, in the only time they will meet before this month's 1992 nationals.

Harding even became pretty serious about a young man she met in Canada, a banker. She met him at a dance club in Vancouver, where, with characteristic assertiveness, she asked him to dance. He came to visit her in Portland in October, and her friends and family liked him. He seemed to have a calming effect on Harding. She talked about taking him elk hunting with her father. "She wanted me to meet him," David Webber recalls. " 'I really love him, Pop,' she said. I told her, 'Tonya, you can't just meet a guy and fall in love with him like that. Love grows.' But that's just how fast she goes."

That *is* how fast she goes. A few days after the young man had returned to Canada, Harding shocked everyone — her lawyer, her agent, her father, her mother, her coach, the Webbers — by announcing she was getting back together with Gillooly. They had talked things out. He had not bought a shotgun, after all.

seemed like I was happy, but something was missing, and now I know what it was. Jeff and I love each other more than ever. We're going to get a counselor and work it out. I know he's changed. I see it in his eyes, and I believe in him. I'm going to be married once in my whole life, and that's the way I'm going to look at it. I don't want to lose him. I really don't."

Gillooly, who declined to be interviewed for this article, would only say, through Harding, that he was happy they were back together and that they were going to make the marriage work.

"She wants more than anything to have a happy home life," says Teachman.

So we shall see. Life unfolds for even the most stable of us in unpredictable ways, and few lives are less predictable than Tonya Harding's.

"You read about these perfect lives in magazines and all," says David Webber, the man whom Harding calls Dad. "But that's not the real world. Tonya's lived in the real world. That's where she gets her toughness. Years ago, when I first met her, her goal was to win the Olympics. Not the world championships. The Olympics. That's what she wanted, and if she keeps her act together" — here he pauses, as if considering that possibility, and adds — "I think she'll make it."

JANUARY 13, 1992

This terribly revealing profile was published just before the U.S. Nationals in '92, when Tonya Harding and Kristi Yamaguchi were favored to win. It was the perfect crossroads moment. Yamaguchi, of course, went on to a smashing victory, and then to earn the gold medal and riches. Harding's performance was so desultory that there was much speculation that this story by ED SWIFT *was responsible. It is unlikely that the messenger was to blame, though, particularly as the skater continues to slip back. You may want to know that she competes now as Tonya Harding Gillooly. — F.D.*

RON FIMRITE

The Amazing Madigan

FROM SPORTS ILLUSTRATED CLASSIC

SLIP MADIGAN SAT STARING moodily out the window at the fleeing countryside as his train rumbled across America's heartland toward New York City. The Slip Madigan St. Mary's—Fordham Special was the affectionate name of this transcontinental party on rails, an annual affair of Madigan's creation that had become the stuff of legend. It was an early evening in mid-November 1939, an hour when Slip would ordinarily be in full social bloom, traipsing through the cars glad-handing his fellow football travelers or stopping by to trade jokes in Joe Millett's private compartment, where the revelry continued without cessation day and night.

Madigan was forty-four and coach for the nineteenth season at little St. Mary's College in Moraga, California, a school he had single-handedly transformed from an athletic nonentity into one of the nation's ranking football powers and the reigning Cotton Bowl champions. Revered as a coach, he was equally famous as a personality, a wild Irishman who thrived in a circus atmosphere, the P. T. Barnum of football.

But Slip was feeling rotten this night. His ulcers were acting up, his team was playing poorly, attendance was down, and a new board of athletic control at the college was attempting to further strip him of his once absolute powers, harassing him to the point where he was being required to actually account for his expenditures. Imagine!

The glass of Scotch before him rested untouched. He had climbed into his powder-blue pajamas earlier than usual in the vain hope of getting a decent night's sleep, but a knock on the door of his drawing room roused him from his windowside reverie. He slipped into a burgundy dressing gown and admitted Art Cohn, the acerbic young sports editor of the *Oakland Tribune,* a good friend and, as far as Cohn's ironic nature permitted, a loyal Madigan supporter.

"The boys are missing you out there," Cohn said, swaying with the movement of the train. "I must say, though, you look like you could use some rest."

"I could."

"You know, Slip, they're saying if you don't beat Fordham, you're through."

The needling seemed to ignite some of the old fire inside. "So that's what they're saying, are they?" Madigan retorted. "O.K., Art, I've got a proposition for you."

"Of course you do."

"No, seriously, since you're obviously a genuine football expert, I'll tell you what I'm going to do. After Fordham, and after our little side trip to Mexico City, we've got one game left, with Loyola in Los Angeles."

"Right."

"So here's my proposition: If by some chance we don't beat Fordham, I'll let you coach the team on the field against Loyola. What do you say?"

"Are you kidding?"

"Certainly not."

"Then you got a deal." And Cohn bolted from the room to begin spreading the word among his fellow scribes.

Slip removed his dressing gown and headed, at last, for bed. "Well, what's the harm," he asked himself, as the train thundered through the impersonal night, "of one last little joke?"

Brother Gregory, the president of St. Mary's College, opened his office door one rainy afternoon in late December 1920 to see a rain-drenched youth standing there with matted black hair and a dimpled smile. The forty-three-year-old brother was certain this must be a student applying for the spring semester. The intruder was obviously new to the campus, because Brother Gregory personally knew every one of the 135 undergraduates in this college run by the order of Christian Brothers.

"I'm Slip Madigan," the young man quickly advised Brother

Gregory. "And I could be just the Christmas present St. Mary's is looking for."

Edward Patrick Madigan, the son of Irish immigrants, was twenty-five then, newly married and not yet a year out of Notre Dame, where he had been a 160-pound varsity lineman for three seasons, with a year off for naval duty in World War I. In 1919, his last season at South Bend, he had been a teammate of George Gipp's on Knute Rockne's first undefeated and untied team. After graduation, in June '20, Madigan coached one season at Columbia Prep in Portland, Oregon, taking a team that had not won a game the year before to the city prep championship. His success in Portland was duly noted by a visiting Christian Brother, who urged Madigan to apply for the vacant football job at St. Mary's, then occupying a single building — called the Old Brickpile — near downtown Oakland.

And now Slip Madigan stood before Brother Gregory, who, impressed by the applicant's brass and by his Notre Dame credentials, hired him on the spot. "You'll have to coach everything, though," he told the young man. "You might even have to collect tickets." And he might well have added, "See if you can find enough players to make a team."

As coach of football, baseball and basketball and as an instructor in law, economics and history at St. Mary's, Madigan received an annual salary of only $1,200. To make ends meet, he and his wife, Charlotte, opened a sandwich shop across the street from campus. His mother-in-law was the cook.

It would be an understatement to say that as football coach Slip faced a major rebuilding job — St. Mary's 1920 football season could charitably be described as having been catastrophic. After opening losses of 6–0 to the Mare Island Marines and 41–0 to Stanford, St. Mary's next played the University of California's first vaunted Wonder Team in Berkeley. The Golden Bears won 127–0; Brother Gregory immediately canceled the remainder of the schedule.

Madigan had just seventeen candidates turn out for the 1921 squad. He outfitted them with hand-me-down uniforms and shod them with cut-rate shoes into which he himself screwed the cleats. On game days he supplemented his squad with "recruits" from among nonplaying students, oversize high school kids and a few local dockworkers, who just sat on the bench to give the opposition the illusion it was facing a real team.

From his old mentor, Rockne, he borrowed the famous Notre Dame backfield shift as well as the conviction that games are won on the practice field. Like Rockne, Madigan made sure that his players were spectacularly well conditioned — no mean advantage in an era when players were obliged to perform on both offense and defense, sometimes for the full sixty minutes.

Madigan's 1921 team was ragtag but rugged and finished the season 4–3. It was one of the losses, in fact, that was the season's great triumph: St. Mary's fell to Cal's second Wonder Team, but by a 21–0 score, a 106-point improvement over the previous year. Slip forever after hailed this moral victory as the coaching feat of the century. In his second year Madigan went 3-5-1; he would not suffer another losing season until his last.

The bench props were soon supplanted by players that Madigan, a most persuasive recruiter, discovered in the Irish and Italian working-class neighborhoods of San Francisco and Oakland and on the farms of the vast California Central Valley. These were young men who might not ordinarily have gone to college but who, upon arriving there on a Madigan scholarship, worked diligently to stay.

In 1924 Madigan got the break he needed to crack the big time when a dispute between Stanford and USC over player eligibility caused cancellation of their game that season. Madigan offered St. Mary's to fill the hole in either schedule. Stanford said no; Southern Cal, coached by Gloomy Gus Henderson, condescended to play Madigan's team. In six games that season the Trojans had lost only to Cal and were considered, as usual, one of the better teams in the country. But Madigan was ready with his best, including workhorse fullback Norman (Red) Strader, a smart quarterback in Louis (Dutch) Conlan and a rotating trio of halfbacks — Jimmy Underhill, Leo Rooney, Hugh (Ducky) Grant — a unit that the press, in emulation of Rockne's famous equine quartet, dubbed the Pony Backfield.

A relatively meager crowd of some 35,000 turned up in the Los Angeles Coliseum to watch this band of unknowns play mighty Southern Cal. St. Mary's didn't even have the requisite fight song then, so the Trojans' band director, improvising, played the popular tune *The Bells of St. Mary's,* which Madigan instantly adopted as the school song.

The game, however, began on a distinctly sour note: Fifteen seconds after the opening kickoff, USC's Hank LeFebvre scored on a 73-yard reverse. But with Strader carrying the load, St. Mary's rallied and trailed at halftime by only 10–7. Still, Madigan was not pleased. "This generation of Irish has lost its guts," he shouted into the upraised Gaelic faces in the locker room at intermission.

St. Mary's scored a go-ahead touchdown in the third quarter. Then, with three minutes remaining in the game, the Trojans launched a final drive from their own 37-yard line, desperate to stave off a humiliating upset, and moved to the St. Mary's six with less than a minute left. Three line plunges carried the ball to within a foot of the goal with seven seconds on the clock, but with no timeouts remaining, USC could not get off another play. St. Mary's had held against one of football's elite.

The 14–10 upset had far-reaching consequences. Henderson resigned under pressure. Stanford, not Southern Cal, went to the Rose Bowl, where it lost to Rockne's Four Horsemen. And little St. Mary's became the game's newest sensation. Madigan never looked back.

These are the Roaring Twenties, and for Slip Madigan and his boys the good times roll on and on and on. . . . In 1926 St. Mary's beats California for the first time, 26–7, inspiring Pat Frayne of the San Francisco *Call-Bulletin* to dub the team the Galloping Gaels, a nickname that sticks. The '26 team finishes undefeated. In '27 Pop Warner's Stanford Indians fall 16–0 in a game so rough and injury-riddled that Stanford thereafter refuses to schedule another Madigan-coached team. All seven of the wins of the '27 Gaels are shutouts, validating Madigan's creed that defense wins more often than offense.

"He was a defensive genius," says one of his linemen, George Canrinus, now eighty-two. "He had us blitzing and stunting long before its was common. We didn't have to score much to win."

In 1929 the Gaels go undefeated and unscored upon until the last quarter of their ninth and final game, when Oregon's Bob Robinson connects on a 20-yard touchdown to Al Browne. St. Mary's wins anyway, 31–6.

Rockne, who refuses to schedule St. Mary's, advises Slip that if he really wants to make the collegiate big leagues, he has to play in New York. Madigan, taking this to heart, is able to fill an open date on the home schedule of powerful Fordham for 1930. Intersectional games between schools from opposite coasts are rare because of the time and cost involved in traveling cross-country by train, but Slip sees this as no obstacle. That summer, with the game safely scheduled for November 15 in New York's Polo Grounds, he writes to his players. "From the rock-bound shores of Maine to the beaches of sunny California, the St. Mary's Gaels are about to make history."

And money. Madigan forms his own travel agency and, with the cooperation of the Santa Fe railroad, organizes a two-week excursion to New York for players and fans, with a side trip to Washington, D.C., thrown in. One hundred fifty "streetcar alumni" and six actual alums sign on for the maiden voyage of the Slip Madigan St. Mary's–Fordham Special, thereafter known as "the world's longest bar."

To prepare New York for his arrival, Madigan dispatches an enterprising student public-relations assistant named Will Stevens as his advance man, arming him with a thousand dollars in cash and a satchel packed with 'Coon Hollow bootleg whiskey. Stevens, later a popular San Francisco newspaperman, arrives a week before the Special. He hounds Damon Runyon, who finally writes a column about the upcoming game. By swallowing a slab of uncooked meat, Stevens persuades Grantland Rice to write that the St. Mary's crew is so tough they eat raw steak.

"I was never so sick in all my life," Stevens later recalls, "but it was worth it."

For Madigan's players this inaugural tour is a storybook adventure. For the rest of the entourage, it is a nonstop party. Madigan entertains nightly in his twin drawing rooms on the train. Joe Millett, a Bay Area businessman, recognizes no closing hour and knows no shortage of bootleg hooch in his compartment. Another booster, Dan Maher, sets off such a racket with his firecrackers at Chicago's Union Station that the homicide squad is summoned to quell what bystanders fear is another gangland shootout.

In New York, Madigan stashes his team at the posh Westchester Country Club in suburban Rye and his fans at the Vanderbilt

Hotel in Manhattan, where two nights before the game he tosses a press party that one celebrant describes as combining "the most spectacular features of an old-fashioned Irish wake and the last days of Pompeii." Madigan explains, perhaps seriously, "It doesn't cost any more to go first class."

All that remains is the game. Fordham, coached by the Iron Major, Frank Cavanaugh, is unbeaten and has outscored its opponents 181–9. The Gaels have lost only to California, 7–6. The coast-versus-coast matchup draws such attention that it is broadcast nationally by CBS radio, with star announcer Ted Husing at the microphone. But Fordham scores two easy touchdowns in the first half and appears headed for a runaway victory. The Gaels troop miserably into the locker room at halftime, fearing lord-knows-what from their fuming coach.

Halftime oratory, in this era, is considered as essential to gridiron success as any combination of X's and O's, and Madigan is a master of the genre, a spellbinder beyond compare, a veritable Barrymore of the bathhouse.

"He had a kind of magic," recalls Lou Ferry, seventy-eight, one of Slip's quarterbacks. "Even the most cynical veteran players were ready to run through the walls after he finished talking."

No oratorical ruse is beneath Madigan. Close members of his family are perpetually invoked, always on their deathbeds, pleading with Slip to win just one more before they pass into the great beyond. Madigan's young son, Ed, lies on the edge of extinction virtually every week. Slip does not skip a beat when, during one such locker room lament for the terminally ill child, young Ed himself wanders in to hear what all the fuss is about. He, too, begins weeping over his own fate.

And so now, sitting there in the bowels of the Polo Grounds, his players wonder, What will the coach come up with this time? Madigan fixes them with his turquoise-blue eyes, then, tongue to the back of his teeth, he recreates the sound of a clicking telegraph key. "Tick, tick, tick," he clicks. "The news is crossing the country that the Gaels are failures. Tick, tick, tick." Then, tearfully recounting the team's climb from the obscurity of the Brickpile to national favor, he cries out, "The fighting human heart is made to win! Do you hear me? The fighting human heart is made to win! Now, who will fight for old St. Mary's?"

From the rear of the room, one voice rises above the din: "I will, Slip! I will!" It is Angelo Brovelli, a sophomore second-string fullback.

"Then you'll get your chance," Slip rejoices, tears cascading down his rubious cheeks. "You'll get your chance!"

Brovelli starts the second half and, carrying tacklers with him, hurtles forward four straight times, to the Fordham 19. The Gaels score on a pass from Fred (Stud) Stennett to Dick Sperbeck. Twice more they score, spurred on by the helmetless Brovelli, his thick black hair cushioning his ferocious line plunges. Fordham is held scoreless in the second half.

The upset is hailed nationwide. Copeland Burg of the International News Service writes, "From Maine to Mineola they are bowing to Slip Madigan's blue ghosts, who slipped through the fog and murk of the Polo Grounds Saturday afternoon to turn back the unbeaten, untied Fordham, 20–12."

Back home the Gaels, wearing derby hats, ride at the head of a parade up San Francisco's Market Street — this after a stopover to meet President Hoover in the White House. Fordham demands a rematch. Madigan accedes after first negotiating a guarantee of $10,000 to cover travel expenses. It is a small price to pay, he suggests, for a legend in the making.

"Years and years ago, out in the beautiful Valley of the Moragas where Don Moraga and his vaqueros rode forth from the shelter of his adobe casa on a little knoll overlooking the valley, they saw the stately trees, gowned in brown and gold, that a few days before had been clothed in shining green. They knew that autumn had come; that days of peace and rest had come to the beloved valley and hills."

Thus, in prose, did belletrist Madigan consecrate the new St. Mary's campus in the Moraga Valley. The move from the dreary Brickpile to this pastoral setting east of the Oakland-Berkeley hills was made in 1928, and Madigan personally raised an additional $115,000 to build the gymnasium that yet bears his name. The St. Mary's student body had increased fourfold since Madigan's first season, not merely coincidental with the growing fame of the football team and its histrionic head coach.

"Sit down, Slip! Sit down, Slip!" the multitudes chanted happily as Madigan strode like a Caesar before his bench. Snappily dressed in a blue serge suit and navy blue topcoat, a checkered silk scarf fluttering beneath his noble chin and a pearl gray fedora atop the sable locks, he roamed his stage, braying at the officials, "What're you doing out there, you horse thieves?"

It was Madigan's view that football — and society at large — had far too many rules. Did Prohibition make sense? Unnecessary roughness? Games and life itself, he said, were better when played with "wild abandon." And so when some referee indiscriminately tossed his flag, Madigan, in unbearable anguish, ripped that pristine fedora from his head, smashed it to the turf, stomped it to ruins and hurled the remains at the offending authority. "That hat," recalls Gael fullback Andy Marefos, now seventy-five, "was on the field as much as we were."

It was all, of course, part of the Madigan persona. "In every St. Mary's crowd of, say, 50,000," wrote San Francisco *Examiner* columnist Prescott Sullivan, "25,000 are there to see Madigan get licked, 25,000 to see him win."

The Cal game at Berkeley annually drew 70,000 or more. The Fordham series filled the Polo Grounds to its 55,000 capacity. The 1931 game against USC, which the Gaels won 13–7 over coach Howard Jones's otherwise undefeated national champions, was watched by 70,000 at the L.A. Coliseum. And the annual clash with Santa Clara became known as the Little Big Game, drawing raucous crowds of 60,000 to expanded Kezar Stadium in San Francisco.

Madigan had more than a rooting interest in big turnouts. With St. Mary's on the rise, he had negotiated a sweetheart deal with the Christian Brothers that, in addition to a modest salary, gave him ten percent of the net gate at every game. By the mid-1930s, deep in the Great Depression, he was the highest-paid coach in the country, with earnings estimated at more than $30,000 annually, virtually all of it from his percentage arrangement. As fellow coaching legend Bo McMillin remarked, "It's wrong to say that little St. Mary's College cut Slip Madigan in on the receipts. The truth of the matter is that Slip actually cut little St. Mary's in for a share." And yet, as Madigan later boasted, "There was always money in the till when I was coaching."

No one could complain that he didn't give the fans a run for his money. His showmanship even extended to costume design. From the early 1930s on, he dressed his bruisers in multicolored satin and silk; compared with more conventionally attired opponents, they looked like so many courtiers in a court of the Bourbons. In '36 his giants were turned out like leprechauns, all in green pants and jerseys, with gold harps on the bodices. For the most part, though, game wear was a modest ensemble of red silk pants, red helmets and royal blue silk jerseys with white epaulets, which Henry McLemore of UPI described as "patterned after the formal dress coat of a high-ranking French Army officer. . . . Heaven help the St. Mary's player who catches a pass in such a position that he wrinkles his suit."

Each year the Fordham excursion grew longer and more ambitious. On one of these Madigan and a cohort named Max Podlech were separated from the group during a tour of the White House and blundered into a private study. "What can I do for you, my good men?" the occupant inquired. "Oh, hi, FDR," Podlech responded, backing away respectfully.

The 1934 junket covered 8,072 miles, seventeen states and six Canadian provinces. In '37 Madigan took his team and some 250 revelers to Havana, where he had his photograph taken with the president of Cuba; he used the picture on the Christmas cards he sent that year. En route to the '38 game he had his punter, Jerry Dowd, who had led the nation in '37 with a 44-yard average, boot a ball into the Grand Canyon to confirm Madigan's boast that "Jerry can *really* kick the ball a mile."

Madigan prided himself on training his press agents, and in Tom (Tom-Tom) Foudy, class of 1935, he found a dream drumbeater. A week before fall practice was to begin in '36, Foudy spotted star end Jimmy Austin on campus. Austin, a handsome lad, told Foudy that he had such a good summer job as a handyman on the MGM lot in Hollywood that he was thinking of quitting school and maybe taking a crack at acting himself. Foudy then asked if, by chance, Austin had actually met any of the MGM stars. Austin said that, yes, Jean Harlow, the Platinum Blonde, waved to him once — or at least he thought she did.

Foudy needed no more. Headlines in the *Oakland Tribune* the next day declared that Austin was giving up football for Jean Harlow. A nice piece of publicity, thought Foudy, and Madigan heartily concurred. Within hours, newspapers across the country besieged both St. Mary's and MGM for details of the affair between the gridder and the glamour girl. Studio press agents responded predictably that Miss Harlow and the football player were "just good friends." Austin sequestered himself in the home of relatives; Foudy hinted to the press that he may have been kidnapped. Madigan philosophized that while the fighting human heart is made to win, it can all too easily be broken by love. Austin finally reappeared and announced he was ready to play football for St. Mary's. Foudy told reporters that Austin was renouncing Harlow for Madigan.

Alas, this was one stunt the Christian Brothers did not find amusing. Brother Albert Rahill, the St. Mary's president, even wrote to the actress apologizing for the mischief. Much to his surprise, she responded amiably and invited him to drop by the studio the next time he was in Los Angeles. Much to her surprise, good Brother Albert did, and over a bottle of Scotch they shared lamentations on the burdens of celebrity.

Before the Little Big Game of 1938, with a rumored Cotton Bowl bid in the offing, Madigan had Foudy make certain that Cotton Bowl founder J. Curtis Sanford was surrounded by St. Mary's operatives during the game. When the Gaels won 7–0, Foudy hurried Sanford downstairs to meet Madigan for dinner. "I caught up with them later that night having a high old time at Shanty Malone's bar," Foudy, now eighty, recalls. "Slip had taken Sanford to the Fairmont Hotel, where he'd introduced him to Marlene Dietrich, who was performing there. How Slip knew Marlene, I'm not sure. But I understand Sanford actually danced with the woman. We got the Cotton Bowl bid."

And the Gaels beat Texas Tech 20–13 in Dallas on New Year's Day, limiting the Red Raiders' star halfback, Elmer (the Great) Tarbox, to just eight yards on seven carries. It would be Madigan's last big win.

Slip and Charlotte had enjoyed a rare night on the town together. What with the demands of coaching, his immense popularity as an after-dinner speaker and his general predilection for staying up to all hours, Slip hadn't had much time to spend with his wife and three children at their fine Spanish-style home in the

Oakland hills. But on this night, March 10, 1940, they had gone
to Mass and then to the movies to see *Northwest Passage*, starring
Slip's good friend Spencer Tracy.

For a few hours at least, Slip had been able to put the disas-
trous 1939 season behind him. The Gaels had indeed lost to
Fordham in New York, and true to his word, Slip had let columnist Cohn direct the team in their final game, against Loyola in
Los Angeles. In fact, Slip's ulcers had confined him to his bed at
the Biltmore Hotel during the game, which, Cohn would glee-
fully brag, St. Mary's won 40–7.

After the season, fourteen St. Mary's players had been declared ineligible by the school for scholastic reasons, a serious
blow to any hopes for 1940. Slip knew also that the college had
been in serious financial straits for much of the Depression. His
percentage-of-the-gate deal had been discontinued by the athletic board, which had insisted, albeit in vain, that he either toe
the line on expenses or resign.

Still, Slip went to bed that night convinced, as always, that
somehow he would work his way through this. He got the bad
news the next day. Athletic board chairman J. Philip Murphy, a
tackle on Madigan's great 1929 team, announced flatly that Slip's
contract would not be renewed. No reason was given for the action, but the message was clear: Slip Madigan was fired. THE
SHOW'S OVER read the headline in the *Call-Bulletin*.

Madigan at first protested, blaming irresponsible enemies on
the athletic board. But the fact was, the financially strapped college could no longer afford such a big spender. The Brothers
were also concerned that far too many visitors to the college were
translating the white SMC block letters set into the hillside above
the campus as Slip Madigan College. The athletic tail had
wagged the academic dog too long.

Murphy further announced that the famous Fordham junk-
ets "are things of the past. From now on, St. Mary's teams will
go by direct line to New York and come back as fast as possible.
We will never again visit a foreign country during a football
trip."

Madigan reluctantly accepted the verdict. "I suspected from
the start it wasn't steady work," he told reporters.

In nineteen years he had built a record of 116–46–12 against some of the best teams in the country. From 1928 to 1939, his winning percentage of .729 was among the best anywhere. Now it was time to get on with the rest of his life. "Dad took football for what it was," says his son, Ed. "He had other interests."

For a time he was general manager of a Bay Area racetrack. He sat in for an old teammate, Eddie Anderson, as the coach at the University of Iowa for two wartime seasons while Anderson was in the service. He was general manager for a year and a half for the professional Los Angeles Dons of the All-America Football Conference. And then, in partnership with Ed, he rather quietly made a fortune in real estate development in the Bay Area. On October 10, 1966, after spending much of the night talking with Ed about football and old friends, Slip Madigan, wealthy and happy, died in his sleep of a heart attack at the age of seventy.

Although many of the housing subdivisions he built in his last years were within a few miles of St. Mary's College, Madigan never set foot on the campus from the day he was fired to the day he died. But that's not to say he didn't drop in at least once afterward.

It was the fall of 1983, and St. Mary's, which had dropped football in 1951 for financial reasons, had returned to the gridiron, now as a Division II team. After a tough practice session, a defensive lineman named Steve Jacoby decided to take a snooze before showering in the Madigan Gym. He grabbed a wrestling mat, plopped it down in the middle of the basketball court and, almost instantly, fell asleep. He awakened hours later to a strange vision. There, atop the bleachers, he could make out the form of a man swiftly pacing back and forth. "Hello up there," Jacoby called out. The distant figure made no response, continuing to pace back and forth.

Jacoby was wide awake now. He climbed to his feet and moved in for a closer look. Moonlight was seeping in through the gymnasium windows. While the restless figure remained mostly indistinct, Jacoby could see in the fresh light that he was dressed in a dark suit of an old-fashioned cut and had on a topcoat and scarf. He was wearing a battered gray hat that looked strangely out of place with the rest of his neat clothes. Jacoby could hear a faint sound, almost like the roar of a distant crowd. "Hello, mister," he tried again.

No answer. Then the mystery man took one more turn and, as suddenly as he had appeared, was gone. Gone, although there was no nearby exit. Jacoby got out of there as fast as his legs would carry him.

Had the spirit returned to the place where the man refused to go? We'll never know. But it was autumn then in the beautiful Valley of the Moragas, and "the stately trees were gowned in brown and gold." They were playing football again at St. Mary's. Surely Slip Madigan couldn't stay away forever.

FALL, 1992

I don't understand why sports editors don't assign more stories about the past. Why let the card collecting and fantasy week businesses corner the nostalgia market? RON FIMRITE *has become the master of this fruitful realm, and this piece on a football coach who has been largely forgotten is, surely, the most engaging read in this collection.* — F.D.

PAT JORDAN

The Wit and Wisdom
of the White Rat

FROM THE LOS ANGELES TIMES MAGAZINE

THE WHITE RAT tells jokes. Sexist jokes about the spinster and the foul-mouthed parrot. Racist jokes about the black dude in the elevator. Redneck jokes about the gay cowboy in the bar. He sits there, in the dugout, chewing tobacco, spitting into a plastic bottle, talking. He is surrounded by younger baseball players. They look down at him and smile.

A pugnacious-looking man from another time and place. He is sixty years old. He has a bristly, rust-colored crew cut; a bullet-shaped head; a jutting jaw; a big, hard belly, and, curiously, a child's bottled-up energy. He rocks back and forth as he talks. He reaches out to touch a player on the arm, the shoulder, anywhere, just to make contact, to draw him closer. "And so," he says, "this cowboy looks up from the bar and says, 'Moo moo, Buckaroo!'" The players laugh, shake their heads. "That's funny, Rat." And trot off to batting practice.

It is a hot afternoon in the desert. Yuma, Arizona, is the spring-training home of the San Diego Padres, who, this day, are playing the California Angels in the first exhibition game of the spring. The stands are filled with older men and women not unlike the White Rat. Between innings they stop by to chat with the Rat, who is now sitting in the stands along the first-base line. They go up to him smiling, acting a little nervous, but they speak to him with familiarity, as they would with an old friend, someone like themselves but more successful.

"Hi, Whitey," says a big man wearing a trucker's cap. "My cousin Claude met you at a Little League banquet in Festus. Remember?"

Whitey Herzog looks up into the brilliant sun and shades his eyes with the flat of his hand. "Sure do," he says, but he doesn't. "Festus, south of St. Louis."

The man smiles. "We seen you lotsa times with the Cardinals," he says. "You did some job with them."

"Well, thank you." Herzog spits tobacco juice into his bottle.

The man nods, grins, is silent for a moment as he thinks of something else to say to cement his friendship with his idol. He finally blurts out: "Say, Whitey, why didn't you sign [Dave] Winfield?"

"Tried to," says Herzog. "But you know how it is today. The whole damned deal is money."

The man shakes his head in despair at the players' greed. Then he says, "Say, Whitey, you like to fish, don'cha? Well, there's this river up in Alaska . . ."

"I'll be sure to try it." Herzog turns back to the field now to watch a young pitcher for the Angels. The man in the trucker's cap senses his time is up.

"Before I leave you alone, Whitey," he says, "could you sign this for my grandson?" He hands Herzog a pencil and a scrap of paper. Herzog signs his name. The man says, "Thanks a bunch, Whitey. Good luck this year."

When he's gone, Herzog says, "Aw, it don't bother me. Signing autographs." He laughs, then says: "I'll tell ya what bothers me. Every guy's got the best damned river to fish in. When you go there, the fish ain't there. Where'd they go? Shoot, the last time I fished in Alaska the only thing I caught was mosquitoes. They were so big they could stand on their hind legs and screw a turkey." Which reminds him of a sexist joke. He tells it, then says: "I should be careful today, huh? Can't go 'round tellin' my secretary she's got a cute ass or else I'll never become a Supreme Court judge."

He laughs again, then gets serious, as he always does when he talks baseball. "You know, Winfield built this big house in the area," he says of the departed Angel outfielder. "You'd think he'd have wanted to stay there. We offered him three million a year, but he turned it down to go with the Blue Jays." Herzog just shakes his head. Three million dollars! Such figures were beyond his comprehension when he was a teenager digging graves for a funeral parlor for spare change. Those days are behind him now. He's the California Angels' senior vice president in charge of player personnel. He signed with the Angels last September because of his long friendship with "the Cowboy," as he calls Angels owner Gene Autry. "I wanted to bring the Cowboy a world championship," Herzog says. "He always helped me out when I needed money."

Last summer the Cowboy called his good friend Whitey Herzog, who had quit his job as manager of the St. Louis Cardinals in mid-season after ten years with the club, and pleaded with him to help straighten out the Angels' organization. For three decades, the Angels, who finished last in the American League West last year, have had the reputation of an underachieving franchise that constantly traded off its talented young players and spent large amounts of cash, foolishly, on free agents, few of whom consistently came through. ("They never had a plan," says Herzog, who is never without one.) Herzog told the Cowboy he had planned to spend the rest of the year playing golf and fishing. Then the Cowboy made him an offer he couldn't refuse. Herzog called his financial adviser, who told him that he didn't need the Cowboy's money, but that if he took it, he'd be able to retire at sixty-two with $25,000 a month, tax-free, for life.

"I can't ever spend that much money in my lifetime," Herzog told his adviser, then signed with the Angels anyway, partly because they let him live in St. Louis during the season while keeping an apartment in Anaheim, but mostly because it was a challenge, he said, "to make the Angels one of the better organizations on the field, with their fans and in their farm system." Then, like a good company man, he said he believed the organization had been unfairly blamed for its bad trades and acquisitions in the past. His primary duties would be to rate talent and suggest trades and free-agent signings. That would include his particular strong suit: grabbing up players other teams were ready to let go of cheap — good players coming off injuries or a bad year and undervalued by their present bosses.

Since the 1991 season was almost over and Herzog knew little about the Angels, he'd have to wait until well into the 1992 season before asserting his presence. "I ain't gonna do anything rash," he said, "just because I'm here." The Angels' senior vice-president of operations, Dan O'Brien, says Herzog has carte blanche: "If he wants to do something, he can. We have no expectations he's gonna turn it around immediately." Richard Brown, the Angels' president, says, "I didn't hire Whitey to overrule him on baseball decisions," but on other occasions Brown has said that he, O'Brien and Herzog will rule together on suggestions by any of the three.

By the time Herzog reached Yuma for the first exhibition game, he was familiar enough with the way the organization was being run to say: "One of our big problems is that some of the dickheads we got working for us think we're competing with the Dodgers, and we're not." He refers to the Angel front office's annoying habit of looking over its shoulders at how much publicity and attendance the Dodgers are getting, rather than concentrating on producing a winner in the American League West.

Then he adds in disbelief: "You know what the hell's really wrong with the Angels? Some people don't get to work until 10 A.M., West Coast time. Everyone in New York is out to lunch by then. When the Angels go to lunch at noon, the New Yorkers are just getting back from lunch. By the time the Angels get back from lunch it's 6 P.M. in New York, and everyone there has gone home. How the hell can you make a deal? You'd think they [the Angels] would get to work at 7 A.M., wouldn't ya?"

Several weeks after opening day, Herzog began to show enthusiasm for his new team. He was particularly pleased with the early pitching of Jim Abbott, Joe Grahe, Don Robinson and rookie Julio Valera, who carried the team while ace left-handers Chuck Finley and Mark Langston were sidelined by injuries. "But I'm still concerned that we're going to have trouble scoring runs this year," said Herzog, to no one's surprise.

On the surface it would appear that Dorrel Norman Elvert Herzog is a typical product of his background and age. He was born in 1931 and raised in one of those small, pinched, hardscrabble Midwestern towns so well delineated in the stories of Sherwood Anderson — a town where people tend to remember a native son's failures more than his successes. When Herzog returned to his hometown as a big-league baseball player in the 1950s, people would say to him, "Your brother Herman was a better player than you." Herzog would snap back, "Why don't you ask *him*? He's carrying mail right here in town."

New Athens (pronounced Ay-thens), Illinois, population 2,100, lies forty miles east of St. Louis. Sixty years ago, much as it is today, New Athens was a farming and coal-mining town with two lumber mills, strip mines, a foundry, a brewery and sixteen bars. Its inhabitants, mostly descendants of German immigrants, were neat, clean, orderly, punctual, hard-working and hard-drinking people who, inexplicably and proudly, referred to themselves as hard-headed Dutchmen. They saw the daily sameness of their lives as comforting, not confining. A day in the mines. Shots and beers on the way home. Checkers on Saturdays at the barbershop. The big Sunday dinner. Laundry on Monday. When Herzog passed through town with a U.S. Army baseball team in 1953, he took his teammates on a tour. He told them who would be sitting where in which bar at what time, and they were. Thirty-four years later, Herzog would write in his autobiography, *White Rat*: "And unless they're dead, that's where they are right now."

Herzog is reticent about his parents. He says only that his mother worked hard in a shoe factory and was so fanatically strict about cleanliness that he preferred to stay away from home as long as possible, playing sports and working at the Mound City Brewing Co., where he learned to drink beer like his father. Edgar Herzog worked at the brewery, where he had the distinction of never having missed a day of work. Herzog remembers his father telling him: "Be there early and give them a good day's work, so when it comes time to lay someone off, it'll be the other guy."

If Herzog's childhood sounds parched and devoid of affection, he glosses over that and points out the positive things he learned. How to make his own bed, a habit he retains to this day. The value of a dollar. Hard work. Punctuality. Self-reliance. He talks disparagingly about kids today, who wouldn't think of playing Little League baseball unless they had the best uniforms and equipment and parents cheering them on. Herzog and his friends played baseball endlessly, in open fields, by themselves. Their parents had no interest in games. They worked too hard.

"But I really think we had it better," Herzog says. "For kids today, everything is organized. I don't see kids having much fun."

Herzog claims there is still a lot of New Athens in him today. When he meets a couple for dinner in Yuma, he is fifteen minutes early. When they arrive, ten minutes early, Herzog is already pacing in front of his car. He says he's worried because he doesn't have a sport jacket. "Do you think it will be all right?" he asks. "In Yuma?" says the man. Inside the restaurant, most of the customers are wearing jeans and T-shirts. The hostess tells Herzog's party to wait at the bar. Precisely at 7 P.M., Herzog goes to the hostess and asks to be seated. She says it'll be ten more minutes. "But our reservations are for seven," he says, almost panicky. When they are all finally seated, he checks his watch again. Fifteen minutes late. He fidgets, says: "My kids, they're always late. I don't know how they hold a job." Then he adds proudly, "But they all got their master's degree."

His three grown children were raised differently than he was. When asked how he was brought up, Herzog doesn't answer. Was he close to his father? He looks pained, angry. "Every kid is close to his father, isn't he?" He calms himself, looks down and says: "We were poor. Dad drank a lot. Women did the work. He never talked to me. The goddamn Germans are like that. My father only asked me if I needed money when he knew I had it. I supported myself since the seventh grade."

In high school, Herzog was a star athlete in baseball and basketball and, despite his considerable intelligence, a lackluster, hardly studious pupil. He used to skip school and hitchhike to St. Louis to watch the Cardinals play. He wanted to leave New Athens, he says, "because there ain't nothin' there."

He got his wish when he graduated from high school. He signed a contract with the New York Yankees, for a $1,500 bonus and $150 a month, to play in their minor league system. "More money than Mickey Mantle got," he says, smiling. They were both center fielders, which was only part of Herzog's problem during his fifteen-year playing career. He was a good outfielder who always hustled but couldn't hit a curveball. While Mantle was hitting 50 home runs a year for the Yankees, Herzog managed to hit only 65 home runs during his entire career, both in the minors and the majors.

Herzog never made more than $18,000 a year playing ball. In the off-seasons, he supported his wife, Mary Lou Sinn, and their growing family by working in a bakery, in a brewery and for a brick and pipe company. They lived in a trailer that Herzog dragged from town to town until 1958, when he attended a technical school so he could learn how to build their first house, which he did.

Herzog never did play for the Yankees (he was a bit player with Washington, Kansas City, Baltimore and Detroit from 1956 to 1963, with a lifetime .257 batting average), except during spring training. In the spring of 1955 he got his Rat nickname because of his resemblance to Yankee pitcher Bob (The White Rat) Kuzava. Both men had short, bristly, pure-white crew cuts that looked like bleached-out spring grass. (A minor league sportscaster had previously dubbed him Whitey.) He also met and became the pet of Yankee manager Casey Stengel that spring. "He took a liking to me," Herzog says. "I was his Boo Boo. Casey said I was a great leader. I don't know why. He just did."

The Yankees' flamboyant, eccentric manager was in his sixties when Herzog met him. Stengel had a reputation for taking modestly gifted players, like Billy Martin, and encouraging them to exceed their limits. He spent a lot of time talking about the intricacies of baseball with his pet Rat, as if sensing even then that Herzog's future lay not on the field but in the dugout or front office. He impressed upon Herzog the importance of the media in a manager's career.

"Stengel taught me how to control an interview," Herzog says. "Spend a lotta time answering their first question so they don't get a chance to ask another." He laughs, then says, "I enjoy writers. They work hard today. But they can create controversies. We had just as many players who were assholes when I played as there are now. But the media didn't write about that stuff then."

Stengel may have taught Herzog how to handle the press but he couldn't talk him into rising above his talent. On April Fools' Day, 1956, Stengel told Herzog he was going to trade him to the

Washington Senators, but then he added: "I'll get you back if you have a good year." Herzog never did.

When Herzog was released by the Detroit Tigers in 1963, he said, "We can't all be Mickey Mantle, can we?" And then, "It's a tough thing for a ballplayer to come to grips with the limits of his talent." It was something he never forgot. Years later, when he had to release 36 players himself, he tossed and turned in bed the night before. His first job outside of baseball during the winter of '63 was as a construction foreman in Kansas City. One afternoon his boss told him to lay off twenty men, based on seniority, not performance. He told his boss, "I don't need a business where you have to fire the good guys and keep the dogs," and he quit.

Herzog assumed that he would live out an ordinary working-man's life. But in 1964, Charley Finley, owner of the Kansas City A's, offered him a major league scouting job. Herzog grabbed it, and it turned into a coaching job the next year. Herzog's destiny now, it seemed, was that of a marginal baseball man, a coach, a man who owes his career to a kindly owner or manager precisely because he threatens no one. Managers pick coaches from among friends less famous than themselves. Managers often take their coaches with them, from team to team, when they're fired and rehired, so long as that coach is loyal, hard-working, not too bright, and grateful for his job, which often can be as mind-numbingly boring as a New Athens job. Coaches hit ground balls to infielders until their hands are callused. They sustain a false good cheer — "Atta boy, pick it up, good kid!" They drink late into the night with their manager. They listen to his monologues without disagreeing.

But that was not Herzog's destiny. He took his coaching duties so seriously at Kansas City that Finley called him the "best coach" he'd ever had. If so, Herzog said, then why are you paying me less money than coaches Luke Appling and Eddie Lopat? He already knew the answer. The latter two were more famous than he. When Finley refused to give Herzog a raise, Herzog told him to "get your donkey to coach third base," referring to the A's mascot, a mule, and left the team.

Herzog wasn't out of work long. The Baltimore Orioles hired

him as minor league manager in 1965; then the Mets hired him
as their third-base coach in '66. He became the team's director of
player development in '67 and was partly responsible for bringing along such Met pitching stars as Tom Seaver, Nolan Ryan
and Tug McGraw. The Mets promised Herzog he would be their
manager when Gil Hodges stepped down. But when Hodges
died unexpectedly of a heart attack in 1972, the Mets hired the
more famous Yogi Berra to manage the team. Herzog completed
his contract, then quit and was immediately hired by owner Bob
Short of Texas to manage his floundering Rangers. Herzog
called his first press conference as a manager and said: "This is
the worst excuse for a big-league club I ever saw." He was both
honest, as always, and right.

The Rangers were in sixth place in mid-season when Herzog
was fired and replaced by the flamboyant Billy Martin. It must
have galled Herzog, always being passed over for men more famous but not necessarily more talented. People always underes-
timated him, which may be why he has a penchant for tooting his
own horn. He is quick to claim he was the best third-base coach,
the best manager, the best player-development man — but not
the best player — to anyone who asks. He's quick to mention that
whenever newspapers conduct polls to find the manager players
would most like to play for, his name usually tops the list.

When Herzog left the Rangers, the Cowboy came to the rescue; in 1974 Herzog served briefly as the Angels' third-base
coach. In Kansas City, in 1975, he was managing again. In four
years he won three division titles and finished second, then
switched over to the Cardinals. He managed in St. Louis for nine
seasons, winning three pennants and one World Series and periodically served simultaneously as the Cardinals' general manager. He was named Manager of the Year in 1976 by UPI and
again in 1982 by the *Sporting News* and UPI, which also selected
him as Executive of the Year in 1981 and 1982. The *Sporting
News* chose him as Man of the Year in 1982, the Baseball Writers
Association of America awarded him Manager of the Year honors in 1985 and *Sports Illustrated* named him Manager of the
Decade for the 1980s.

Cardinals owner August A. Busch Jr. was the first to trust Herzog's judgment and innovative theories, which is why Herzog

considers him "the greatest owner I ever worked for." When Busch died in 1989, Herzog lost heart. He quit and went to work for another old man he respected, the eighty-four-year-old Cowboy. Herzog immediately found himself in the middle of a contract dispute between the Angels' hard-hitting first baseman, Wally Joyner, on one hand, and the Cowboy and his wife, Jackie, on the other. Joyner — offered a four-year, multimillion-dollar contract containing, the club said, everything he had asked for — left at the last minute to accept a less-money, one-year contract with Kansas City. Herzog's first impulse was to side with his player. When the squabble reached an impasse, however, he said the bottom line was, "I work for the Autrys."

Herzog's respect for older men has a lot of New Athens in it. It is the respect of the workingman for his boss. Herzog sees himself fingering his hat in his hand, at one end of a vast expanse of office where his boss sits behind a burnished, mahogany desk. "Yes, sir," he says, and backs out the door. Today, as an older man himself, Herzog seems to enjoy more the company of younger men, his players. He greets them all by name, with a smile, a slap on the back, a dirty joke, and then, serious now, sotto voce, a solicitous inquiry into a wife's pregnancy. The players' faces light up when talking to the White Rat. He is more like them than he is like a front-office man. He is still profane, raunchy, like a jock. "I want them to be my friends," he says of the players, "yet to respect me as a person, too."

Herzog's nickname is a misnomer. His hair is not really white, but orange. There is nothing ratlike about him. He is not secretive, underhanded or untrustworthy. Herzog is honest to a fault. He says he persuaded the Angels to sign Mark Langston to a long-term contract because he knew the pitcher wanted to stay in southern California to further his wife's acting career. "But she ain't that pretty," says Herzog. Of another Angel, Junior Felix, Herzog says: "He's a dog. Always has been. They say he's got talent, but a lotta players got talent." (True to form, Herzog later owned up to this rash statement. Two weeks into the season he said: "Junior Felix has hustled and done things he wouldn't have done a year ago. I don't know how he'll do all season, but after the first two weeks I'm enthused about his play.")

Todd Worrell, Herzog's ace relief pitcher at St. Louis, was a wimp, the Rat says, until he married a tough-minded woman Herzog calls a "bulldog." Herzog is not even afraid to criticize his beloved Cowboy, when it comes to the Angels. "The Angels have never been a factor with Latin-American players," he says, "because the Cowboy always wanted California boys." He raises his eyebrows and waits for his listener to get the picture. California boys. Blond, blue-eyed, white. Then he goes on: "The Cowboy says, 'That kid's from southern California. Why didn't we draft him?' " Herzog shakes his head.

Last winter, Herzog had a much-publicized dispute with Dennis Gilbert, agent for former Pittsburgh All-Star outfielder Bobby Bonilla, now a New York Met. Gilbert used the Angels in a bidding war to get higher offers from other teams. Herzog was furious, not because Gilbert used the Angels but because he didn't tell Herzog he was using them. "That s.o.b. lied to me," Herzog says. "If he'd have asked me not to withdraw our offer so he could use it with other teams, I woulda said, 'The offer's there for you.' But he didn't *ask* me!" Herzog vowed never to deal with Gilbert again, then began bargaining with him over the services of another free-agent client, Kansas City outfielder Danny Tartabull, who wound up with the Yankees. "He wanted a five-year contract," Herzog says. "But at Kansas City he had a five-year contract and only played good his first and last years. So I offered him a three-year contract. I figured that way he'd only have one bad year for us."

One morning in Yuma, the Padres–Angels game was in a rain delay, and Herzog wandered over to the pressroom. He sat at a corner table with an old friend, Kenny Parker, a scout. Parker is in his fifties, a pink-faced man with white hair, a deep-South drawl and a riverboat gambler's straw hat. Parker laughed with Herzog about the time they got drunk in a Mississippi hotel room. Herzog then told Parker a joke about a guy who gets killed by a car in front of his friends. The friends decide to send their most sensitive cohort to break the news to the man's wife. The sensitive man knocks on the door. The wife opens it. "You the Widow Jones?" the man asks. "I'm not a widow," she says. "The hell you ain't!" says the man.

Parker laughs so hard his face turns crimson. When he stops, he looks around, as though for eavesdroppers. He leans forward to whisper in Herzog's ear about a ballplayer he's been scouting. Herzog nods, then says, "No, I think he can still play." Parker says, "Thanks, Whitey."

Before the rain stops and Herzog leaves, he and Parker will be interrupted a number of times during their conversations. The men are mostly old-time scouts. They stand respectfully in front of Herzog as if waiting for an audience. He greets them all with a smile, as if he remembers them. They lean down to whisper another question in his ear. Herzog shakes his head. "I don't know," he says. "He's got a bad attitude." The men nod, "Thanks, Whitey" and leave.

Parker says baseball men are always picking Herzog's brain, not only because he's such a great judge of talent, but also because "Whitey don't lie. If you're horseshit, he tells you to your face." Cleveland General Manager Hank Peters once called him "the best judge of talent I ever saw." Others have called him the most talented baseball man of his era. The most innovative. A baseball genius, because he can see the obvious, then act on it, no matter if it had never been done before in baseball.

Herzog questions everything. Why do pitchers run lazy wind sprints day after day in the outfield? "It don't do them no good," he says. Why do managers insist that players not drink at the bar in the hotel where the team stays on road trips? It only forces the players to spread out at different bars where they are more inclined to get in trouble. It's safer to keep them together in the hotel bar where they're staying. "I gave my players the hotel bar," Herzog says, "and I found another one."

Herzog was the first manager in baseball to tailor his team to the realities of artificial turf. During his years with St. Louis, he was saddled with mediocre starting pitchers and punchless hitters. He simply adjusted, by relying heavily on his relief pitchers and by building his offense around speed and defense, which perfectly suited the fast artificial turf of Busch Stadium. A typical Cardinal rally would produce a run on a walk, a stolen base, a sacrifice bunt and a sacrifice fly. Whitey Ball. In 1982, the Cardinals hit only 67 home runs all season, then went on to beat the Milwaukee Brewers, who had hit 216 home runs, in the World Series.

The White Rat tells stories. Baseball stories about people. Like the minor league pitcher called up to the Mets one year. He went home first to get his good suit coat for the Big Apple. "He got syphilis," Herzog says, "and never pitched again." He shakes his head, a bulldog of a man sitting in the sun in Yuma along the first-base line, watching a baseball game.

Lance Parrish, the Angels' veteran catcher, walks past Herzog's seat on his way toward the bullpen. He smiles and waves to Herzog, who stares after him, a big lumbering man, perhaps in the twilight of his career.

"Now that bothers me," Herzog says. "Lance is on the last year of his contract, and if I sit him on the bench and play John Orton [a rookie catcher], Parrish won't put up any numbers to bargain with next year. But this year I want to give the kids an opportunity to play. The Angels never did that before. They just signed free agents. But you gotta find out about these young kids. We got Tony Perez's kid [Eduardo] in the minors, and he can play. We got this pitcher Paul Swingle; he's got the best arm in camp. He use ta be an outfielder until they made him into a relief pitcher." Herzog opens the Angels' press guide to check Swingle's statistics. "Look!" he says. "Eighty-eight innings in three years. I wanna know why he wasn't pitchin' two hundred innings a year, to get some experience, then put him in the bullpen."

Herzog stares down toward the bullpen. Parrish, sweating in the heat, warms up the next pitcher. "He's a good person," Herzog says. "He's been good for baseball. Goddamn, I worry about him!"

One reason Herzog wants to see if his young players can play is that the usual avenues for building a team, trades and free-agent signings, are largely closed to him. The Angels aren't likely to spend millions on free agents anymore because they are in financial trouble, according to Jackie Autry, who has been running the team's financial affairs for much of the past decade. She claims that because of escalating salaries the team lost $3.6 million last year and could lose $8.5 million this season. "By August we'll be $21 million in debt," she says. Herzog, true to his New Athens background, is not averse to pinching pennies. In fact, it seems to be a challenge — to build a contending team without bursting the owner's budget.

As for trades, the Angels don't have much talent that anyone wants. They lost Winfield and Joyner, who represented most of the team's home run and RBI production, and they failed to sign any big names to replace them. The only Angels any team would want are its three left-handed pitchers, Langston, Abbott and Chuck Finley, and their ace reliever, righthander Bryan Harvey. But unlike most baseball men, Herzog doesn't believe in trading an ace pitcher for an everyday player, no matter how good the player is. That doesn't mean he won't make trades, however. He's a master at finding players with selective skills who fill a need on the kind of club Herzog and Angels' manager Buck Rodgers are trying to build.

Herzog believes that the days of building a team by simply buying or trading for superstars is over. It's too risky, too expensive and often counterproductive; teams loaded with superstars are often less than the sum of their parts. That doesn't mean he's averse to keeping the stars his club already has. Take Abbott, an eighteen-game winner last year, for instance. He made under $400,000 last year, and the Angels promptly signed him to a $1.8-million one-year contract. Herzog thought that was foolish, that the Angels should have locked Abbott into a long-term contract for a lot more money. "The time to sign him to a long-term contract is before he has a big year," Herzog says. "You got to stay ahead of the hounds."

Herzog also doesn't believe in the Angels' policy of waiting until the season is over before negotiating with a player whose contract is up. "I'm not sure you can wait until a player's in his 'walk year.'" he says. He believes that it is often cheaper to sign a player in mid-season, before other teams begin sniffing around.

Because of the intricacies and risks involved in signing superstars, Herzog prefers instead to pursue high-quality players who are relative bargains because they struggled the previous season. Two examples are designated hitter Hubie Brooks, whom Herzog obtained from the Mets, and outfielder Von Hayes, late of the Philadelphia Phillies. Both had below-par seasons in 1991, and trading for them wasn't too costly; both have done well for the Angels in the early stages of 1992.

"I'll follow a guy from team to team," says Herzog, "look for things, then grab him. I like to get a guy after a bad year. Hell, you can't touch him after a good year." Besides, Herzog says, if you keep stealing other teams' stars, soon nobody will want to trade with you. "The secret is to make trades that help the other club, too."

Herzog also isn't afraid to trade for other teams' headaches. When Joaquin Andujar pitched for manager Bill Virdon at Houston, he drove the placid Virdon to distraction. "He wants to pitch every day," said Virdon. I can live with that, Herzog thought, and traded for Andujar. Herzog says that when he went out to the mound to take out Andujar, he'd tell him: "Great job, Joaquin! You're pitching Tuesday." Andujar would smile and say, "O.K., Skip," and walk off the mound.

Herzog smiles at the simplicity of his solution to the Andujar problem. It was so obvious — the secret to his success — he must wonder why others hadn't thought of it. Then, remembering Andujar, he says with affection: "He was wacky, ya know, but he had a heart of gold. I called him the other day. Just to talk to him. He lives in the Dominican Republic. Maybe he could do some scouting for us down there."

Although Herzog often traded for problem players, he just as often got rid of his own when he saw they were disrupting the delicate balance of his team. He parted with the Cardinals' Garry Templeton, whom he called "the most talented athlete I ever saw," because, he says, Templeton wouldn't hustle. He traded off Lonnie Smith, only after repeated drug-related problems, and finally Andujar himself, the season after he'd won twenty-one games, for the same reason.

"A leopard can't change his spots," Herzog says. He mentions Yankee pitchers Steve Howe, arrested on drug charges this past winter, and Pascual Perez, banned from baseball for failing a drug test during spring training. Hiring them is "bad management," he says. "It's not only talent. You got to find his personality, too."

The Angels–Padres game is in the late innings now. A lazy, spring-training kind of game in the hot sun. A lot of delays. Pitching changes. Fans growing restless, looking over their shoulder at the White Rat. They still go up to him between innings.

"Hey, Whitey! Remember me?" asks a man with a sunburned face. "I was in Korea with you."

"Sure do," says Herzog. The man hands him a beer, crouches down to talk awhile, then leaves. Herzog hides the beer under his seat. In a way, he's still an old-fashioned man, conscious of his image in public. He may curse and tell raunchy jokes, but never around people he doesn't know.

"Whitey, can I have your autograph?" says a teenage boy with stringy hair, handing over a baseball. Herzog notices all the other signatures on it.

"Whaddaya gonna do, sell it?" he asks, and signs.

"Wow!" the boy says. "Right on the sweet spot!" It is that spot always reserved for the biggest stars on a team.

Herzog turns back to the action on the field. He sits there, rocking back and forth, touching his companion on the arm to make a point, commenting, questioning, remembering a life lived in the game he loves. Jim Abbott, who's missing his right hand, lines a foul ball down the first-base line. "Pretty good swing for a one-armed man," Herzog says. "If he gets a hit off this pitcher, I'd release the s.o.b."

Apropos of nothing, Herzog blurts out, "Ya know what the two most amazing stats in baseball are? Ted Williams hit .400 against Herb Score, and Nolan Ryan pitched 170 consecutive innings without losing the lead after the seventh inning. I never did think Nolan would make it in New York. He needed a relaxed atmosphere. Some guys can't play in certain cities." Such intangibles are what Herzog looks for when he makes a trade.

When the Angels score a run on a ground-ball single, a stolen base and two sacrifice fly balls, Herzog says: "Helluva rally! If I was our manager, I'd tell 'em, 'There's our run, boys, now hold 'em.' " Then he answers an unspoken question before it's asked. "I ain't here to manage the Angels." He raises his eyebrows, then adds: "But it ain't written in stone I won't manage the Rhode Island Reds or some Korean team. I was a good manager, ya know. You can check it out. But today, a manager doesn't control his destiny. And that would bother me."

After the game, Herzog stops off at the hotel bar to unwind. He has a few drinks, explains how today's ballplayers confuse him. "They're programmed to deal with failure," he says, "not success. They're always talkin' about pressure. I'll tell you what pressure is. A guy's got to put food on the table for his family." He drains his drink and orders another. When it comes, he holds up the glass, and says: "Drinks are like a woman's breasts. One ain't enough and three are too many." He takes a sip and settles back into his chair. Comfortable. A sixty-year-old man from a small, pinched town who has risen above it all — who's achieved fame, wealth, success, respect, the good life beyond his wildest dreams. He can play golf and go fishing whenever he wants to. He can watch four different baseball games on the four TVs he owns. He can buy his brother a pet Vietnamese pig as a joke. "He's got all this pig crap," Herzog says. "Ashtrays and stuff. So I said, 'You like pigs, huh? Let's see if you like this one.' And damned if he don't."

Herzog today seems less passionate about the game he loves, though still intellectually involved. He seems more determined to enjoy his life outside of baseball, too. So he accepted a no-lose situation. The Angels can only get better, not worse, and the credit will go to Herzog. So what if he was overruled about Joyner and Abbott, if he must listen to Jackie Autry say she has no money to throw around, and to Richard Brown warn that all Herzog's suggestions must be filtered through a committee.

A younger Herzog might have raged, or even quit, over such things, insisting on the last word. The loss of such power doesn't seem to bother him now, because the game has changed and so has his place in it. The power has shifted to the players, and that rankles him.

Suddenly he lurches forward, his elbows planted on the table. "You know what I don't understand," he says. "One year I made six thousand dollars as a player and I had to buy my own tickets to the game for my family. Today, you got players making two million a year and they want five hundred free tickets." He shakes his head in despair. "I just don't understand it," he says. "I never saw so many unhappy millionaires in my life."

MAY 10, 1992

The subtext of this wonderfully engaging visit with an old baseball noggin is that the subject — Whitey Herzog — stayed in the game forever despite limited gifts, while the author — PAT JORDAN — was signed to a huge bonus contract as a teenager, yet failed to grow to his full promise. Pat has succeeded as a writer, so the irony is almost incidental by now. It is simply these two people's love for baseball that shines through. — F.D.

DONALD KATZ

The Master Grappler

FROM OUTSIDE

BY THE TIME I saw the huge snake cruising in, its black eyes rising just a quarter-inch above the primordial bog, I was submerged to my earlobes in a Louisiana bayou so completely decorated by plant and insect life and so thickly muddied by alluvial silt that the master catfish grappler beside me looked for all the world as if he'd been buried alive. We were two disembodied faces, pointing up into a ghostly, ancient forest of desiccated cottonwoods heavily festooned with gauzy moss.

The dense curtains of moss sucked the noise of the day from the air, though the huge mosquitoes sitting atop the water beside me sounded like helicopters, and nearby bullfrogs the size of two-month-old kittens sounded like foghorns on ocean vessels.

And I could hear the big snake swimming my way. It sounded not unlike a rowboat oar being dragged through a still lake.

"Pat," I hissed. "Big snake."

But Pat Mire was concentrating. He kept disappearing under the surface of the cold and viscous Bayou Mallet. He was feeling around in the bed of the bayou, searching for holes big enough to house a 20- or 40- or 50-pound catfish, which he intended to catch with his bare hands.

"Pat, you got water moccasins down here, don't you?" I wondered, casually as I could.

"Yes sir," said Pat. Then he took another breath. When he came back up, several gigantic mosquitoes lighted on his high forehead and began to poke him with prongs that looked like safety pins.

At thirty-nine, Patrick Mire is considered both an accomplished student of Cajun folk culture and the best of all the grapplers — or *pêcheurs-le-main,* a term that translates as "hand fishers" — in the entire tri-parish region of Louisiana's Prairie Cajun country. Mires going back several generations have risen early in the morning, dressed up as if to go duck hunting, and proceeded, with their shoes and hats still on, into the local bayous, there to catch very big, uncommonly strong fish with their hands.

A grappler dives directly into the holes and huge hollow logs and stumps where the biggest catfish live. Once inside, he attempts to entice the heavily barbed animal, which looks and behaves like 10 to 60 pounds of pure muscle packed into a slime-coated wetsuit, to swallow a bare hand. At the first tentative nibble, the grappler kind of pets the great grotesque head of the fish. Slowly at first, and then with whatever violence becomes necessary, he slides his other hand ever deeper into the fish's gullet, hoping to reach out through one pulsing gill slit and grab hold of the other hand.

The fish perceives this violation as you might perceive a strong man threading his hand into your mouth, through your sinuses and auditory canal, and out into the light through your ear. The violent underwater confrontation that ensues often results in a 225-pound tough guy being dragged underwater and down toward the Gulf of Mexico by an animal with a pedigree dating back to the dinosaurs. On a good day — depending on the hand fisher involved — the man wins.

"You got to grab 'em there," Pat said when I asked if there wasn't a less disputed spot by which to lay hold of the fish. "They just too damned slick 'n' slimy and strong to grab anywhere else."

Most cajun hand fishers will readily note that a catfish can "make you a bad sore," a reference to the fact that through a combination of particularly powerful jaw muscles and a mouth lined with high-grit sandpaper, a catfish can flay back the skin of a human arm and hand like so much peel off a ripe banana.

A typical catfish lying on the ground next to a river wears one of the meanest faces observable in all of nature. Given a few drops of water and a little mud, a catfish can kind of crawl off a bank and go home. (One exotic Asian breed is said to manage long portages through sheer willpower.) Catfish can bleat like wounded mammals at times, and if you stare hard enough, you can easily become convinced that an angry cat is just a half an evolutionary step from rising up, kicking your ass, and eating you whole.

The Catfish Book, a wonderful volume by Linda Crawford, reports Russian catfish measuring fifteen feet in length and weighing in at 750 pounds. Mark Twain once reported the sighting of a 250-pound specimen on the Mississippi, and this fish can still weigh as much as 200 pounds. Catfish apocrypha are of an appropriate scale: Waterfowl, various pets, and one small child — the poor youngster placed in stories all over history and locale — have all been snapped up by hungry cats. Innumerable *pêcheurs-le-main* have been dragged to their deaths, locked up shoulder-deep in some big cat's jaws, though you won't find any names or dates.

"An Obsoloosa cat will just destroy a hand," Pat had said when we stopped in at Mowata Store, his friend Bubba Frey's country eating place, for supplies (ice and lots of beer) before wading into Bayou Mallet. Mowata Store lies eight miles outside Eunice, Louisiana, right in the middle of Cajun country.

"A flathead is easier to handle," Pat continued. "Grab his lip just right and get his jaw outa position, and you're O.K."

"You really goin' in?" Bubba asked me, just enough disbelief in his voice to make me nervous.

I'd agreed to be the guy who blocks the fish's escape route. I had no intention of feeling the inside of a catfish's mouth. There are few things better to eat than a well-cooked catfish, but the truth is I've always found the live version of the meal too repugnant of aspect even to touch.

Bubba pulled out from a great steel pot a couple of his hand-packed boudin sausages, delicious Cajun creations just hot enough to singe your nose hair. Bubba is known far and wide for his boudin and for his capacity to play an extremely clean Cajun fiddle, but his loyalty to the proud traditions of his culture stops just short of grapplin' with the cats in the bayou. "They'll roll you on over and take you down," he said, tugging at his T-shirt.

Bubba showed me a significant scar on his thumb where one

of the local loggerhead snapping turtles once removed a bit of flesh. Loggerheads, Pat had explained, favor the same kind of holes catfish do.

"Loggerhead's got a head on him big as a twelve-inch softball," Bubba said. "Things can take half your foot away."

He grinned at me. "So you really goin' in?" he asked again. I just smiled and shot a trusting look at Pat.

Out at the bayou, Pat and I donned suitable protective hand-fishing gear — jeans, sneakers, and long-sleeved flannel shirts. Pat loitered quite a while alongside his pickup, heartily diminishing a case of beer and talking of catfish battles past. He sorted out piles of red and purple mesh crawfish sacks that would be used both to stop up escape holes and bring the fish to shore. He wound a rope around his waist to hold the sacks, just as his father had taught him to do when Pat was only six.

Felix Mire, a farmer and retired butane delivery man, still joins Pat in the mud at age seventy. He likes to string a rope through the fish's mouth and out the gill slit when he grapples it, which makes it easier to drag the catch up onto the bank.

"You really comin' in?" Pat said, his tone causing me to think upon the preimmersion beer as part sacramental Cajun tradition and part application of a liquid foolhardiness sufficient to the craziness at hand. Then we got wet. Walking in a slow-moving bayou is a special sensation. You'd move slowly even if you hadn't heard it was safer that way, because each step deposits you thigh-deep in fine delta silt. This water was icy, and the air didn't move at all.

Up along the tributorial edges of the Kankakee River in Illinois, where I first heard about men catching the least sightly of all freshwater fish with their bare hands, the little-known pastime is called "hogg'n'." In Arkansas, where it's against the law, they call it "noodlin'." In East Texas, it's called "grabblin'," while in certain parts of Louisiana it's called "grapplin' " or "grabbin'." In Mississippi, where the emphasis falls more to the tactile mesmerization of the fish than to the actual wrestling of the animal onto the land, they call it "charming." "Graveling" and "hand grabbing" are other variations on the same sport — if sport is what this tribal bit of manly endeavor can accurately be called.

Technique and style vary according to region and relative
claim to historical tradition — the most outlandish variation I've
come across being the application of a protective layer of duct
tape to the hand and forearm. All practitioners share a reverent
tone when they claim to understand certain transcendent secrets
tethered to the dying art. I often heard that a grandfather or a
great-grandfather had learned how to do it, usually from somebody who lived downriver, farther to the south. I kept asking
who invented hand fishing — who was the first to even imagine
such a thing — and I asked all the way down to the bayous of
south-central Louisiana until I found a window to a deeper past.
In Pat Mire's isolated piece of the republic, Cajun men say they
learned to put their hands into a big fish's mouth from the local
Indians, and the local Indians claim they've just known how to
do it all along.

A few years ago, Pat Mire made a film about hand fishing in
the bayous called *Anything I Catch: The Handfishing Story*. In it, he
reported that an old-timer was once asked what he did when a
snake occupied the hole he was exploring instead of a fish.

"Why, you jus' find yo' another hole," the old-timer said.

I kept thinking about the line as the big snake swam closer. I
was sure I saw it smiling. I kept looking over at Pat, just to make
sure he saw it too. I sensed that an intricate etiquette was involved in joining the animals in the swamp. I tried to stay cool
like Pat.

"Whoa, Pat," I said. "Before you go back down, just tell me if
this big snake here is poisonous."

I watched four huge mosquito bites enlarge on Pat's head like
small balloons. He seemed oblivious now, as if he'd moved into
some altered, meditative state. He was actually "fishing," feeling
things with his feet, occasionally touching submerged logs with
his hands and then diving down to feel the edges of holes in the
banks. He'd said the catfish — *goujon*, as the Cajuns call them —
tend to smooth out the entrances to their holes.

"Don't worry," he said. "I can smell water moccasins. You
know, my dad, he won't ever back away from a snake. He feels
one in a hole, and he grabs it by the tail and tosses it up on the
bank. I've seen him throw water moccasins out many a time.
Now, come on under and feel this log," he said. I jumped when

he grabbed my hand under the clouded water. He directed me to a huge log, the hole in its side marked by rough and deep ax cuts.

"Very old," Pat said. "Even in the late nineteenth century they would have used a rough-cut saw. Not many people have ever felt this log. They put the hole there to block off one side of the log. O.K., now. Let's just see if we got a fish inside."

I bunched up some crawfish sacks as Pat instructed and plunged my hands into the hole. I could barely keep my mouth above the surface, and I was sure that much of one hand was still exposed to whatever lurked inside the log.

"If you feel a bump, don't move," Pat said as he felt his way to the far side of the log, moving in huge, elliptical steps, like an astronaut across a stretch of moon. "The hardest thing to learn is not to move when he touches you. Just try. If you jerk back from a loggerhead, that's when he clamps off whatever he's got in his mouth."

"Can they see us, Pat?"

"Who?"

"The fish."

"Who knows?" he said, drawing in a big breath.

And with that, Pat went under, and in the next second I felt a powerful, wriggling force slam like a hard-swung baseball bat against my bare hand.

The Cajuns are descended from the French Acadians, whom the British deported from Nova Scotia in 1755. They began fishing with their hands because the nets and weirs their fishermen brought south didn't work in the tideless swamps and bayous of Louisiana. Over the years, as the refugees and their descendants and additions settled in the boggiest realms of the Deep South, they were known first as Cadiens and finally as Cajuns, the term applied by locals with whom they blended through the years. " 'Cajun' — as 'Indian' became 'Injun,' " Pat explained.

Most of Pat's films are based on his research into Cajun folkways. He left Eunice after college and grew out his hair. He hit the gringo trail in South America and lived on the Kenai Peninsula in Alaska.

"I came back starving for this," Pat said as we floated and shivered in the morass. "I came back for the music, the food, the talk, and to do things like this — things that set us apart from other people." The previous evening, out at Bubba's uncle's camp, some men had gathered for Cajun music and Cajun food and, apparently, to compare their scars. A local rice farmer was contending that it was a "big ol' blue cat" that had years ago pulled the skin off his left thumb.

"That's not what you said last time," somebody replied.

Camps are a Cajun institution. The one owned by Bubba's uncle is a ramshackle two-room dwelling with a big table and a bunch of plastic kitchen chairs. The 13,000 inhabitants of Eunice have seen better times than now, with the oil business dried up. The camps become more important when it gets like this. Though the camp is not far from town, the area nearby is heavily wooded. Hooks and chains for skinning fish and game protruded from several trees. An extremely heavy iron pot, very black, was sitting on a fire. Pat whipped up a fragrant catfish étouffée; a tray full of fat catfish steaks and another full of bullfrog legs the size of jackrabbit hinds sat nearby. Cayenne pepper was poured into the pot, and strangely sad and medieval music filled the night.

Pat was stirring in time with the music when somebody said, "We shoulda invited some women."

"What, and fuck the whole thing up?" Bubba replied.

I told Pat that a senior parks-and-wildlife official in Texas had told me that Texas, like Arkansas, outlawed grapplin' because it was thought unsporting, tantamount to dynamiting or electrifying a body of water. The official had added that catfish that will let you get a hand in their mouths are usually spawning. "One of those boys gets real good at it," the man had said, "and he can clean out a river."

"First," Pat said, "it's the male that guards the hole. The male shoves the female in there, but then she leaves. He stands guard until the eggs are hatched, upon which he begins to eat as many of his children as he can. I pull out a big old male, and the babies live. As to it not being sporting — compared to the sporting way of tricking a fish into thinking there's no steel hook inside his food — I jus' don't know what to say."

Several of the men at the camp offered me ironic compliments about my plan to follow Pat into a swamp full of snakes, turtles, and a particularly trashy sort of fish that's changed little since the Eocene epoch. One or two put their one arm not holding a beer around me and said that I must be fully accoutred in the anatomical sense. By the time his transcendent étouffée was ladled over plates of steaming rice, Pat was sitting on one of the frayed plastic chairs, waving away mosquitoes and trying to explain what you have to know to risk the primal vagaries of deep, dark holes. He tried to talk of what you had to feel inside to be able to convince a great big fish to fall into your grasp.

"You have to become part of the environment; you have to feel part of the same exact thing as that fish. You have to become larger than your own impulses. And you have to really use those hands." As he spoke, I thought about watching my six-year-old daughter playing in a pond a few weeks earlier. Several of her friends had been trying time and again to capture one of the hundreds of darting newts that teemed below the pond's surface. As the others gave up in frustration, my daughter — who likes to stand back and take in a scene before plunging in — slowly put one hand into the pond and waited. She drew it out and handed a wriggling newt to one of her friends. Then she reached back in and came out with another, handing a newt to each of her playmates, steady and calm. I waded in and tried to catch one for ten minutes, obviously out of sync, utterly in awe.

"I do it because it won't be done much longer," Pat was saying by the time the fiddles were being packed away. "I fish with my hands, well, jus' 'cause I can."

"Be mentally prepared," Pat said before he went down after the fish again. "Concentrate on not drawing back."

By now my feet had floated to the surface, but I was determined to block up the hole. A hogger from up north had told me that in the eight-foot waters he fished, one man will stand on a submerged hogger's back and others will pile on until sufficient weight is brought to bear to keep the bottom guy down; other times, two men will dive down and physically insert another into a deep hole.

Pat was under water for a very long time. He had told me that in the old days a hand fisher who could spend a few minutes under water was revered as a true *plonger*. Pat said it often takes some time to stroke and pet the fish.

"Otherwise they get wild," he said. (All the talkers on the subject pronounce it "while.") "And a wild cat you really don't need. You have to slowly feel what you've got. Then you've got to move in."

I felt another hard bump. Whatever hit me was very hard and even colder than the frigid water. Seconds later Pat shot out of the bayou, rising up like a Polaris missile, gasping for air. His left hand was spurting blood from having been deeply spined, but he was hugging a hideous-looking bit of prehistory to his chest, clutching as the fish slapped him hard in the gut. When the fish was finally glowering in the dust beside the bayou, two bare-chested teenagers in feed-store caps strolled onto the bank. "You the boy made the fee-ulm," one of them said to Pat.

"You teach us to fish?" said the other. "My great-grandfather could do it, but I don't know anybody who still knows how."

"Yeah, sure," Pat said, panting, bleeding, his wound swelling up like an extra digit, insect bites rising from his pate, mud coating his soaked clothes. "I'll teach you." The two boys smiled broadly as the incensed catfish below them just stared off into the eerie woods.

OCTOBER 1992

To be honest, I am not an outdoorsman. Furthermore, the only thing I like less than hunting or fishing is reading about someone else hunting or fishing. But DONALD KATZ'*s fine piece on a most curious art is both instructive and entertaining. Trust me — even if you can't stand the great outdoors either.* — F.D.

HOWARD KOHN

The Art of the Sprint

FROM THE LOS ANGELES TIMES MAGAZINE

EACH OF THE SIX, thinking he might someday be the fastest man in the world, went to Houston to check out the track coach Tom Tellez, and each of the six remembers Tellez telling him, straight off: "There are two ways to run a race. The right way, and the wrong way." Or, not beating around the bush: "The right way, and the way *you* run." Tellez did not pat any of them on the back. He did not smile. He just looked them in the eye, deadpan. The more they heard him go on in earnest detail about biomechanics and physics and kinesiology, never easing up, the more they had to wonder: *When is this old crank going to tell me how great I am?*

For each of them, even for Carl Lewis, the most dominant sprinter of all time, the question is still pending. Each of them, even Lewis, who as a high school senior in 1979 was chased right and left by recruiters but paid his own way to Houston to interview with Tellez, is still waiting to hear the coach say, "You did it! You ran it exactly right!" And Tellez is still waiting for one of them, perhaps Lewis, perhaps Leroy Burrell or Mike Marsh, or perhaps Joe DeLoach or Floyd Heard or Mark Witherspoon, to speed down the track with absolutely perfect form: arms stroking, strides long and easy, shoulders squared, no early lunging at the tape, earth-to-earth lightning from start to finish. Each of the six, every time he races, takes another run at reaching maximum potential.

But last May, under a piercing Texas sun, they had gathered solely to prepare and train. They tossed gym bags on the grass near a reddish-brown oval on the grounds of the University of Houston, the base of operations for Tellez, a native Southern Californian. They stretched and contorted themselves gracefully, methodically, as dancers do. All six were committed body and soul to Tellez. All were the eager subjects of that cheerless, brutally honest, scientifically guided perfectionist. Where other coaches might have seen runners destined to be good or even excellent, Tellez saw young men into whom he could pour his consummate knowledge of the sprint, transforming them into ten-second wonders. His quest had become their quest. Although they were all members of California's Santa Monica Track Club, they had taken up residence in and around Houston to be near Tellez. They had sworn off parties and worked with free weights and trimmed their diets to the essentials until their bodies were as splendidly exquisite as Greek statues. And they had exercised their minds, sharpening their focus, learning moxie, practicing mental reflexes, rehearsing a plan, because in that brotherhood of the righteous, select few, there was no one who won on sheer talent.

Tellez stood by while they loosened up. He was short and slim and deeply tanned, young-looking at fifty-eight save for hair gone white. His gaze was fixed on their every movement. "We're doing O.K., but we have to do better," he said, drolly pessimistic. "It's time to step it up." This was a month before the U.S. Olympic Track and Field Trials in New Orleans, two months before next week's opening of the Barcelona Games. That day in May, the six definitely ranked among the top fifteen in the world for the two sprint events, the 100 and 200 meters; they were arguably within the Top Ten, and conceivably they composed the top six.

But none of that assured them of the goal at hand: getting to Barcelona. "Other runners out there can beat them," Tellez said matter-of-factly (and prophetically, though he could not know it then). He constantly had to remind them of that.

This was all they knew in May in Texas: Each of them needed to reach maximum at the Games, not six weeks out in New Orleans. Yet no one could afford to hold back in the trials. All of them were twenty-five or older, well into their prime sprinting years. There might not be another Olympics for them. They *had* to qualify. They had to get to Barcelona, to the bright, flood-lighted track circling inside a Spanish stadium, the perfect place to show the world the meshing of their talent and his genius. The perfect opportunity to pursue once more the elusive purity of the perfect race.

Warm-ups over, Leroy Burrell and Mike Marsh are the first into the blocks. Burrell sports a mustache and a chronic five o'clock shadow. Thickly built, he has a body for heavier-duty sports but says he is not interested in a second love like pro football. Marsh, on the other hand, is the picture of smoothness. His head is shaved. His arm and leg muscles are slicked up under the skin instead of bulging through.

For as long as Burrell and Marsh have been racing, way back to high school, Carl Lewis has been The Man, but in the '90s these two have begun to give him a run for his money. In the past two years, Burrell's overall times have evened out as the best in the world in the 100 meters, and this year Marsh has come on, posting the fastest pretrials times for an American in both the 100 and 200.

A pistol is fired, and Burrell and Marsh charge ahead. "Keep turning over, keep turning over," Tellez barks out, by which he means, put one foot in front of the other as fast as possible, a concept so prehistoric it seems simple-minded of him to keep re-peating it to a pair of world-class athletes.

But the most basic elements of running take on new meaning when Tellez is your coach. "Swing through, swing through," he shouts at them. Under his breath he mutters to me: "Their knees are too high. Extra knee-lift doesn't do jack for you. You've got to swing your leg through." He stops to sniff a medicated in-haler. At the previous Saturday's meet in New York, he caught a cold when the temperature fell 40 degrees in four hours. "Your forward motion," he says, pantomiming the motions, "is based on the revolutions you make with your legs, and for every revo-lution, your feet have to hit the ground. The higher your knees are, the farther from the ground your feet are." He glares as Burrell and Marsh walk back 100 meters to the starting point. "Actually, there's a little more to it. With your knees too high, you sit back and lose momentum."

Actually, there's *a lot* more to it. Competitive running is hardly what it seems to be: ready, set, and go like hell. Every move is endlessly practiced and choreographed, based on the laws of Newton and assorted biomechanical principles. Other track coaches may understand psych-outs and the rest of the head game better than Tellez, but no one beats him at the science. Lewis, the phenom from suburban Philadelphia, surprised people by seeking out and choosing Tellez to be his college coach despite receiving the royal treatment from several bigger names, such as Jumbo Elliott of Villanova University, but in Lewis' mind his decision was not a close call. Tellez was different from everyone else because, rather than take Lewis' future greatness as a given, he told this long whip of a kid that only if he perfected his style would he have a shot at being great. The subsequent years are sports history.

Talking about the made-over Lewis, Tellez says: "Carl had a habit back then of really getting his knees up, which looked marvelous to fans and to sportswriters, and Carl was proud as can be. I had to tell him his knee-lift was a waste of energy and motion." Nothing in Tellez's expression changes, no chuckle, no half grin, nothing. He is as serious now as he was thirteen years ago. "Carl listened and went out and lowered his knees. He's an instinctive learner, completely tuned in to his body. Whatever I showed him, two minutes later he'd be out on the track implementing it." The perfect mimic, the perfect accentuator of the positive, Lewis won so many blue ribbons everyone lost count.

From the start, the relationship has been a two-way street. By the very nature of his incredible skills, Lewis has been an object lesson to Tellez. He was the sprinter who would define his sport, a breakthrough champion, the embodiment of all the abstracts of geometry and math and physics that Tellez had so studiously researched.

The traditional way of running a short race was to go all out, pretty much in freestyle fashion, and for most of Tellez's time in California, through his student years as a so-so hurdler and a jack-in-the-box halfback at Whittier College and as an up-and-coming coach at Buena Park High School, Fullerton College and UCLA, he was a traditionalist, coaching his runners as he had been coached. "All you used to hear a coach say was, 'Go, go, go.'

Running was thought of as voodoo. One guy was faster than another because of some mysterious power he had," he says. Eventually he noticed that the fastest runners had certain things in common, and it occurred to him that running freestyle was haywire: "I wanted to create a scientific model every runner could use."

Tellez boned up on basic notions about velocity and levers and anatomy. He took notes from scientific journals and the classic track textbooks. In the library, to his amazement, he also found a treasure trove of dusty master's and doctoral theses about the mechanics of running. He read them all. He assembled his own library: journals from Europe and the Soviet Union, every available piece of film, shots from every angle, every era, even those predating Jesse Owens. He watched them over and over. "Most coaches notice the dissimilarities between runners. I was looking for similarities. When you look carefully, you see the body works best only one way," Tellez says.

Studying Owens and the other greats on film, scanning their blurred bodies frame by frame, matching action against biomechanical principles, Tellez began to see how a race should be run. A lot of what he learned went against the grain. It was always assumed that you should start a race with your eyes on the finish line, but Tellez decided you should have your head aimed downward, as though to pitch face first onto the track. Unconventional and uncomfortable, yes, but it forces the rest of your body into the proper position for takeoff. From start to finish, he identified the other elements of mechanical perfection: a straight spine, head in alignment, an even backswing with the arms, long leg strides, knees bent at a natural point in the upswing and so on.

It seemed logical that a runner with good mechanics would be a faster runner. Armed with this theory, Tellez left an assistant's job at UCLA in 1976 for the head job at the University of Houston. There, the theory did produce all-conference runners out of typical student athletes. Then, three years later, along came the atypical and preternatural Lewis. Could Tellez turn a star into a superstar? Indeed he could. "Watching Carl get better and better was truly gratifying," he says. "I'd tell him about parabolic curves and acceleration curves, all the information I had, and he'd put it into action." Every time Lewis stepped onto the track, the science of running came stupendously to life.

Up until the Lewis era, the ten-second 100 had seemed virtually unattainable, except for a freakish 9.95 run by Jim Hines at the 1968 Olympics. In the past decade, however, Lewis, Burrell and Marsh, as well as two runners who don't train with Tellez but who belong to the same school of scientific thought, Calvin Smith and Dennis Mitchell, have shattered the barrier numerous times.

As word has spread, one potential Olympian after another — not only sprinters, but hurdlers, long jumpers, high jumpers, vaulters, javelin throwers and decathletes who understand that their performances depend in large measure on how well they can take advantage of the laws of motion — have arrived with their bags at Tellez's sweaty, Spartan quarters in the Jeppesen Fieldhouse, an old piece of flat architecture splotched throughout with Texas red. Tellez accepts some of the athletes and turns the others away. His criteria have less to do with their stat sheets than with their work ethic and their willingness to take criticism on the chin. And if they qualify, Tellez's expertise is offered essentially gratis. The Santa Monica Track Club, for instance, pays his expenses when he accompanies the sprinters to meets, but it is the university job, not coaching Olympians, that butters Tellez's bread.

Marsh and Burrell return to the blocks and, in tandem, run again. This time their movements seem at once more deliberate and more rhythmic.

'O.K., that's a little better," Tellez says, a high compliment, and the two take a break.

Burrell, who is twenty-five, grew up in the Delaware Valley not far from the scene of Lewis' schoolboy exploits, and he knew early on he wanted the same college coach as Lewis. In 1985, he arrived in Houston as a freshman and has been training with Tellez since. "The rah-rah coaches are fun, but you are basically on your own. Coach T is the opposite. He never fails to tell you what you're doing wrong," Burrell says, flopping down on the grass. "Some coaches are afraid to hurt your feelings. Not Coach T. He doesn't hesitate."

Marsh, also twenty-five but a relative newcomer in Houston,

goes over to scold two hurdlers, a man and woman, who are engaged in mock wrestling on the infield. "Hey, cut that out," he warns. "Somebody's going to get hurt." Tellez glances over, and the couple, flirting a bit as they go, head back to the track. On orders from Tellez, there is not supposed to be any horseplay that might result in injury.

Marsh sits down. "Coach T is in charge," he says. "We go to meets when he says and stay home when he says, even if we lose out on appearance fees. Money is never part of his decision-making. We trust him. He has a vision and a plan for our careers. Right now it's how to get to Barcelona." Right now Marsh would follow his coach over a cliff. After a long career as a middle-of-the-pack runner, through school in Hawthorne and undergraduate years at UCLA, Marsh came to Tellez in 1990, hoping that a new coach and a new approach would change his luck. At first, it didn't. At last year's U.S. championships, he struggled to fifth place in the 200 and seventh in the 100. But this year, just in time for the trials, Marsh all of a sudden was a legitimate contender.

The man to beat, though, was still Lewis, and after him, Burrell, who held the world record for the 100 through much of the 1991 season only to lose it to Lewis at the very end. There have been mechanical lapses for Burrell this year, but recently he has regained his form. "I kept telling him he had to bring his legs all the way through," Tellez says. "About a week ago, it clicked." Burrell gets to his feet at a signal from Tellez, a slight nod. No yogi ever controlled his surface demeanor better.

Over his shoulder, Burrell says: "When we're on the track with Coach T there are no stars." A smile and a wink. "Except for him."

The quiet one, Floyd Heard, leans against a cement wall, suffering from mental fatigue. "At this level, it's one hundred percent mental," Heard says. "Like Coach T is always telling us, 'Your body wants to work perfectly. It's your mind you have to concentrate on.'" Yesterday Tellez caught him overreacting to the gun, his head snapping up, and today Heard is working on that single flaw, over and over. Tellez calls for at least four practices a week, from 1:30 to 3:30 in the afternoons. Speed is the emphasis at half the practices, technique at the other half. The former leaves the runners with their tongues hanging out, but the latter is far more exhausting. They work on their technique until their brains feel fried.

Every flaw is worth a fraction of a second, and a fraction is all that separates Heard from Lewis, Burrell and Marsh. He has been a few hundredths of a second away from the magical ten-second 100, and this year he is the fourth regular, along with the three of them, on the Santa Monica Track Club 4 × 200 relay team, a quartet that broke the world record in April, at the Penn Relays in Philadelphia, despite one poorly executed handoff.

Baby-faced, with eyes that seem both merry and serious, the twenty-six-year-old Heard has been with Tellez since 1988. He had tried for a Houston track scholarship earlier, fresh from high school in Milwaukee, but the university was at its limit, so he settled for one from Texas A&M. After two years he left school and joined the Santa Monica club, training with Tellez. "At A&M I ran tensed up. My face was scrinched up. My shoulders were scrinched up. Coach T taught me to run relaxed," he says. "Being relaxed is the secret to my success."

Mark Witherspoon goes to the blocks and is next to get the hard once-over from Tellez. Witherspoon is twenty-eight, a long-legged, lean, rippling sprinter and relay man who heard of Tellez while at Abilene Christian College and began training with him in 1986. Though Witherspoon has not yet competed in a big international meet, he has been running some good times this year. He has always had the ability, Tellez says, but he just had to harness it.

"Running relaxed, that's the ticket," says Witherspoon. Each of the six will tell you the same thing. Tellez himself, when he's not zeroing in on specifics, chants a mantra, "Relax. Don't get quick. Slow down."

Slow down? It's one thing to turn conventional track-and-field wisdom on its head, but to tell a sprinter to run slowly? It is so opposed to what most people intuit about racing that it doesn't seem to make sense. Yet Tellez shakes his head, insisting, "Slow down! Slow down, and you'll go faster."

Of course, the riddle is obvious. It's Zen. Running a race is like running a life. Conserve yourself, pace yourself, attend to everything in its own sweet time, and you'll reach the finish in great shape. Notwithstanding that only a rare number of us get the hang of pacing ourselves over a span of seventy or eighty years, Tellez expects his runners to do this through a race that lasts all of ten seconds, not significantly longer than it takes to turn a page or blow a kiss. He expects them to do it because scientifically it makes total sense.

Tellez's runners know by heart the five phases of a sprint, which, when divided into percentages, provide the perfect game plan for a race. Phase 1: Reacting to the gun (1 percent). Phase 2: Clearing the blocks (5 percent). Phase 3: Accelerating to peak velocity (64 percent). Phase 4: Maintaining peak velocity (18 percent). Phase 5: Decelerating (12 percent).

According to a law of physics, runners must slack off once they've hit top speed just as objects that go up must come down once they've reached their highest point. At best, a runner has a second or two before deceleration sets in. Clearly most races are won or lost in Phase 3. Revving up too quickly means spending too much of a race trying to resist an implacable fact of science. You will start running on empty. "Here's a common situation. A guy gets the jump on you. Do you follow your instincts and turn on the afterburners? Well, if you do, you'll lose" is what Tellez tells his runners.

There are dozens of body motions that Tellez teaches, but he is not like some high-tech coaches who cannot simplify themselves. The whole of his philosophy can be summed up in his seemingly contradictory one-liner: *Slow down* (near the beginning of a race) *and you'll go faster* (into the finish). A hot flash in the first half of a race is a guy with a scrinched-up expression, clenched muscles, fading willpower and shortening strides in the homestretch, whereas one of Tellez's steady, easygoing runners is still gliding along with long kicks.

"*Just go!* — that's how I was brought up. It's taken me a long time to learn to race with a game plan," Marsh says.

The game plan does not come naturally, least of all to Joe De-Loach, and least of all to Joe DeLoach today. He is babying a sore quadriceps and has to go over the game plan only in his head. "All my life I've been somebody who likes to put the hammer down. On-your-mark-BOOM! I've had to fight to get control of that urge. I've had to fight to learn discipline and patience," DeLoach tells me. He has the scrubbed-clean handsomeness of the kid next door and a smile as big as a country mile. DeLoach, twenty-five, is the reigning Olympic gold medalist in the 200, and he was in tiptop condition, never running better, until the quad popped a week ago. It's not a serious injury, but the timing is terrible, and it's got him searching his soul. His entire career is up in the air.

This state of affairs is nothing new for DeLoach. He grew up in Bay City, Texas, 100 miles south of Houston, and DeLoach was thrilled in 1985 when Carl Lewis personally rode down to Bay City on a recruiting visit. DeLoach thereupon signed with Houston, only to discover Lewis' visit had been in violation of NCAA rules. The thrill ended up costing DeLoach a year of eligibility. During that year, Tellez expected DeLoach to keep himself primed, and when DeLoach got flabby mentally and physically he fell out of favor. The saving grace was that DeLoach, up close, is enormously likable, and Tellez, aided and abetted by Lewis, gave him a second look and decided to turn him into a special project.

The Tellez effect did not take hold right away, but when it did, DeLoach found himself at the 1988 Olympics in Seoul making the cut for the 200. Two lanes away from him in the finals was Lewis, the invincible man, high-stepping for the crowd. The two runners had become best friends, close as blood, but DeLoach had remained the little brother, the protégé. Up to that point Lewis had won six Olympic gold medals in six attempts. DeLoach looked up and down the track rather than sideways at Lewis. *The only person you're competing with is yourself.* Tellez had beaten that into his brain. DeLoach tried to visualize the race ahead, his body switching gears through the five phases *(slow down!)* and suddenly, "I could see myself doing it, just the way Coach T described it." And then suddenly he *was* doing it. Lewis, the runner-up, walked over to offer congratulations, feeling stunned, though not half as stunned as DeLoach.

Within months, however, DeLoach had to undergo surgery for a torn hamstring, and for the next three years other injuries kept him from running at 100 percent. Then his wife gave birth to Joe the third, and with the responsibility of a child on top of his medical problems, DeLoach began to think of retiring from competition. "I asked Coach T, 'Can I ever get back to where I've been?' Coach T is like a father. We love him and believe him on faith because he's never lied to us. He told me how badly I had to want it and how hard I had to work to come back," DeLoach says, "and I realized I could do it."

At a practice eight days ago, at long last, that superman glow began radiating through him again. The next day, still flushed, DeLoach came jogging around a curve to see Burrell and Marsh, legs cocked for a one-on-one, and in a split second he dropped into position alongside them and put the pedal to the metal. "Talk about falling into bad old habits, talk about dumb," he says. The pain in his quadriceps flared immediately.

"I've told them a thousand times you can't be careless, not this close to the trials," says Tellez, exasperated. Though DeLoach is the defending Olympic champion, he must run a qualifying time of 20.4 or better this year in the 200 merely to be invited to the trials. As things stand, he will have only one chance to do so, at a meet in Indianapolis on June 10. He rubs and massages his leg. "I can feel the knot, but it's getting looser every day. I'll be ready for Indianapolis," he says, and adds this, as if it were the lone variable: "Just pray the weather's good."

The reality is far more pessimistic. "It's a long shot," Tellez says candidly. He has a weary economy of expression that bespeaks a lifetime of experience. "I was watching Joe when it happened, but what could I do? He has to be responsible for himself," Tellez says, pausing. "I don't know. Maybe it is my responsibility. Joe was depending on me. I should've made him be more careful." There is more than a little heartbreak in his voice.

A sports car slides into the parking lot, and out bounds Carl Lewis, late again. "I'm here, I'm here!" Unquestionably the grand master, the oldest and boldest of the Santa Monica Six, he grabs a few hands and strips down to a pair of three-tone running shoes and tight, high-waisted blue shorts. He looks a bit otherworldly in this half-naked state, only hairless skin showing. "I feel good," he says. A chiropractor has been treating Lewis for tightness in his back, but he stretches out with no difficulty. "I think it's time to start stepping it up."

Hearing Lewis' pronouncement, Tellez cracks a smile, his first of the day. A while later there is a second smile, when I ask if any race has come close to perfection. "The finals last year in Tokyo," he answers, "when Carl set the record." This was in August at the world championships, which are held every two years. Lewis won the 100 in 9.86 seconds, the fastest officially recognized time ever, even though he was an underdog to Burrell going in. "Carl ran a beautiful race. He didn't hurry himself, he didn't take the lead till the last five meters, but I've never seen anyone finish so strong," Tellez says. "He was ninety-nine percent perfect. His only hitch was at the start, as usual."

It is no secret that, great as Lewis is, he has always reacted slowly to the gun. Against top competition he almost never is ahead in Phase 1 or Phase 2. A coach with a different perfectionist's bent would have fired starter's pistols at Lewis in practice until he was jumping out of his skin. But Tellez instead taught him a few compensatory tricks, such as pushing hardest out of the front block for better forward thrust, and convinced him that with his exceptional eight-foot strides, he need not worry about being behind early in a race. "He convinced me it could be to my advantage. Let the other runners worry about me catching up," Lewis says. "Coach T is such an unbelievable teacher, and the main thing he's taught me is to have confidence in the game plan. When you have confidence you can relax."

Before the Tokyo race Tellez did a couple of things he rarely does anymore. He gave Lewis a pep talk and openly predicted his victory. When the chips are down, he told Lewis, a true champion summons up massive will. You can't miss the bond between the two men, and, as much as anything, it is their deep-down belief in each other that unites them.

Given that Lewis will forever be Tellez's favorite, and given what I'd heard about the kind of guy Lewis is supposed to be, his reputation of being "a child who has climbed a tree and lost himself in the self-absorption of how far out on a limb he can go," as *Sports Illustrated* once put it, not to mention his high-rent wardrobe and his zest for publicity, you have to assume there is some resentment of him among his teammates. Maybe there is, but it's not detectable. On the contrary, Lewis' teammates will adamantly argue that he has endured a lot of bad press in order to give the sport of track more pizzazz and drama, as Muhammad Ali once did for boxing, thereby attracting sponsorship money for an annual six-month season of outdoor track meets.

Bonus money is divided among the top finishers, enabling runners who are long on speed but short on contracts to earn enough of a living to be out every afternoon with their coach rather than at day jobs. Lewis himself is financially well-off thanks to contracts with Panasonic Corporation, Kodak and other companies (it's estimated that he has earned $3 million to $4 million a year), but Lewis has continued to campaign nonstop to give his sport more professionalism and more equitable profit sharing. On a personal level, as far as his teammates go, he's involved them as partners in a sportswear merchandising business, called Modern Men Inc., that relies heavily on his commercial image. The company features African prints and designer running suits, including the nude-look suit made semi-famous by Lewis. The Lewis style is the rage of the European circuit, where mail-order sales have been brisk, and in January, the company opened a retail store in Houston.

Where Lewis really contributes to his teammates' careers, though, is on the practice field. Nothing focuses a runner like a chance to beat The Man. His training partner today will be Witherspoon. The rap on Witherspoon is that, because of injuries and perhaps a lack of mental toughness, he's never lived up to his potential. (His best performance was during a 1987 national championship in San Jose, where he defeated Lewis.) Now, when Lewis makes his move toward the blocks, Tellez tells Witherspoon: "I want you to run with Carl as long as he stays out here. He's going to be stepping it up, which is what you need." Witherspoon looks tired. The 88-degree temperature has been baking the pep out of us. But he follows Tellez's orders.

The irony is that this year, it's Lewis who needs the motivation. Lewis' performances in the early season have been sporadic, his attitude nonchalant. He has run the 100 and 200 only on occasion. Partly it's the distractions, the usual hounding by reporters and fans, plus time spent on expansion plans for Modern Men and a busy schedule shooting Panasonic commercials for a $17-million ad campaign to be launched during the Olympics. But there also are questions brought on by the fact that Lewis is turn-

ing thirty-one. And though it's true his physical skills remain second to none, as demonstrated so remarkably in Tokyo, he admits
to feeling a certain ennui. "Unless it's a big race I have trouble
getting myself up psychologically," he tells me. "There are kids
who go crazy trying to win every race, which is how I used to be,
but I've been around for such a long time that now I have to pick
my races where I really and truly want to get into it. I need the
adrenaline to flow."

Tellez, honest man that he is, says: "There is such a thing as
being too relaxed, and so far this year Carl is too relaxed. And
time is getting short." He crosses his arms and goes back to
watching his runners, watching for their imperfections.

As it would turn out, three of the Santa Monica Six would make
the Olympic sprint team, and three would not. DeLoach was the
first to lose out. His leg did not heal by the time of the Indianapolis meet, and he was rendered ineligible. "Now he will have to
decide how dedicated he's willing to be," Tellez said. "If he's dedicated enough, and I think he is, he'll be back running in Europe
by the end of the summer. And then next year there's the World
Championships."

For the fan who tunes in to track only on occasion, however,
what happened at the trials from June 19 to 28 in New Orleans
had to be more than a little confounding. Although Burrell qualified in the 100, as expected, he was uncomfortable in the blocks
and was called for a false start in the finals. And two virtual unknowns, Witherspoon and Marsh, stole the show. Witherspoon
ran the race of his life to qualify in the 100, and Marsh lived up
to his early-season promise, qualifying in the 200. Witherspoon
and Marsh, along with Burrell, qualified for the 4x100 relay
team as well.

On the other hand, Heard faded into the middle of the pack
in both the 100 and 200, and, of all people, Lewis faded, too. He
was fourth in the 200 and a desperate sixth in the 100. That was
good enough only for an alternate's spot on the relay team,
which he declined. Lewis intimated after the 100 race that he was
not feeling well. In fact, he was found to have a sinus infection.
Not since 1976, when he was fifteen, has Lewis not been among
America's Olympian runners. "It's nobody's fault but my own.

I've just felt flat all week long," he said, adding graciously, "I guess it's my turn to be on the sidelines rooting for my teammates."

There seems to be two ways to assess the outcome of this year's trials. One is to say that Witherspoon's and Marsh's performances, placing them in excellent positions for medals in Barcelona, have nicely proved Tellez's philosophy. The other is to say that Lewis' failure, which was the talk of the whole week, has done the opposite. Leave it to Tellez to have a third perspective. He does not want to diminish the value of winning or losing, he says, nor the value of the Olympics, but he wants it made clear there is a bigger picture. "When you lose, all you've done is lost a race. You haven't failed. Your philosophy hasn't failed," he says. He figures the philosophy itself is not as important as the fortitude it takes to carry through the ups and downs. "The real test is to go back out, work hard and succeed. Don't give up. The goal is to run your best race. Ultimately the goal is to run the ultimate race. Maybe I'll live long enough to see it."

JULY 19, 1992

This story illustrates how, in sports writing, the most interesting work can be done by someone new to the subject, who isn't burdened with knowledge of the X's and O's. An expert in track and field probably would have passed over the detail that fascinates HOWARD KOHN, *the archaeologist, as he studies this new culture with an altogether fresh eye.* — F.D.

MARK KRAM

No Pain, No Game

FROM ESQUIRE

OBSERVE, PLEASE, the human skeleton, 208 bones perfectly wrought and arranged; the feet built on blocks, the shinbones like a Doric column. Imagine an engineer being told to come up with the vertebral column from scratch. After years, he might produce a primitive facsimile, only to hear the utterly mad suggestion: Okay, now lay a nerve cord of a million wires through the column, immune to injury from *any* movement. Everywhere the eye goes over the skeleton, there is a new composition: the voluting Ionic thigh, Corinthian capitals, Gothic buttresses, baroque portals. While high above, the skull roof arches like the cupola of a Renaissance cathedral, the repository of a brain that has taken all this frozen music to the bottom of the ocean, to the moon, and to a pro football field — the most antithetical place on earth for the aesthetic appreciation of 208 bones.

After nine years in the NFL, Joey Browner of the Vikings is a scholar of the terrain and a rapt listener to the skeleton, the latter being rather noisy right now and animated in his mind. It is Monday morning, and all over the land the bill is being presented to some large, tough men for playing so fearlessly with the equation of mass times velocity; only the backup quarterback bullets out of bed on recovery day. The rest will gimp, hobble, or crawl to the bathroom, where contusions are counted like scattered coins, and broken noses, ballooned with mucus and blood, feel like massive ice floes. Browner unpacks each leg from the bed as if they were rare glassware, then stands up. The feet and calves throb from the turf. The precious knees have no complaint. The thigh is still properly Ionic. The vertebral column whimpers for a moment. Not a bad Monday, he figures, until he tries to raise his right arm.

The bathroom mirror tells him it's still of a piece. It's partially numb, the hand is hard to close, and the upper arm feels as if it's been set upon by the tiny teeth of small fish. Pain is a personal insult — and not good for business; he knows the politics of injury in the NFL. Annoyed, his mind caroms through the fog of plays from the day before, finally stops on a helmet, sunlit and scratched, a blur with a wicked angle that ripped into his upper arm like a piece of space junk in orbit. He rubs *dipjajong* — an Oriental balm — on the point of impact, dresses slowly, then slides into an expensive massage chair as he begins to decompress to a background tape of Chopin nocturnes, quieting and ruminative, perfect for firing off Zen bolts of self-healing concentration to his arm.

By the next morning, after re-creating his Monday damage probe, he appears more worried about his garden of collard greens and flower bed of perennials; given the shape of his arm, most of hypochondriacal America would now be envisioning amputation. That is what Browner would like to do, so eager is he to conceal the injury, so confident is he that he could play with one and a half arms. At six-three, 230 pounds, he is a diligent smasher of cupolas, who has made more than one thousand tackles in his career. He is the first $1 million safety in NFL history; a six-time All-Pro; and a two-time conscriptee to the all-Madden team, an honor given out to those who have no aversion to dirt, blood, and freeway collision.

His only peer is Ronnie Lott, with whom he played at USC. Lott put the safety position on the map, invested it with identity, separated it from the slugging linebackers and the butterfly cornerbacks. It is the new glamour position in the NFL, due in part to CBS's John Madden, a joyful and precise bone counter who always knows where the wreckage will lie. With schedule parity, the outlawing of the spear, the clothesline, and the chop block, with excessive holding, and so many tinkerings to increase scoring, pro football veered toward the static on TV. Madden, it's clear, wanted to bring some good old whomp back to the game, and he found his men in players like Lott and Browner. Now the cameras are sensitive to the work of safeties, the blackjacks of the defensive secondary.

Of all hitters, they have the best of it: time and space for fierce acceleration, usually brutal angles, and wide receivers who come to them like scraps of meat being tossed into a kennel. Lott delineates their predatory zest in his book, *Total Impact,* saying that during a hit, "my eyes close, roll back into my head . . . snot sprays out of my nostrils, covering my mouth and cheeks." His ears ring, his brain goes blank, and he gasps for air. He goes on to broaden the picture: "If you want to find out if you can handle being hit by Ronnie Lott, here's what you do. Grab a football, throw it in the air, and have your best friend belt you with a baseball bat. No shoulder pads. No helmet. Just you, your best friend, and the biggest Louisville Slugger you can find."

Like medical students, pro players do not often dwell on the reality of the vivisection room, so Lott is an exception, a brilliant emoter with a legitimate portfolio, but still a man who has a lot of pages to fill with body parts and brute-man evocations. Browner has no marquee to live up to — except on the field. He is a star, though not easily accessible in media-tranquil Minnesota, distant from the hype apparatus on both coasts, part of a team that always seems to avoid the glory portioned to it annually in preseason forecasts.

Tuesdays are black days at a losing team's quarters, soft on the body and miserable for the mind. It is the day when coaches slap cassettes of failure into machines, vanish, then emerge with performances graded, carefully selecting their scapegoats. Good humor is bankrupt. On this Tuesday, Viking coach Jerry Burns looks much like Livia in *I, Claudius,* who in so many words scorches her gladiators, saying: "There will be plenty of money for the living and a decent burial for the dead. But if you let me down again, I'll break you, I'll send the lot of you to the mines of New Media." Browner smiles at the notion. "That's it — pro football," he says. "You don't need me."

"No tears like Lott?" he is asked.

"No tears," he says. "I guess I don't have much of a waterworks."

"No snot?"

He laughs: "He must have some nose."

"What's total impact?"

"Like a train speeding up your spinal cord and coming out your ear. When it's bad."

"When it's good?"

"When you're the train. Going through 'em and then coming out and feeling like all their organs are hanging off the engine."

"You need rage for that?"

"Oh, yeah," he says. "The real kind. No chemicals."

"Chemicals? Like amphetamines?"

"Well, I don't know that," he says, shifting in his chair. "Just let's say that you can run into some abnormal folks out there. I keep an eye on the droolers."

"Your rage, then?"

"From pure hitting," he says. "Controlled by years of Zen study. I'm like the sun and storm, which moves through bamboo. Hollow on the inside, hard and bright on the outside. Dumb rage chains you up. But I got a lot of bad sky if I gotta go with a moment."

"Ever make the perfect hit?"

"I've been looking for it for years."

"What would it feel like?"

"It would *feel* like you've launched a wide receiver so far he's splashed and blinkin' like a number on the scoreboard. That's what you're after mostly."

"Sounds terrible."

"It's the game," he says, coolly. "If you can't go to stud anymore, you're gone."

"I get the picture."

"How can you?" he asks, with a tight grin. "You'd have to put on the gear for the real picture."

There is no dramaturgy with Browner, just a monotone voice, a somnolent gaze that seems uninterested in cheerful coexistence. Or, perhaps, he is a model of stately calm. His natural bent is to listen. He does come close to the psychological sketch work of Dr. Arnold Mandell, a psychiatrist with the San Diego Chargers some years back who visited the dark corners of a football player's mind. Now in Florida, Mandell says: "Take quarterbacks: two dominant types who succeed — the arrogant limit-testers and the hyperreligious with the calm of a believer. Wide receivers: quite interested in their own welfare; they strive for elegance, being pretty, the stuff of actors. Defensive backs: very smart, given to loneliness, alienation; they hate structure, destroy without conscience, especially safeties."

Is that right? "I don't know," says Joey. "But it's not good for business if you care for a second whether blood is bubbling out of a guy's mouth." Highlighted by cornices of high bone, his eyes are cold and pale, like those of a leopard, an animal whose biomechanics he has studied and will often watch in wildlife films before a game. An all-purpose predator with a quick pounce, no wasted motion, the leopard can go up a tree for a monkey ("just like going up for a wide receiver") or move out from behind a bush with a brutal rush of energy ("just what you need for those warthog running backs"). The mind tries for the image of him moving like a projectile, so massive and quick, hurling into muscle and bone. It eludes, and there are only aftermaths, unrelated to Browner. Kansas City quarterback Steve DeBerg served up the horrors in a reprise of hits he has taken: his elbow spurting blood so badly that his mother thought the hitter used a screwdriver; a shot to the throat that left him whispering and forced him to wear a voice box on his mask for the next six games; and this memorable encounter with Tampa Bay's Lee Roy Selmon: "Lee Roy squared up on me. The first thing that hit the ground was the back of my head. I was blind in my left eye for more than a half hour — and I didn't even know it. I went to the team doctor and he held up two fingers. I couldn't see the left sides of the fingers — the side Selmon had come from. I sat on the bench for a quarter."

Browner offers to bring you closer to the moment of impact. He puts some tape into the machine and turns off the lights. The figures up on the screen are black and white, flying about like bats in a silent, horrific dream. Suddenly, there is Christian Okoye, of the Chiefs, six-one, 260 pounds, a frightful excrescence from the gene pool, rocketing into the secondary, with Joey meeting him point blank — and then wobbling off of him like a blown tire. *"Boooom!"* he says. "A head full of flies. For me. I learned. You don't hit Okoye. He hits you. You have to put a meltdown on him. First the upper body, then slide to the waist, then down to the legs — and pray for the cavalry." Another

snapshot, a wide receiver climbing for the ball, with Browner firing toward him. *"Whaaack!"* he says. "There goes his helmet.
There goes the ball. And his heart. Sometimes. You hope." The
receiver sprawls on the ground, his legs kicking. Browner looks
down at him. Without taunting or joy, more like a man admiring
a fresco. "I'm looking at his eyes dilating," he says. "Just looking
at the artwork. The trouble is, on the next play I could be the
painting." Can he see fear in receivers?

"You don't see much in their eyes," he says. "They're con men,
pickpockets."

"Hits don't bother them?"

"Sure, but you tell it in their aura. When you're ready to strike,
you're impeding it, and you can tell if it's weak, strong, or out
there just to be out there."

"So they do have fear?"

"Maybe for a play or two. You can't count on it. They may be
runnin' a game on you. Just keep putting meat on meat until
something gives. But a guy like Jerry Rice, he'll keep comin' at
you, even if you've left him without a head on the last play."

"The film seems eerie without sound."

"That's how it is out there. You don't hear. You're in another
zone."

"So why not pad helmets? That's been suggested by some critics."

"Are you kidding?" he says. "Sound sells in the living rooms.
Puts backsides in BarcaLoungers for hours. The sound of violence, man. Without it, the NFL would be a Japanese tea ceremony."

The sound, though, is just the aural rumor of conflict, much like
the echo of considerable ram horn after a territorial sorting-out
high up in the mountain rocks. NFL Films, the official conveyer
of sensory tease, tries mightily to bottle the ingredient, catching
the thwack of ricocheting helmets, the seismic crash of plastic
pads, and every reaction to pain from gasp to groan. Network
coverage has to settle for what enters the living room as a stran-
gulated muffle. But in the end, the sound becomes commonplace, with the hardcore voyeur, rapidly inured in these times,
wondering: *What is it really like down there?* It has the same dulling
result as special effects in movies; more is never enough, and he

knows there is *more*. Like Browner says: "Whatever a fan thinks he's seeing or hearing has to be multiplied a hundred times — and they should imagine themselves in the middle of all this with an injury that would keep them home from work in real life for a couple of weeks."

What they are not seeing, hearing — and feeling — is the hitting and acceleration of 250-pound packages: kinetic energy, result of the mass times speed equation. "Kinetic energy," says Mandell, "is the force that dents cars on collision." He recalls the first hit he ever saw on the sidelines with the Chargers. "My nervous system," he says, "never really recovered until close to the end of the game. The running back was down on his back. His mouth was twitching. His eyes were closed. Our linebacker was down, too, holding his shoulder and whimpering quietly. I asked him at halftime what the hit felt like. He said: 'It felt warm all over.'" TV production, fortunately, can't produce Mandell's response. But there still remains the infant potential of virtual reality, the last technological stop for the transmission of visceral sensation. What a rich market there: the semi-reality of a nose tackle, chop-shopped like an old bus; the psychotic rush of a defensive end; the Cuisinarted quarterback; and most thrilling of all, the wide receiver in an entrechat, so high, so phosphorescent, suddenly erased like a single firefly in a dark wood.

Quite a relief, too, for play-by-play and color men, no longer having to match pallid language with picture and sound. Just a knowing line: "Well, we don't have to tell you about that hit, you're all rubbing your spleens out there, aren't you, eh?" But for now, faced with such a deep vein of images, they try hard to support them with frenetic language that, on just one series of plays, can soar with flights of caroming analysis. War by other means? Iambic pentameter of human motion? The mysterioso of playbooks, equal to pro football as quark physics? For years they played with the edges of what's going on below as if it might be joined with a 7-Eleven stickup or the national murder rate. It is Pete Gent's suspicion (the ex-Cowboy and author of *North Dallas Forty*) that the NFL intruded heavily on descriptions of violence, as it has with the more killer-ape philosophies of certain coaches. If so, it is a censorship of nicety, an NFL public relations device to obscure its primary gravity — choreographed violence.

But claw and tooth are fast gaining in the language in the

booth, as if the networks are saying, Well, for all these millions, why should we struggle for euphemism during a head sapping? Incapable of delicate evasion, John Madden was the pioneer. Ever since, the veld has grown louder in decibel and candid depiction. Thus, we now have Dan Dierdorf on *Monday Night Football,* part troll, part Enrico Fermi of line play and Mother Teresa during the interlude of injury (caring isn't out — not yet). There's Joe Theismann of ESPN — few better with physicality, especially with the root-canal work done on quarterbacks. Even the benignity of Frank Gifford seems on the verge of collapse. He blurted recently: "People have to understand today it's a violent, vicious game." All that remains to complete the push toward veracity is the addition of Mike Ditka to the corps. He said in a recent interview: "I love to see people hit people. Fair, square, within the rules of the game. If people don't like it, they shouldn't watch."

Big Mike seems to be playing fast and loose with TV ratings — the grenade on the head of the pin. Or is he? He's not all *Homo erectus,* he knows the show biz fastened heavily to the dreadful physics of the game. "Violence is what the NFL sells," Jon Morris of the Bears, a fifteen-year veteran, once said. "They say they don't, but they do." The NFL hates the V-word; socially, it's a hot button more than ever. Like drugs, violence carries with it the threat of reform from explainers who dog the content of movies and TV for sources as to why we are nearly the most violent society on earth. Pete Rozelle was quick to respond when John Underwood wrote a superb series in *Sports Illustrated* on NFL brutality a decade back. He condemned the series, calling it irresponsible, though some wits thought he did so only because Underwood explored the possibility of padding helmets.

Admittedly, it is not easy to control a game that is inherently destructive to the body. Tip the rules to the defense, and you have nothing more than gang war; move them too far toward the offense, and you have mostly conflict without resistance. Part of the NFL dilemma is in its struggle between illusion and reality; it wants to stir the blood without you really absorbing that it is blood. It also luxuriates in its image of the American war game, strives to be the perfect metaphor for Clausewitz's ponderings about real war tactics (circa 1819, i.e., stint on blood and you

lose). The warrior ethic is central to the game, and no coach or
player can succeed without astute attention to the precise fash-
ioning of a warrior mentality (loss of self), defined by Ernie
Barnes, formerly of the Colts and Chargers, as "the aggressive
nature that knows no safety zones."

Whatever normal is, sustaining that degree of pure aggression
for sixteen, seventeen Sundays each season (military officers will
tell you it's not attainable regularly in real combat) can't be part
of it. "It's a war in every sense of the word," wrote Jack Tatum of
the Raiders in *They Call Me Assassin*. Tatum, maybe the preemi-
nent hitter of all time, broke the neck of receiver Darryl Stingley,
putting him in a wheelchair for life; by most opinions, it was a
legal hit. He elaborated: "Those hours before a game are lonely
and tough. I think about, even fear, what can happen." If a mer-
ciless intimidator like Tatum could have fear about himself and
others, it becomes plain that before each game players must find
a room down a dark and distant hall not reachable by ordinary
minds.

So how do they get there, free from fear for body and performance? "When I went to the Colts," says Barnes, "and saw giant
stars like Gino Marchetti and Big Daddy Lipscomb throwing up
before a game, I knew this was serious shit, and I had to get
where they were living in their heads." Job security, more
money, and artificial vendettas flamed by coaches and the press
can help to a limited point. So can acute memory selection, the
combing of the mind for enraging moments. With the Lions,
Alex Karras took the memory of his father dying and leaving the
family poor; the anger of his having to choose football over
drama school because of money kept him sufficiently lethal. If
there is no moment, one has to be imagined. "I had to think of
stuff," said Jean Fugett of the Cowboys. The guy opposite him
had to become the man who "raped my mother."

But for years, the most effective path to the room was the use
of amphetamines. Hardly a book by an ex-player can be opened
without finding talk about speed. Fran Tarkenton cites the use of
"all sorts" of uppers, especially by defensive linemen seeking
"the final plateau of endurance and competitive zeal." Johnny
Sample of the Jets said they ate them "like candy." Tom Bass
even wrote a poem about "the man" (speed), a crutch he de-

pended on more than his playbook. Dave Meggysey observed that the "violent and brutal" player on television is merely "a synthetic product." Bernie Parrish of the Browns outlined how he was up to fifteen five-milligram tablets before each game, "in the never-ending search for the magic elixir." The NFL evaded reality, just as it would do with the proliferation of cocaine and steroids in the eighties.

The authority on speed and pro football is Dr. Mandell, an internationally respected psychiatrist when he broke the silence. He joined the Chargers at the behest of owner Gene Klein and found a netherland of drugs, mainly speed. One player told him "the difference between a star and a superstar was a superdose." Mandell tried to wean the players off speed and to circumvent the use of dangerous street product. He began by counseling and prescribing slowly diminishing doses, the way you handle most habits. When the NFL found out, it banned him from the Chargers. Mandell went public with his findings, telling of widespread drug use, of how he had proposed urine tests and was rebuffed. The NFL went after his license, he says, and the upshot was that after a fifteen-day hearing — with Dr. Jonas Salk as one of his character witnesses — he was put on five-year probation; he resigned his post at the University of California–San Diego, where he had helped set up the medical school.

"Large doses of amphetamines," he says now, "induce prepsychotic paranoid rage."

"What's that mean?" he is asked.

"The killer of presidents," he says.

"How would this show up on the field?"

"One long temper tantrum," he says. "Late hits, kicks to the body and head, overkill mauling of the quarterback."

"How about before a game?"

"Aberrant behavior. When I first got up close in a dressing room, it was like being in another world. Lockers being torn apart. Players staring catatonically into mirrors. I was afraid to go to the center of the room for fear of bumping one of them."

"Is speed still in use?"

"I don't know," he says. "I'd be surprised if it wasn't, especially among older players who have seen and heard it all and find it hard to get it up. Speed opened the door for cocaine. After speed, cocaine mellows you down." He pauses, says thoughtfully: "The game exacts a terrible toll on players."

Joey Browner is asked: "At what age would you take your pension?"

"At forty-five," he says.

"The earliest age, right?"

"Yeah."

"Should the NFL fund a longevity study for players?"

"Certainly."

"Are they interested in the well-being of players? Long term or short term?"

"Short term."

"Any physical disabilities?"

"Can't write a long time with my right hand. This finger here [forefinger] can't go back. It goes numb."

"How hard will the transition be from football?"

"I'll miss the hitting," he says.

"If someone told you that you might be losing ten to twenty years on your life, would you do it again?"

"Wouldn't think twice. It's a powerful thing in me."

"They say an NFL player of seven years takes 130,000 full-speed hits. Sound right?"

"Easy. And I remember every one."

Browner was answering modified questions put to 440 ex-players during a 1988 *Los Angeles Times* survey. Seventy-eight percent of the players said they had disabilities, 60 percent said the NFL was not interested in their well-being, and 78 percent wanted a longevity study. Browner was with the majority on each question. What jolted the most was that pro football players (66 percent of them) seem to be certain they are dying before their time, and that 55 percent would play again, regardless. The early death rate has long been a whisper, without scientific foundation. "We're now trying to get to the bottom of this idea," says Dr. Sherry Baron, who recently began a study for the National Institute for Occupational Safety and Health. "From the replies we get, a lot of players are nervous out there."

The Jobs Rated Almanac seemed to put the NFL player near the coal miner when it ranked 250 occupations for work environment. Judged on stress, outlook, physical demands, security, and income, the NFL player rose out of the bottom ten only in income. With good reason. The life is awful if you care to look past the glory and the money; disability underwriters, when they don't back off altogether, approach the pro as they would a career bridge jumper. Randy Burke (former Colt), age thirty-two when he replied to the *Times* survey, catches the life, commenting on concussions: "I can talk clearly, but ever since football my words get stuck together. I don't know what to expect next." And Pete Gent says: "I went to an orthopedic surgeon, and he told me I had the skeleton of a seventy-year-old man."

Pro football players will do anything to keep taking the next step. As it is noted in Ecclesiastes, *There is a season* — one time, baby. To that end, they will balloon up or sharpen bodies to murderous specification (steroids), and few are the ones who will resist the Novocain and the long needles of muscle-freeing, tissue-rotting cortisone. Whatever it takes to keep the life. A recent report from Ball State University reveals the brevity and psychic pain: One out of three players leaves because of injury; 40 percent have financial difficulties, and one of three is divorced within six months; many remember the anxiety of career separation setting in within hours of knowing it was over.

What happens to so many of them? They land on the desk of Miki Yaras, the curator of "the horror shop" for the NFL Players Association. It is her job to battle for disability benefits from the pension fund, overseen by three reps from her side, three from the owners. For some bizarre reason, perhaps out of a deep imprinting of loyalty and team, players come to her thinking the game will be there for them when they leave it; it isn't, and their resentment with coaches, team doctors, and ego-sick owners rises. Her war for benefits is often long and bitter, outlined against a blizzard of psychiatric and medical paperwork for and against. She has seen it all: from the young player, depressed and hypertensive, who tried to hurtle his wheelchair in front of a truck (the team doctor removed the wrong cartilage from his knee) to the forty-year-old who can't bend over to play with his children, from the drinkers of battery acid to the ex-Cowboy found wandering on the desert.

"It's very difficult to qualify," Yaras says. "The owners will simply not recognize the degenerative nature of injuries. The plan is well overfunded. It could afford temporary relief to many more than it does. I even have a quadriplegic. The doctor for the owners wrote that 'his brain is intact, and he can move his arm; someday he'll be able to work.' They think selling pencils out of an iron lung is an occupation."

On Saturday, Joey Browner begins to feel the gathering sound of Sunday, bloody Sunday. He goes to his dojo for his work on *iaido*, an art of Japanese swordsmanship — not like karate, just exact, ceremonial patterns of cutting designed to put the mind out there on the dangerous edge of things. He can't work the long katana now because, after thirty needles in his arm a couple of days before, it was found that he had nerve damage. So, wearing a robe, he merely extends the katana, his gaze fixed on the dancing beams of the blade, making you think of twinkling spinal lights. What does he see? The heads of clever, arrogant running backs? Who knows? He's looking and he sees what he sees. And after a half hour you can almost catch in his eyes the rush of the leopard toward cover behind the bush where he can already view the whole terrible beauty of the game, just a pure expression of gunshot hits, all of it for the crowd that wants to feel its own alphaness, for the crowd that hears no screams other than its own, and isn't it all so natural, he thinks, a connective to prehistoric hunting bands and as instinctually human as the impulse to go down and look at the bright, pounding sea.

JANUARY 1992

As with Pat Jordan, MARK KRAM started off on the other side in sports, as a minor league ballplayer. Much of Mark's memorable work, though, has been in the more primevil world of boxing. His fascination with the brutality that men do to their fellows in the name of sport has never seemed more eloquently put than in this piece on football violence. This article is important, too, because the subject needs to be more honestly aired by football writers. — F.D.

DAVE BARRY

The Old Ball Game

FROM TROPIC

YOU KNOW THAT next year Florida will have a major league base-ball team, the Florida Marlins. But what you might not know is that this year, the Marlins have a minor league team, the Erie Sailors. A fortunate few of the hopeful young players in Erie this summer could some day realize their ultimate dream — to make the big leagues, and to step onto the field at Joe Robbie Stadium. Of course, they'll probably drown, inasmuch as the field will be under eight feet of water from the typical frog-choking South Florida summer thunderstorms. But that's part of the excitement that makes us love the game of baseball.

In fact, the editors of *Tropic* magazine love baseball so much that they decided to take the time out from their busy schedule of playing golf during work hours to send me up to Erie to check out the Sailors. I was the logical choice for this assignment, because I am known to be a real baseball "nut." I'm always talking about the game with my assistant and fellow fan, Judi Smith:

JUDI: "Did you believe Lemke last night?"

ME: "Lemke?"

JUDI: "The second baseman. For the Braves. In the World Series."

ME: "They're having the World Series?"

And so, after doing some preliminary research to determine exactly which state Erie is located in (Pennsylvania), I set out to find the Sailors. Here is my scouting report:

Friday

I arrive in Erie on a connecting flight from Detroit aboard one of those bouncy propeller planes that are always flown by what appear to be teenagers. Although it's August, the Erie weather is cold and rainy, possibly because of a nearby lake, which by an "eerie" coincidence *(rim shot)* is also named "Erie." It appears to be quite large.

I rent a car and tune the radio in to a station broadcasting a Cleveland Indians pre-game show. The announcer is interviewing former major league pitcher Mel "Chief" Harder, who pitched against Lefty Grove sixty years ago in the first game ever played at Cleveland's Municipal Stadium. The announcer is asking the kinds of questions that only sports announcers are capable of asking.

"Were you cognizant of the thrill, Mel?" he asks.

Mel acknowledges that, yes, he was cognizant of the thrill, but mainly he was cognizant of trying to get guys out.

A few minutes out of the airport I become cognizant of reaching my motel, the El Patio. It's on the west side of Erie, just down the road from a place called the Lager Café, which has a sign that boasts "All Legal Beverages."

The El Patio motel is getting on in years, but it's clean and the staff is friendly. I check into my room and head for the lounge, which is called Choo-Choo's and has an electric train running around on a track up by the ceiling. Choo-Choo's is filling up with a happy-hour, TGIF-type of crowd, keeping the waitress busy.

"I need a bourbon and cranberry juice," she is saying to the bartender.

"A bourbon and *what?*" he says.

"Cranberry juice," she says.

"Yuck," observes the bartender.

Meeting me in Choo-Choo's are two journalists from the *Erie Times:* Kevin Cuneo, who's the sports editor and an Erie native; and Dave Richards, who's a sports writer AND the paper's rock critic, writing under the name "Dr. Rock." They describe Erie as an ethnic, blue-collar, wings-and-pizza, neighborhood-tavernon-the-corner kind of town. They say that although Erie is the third-largest city in Pennsylvania (the metropolitan-area population is close to 300,000), it tends to have an inferiority complex, living in the shadow of Pittsburgh, Buffalo and Cleveland, all of which are about one hundred miles away.

"The feeling some people have," says Cuneo, "is that, if it's from Erie, it can't be any good." It would not be easy, living in the shadow of Cleveland. This is not to say that Erie has nothing to boast about. Consider the following:

• During the War of 1812, the American ships used in the Battle of Lake Erie were built in Erie. (The actual battle, however, was fought near Sandusky, Ohio.)

• Bob Hope was married in Erie. He was on his way to Niagara Falls, but apparently he couldn't wait.

• In a cemetery right next to the El Patio motel, there's a gravestone that says, in large letters, "HAMBURGER." Almost directly across the street is . . . a McDonald's. (While I was in Erie, several people told me about this point of interest.)

• According to Dave "Dr. Rock" Richards, "some tourism people claim that Erie has the second-best sunsets in the world."

But one of the best things about Erie, at least for sports fans, is professional baseball. The Sailors have been in Erie since 1890, when they played in the Iron and Coal League. Over the years they've been affiliated with a number of big-league teams, including most recently the St. Louis Cardinals and the Baltimore Orioles. They currently have a one-year contract with the Marlins, expiring at the end of this season. The basic deal is that the big-league team provides the players and coaches, and pays them; the minor league organization provides a place to play, and gets its income from ticket and concession sales.

The Sailors play in the New York–Penn League, against teams like the Elmira Pioneers and the Niagara Falls Rapids. These are short-season, Class A teams — the second-lowest rung on the baseball ladder. (The lowest rung is the rookie league; the Florida Marlins' only other farm team this year is a rookie-league team, called the Marlins, based in Kissimmee.) From short-season Class A, the players hope to climb to full-season Class A, then Class AA, then Class AAA, and finally to the major leagues. Most will never come close. But there's always hope: Of the hundreds of guys who've played for the Sailors since 1981, nineteen have made it to the majors. None of them became big stars, but they got there. That's the dream.

The Sailors play at Ainsworth Field, which was built in the early 1900s, with a new grandstand added as a WPA project in the 1930s. Future superstars Pete Rose and Tony Perez played there as minor leaguers, and old-time Sailors fans will tell you about the 1932 exhibition game at Ainsworth in which Babe Ruth hit a home run so hard that the ball came down in approximately 1934.

So Ainsworth is a semi-historical landmark, but it's also a headache: Major league officials have decided that it's below minimum stadium standards. Unless Erie builds a new stadium by 1994, the Sailors will be unable to affiliate with a big-league team. Cuneo is part of a group trying to get a new stadium built, but there's a big political hassle about where to put it and how to pay for it. So the Sailors' fate is up in the air, like a high fly ball on a gusty day.

Speaking of weather, the game is rained out the day I arrive, so Cuneo takes me to Hector's, a legendary local Italian restaurant named for the late owner, Hector DiTullio. Kevin tells me that back in 1967, when the Sailors were a farm club for the Detroit Tigers, Hector and his wife, Angie, played an important role in keeping the team going when the Sailors' owner ran out of money.

"He couldn't afford to pay the players," Cuneo says, "so he made Hector a partner. What this meant is that for a month, Hector and Angie fed the players for free."

Hector died in 1991, but his spirit lives on in the form of pictures of him on the wall with celebrity patrons such as Perry Como and Vic Damone. Cuneo tells me that another famous Hector's patron is Los Angeles Dodgers Manager Tommy Lasorda, who is especially fond of a dish called "tripe," which I believe is the stomach of a cow.

Cuneo says that during the 1988 World Series between the Dodgers and the Oakland A's, he reminded Lasorda that they had met at Hector's, and Lasorda said, "Tell that s.o.b. Hector to send me some tripe!" And so Hector did, express-shipping fifty pounds of it out to California. Perhaps this is mere coincidence, but the Dodgers went on to beat the A's in four straight games. Cuneo says that in the triumphant world-champion Dodger locker room, Lasorda was drinking champagne and eating Hector's tripe. It was major-league tripe.

I myself would rather eat old linoleum than the stomach of a cow, so I order ravioli with Italian sausage. It comes in a huge portion, and it costs less than you pay for a small salad at many restaurants in Miami. As we're eating, Angie comes out from the kitchen to check on the customers. She seems to know everybody in the restaurant. The ravioli is delicious. I'm starting to like Erie a lot.

Saturday

Saturday is beautiful — the sky bright blue, the temperature in the seventies, a perfect day for baseball. I spend the morning driving around Erie. Most of it doesn't seem to have changed much since the 1930s or 1940s — neighborhood after neighborhood of tree-lined streets with rows of neat wood-frame and brick houses, American flags fluttering over carefully tended little yards. People are washing their cars, mowing their lawns, walking to the corner store, sitting on their front porches; kids are playing catch, riding their bikes. The whole town looks like a commercial for something extremely wholesome.

At noon I head for the West Erie Plaza, where a Sailors promotional event is scheduled. The plaza is a nonenclosed, strip-type shopping center, and when I arrive, two figures are sitting behind a battered green table set up outside Watson's Men's Wear. One of the figures is a person wearing a well-worn sea gull costume, with a large droopy yellow bill sticking out the front, a tail in the back and a sailor's cap on its head. This is the Sailors' comical mascot, the Sea Gull.

The other figure is Sean Gousha, a twenty-one-year-old catcher from Escondido, California. He's your white-bread, all-American boy: tall, lanky, red-haired and freckled. He looks exactly like a flesh-and-blood version of Archie, from the comics. You expect Betty, Veronica and Jughead to show up at any moment.

Gousha is not exactly a hot prospect. He was picked in the 39th round of the 1992 draft, and has played in only nine of Erie's 44 games so far. He's batting .138. He's a long shot in a long-shot league. But you'd never know it to talk to him: He's cheerful, friendly, smiling, positive. He has been sent to the West Erie Plaza to promote the Sailors, and by gosh he is promoting them.

No crowd has gathered for this promotion, so Gousha corrals shoppers as they walk past.

"Hi!" he says to a man with two boys. "You guys baseball players?"

"No," says the man. "Soccer."

"I'm with the Sailors," says Gousha. "My name's Sean. I'm the catcher. One of the catchers. You guys want a bumper sticker?"

"O.K.," say the boys.

Sean signs a bumper sticker, and so does the Sea Gull, who writes "Mr. C-Gull."

Sean gives the sticker to the boys. "You want to come see us play tomorrow night?" he asks. "They're giving away tickets in the men's store."

"O.K., maybe," says the father. They go into the store.

A little boy, maybe nine, walks up.

"Hi!" says Sean. "You a big Sailors fan?"

The boy says: "My mom saw in the paper? That there was Erie Sailor tickets?"

"Sure!" says Gousha. "They'll give 'em to you inside. Tell 'em how many you need. You want me to sign a bumper sticker? My name's Sean. I'm a catcher on the team."

"O.K.," says the boy.

Gousha, like the other Sailors, makes $850 a month, plus $16 a day for meal money. Bear in mind that, in the major leagues, the *average* salary is $1.1 million a year. The superstars make much more, of course: $5.4 million a year for Jack Morris; $5.8 million for Bobby Bonilla; $7.1 million for Ryne Sandberg. (When Sandberg signed his contract, Jose Canseco, scraping by on $4.7 million a year, was quoted as saying: "They can't complain about my contract. I'm one of the poorest guys in baseball.")

And of course you do not see these highly paid players spending their afternoons at shopping centers, chatting with people, signing bumper stickers, hustling tickets. Some major leaguers don't like to give autographs, or even get near the fans. Some of them seem to view the public as nothing more than a pain in the butt.

I ask Sean Gousha about this.

"I can see how dealing with the fans all the time would become tedious," he says. "But you have to realize that these people look up to you. They're putting out an effort to support *you*."

A man walks past.

"Hi!" says Gousha. "You want to see the Sailors play tomorrow night?"

"I'm a truck driver," the man says. "I'm on the road."

"Too bad," says Gousha.

Gousha's plan is to stick with baseball as long as he can, see how far he can get up the ladder.

"When else can you do it?" he asks. "If you're not good enough, you get on with your life, get a suit and tie, a nine-to-five job. But right now, I'm happy. I'm playing baseball every day. It's my *job*."

He shakes his head, amazed by this stroke of good fortune.

Sweating inside the Sea Gull costume is Steve Factor, twenty-six, who, when he's not being a comical mascot, is a computer specialist and woodworker. He doesn't talk when there are civilians around — that would be contrary to Standard Mascot Procedure — but he opens up when it's just the three of us.

He says it isn't all fun and games, being the Sea Gull.

"I get called a *duck*, a *pigeon*, an *eagle*," he says. "And they pull my tail *constantly*. But basically, everybody likes the Sea Gull. Except when I beat a kid in the Base Race."

The Base Race is a promotion at Sailors games wherein a fan races the Sea Gull around the bases, hoping to win a $25 gift certificate.

"The players are always telling me to win, so if I *lose*, the players hate me, but if I *win*, the crowd hates me."

Gousha looks sympathetic. "It's a Catch-22," he says, seemingly without irony. "A no-win situation."

"Yup," says Factor, nodding his Sea Gull head.

I ask Factor who his major professional influences are.

"The San Diego Chicken is the best," he says. "Also the Pittsburgh Pirate. I've learned a lot from both."

He stops talking as a man approaches.

"Hi!" says Gousha. "You a Sailors fan?"

"Not this year," says the man, walking past.

Factor continues: "My dream is to go to the majors, too," says Factor. "That would be neat, if the Marlins would ask me to be the mascot."

Everybody wants to make the big leagues.

As I leave, Sean Gousha, professional baseball player, is explaining to some fans that they should clean off the bumper before they put the sticker on.

I drive all the way across Erie, to the east side, where another Sailors promotion is under way in the parking lot of A. Duchini Inc., a hardware store. Set up around the parking lot are displays of various types of merchandise, including a nice selection of toilet seats. Over to one side, representing the Sailors, are two pitchers, Jerry Stafford and Pat Leahy, both big, blond guys. Like Sean Gousha, they're sitting at a beat-up table; in front of them are little paper cups filled with paint, so they can do face paintings on any fans who are interested.

I ask Stafford and Leahy if anybody told them, when they got into professional baseball, that they'd need to know how to paint faces.

"They forgot to mention that," says Leahy.

"But we're pitchers," says Stafford. "We can adjust."

On hand is a crowd of a few dozen people, but they're not paying any attention to the Sailors. They're more interested in four cheerleaders for the Buffalo Bills pro football team, which is in Erie today for a scrimmage. The cheerleaders, called the "Buffalo Jills," will also be appearing at the Sailors game tonight. Their shorts are so tight that it's hard to imagine anybody wearing them and breathing at the same time.

The other big attraction is the Rocket 101 booth. Rocket 101 is a radio station doing a remote broadcast from the parking lot. The crowd has lined up to spin a carnival-type wheel; depending on where it stops, people can win six-packs of Pepsi, hats, T-shirts, Sailors tickets, or — if they're lucky — a chance to get inside the Money Machine.

The Money Machine looks like an oversize telephone booth. Inside, scattered on the floor, are a few dozen dollar bills. When a contestant gets inside, a powerful fan is turned on, causing the bills to swirl wildly around while the contestant tries to grab as many as possible and shove them through a slot before the fan shuts off. Contestants get to keep whatever money they push out.

Emceeing the promotion is a disc jockey who identifies himself as "The Weasel."

"It's my given name," he announces.

The Weasel strides around the parking lot with a wireless microphone, schmoozing with the crowd, doing a play-by-play of the wheel spins, announcing the prizes. A cheer goes up when a large woman named Eileen wins a chance in the Money Machine. She puts on a pair of safety glasses, then climbs into the booth. The Weasel turns on the fan. The dollar bills fly up and flutter violently around Eileen, who tries frantically to snatch them, waving her arms wildly, looking not unlike Tippi Hedren being attacked by the birds in Hitchcock's *The Birds*. The crowd, encouraged by The Weasel, cheers.

In a few seconds the fan shuts off and Eileen gets out. The Weasel dramatically counts out her winnings: ". . . nine, ten, eleven, twelve DOLLARS!" The crowd applauds. So do the Buffalo Jills. So do professional baseball players Jerry Stafford and Pat Leahy, sitting alone at the face-painting table.

I leave and drive over to historic Ainsworth Field, home of the Sailors. It's in a neighborhood of small but well-maintained homes. There's no parking lot; the grandstands are right across a narrow street from the houses. The fans park on neighborhood streets. Ainsworth also has no locker room: The Sailors change and shower in a junior high school next door. In fact, the school is a little *too* close, occupying an area where a good chunk of right field should be. The result is that the right-field fence is a very short 290 feet from home plate; this is a big reason why major-league baseball is unhappy with Ainsworth. It was good enough for the Babe, but times change.

I enter the stadium through the Sailors office, a tiny, cluttered room with boxes of fruit on the floor (for the players). I walk out onto the field and look up at the grandstands, which hold 3,500 people. They're old and dingy, but they're close to the field, wrapped around from first base to home to third; not a bad seat in the house.

The field looks like it's in pretty good shape, the grass lush from all the rain. The outfield fence is covered with advertising signs, including one for Choo-Choo's ("Wet Your Whistle"). In center field there's a small electric scoreboard. In left there's a big old scoreboard, the kind where somebody has to put up the numbers by hand. Painted on it, in large letters, are the words WASTE MANAGEMENT.

I walk across the infield, out into right field, and turn to look back toward home. My mind fills with boyhood memories. All of them are bad. I played Little League baseball in Armonk, New York, and spent many an inning standing in right field, where I was supposed to catch the ball if, God forbid, anybody ever hit it to me. I prayed that this wouldn't happen, because I never, not once, caught an airborne ball. Defensively, my team would have done just as well to put a floor lamp out there. Most innings I had nothing to do, but every once in a while there'd come a sickening moment when the batter would swing and the ball would come flying in my direction, way up in the air, and people would be yelling at me, and I'd start running, not necessarily in any specific direction, just *running*, and, whump, the ball would land somewhere, never where I was, and people would be REALLY yelling at me now, and I'd run over and pick up the ball and throw it as hard as I could in the general direction of the yelling people, but by then the other team had scored eight or ten runs.

I never dreamed about playing in the major leagues. I just dreamed that Little League would be *over*.

I walk through a door in the outfield fence, directly behind which is the massive wall of the junior high school, and another door. I enter the school and climb some stairs, then find myself in the Sailors locker room, which is actually the school gym, with temporary lockers set up in the middle of the basketball court. It's a spacious arrangement.

Off to the side is the door to the girls' locker room; over the door are some strips of tape, on which is written:

MANAGER'S OFFICE
FREDI GONZALEZ

Fredi Gonzalez is inside, sitting at a desk, looking at a page of names and numbers. He's listening to something through earphones. I figure he's checking out the stats for tonight's opponent, maybe listening to a scouting report. But he laughs and tells me he's just browsing through a book listing all minor league players, seeing what happened to guys he has known over the years. He's listening to a Santana album.

Gonzalez, twenty-eight, is an easygoing guy with a stocky build. Born in Cuba, he came to Miami at age three and became a star catcher at Southridge High. He was drafted by the Yankees and spent six years in the organization, but he never got out of Class AA ball. Couldn't hit. He went into coaching, first at the University of Tennessee and then for the Miracle, an independent Class A team based in Pompano. And now he's in the Marlins organization, with another shot at the big leagues. But he has no complaints about being in Erie.

"The people here are great, incredibly friendly," he says. "When we first got here, we got off the plane, and right there at the airport people were offering the players places to stay. They'd say, 'I got an extra room, $50 a month, and you get meals.' It was amazing. These people really love this team."

I ask him how he likes Ainsworth Field.

"It has a *lot* of charm," he says, laughing. "Really, look at this view."

He opens his office window, and we both lean out. We're looking down onto right-center field, with the infield and grandstands beyond. A nice breeze is blowing toward us. The sky is a brilliant blue, the ballfield grass a deep, glistening green. I'm expecting to see Kevin Costner out there playing catch with his dad's ghost.

"How many managers have a view like this from their offices?" Gonzalez asks. "This is great. This is minor league baseball. I'm in a profession that's *fun*. How many people can say that?"

As I leave, Gonzalez is settling back at his desk in the girls' locker room, picking up his players book, checking on guys he's known, seeing who ended up where in baseball.

Tonight's Sailors game is a double-header against the Geneva (New York) Cubs, scheduled to start at 6:05. By 5:30 a couple of hundred people are lined up outside the Ainsworth Field ticket booth. Grandstand seats are $3.75; reserved grandstand seats are $4.50. The bleachers are $3.

It's a cheerful, family crowd; there are a lot of kids. There's a high percentage of guys with potbellies and baseball-style caps that they probably never take off except maybe to attend the funeral of somebody they really liked. A lot of the people seem to be regulars, very comfortable with this ballpark, *their* ballpark. Many wander over to the fence to watch the Sailors warming up on the field.

Just inside the stadium entrance is a guy with a grill selling hot dogs for $2. Two kids walk past.

"Two dollars for a *hot dog?*" one is saying. "No *way.*"

Up in the stands, in a little alcove, is the official card table of the Erie Sailors Boosters. Overseeing the table, as she does every game, is Club President Mary Shchouchkoff, twenty-seven, who is a billing clerk in a hospital pharmacy and a true Sailors fanatic. She's selling club memberships for $5; members get to take bus trips to away games, choose the Player of the Week, hold a picnic for the players, and bring them cards and cakes on their birthdays. Shchouchkoff also helps the team find Erie residents willing to house players.

As I pass by, she's talking to some fans, promoting an upcoming road trip.

"If we get the same bus driver as last time," she says, "we may stop at Niagara Falls on the way back."

I head up to the press box, at the top of the grandstand behind home plate. There I find Skip Weisman, who's the Sailors' president and general manager, which means he's responsible for nine billion details: the tickets, the programs, the lights, the press, the field, the souvenirs, the Sea Gull, the hot dogs, and whatever else is needed. During games, he's in constant motion, talking to people, checking on things, handling problems, always calm.

To keep the fans entertained, Weisman runs a lot of special promotions: Batting Glove Night, Bob Uecker Night (really), Umbrella Night, Fanny Pack Night, etc.

"In June we had Beach Towel Night," he says. "It was fifty-five degrees and rainy. That didn't do so well."

Tonight is Buffalo Jills Night, and there's a good crowd on hand, nearly three thousand people. The promotion coming up Monday (it kills me that I'm going to miss this) is The Dynamite Lady.

"Her big thing," Weisman says, "is she builds this little Styrofoam Coffin of Death. Then she goes inside, closes it up, sets it off, and KABOOM, there's a *real* loud noise and it blows apart. And then hopefully she walks away."

Weisman's goal is to own his own minor league team.

"Everybody always assumes I want to get a job with a major league team," he says. "But if I ran a team in the majors, what would I do? Argue with players' agents all the time? Write checks for seven million? Here, I get to do everything."

One thing he gets to do is carry the ballpark organ up to the press box. The organ is actually one of those plastic electronic keyboards, which gets plugged into the PA system. The official organist is Margo Wright, Erie native and first-grade teacher. She also sings the national anthem. She's been doing this at Sailors games for seven years, and has developed a loyal fan following. She sings the anthem from the press box, holding the PA microphone. The crowd cheers her as she hands the microphone back to the announcer, Bob Shreve, who tells the fans that tomorrow afternoon, they might want to drive down to Pittsburgh, because Wright will be singing the anthem at the Pirates–Cardinals game. This elicits a big hand and shouts of "Yayyyy MARGO!" An Erie talent, making it to the big leagues.

Wright tells me that she had to try out for the Pirates, along with seventy-five other people, which meant she listened to seventy-five versions of the anthem.

"They told everybody to keep it short," she says, "but one woman went *four minutes and twenty-seven seconds*." Wright says she tries to keep it under 1:15. You young would-be anthem singers out there would do well to bear this tip in mind.

Meanwhile, on the field, the actual baseball game has started. I understand that the quality of play is not quite up to major league level, but the difference is hard for the untutored eye to see. Guys are throwing, catching, batting, running, scratching, spitting, adjusting their supporters and making mysterious signals to each other; the umpire is indicating strikes by pointing violently to his right, as if he's angry at some imaginary person over there, at whom he yells "ZHREEEEEEEEEEEIIIIICHHH!" To me, it looks just like the major leagues, except that (a) you can see everybody a lot better, because the grandstands are so close to the field, and (b) the players look absurdly young. An alarming number of them were born in 1970.

I could already *vote* in 1970.

I'm sitting in the press box between sports writer/rock critic Dave "Dr. Rock" Richards and the official scorekeeper, Les Caldwell. Caldwell has several complex scoring forms in front of him, covered with little boxes to be filled in, and a lot of abbreviations. I recognize some of these, such as "AB," "R," "H," and of course "RBI," but I'm stumped by others, such as "GDP" and "CI."

I ask Caldwell about these.

"Ground Double Play and Catcher's Interference," he says, writing busily.

"Do you do your own income taxes?" I ask.

"Yes," he says.

In the bottom half of the first inning, Sailors shortstop Tony Sylvestri gets up to bat. Caldwell informs me that Sylvestri just joined the team; he had been playing in the San Francisco area for a semi-pro team called the Galoob Fog.

"He's staying at my house," Caldwell says. "C'MON TONY!"

Sylvestri hits a double.

"ALL RIGHT, TONY!" shouts Caldwell. Then, switching smoothly from rooter/landlord to official scorer, he records the hit.

A short while later, Caldwell glances at the electric scoreboard.

"Hey Jerry," he says to official scoreboard operator Jerry Pryber. "Why do they have six runs?" That's what the scoreboard says, even though Geneva in fact has only two runs. Nobody else in the stadium appears to have noticed this.

"Whoops," says Pryber, fixing it.

The press-box atmosphere is loose. In addition to official press-box activities, there is a great deal of eating, bantering, and professional-level scouting of the crowd for previously undiscovered talent.

"On the right!" somebody will say. "Second section, second row! Red hair, blue halter top!" Instantly, regardless of what is going on in the game, several pairs of binoculars are snatched up and aimed at the stands.

"I dunno," a voice says.

"Kind of old," adds another.

Clearly this is not Political Correctness Night.

Announcer Shreve informs the crowd that the Buffalo Jills are here. There are four of them; they dance along the aisle below

the press box, followed by the Sea Gull, who is holding his bill
down so he can get a good view out his eye holes.

"Did you play *Tequila?*" asks the general manager and president, Skip Weisman, arriving in the press box.

"I just did," says official organist Margo Wright.

"Well, did they dance?" asks Weisman.

"The first one was really boogie-ing," observes announcer
Shreve.

"Maybe we should play it again," says Weisman, making a
management decision.

The Jills dance back the other way. They have the full attention of the press box.

"I *love* spandex shorts on a woman," states official scorer Les
Caldwell.

In minor league double-headers, each game goes only seven
innings. This game goes into the top of the seventh with the Sailors leading 6–4. But the Cubs threaten to rally, getting a man on
base.

"Turn the lights off," I suggest to Weisman.

"We already did that once this year," he says. "We had a thirty-
minute blackout delay."

The Cubs rally never materializes, and the Sailors win, 6–4,
their sixth straight victory. Between games, Margo Wright leads
the crowd in singing *Take Me Out to the Ball Game.* One of the Buffalo Jills suffers a bee sting. It is not a career-ending injury, but
she is out for the night. The Sea Gull races a kid around the bases
and loses big when, rounding third, he is tackled by the remaining Jills.

The Jills perform a cheer for the fans, shouting:

"Hit 'em high! Hit 'em low! Go, Sailors, GO!" This seems to be
a football cheer, but the fans don't mind. As the Jills prance off
the field, a voice in the crowd says, "How do they get those shorts
off?"

The Sailors also win the second game, 7–0. Sean Gousha, the
catcher who was hustling tickets in the shopping plaza, plays the
entire game (he didn't play in the first one) and hits a double,
raising his batting average to .156. I'm happy for him. In fact,
I'm feeling pretty good in general, walking out of the stadium
after more than four hours of pretty good baseball and various
other entertainments, not to mention a couple of beers, a hot dog

and a bag of peanuts. Including a reserved-seat admission ticket, the evening cost me a total of $11.

I pass through the gate behind a man who is complaining to his companion. "Double-headers, they only play seven innings," he says. "They don't give you your money's worth."

Sunday

Tonight's game is against the Batavia (New York) Clippers, who last night played at home before an announced attendance of 434. But tonight in Erie — possibly because of those free tickets the Sailors gave away yesterday — there's another good crowd, 3,400 people. This is the best attendance the Sailors have had since the home opener June 15. On that night, both Miami and national media were on hand, not to mention Marlins owner and bazillionaire Wayne Huizenga, who flew up with other high team honchos on one of his various jets. The VIPs sat in a temporary plywood box erected along the third-base line and draped with bunting. The night was cold, and the Sailors lost in thirteen innings, and that was pretty much the end of the out-of-town hoopla.

But this is another perfect baseball night, and a lot of fans have come early to lean against the low chain-link fence next to the outfield and watch the players warm up. The Clippers wear uniforms with a big letter "P" on the front; these are hand-me-down uniforms from the big-league affiliate team, the Phillies.

Up in the press box, the regulars are assembling; they applaud when Margo Wright arrives, fresh from her successful anthem performance at the Pirates–Cardinals game. She tells me she got through it in 58 seconds, a personal record. She also asks me if I can put in a good word for her with the Marlins.

"If I could sing in Miami, that would be so cool," she says. "I *know* people from Erie would go."

So, if there are any Marlins executives reading this: Give Margo a shot. She has a strong voice, good speed and a nice range, and if your starting organist tires in the late innings, she can step in and do the job.

The Sailors' starting pitcher tonight is Jerry Stafford, one of the players manning the face-painting table yesterday in the

A. Duchini Inc. parking lot. The starting catcher, once again, is Sean Gousha, starting to get some playing time. He doesn't have a good first inning: With Clippers on first and third, the man on first attempts to steal second, and Gousha's throw goes into center field, allowing a run to score.

"Throwing error," rules official scorer Les Caldwell. "Unearned run."

The top half of the inning ends with the Clippers up 1–0. The electronic scoreboard, however, reads 0–0.

In the bottom half of the first, the Sailors face starting Clippers pitcher Larry Mitchell, who throws the ball 93 miles an hour, which is fast for any league. The Sailors fail to score, and the inning ends with the Clippers still up 1–0, and the scoreboard continuing to read 0–0.

At this point, some fans yell up to the press box: "HEY, WHAT'S THE SCORE?"

"Whoops," says official scoreboard operator Jerry Pryber, putting up a "1" for Batavia.

"Way to slide that 'one' up there, Jer," says Len Fatica. He's broadcasting the game over radio station WERG-FM, which is affiliated with Gannon University in Erie. Fatica asks me to sit in and do color commentary for an inning, which I do. I announce that the Sailors are running a number of promotions tonight, including Poison Reptile Night, Igneous Rock Night and Urinal Deodorant Night. I'm lying, of course, but nobody seems to care. I'm not sure that anybody outside the press box is actually listening.

General Manager and President Skip Weisman stops by the press box, and I ask him how much it would cost to buy the Sailors. He says the current owners — a group that includes actor Bill Murray — bought the team a year and a half ago for $700,000; he figures that the Sailors are worth about $1 million today. He says there was a time, not too long ago, when you could buy minor league franchises in some areas for $10,000.

"I got into this just a little too late," he says. Then he's off to check on something.

Clippers pitcher Mitchell continues to throw hard, and although my man Sean Gousha goes three for four at the plate — upping his average to .222 — the Sailors lose, 5–0. The seven-game win winning streak is over, but the fans drifting out of the stadium don't seem to mind much.

Just outside the gate, three men, probably in their sixties, are talking about an upcoming away game:

FIRST MAN: Is it cheaper if I go on the Booster Club bus?

SECOND MAN: Well, you get a snack.

FIRST MAN: What kind of snack?

SECOND MAN: You get a diet pop.

THIRD MAN: And chips.

FIRST MAN: I gotta think about it.

Monday

I leave Erie in another bouncy little plane. It's raining again. Tonight's Sailors game is canceled, along with the performance of The Dynamite Lady.

Epilogue

The 1992 Sailors season ended September 1. As I write this, the Marlins haven't decided whether to remain affiliated with the Sailors for the 1993 season. And if Erie doesn't solve its stadium problem by 1994, the Sailors won't be affiliated with any big-league team.

Of course by next year, South Florida won't care about Erie: The Marlins will be playing here. We'll have a big-league team to follow, with big-league stars making big-league money, playing in a big-league stadium in front of big-league crowds. Everything will be bigger.

Although not necessarily better.

SEPTEMBER 13, 1992

It was always an awful cliché to go down to the bushes and see "true" baseball, undefiled by hype and money. Then, when Ron Shelton wrote the wonderful film BULL DURHAM, *The Precious Minor League Baseball Cliché Story was raised by sports editors to another power.* DAVE BARRY *writes with such a keen eye and marvelous wit, he makes the minors seem like his own original discovery.* — F.D.

CHARLES P. PIERCE

The Next Superstar

FROM THE NEW YORK TIMES MAGAZINE

A SUMMER STORM cell breaks, purplish and powerful, over the North Park Baptist Church on the north side of Orlando. Hard rain drums speedy and loud off the rusted tin portico of the recreation center, the bright little gym that Pastor Harry Bush calls "a little beam from God." It is the kind of place where basketball is born in the hearts of the people who play it. Shorn of numbers, salaries and reputations, they come to places like this to bring the game at one another, testing at the roots the fundamental authenticity of basketball's rewards.

The Orlando Magic have begun to filter into town, one or two at a time, as the season approaches. For a moment, several of them sit, and they listen to Pastor Bush, who talks to them of gifts and of God through the steady thrum of rain on the windows. They are veterans, most of them: big Stanley Roberts, soon to be the central player in a three-way trade that will send him to the Los Angeles Clippers; Dennis Scott, a gifted deep shooter trying to come back from a bad knee injury, and Scott Skiles, a twenty-eight-year-old guard with a sweet instinct for the game's geometry and a go-to-hell attitude that makes him, weight for age, perhaps the toughest player in the National Basketball Association. They politely pay attention to Pastor Bush, all of them looking like men in a rescue mission out of the 1930s, willing to accept a sermon as the price for a bowl of soup.

"Some of you have come here without families," Pastor Bush is saying. "Some of you have come down here without pastors."

The youngest of them is also the biggest. Even sitting down, he is perceptibly taller and wider than the older players. When he was a young boy, growing up in Newark first, then on Army posts around the world, Shaquille O'Neal was ashamed of his size. He shot up to six foot eight as a sophomore in high school, but his coordination lagged behind. He slouched, making himself look even more ridiculous. "My parents told me to be proud," he recalls. "But I wasn't. I wanted to be normal."

He first wanted to be a dancer on the television show *Fame*. He wanted to be lithe and smooth and lightly airborne, working on his break dancing until he could make himself appear to flow. He spun on his head, the way the sharpest breakers did. Until, one summer, he got too wide to flow and too big to spin on his head. He had outgrown his dreams. He was fourteen years old.

He picked up a basketball because that is what the biggest children do. At age sixteen, he was the most sought-after high school player in the country, enrolling at Louisiana State University. Last spring, he became the number one pick in the NBA draft, signing in August with the Magic for an estimated $40 million over the next seven years. In addition, he took the first steps toward being a multinational corporation — wholly owned by himself. Reebok, the athletic-shoe company, has made him central to its drive to dominate that lucrative market. Soda companies have come calling. He also will have his own basketball and his own action figures.

The Magic is depending upon Shaquille O'Neal to reverse its sorry history as an expansion team, to make it a competitive basketball operation rather than simply another entertainment outlet fighting for tight discretionary dollars in the Kingdom of the Mouse. The NBA is counting on him to lead it into the next generation and a continuation of the spectacular personality-driven growth of the last decade that has made the league the most astonishing success story in the history of professional sports. "He's a little mini-entertainment complex," says his agent, Leonard Armato, "before he ever steps on the floor." He is seven foot one and 300 pounds. In March, he turned twenty.

There are few doubts about his playing abilities. Of his most immediate contemporaries, he is bigger than Patrick Ewing of the Knicks, stronger than David Robinson of the San Antonio Spurs and a more instinctive defender than Hakeem Olajuwon

of the Houston Rockets, for whom the game seems to have become a burden. Yet, in some ways, O'Neal is still amazingly raw.
In his first exhibition game, against the Miami Heat, he committed nine turnovers, a ludicrous number for a center. There are
moments when he seems to get hugely tangled in himself, and he
has the devil's own time with free throws. What he has is enormous natural ability. All he lacks is acquired wisdom.

Says the Knick guard Glenn (Doc) Rivers, who played with
O'Neal in a series of pickup games this summer: "He's going to
stumble into twenty points and ten rebounds a game just because
he's so big. He's going to have to work on it, but he's just so . . .
grown-up for his age."

In an October exhibition game in Asheville, North Carolina,
the good and bad in him were on conspicuous display. Against
the Charlotte Hornets, he put up 26 points and 11 rebounds, but
he also lost the ball six times. He was duped into silly offensive
fouls when smaller men moved in behind him as he powered
toward the basket. Still, to watch him slap away a shot by Kendall
Gill, a star of the Hornets, and then go 90 feet to drop a lay-up
at the other end is to see almost limitless promise.

O'Neal took all of it with poise and equanimity. "I'm all right,"
he said afterward. "I'm at about seventy percent, or maybe
eighty."

Orlando coach Matt Guokas explains: "People tend to forget
how young he is because of how big he is. He's still learning the
pro game. He doesn't really even know the language yet." And if
he sometimes looks like an Arthur Murray student confronting
the footprints on the floor for the first time (once, against the
Charlotte veteran J. R. Reid, O'Neal tied himself in an enormous
knot, and Reid blocked his shot), he also clearly looks like the
latest coming of basketball's most compelling mythic figure —
the Big Man in the Middle.

Once, a center was called a "pivot man," with good and clear
reason. Everything about the game, from its actual strategy to its
psychic rhythms, revolved around him. Over the past twenty
years, however, basketball has moved up and out, away from the
big men in the middle. First, Gus Johnson and Elgin Baylor took
it into the air, where Connie Hawkins, Julius Erving and Michael
Jordan have followed. Then, Larry Bird and Magic Johnson, nei-

ther of whom could jump conspicuously well, redefined their respective positions, largely through their mutual love for and faith in the pass. Both were six foot nine, but both excelled at positions previously thought to belong to smaller men. Bird played essentially the small forward's slot, and Johnson was a point guard. Centers followed the trend as the game evolved. This led, at its best, to the multiplicity of skills demonstrated by David Robinson, and, at its worst, to the pathetic sight of Ralph Sampson, a seven-foot-four man trying to play himself shorter.

In this, O'Neal may be the perfect synthesis of old myth and new reality. His is essentially a power game, but it is infused with the kind of speed and agility required by modern professional basketball. He will handle the ball on the perimeter if he must (the first play he ever made that caught national attention came in a televised all-star game after his senior year at Robert G. Cole Senior High School in San Antonio, when O'Neal grabbed the ball off one backboard and took it the length of the floor to dunk at the other), and he is working on a jump shot. But his greatest gifts remain in the classic pivot — close in, with his back to the basket. There, he is that thing most beloved by the savants — a "quick jumper," rising apparently from his ankles and calves without ever appearing to gather himself.

The Big Man in the Middle endures as an archetype, largely because he was so much of what first made basketball unique. Wilt Chamberlain once pointed out that "nobody loves Goliath," as an excuse for his enduring unpopularity. He was wrong, of course, even scripturally: the Philistines loved Goliath. If O'Neal comes up a little short of Goliath's six-cubits-and-a-span, his talents and, more important, his personality may make him the living refutation of the Chamberlain theorem. He has a quick smile that instantly takes five years off his age. This is what the Magic and the NBA are counting on — a Goliath everyone can love.

For to be merely a player — even a great player — is no longer all there is in the NBA. The league creates stars now, a culture of celebrity that could not have been anticipated in the late 1970s, when the NBA was in very real danger of collapsing altogether. There is an inexorable blurring of the line that separates entertainers and athletes. Most recently, Charles Barkley appeared in a cartoon brawl with Godzilla. This culture reached its apex at the Olympic Games in Barcelona, when the United States team, featuring Bird, Johnson, Jordan, Barkley and other NBA stars, careened across Europe like some strange, elongated outtakes from *A Hard Day's Night*.

That culture of celebrity has its benefits; for example, Jordan's carefully crafted public image largely insulated him from accusations of high-stakes gambling leveled against him last season. But it's also a fragile culture, largely black and formed during a decade of racial reaction. It needs constant renewal. Bird and Johnson are both retired, and Jordan insists that he will not play much longer. To survive, the celebrity culture that fueled the NBA's rise needs new, young, charismatic players while it continues to finesse the problems of race and class that bedevil every other institution today.

As soon as he left college last spring, Shaquille O'Neal became the de facto leader of that next generation. No less an authority than Magic Johnson sees that. "He's got it all," says Johnson, who worked out with O'Neal in Los Angeles last spring. "He's got the smile, and the talent, and the charisma. And he's sure got the money too."

Indeed, Shaquille has a goofy kid's smile that runs up the left side of his face a little faster than the right. On his first day at a summer construction job at LSU, he jumped off the roof of the house on which he was working, terrifying the occupants. When a couple in Geismar, Louisiana, named their infant son Shaquille O'Neal Long — simply because they loved the name — Shaquille immediately drove out and had his picture taken with the baby.

And he does have something of a sweet tooth for cars. He drives a burgundy Blazer with the license plate "Shaq-Attaq," and his black Mercedes sports a front plate that reads, "Shaqnificent." Both are parked at his new house in Isleworth, a luxury suburb outside Orlando. The first thing he did after signing his Orlando contract was to return home to San Antonio and treat two of his friends to a trip to an amusement park. This, from a newly minted millionaire who announced on his first trip to Orlando that he was looking forward to "chillin' with Mickey," and who explained on the opening day of the Magic's training camp, "I was a child star, just like Michael Jackson and Gary Coleman."

Dennis Tracy, who has signed on as his friend's unofficial media liaison, says: "I can't see him ever changing. He'll always be that kid who jumped off the roof because it was fun to do."

So far, O'Neal has done all the right things. He signed quickly and without rancorous negotiation. He defused a potentially messy situation over his college number 33, surrendering it to his veteran teammate Terry Catledge. Over the summer, he impressed current NBA players with his love for hard work and, oddly enough, with his punctuality. "The most impressive thing is that he's such a mature person," says Doc Rivers. "When we were playing at UCLA, we started at nine o'clock in the morning, and he was there right on the dot every day. You don't see many college kids like that."

O'Neal listens attentively as Pastor Bush winds up his talk, and then he takes the floor. He is playing with Skiles, who is already in game shape and driving his teammates hard. Roberts, a former LSU teammate of O'Neal's, tries to shoot a jump shot over him, and O'Neal slams the ball off the floor in a ten-foot carom. Skiles is not impressed. "Shaq," he says, "block it back to someone on your team." Shortly thereafter, Stanley Roberts has had enough, and he walks off the floor, claiming an injured leg.

Thunder peals outside, and there is a flash that shows the wire threaded through the thick window glass above the bleachers. On the first day that Shaquille O'Neal came to Baton Rouge, the skies darkened and roared, and a small tornado blew through town. Scared to death, he rode around on Dennis Tracy's bicycle with the storm blowing up all around him.

There is portent to the way he plays. His team wins. The lightning cracks.

"O.K.," says Scott Skiles, looking up at his newest teammate. "You guys bring it back."

It is a comfortable world that Shaquille O'Neal joins. Between 1981 and 1991, the NBA's gross nonretail revenue grew from $110 million to $700 million — an increase of 636 percent. Its gross retail revenues, which include the vastly profitable licensing of team jackets and caps, exploded even more vigorously, now totaling more than $1 billion per year.

As recently as a decade ago, there was serious talk of folding at least three and possibly as many as six franchises. Now, the average franchise is worth approximately $70 million, and there is talk about selling the Boston Celtics alone for $110 million. "There is no one place that it changed," says the NBA commissioner, David J. Stern. "A number of things that the owners and players did provided a better stage for all our players." Indeed, on the two most volatile issues of the past twenty years in professional sports — money and drugs — the NBA and its players have developed workable solutions, while largely avoiding the acrimony that has become customary in both baseball and football.

The league's greatest triumph has been to inculcate in everyone a fundamental loyalty to the idea of the league. Hence, Stern talks about "the NBA family." "It may not be a traditional family," he says, "but it is an extended family." This has provided NBA players with a stable foundation from which to kick off their own lucrative careers. Each generation builds on the previous one. Erving's abilities as a player and as a public person made it easier for Bird and Johnson, who made it easier for Michael Jordan, who took the whole business to another dimension. Without Erving, who proved once and for all that black athletes were neither brooders nor cartoons, Jordan's entree into the corporate class would've been that much more difficult. In turn, Jordan's success eases the burden on O'Neal.

He joined the family at the end of last year's college season, leaving LSU with one year of eligibility left. He was tired of being triple-teamed and physically roughed up. "I played my heart out," he says. "But there was one game, I was catching alley-oops all day. So, in the second half, I was doing my spin move, and guys were putting their butts into my leg, coming under me. It was not a money thing. I was taught at a young age that if you're not having fun at something, then it's time to go."

The lesson came from his father. In the early 1970s, with Newark just beginning to turn from the riots of 1967 into something even more lost and hopeless, Philip A. Harrison decided to get out. He joined the Army and, before he could marry Lucille O'Neal, he was shipped overseas. She had their baby without him. Looking through a book of Islamic names, she called him Shaquille Rashaun O'Neal, which, she says, means "Little Warrior." "I wanted my children to have unique names," Lucille says. "To me, just by having a name that means something makes you special."

The couple married soon thereafter. The family held together in the gypsy jet stream that is military life. "The best part for me was just getting out of the city," Shaquille recalls. "In the city, where I come from, there are a lot of temptations — drugs, gangs. Like, when I used to live in the projects, guys'd ride by in their Benzes. Kids want to have the fancy clothes and the Benzes. They say: 'Look at Mustafa. He's done this and done that. I want to do that.' When I was little, I was a kind of juvenile delinquent, but my father stayed on me. Being a drill sergeant, he had to discipline his troops. Then, he'd come home and discipline me.

"The worst part was, like, traveling, you know? Meeting people, getting tight with them, and then having to leave. Sometimes, you come into a new place, and they'll test you. I always got teased. Teased about my name. Teased about my size. Teased about being flunked. You know, 'You so big, you must've flunked.' I'd have to beat them up. It took a while to gain friends because people thought I was mean. I had a bad temper. Guys used to play the 'dozens' game with me where they used to talk about your mother, and I'd get mad and hit them. One day, I just woke up and walked away."

They moved to Germany twice, the last time just before Shaquille entered junior high. It was a tight, regimented existence. In Fulda, where Sergeant Harrison was stationed, there was some anti-American agitation; in one bizarre protest, the townspeople painted American military vehicles a bright blue. It is significant, then, that, for all his travels, Shaquille still calls Newark his home, and that "the projects" loom so large in his personal iconography despite the fact that he spent very little of his life there. "He didn't want to leave," his father explains. "He wanted to stay there with his grandma."

But that was not the way that the sergeant's family functioned, and all four of his children knew it. "Society is always dictating to the parent who's the boss," says Harrison, who will retire as a staff sergeant in September 1993 and move his family one last time — to Orlando. "You know who the boss is today in the family? The children. My dad disciplined me. Your dad disciplined you. What was said about it? Now, everybody's in the middle. Back then, the people in the middle were your friends, so you didn't disrespect them. Now, somebody runs to the court."

One day near Fulda, Shaquille went to a basketball clinic run by Dale Brown, the energetically eccentric basketball coach at LSU. Brown presumed that the big young man was a soldier. Discovering that Shaquille was, in fact, barely a teenager, Brown's coaching antennae vibrated into the red zone, and he asked to meet the sergeant. Five years later, after Harrison was posted to Fort Sam Houston in San Antonio and after Shaquille became a high school All-America at Cole, LSU recruited and won him. It was presumed that Harrison made the choice for his son. "That was him alone," Harrison says. "We pushed the boat away the day he decided to go there. We told him, 'Go out there and take what we taught you and what you learned in life and apply it and do what you have to do.' "

In college, O'Neal became a superstar, despite breaking his leg during his sophomore season. By the end of last season, he was averaging 24.1 points per game. But the Pier 6 strategy of rival coaches was wearing his patience thin. In addition, Brown seemed unable to keep O'Neal as the focal point of the LSU offense, something that drove NBA types mad when they looked at tapes of the Tigers, and something that they blame for the rough edges that still exist on his game.

"I saw one game last year when this kid touched the ball about twice in the entire second half," says one NBA scout. "I said, 'Is this guy kidding or what?' " O'Neal managed to restrain himself until the Southeastern Conference tournament, when he became one of the instigators of an ugly brawl in which even Brown was seen throwing haymakers at the opposition. Shaquille was suspended for the Southeastern Conference championship game the following day. After LSU was eliminated early in the subsequent NCAA tournament, he made his decision to turn professional. He closed his bank account and went home to San Antonio.

His father always had insisted that O'Neal would stay the full four years at LSU. His parents had tried to impress upon their son the value of a college degree. In addition, Philip Harrison had emphasized the vast differences between the college game and the one that is played in the NBA. But the scene at the Tennessee game gave even the sergeant second thoughts. "I told him I wanted to leave," Shaquille says. "It was not that hard. He just thought about it and finally, he said, "If I was you, I'd want to leave, too.' Not because of the money, but because I wasn't having any fun. Everybody thinks he's a dictator. He's not."

His father laughs now. "Everybody's got this myth that, when the sergeant speaks, everybody listens." He points at his wife: "When *she* speaks, everybody listens."

Shaquille announced his availability for the draft on April 3, and he was taken into Stern's NBA family almost immediately. Through Dale Brown, the family had met a Los Angeles–based agent named Leonard Armato, who also represents Hakeem Olajuwon, and who also had helped straighten out the tangled public image of Kareem Abdul-Jabbar. Armato agreed to represent Shaquille. In June, he went to the NBA finals in Portland, where he was interviewed by Ahmad Rashad. Endorsement offers bloomed everywhere. It was a dizzying time, and Shaquille handled an array of new situations with conspicuous aplomb.

Counselors who work with them say that military children adapt quickly, that they develop social skills faster than other children their age. Shaquille was formed within a dynamic that was at once very stable, and at the same time in predictable flux. Every three years, as the sergeant was rotated between duty stations, there were new places to see and new friends to make. Even though he seems to cling to Newark as some sort of cultural touchstone, Shaquille learned very early in his life to function in different contexts with ease and confidence. He has been an urban homeboy and an American abroad, a Texas schoolboy legend and a college star. He is going to be a professional star, a commercial spokesman and a national celebrity.

"Ego is acting like you're all-that," he says. "Like they say on the block, 'all-that.' Can't nobody touch you," he says. "Confidence is knowing who you are."

At various times during his career, the Orlando general manager, Pat Williams, has treated NBA crowds to halftime entertainments involving singing dogs and wrestling bears. He has become known as the league's premier showman, occasionally at the expense of his reputation as a basketball man. Williams needed to sign O'Neal quickly. For the first few seasons, the Magic were content to sell the entertainment side of the NBA experience. But, in an area where there were so many other entertainment options, it became incumbent upon the team to move toward competitive basketball, lest it drop down past Sea World on the food chain of local attractions.

"As great as Disney and Sea World are," explains Jack Swope, the Magic's assistant general manager, "they're not considered something that local people can identify with. It's hard to root for Disney World." It's just as hard, however, to root for a basketball team that wins twenty games a year. O'Neal would be the link between the entertainment function of the Magic and the athletic one.

Immediately after the draft, a nervous Williams couldn't even find his new star. There was nothing coming from the O'Neal camp, he says, like "yippee, we're glad Orlando won the lottery." "There were no warm-fuzzies coming out of that end for about a month," he says. In addition, Williams was having trouble with the NBA salary cap. It stabilized the league's fiscal situation, but it also requires general managers to contort themselves regularly through baffling mathematical gymnastics just to get their rosters filled.

Orlando's situation was complicated further when the Dallas Mavericks signed Stanley Roberts, a restricted free agent, to an offer sheet that totaled $15 million over five years. The Magic had to match that offer within fifteen days or lose Roberts without compensation. Moreover, because of salary-cap restrictions, the Magic had to sign O'Neal before matching the offer to Roberts.

Williams was going in seven directions at once. To make room for O'Neal under the salary cap, he traded guard Sam Vincent to Milwaukee and restructured five other existing contracts. On August 4, O'Neal signed for a reported $40 million over seven years. Orlando also matched the Dallas offer to Roberts, whom the Magic then traded to the Clippers in September in a deal that brought two first-round draft picks, which will be used to put the required supporting cast around O'Neal.

It was a remarkably civil negotiation. "To their credit, Shaquille and his people were bright enough to understand," Williams says. "They worked with us in those fifteen days. Most people thought we couldn't do it. But we did it."

That left Armato free to develop the rest of what he calls Shaquille's "entertainment complex." While the Magic own the rights to everything with their name on it, O'Neal is free to make whatever outside deals he can. (For example, he can do television commercials, but he can't wear his uniform in them without the prior approval of either the team or the league.) Soon, a lucrative deal was signed with Spalding for the Shaquille O'Neal basketball, and one is in the works with Kenner for a line of Shaquille action figures. Since Armato made his reputation primarily as a shrewd money manager — as opposed to as a hardball negotiator like David Falk, the Washington attorney who represents Patrick Ewing — O'Neal feels confident that his long-term interests are secure.

"We've got good investments going," he says. "We've got stocks, T-bills. We're all right."

Armato plans a unified marketing strategy and a logo currently being designed by a team of graphic artists in Los Angeles. "We're thinking of a single image for Shaquille through all of the products in a way that benefits all of them," Armato says. "Let's say it's a soft drink: The 'Shaq-Pack.' On the package as a prize, maybe there's a Shaquille basketball, or a pair of shoes. The NBA is putting Shaquille in one hundred different countries by itself."

The most obvious modern endorsement is a shoe contract. It's almost unfathomable today to realize that Kareem Abdul-Jabbar once made only $100,000 a year to wear Adidas basketball shoes. In 1983, Nike had passed Adidas as the leader in worldwide sales. The following year, however, Reebok, a smaller, Boston-based company, took over the market from floundering Nike, largely by catching the aerobics boom that Nike missed. Later in 1984, though, after Nike signed Michael Jordan to an innovative promotional deal, Nike won back the market again — by September 1985, the company had sold more than 2.3 million pairs of Air Jordans alone — and Reebok now plans to counter Jordan with Shaquille O'Neal, whose size 20 feet will be shod in Reeboks in exchange for a reported $10 million over the next five years. Nike and Jordan made this deal possible, and Reebok and

O'Neal plan to repay the favor by bringing them down out of the air.

"He is going to be the focal point of basketball for us," says Mark D. Holtzman, Reebok's director of sports marketing. "We want to portray him as the strongest man in the NBA, and we want to do it worldwide. We're going to put him in fifty countries." Reebok is hanging new technologies on the "Shaq Attaq" shoes as well, which will retail for more than $100. O'Neal spent part of September shooting the first commercials for them.

Every step he takes now has consequences. Every move he makes sets off tremors, and his first NBA season is barely a week old. When he and Catledge were wrangling over number 33 in Florida, the NBA licensing people grew edgy in New York, since they didn't know what number to put on their official Shaquille gear.

O'Neal is aware that the commercials he so enjoyed making will contribute to a deadly consumer culture that grips the projects where he has anchored his past, to that look he saw in the eyes of the kids who wanted the Benzes long ago. He is going into a culture of celebrity that has been accused of abandoning its most impoverished adherents.

"I'm worried about that," he says. "I'm not going to make myself a superhero that people can't touch. The commercials are going to show both sides of me, what I like to do off the court, like listen to my rap music. The question was asked of me, should athletes be role models? The answer is, yes, to a certain extent. Like, when I was a kid, I could look up to Doctor J, but if I needed some advice about the birds and the bees, I couldn't ask Doctor J. I couldn't call one of these superstars. I had to call Mommy or Daddy. I mean, we should carry ourselves well on TV. We should not do things like beat our girlfriends up, do drugs or alcohol. Now, if all those kids lived with me, then I could be their role model."

The forum club is hopping. Once the NBA was armories in places like Davenport, Iowa, and Rochester. Today it is the Great Western — formerly Fabulous — Forum in Los Angeles. Once it was steelworkers and mill hunks. Today it is agents and movie stars and singers. In the Forum Club, there is taffeta and lace, leather and gold. There is loud talk of agents and properties and the hot places to go later that night. Ice rings like delicate chimes. It is a basketball evening in Los Angeles, and the sky outside is a perfect parfait.

Every August, Magic Johnson hosts a benefit game for the United Negro College Fund. O'Neal has come to play this year. His coach is Arsenio Hall. Coaching the other team is Spike Lee. The singer Al B. Sure sits in one section with the female singing group En Vogue. At midcourt, Jack Nicholson sits with his infant daughter, whose parents will later mutually determine that they no longer want to live together in separate houses. It's a long way from North Park Baptist Church, a great distance from Pastor Bush and his little beam from God's eye.

O'Neal plays with consummate ease and confidence. He blocks shots by catching them. He whips down the lane for a dunk off an inbounds play, and he winks at Leonard Armato's four-year-old son while he does it. He tosses the veteran Pistons center Olden Polynice this way and that, once bouncing the ball off the backboard, retrieving it with a lightning first step, and then slamming it through as the women from En Vogue rock and Arsenio grabs his head. He ends up with 36 points and 19 rebounds. "Shaquille, the best part about him is that he's mean," Magic Johnson says later. "He's going to be one of those guys that, after you play him, you sleep real good. He's gonna put guys to sleep."

He does not look mean. He does not look like a product here. He looks like a twenty-year-old discovering himself all over again. There is a purity that extends from north Orlando to this gathering of gaudy dilettantes. He will be comfortable in both places. He will be a kid and a corporation. He will be for sale and he will be free. He will be a Goliath for everyone to love.

NOVEMBER 15, 1992

CHARLES P. PIERCE is the first writer to make a cottage industry of Sha-quille O'Neal, as he did a first profile on the phenom at LSU at the National. At that time, we put the kid on the cover with the title THE BEST EVER?, but by the time the paper came off the presses the question mark had somehow disappeared. Now that Shaquille is well on his way to possibly becoming the best center ever, Charlie and the National look all the more clever. What I liked especially about this piece — and sports articles in the New York Times Magazine *usually read as if they've been poorly translated from a minor dialect for the benefit of readers who haven't seen an athletic contest in their life — is how well Charlie places the callow rookie in the traditions of the sport and the league.* — F.D.

RICK REILLY

What Is the Citadel?

FROM SPORTS ILLUSTRATED

> Sir, it is a fortress of duty, a sentinel of responsibility, a bastion of
> antiquity, a towering bulwark of rigid discipline, instilling within
> us high ideals, honor, uprightness, loyalty, patriotism, obedience,
> initiative, leadership, professional knowledge and pride in
> achievement.
> — *from the school handbook*

FRESHMAN CHADD SMITH KNOWS why he's hanging from his
closet shelf by his fingers at three in the morning, with his legs
bent and spread. It has to do with football. The Citadel hadn't
lost the Wofford game since 1958. In fact, it had *never* lost the
Wofford game at home. But tonight it did. As usual, somebody
has to pay. As usual, it's the freshmen. That part he understands.
What Smith wants to know is, *What is it? What is that coldness I feel
now and again down between my thighs?*

Smith is hanging because of football and duty. At the Citadel
it is the sophomores' *duty* to run out any freshman who does not
measure up to the Citadel man — to break him down, humiliate
him, run him until he cannot feel his toes, drill him until the arm
with which he holds his rifle is numb, yell at him until his cere-
bellum turns to Jell-O, rack him until he either does things the
Citadel way or goes home blubbering to his mommy. It's a point
of pride among the seventeen companies at the Citadel to see
who can chase out the most knobs, as freshmen are called; a
usual figure is 15 percent of the class. This tradition is called the
Fourth Class System, and if you survive it you are, say Citadel
men, "nine feet tall and bulletproof."

Smith knew knob year would suck, but he knew what to do. You talk to no one and salute everyone. You run when you are inside the barracks. You ask permission to eat, leave, pass, cough, sneeze and scratch your nose. You serve everybody at mess and hope you can stuff in a forkful before mealtime has elapsed. You polish your shoes and your brass until midnight and then your French and chemistry until two, and you hope the guy who blows reveille dies in his sleep.

You do not put a picture of your girlfriend on your desktop. You do not watch TV, because you are not allowed a TV. You do not get Cokes out of the barracks Coke machine. You do not walk on any grass, which means you must walk *around* the football-field-wide quadrangle in the middle of campus. You do not have any answers besides *Sir, yes, sir!* and *Sir, no, sir!* and *Sir, no excuse, sir!* And you do not complain unless you want thirteen weekends of being stuck in your room.

You try to make nice and be invisible, because any sophomore half your size can drop you for fifteen pushups on a lark. For the first week you smell like three-day-old sweat socks, because all you get are ten-second showers — unless, of course, some joker decides to throw you a shower party. This is another Citadel tradition, in which the upperclassmen turn the showers up all the way on hot, dress you in full rain gear and make you exercise until you throw up. Could be worse. There was once an upperclassman, it is said, who would hold a pistol to freshmen's heads, asking them things they should have memorized from the school guidebook. He found that a pistol is a great aid to concentration.

But if things are bad for freshmen, they are doubly bad for freshman athletes. The Citadel may be the only college where the freshman athlete is LMOC, low man on campus. "In high school," says one former knob jock, "you're a big deal. Here you're dirt." In season, athletes get out of the daily marching and Saturday-morning room inspections, which means they're resented by the other cadets, and that means when an athlete returns to the barracks, he must make amends. It doesn't matter that the jock must practice his sport four hours every day instead of marching. It doesn't matter that hazing can be, officially at least, grounds for immediate expulsion from the Citadel — not to mention a misdemeanor according to South Carolina law.

What matters is that the jock has found a loophole in Citadel discipline, and no Citadel man with a pocketful of duty will stand for that.

Right now Smith, a member of the school's cycling team, is wondering how much more duty he can take.

"Smith!" one of the upperclassmen roars into his ear. "Whatever you do, don't drop! Don't drop, Smith!" Smith is not sure who exactly is trying to shatter his tympanum. He hadn't had time to see. The door flew open and the lights were off.

Cadet Smith always wanted to be a Citadel man. He wanted it so devoutly that he and his single mom took out $13,000 in loans to make first-year tuition. You wear the Citadel ring, you get a good job, because Citadel men look out for each other. You could spray a bucket of birdseed in any restaurant right here in Charleston and hit a dozen of them.

At first Smith thought he might slip through freshman year without making a blip on the sophomores' radar screen. But one day during sweep detail a sophomore decided that Smith was sweeping incorrectly. As he screamed at Smith, he spit in Smith's mouth. It disgusted Smith and this showed on his face and the sophomore knew it, so the next day he spit in Smith's mouth again. The following day, when Smith started feeling sick, he was sure he'd caught something from the boy's saliva. He got worse. Doubled over in pain, he tried to make it to the infirmary. On the way a sophomore dropped him for fifteen quick pushups. Citadel men leave mercy to heaven.

Once he was checked into the infirmary, Smith called his mother. She called Citadel authorities. The spitter didn't go down for it, but word got back to the upperclassmen. Cadet freshman Smith was now officially a snitch. And that's when things just got out of hand.

The upperclassmen took turns busting into Smith's room for late-night "inspections." (There are no locks on bunk-room doors at the Citadel.) Three hours of sleep in a night became a luxury for Smith. Many nights he got zero hours. He made up for it by falling asleep in class. His plan to make "killer grades" the first year and thereby get a scholarship was sinking fast.

Then came the Wofford loss, and that's how Smith ended up hanging from his closet shelf, his legs burning, his arms trem-

bling, his fingers slipping and his ears absorbing the insults and
the spit and the constant warning: "Don't drop, Smith! Whatever
you do, *don't drop!*"

What *was* it down there?

"O.K., Smith," a voice finally whispered in his ear. "We're getting ready to leave. But before we go, I want you to look down."

There, gleaming in the reflected moonlight, two inches below
his testicles, was an officer's saber.

The Citadel's 15–12 loss to Wofford on September 14, 1991, was
laid mostly on the burred head of 175-pound cadet freshman
kicker Chad Davis, who missed three field goals. It didn't matter
much to the sophomores that Davis had kicked two field goals
and three PATs in a win against Presbyterian College in the first
game of the season. In fact, the sophomores had made him hang
for fifteen minutes from his closet shelf just so he wouldn't get a
swelled head. But blowing the Wofford game was unforgivable.

On Davis's recruiting visit the football coaches had made the
Citadel sound like the Elks Club. As an all-state kicker from
Union (South Carolina) High School and a *USA Today* Honorable
Mention All-America, Davis had choices. "I thought a little re-
sponsibility and discipline might be good for me," he says.

A little might have been. But one day Davis called a rifle a gun,
and the sophomores smelled a weakness. They hounded him.
They stepped on his shoes and hollered, "Why aren't these
shined?" They jumped into him at formation and threw discreet
elbows into his gut. They busted his chops every night. "I'd lie
awake," he remembers, "wondering when they were going to
come in next." He was taking five packs of Vivarin a week and
drinking two Cokes per class to stay awake.

When he blew the Wofford game, things just got out of hand.

According to several sources, to remind Davis that he had
choked, a couple of cadets made him stand at formation the next
day with his hands around his neck. The screaming and humiliation were delivered in industrial-sized doses. And finally something inside Davis couldn't take it anymore.

"Davis, why'd you miss those kicks?" a sophomore screamed.

No answer.

"Davis, you got an attitude?"

"Sir, yes, sir!"

"You do?"

From that moment until he woke up a day later in the infirmary, Davis can't remember a thing. "I think I went crazy," he says. "They said I was hysterical."

Though the administration says it did not happen, sources say they were told that the sophomores threw Davis a blanket party. This is not to be confused with a towel party, in which you drop a dozen bars of soap into a towel, tie it up and beat a knob with it. In a blanket party the attackers sneak into the victim's room, throw a blanket over his head and do what they may. This time doing what they may meant taking Davis to a utility sink. They dunked Davis's head in the water five, ten, fifteen, twenty times.

They stopped when he passed out.

To be a Citadel man is to be part of a rich Southern tapestry. The school was formed in 1842 by an act of the South Carolina state legislature. Citadel cadets manning four Charleston Harbor cannons fired the first shots of the Civil War, on the Northern supply ship *Star of the West*.

The Citadel has earned a reputation as a good place to send your boy to purge him of all the hogwash and MTV gurgling in his cranium; a place to turn him into a gentleman soldier and a useful citizen. Your average Citadel cadet is a patriotic boy from a conservative family in a small, low-country town in the Carolinas, quite often a boy with a military man in his family or, even more often, a Citadel legacy. He is a boy who would like to test his guts against the Citadel horror stories he has heard. Nobody comes in naive, but nobody comes in ready, either.

You need to post only a 2.0 grade-point and an 800 SAT score to qualify for admission. Last year the Citadel ranked second among South Carolina public universities in entering freshmen's SAT scores. Of course, South Carolina public universities ranked dead last in the nation, so second does not exactly get the commandant invited to the Rose Garden.

An entire military hierarchy is in place here, from the president, Lieutenant General Claudius Watts, to the cadet regimental commander to the platoon commanders to the company commanders right down to the lowliest, gutter-swabbing knob. On any Friday of the school year you can see the Citadel outfitted in its finest appointments, gray and black and buttons and flags, marching precisely on the parade field. It's the best and cheapest show in town. Of course, it's nothing more than that — a show.

Citadel cadets have no more connection to the military than do Harvard undergraduates. Only those students who have signed ROTC contracts will be obliged to be sworn into a branch of the service, and an ROTC contract can be signed on most any campus in the country. Even former Citadel president James Stockdale, a Congressional Medal of Honor winner, likened attending the Citadel to playing soldier. Get up close and you can see it. Those splendid cadet uniforms — and the faculty's, too — are of the sort you might get at a good Army surplus store, vague grays and indefinite stripes and tags. The Citadel uniform is the equivalent of a World War II bomber jacket ordered through a catalog.

What's odd about all this is that the Citadel is a state-funded institution. What's odder still is that the taxpayers who pay for the Citadel are not allowed in the barracks, women are accepted only into the night program, and the school's policy-making body — the board of visitors — is made up entirely of Citadel graduates, all of them with honorary military rank.

Still, if you like that kind of show, there is none in America quite like it. To spend a night in the Citadel barracks is to bunk down in a military time warp. People salute people. Taps is played every night and reveille every morning. Cadets walk outdoors on seventy-year-old balconies to get to their communal shower. The Citadel burr haircut is still given every day at the campus barbershop. Freshmen, not faxes, are still the most common way to send messages. Even the architecture is out of time and place. The Citadel's straight lines and whitewashed, Lego-castle walls evoke a stark Moorish prison. And within those walls the night is cleaved by mysterious screams.

If there is one thing you learn at the Citadel, it's discipline. Every cadet who has been on the parade grounds for a march on a muggy September afternoon knows what happens when a mosquito alights on the neck of the boy in front of him: absolutely nothing. And though the mosquito feasts and the lump rises on the boy's neck, he does not flinch. A Citadel man does not permit himself to itch.

Cadet freshman lineman Karl Brozowski, a towering bulwark of a boy, six foot three, 240 pounds, thought he might like some of that hard discipline. Brozowski figured he could handle anything. He comes from rich football stock. His dad, John, played for Tennessee. His dad's uncle is former Philadelphia Eagle Chuck Bednarik. Karl even turned down an appointment to West Point to be a Citadel man. That was his first mistake.

His second was going to junior cornerback Torrence Forney about all the racking he was getting from the sophomore next door. Mark Rajewski, a five-foot-nine second-year cadet, had graciously chosen to devote his time and energy to driving Brozowski mad. "It's going to be a *long* year," Rajewski had told him. In the second week Rajewski kept Brozowski up most of the night before a test. That's when Brozowski went to Forney. Hello, snitch.

Brozowski's parents could tell things weren't going well for him, so they would drive down from Atlanta on Saturdays and take Karl and a few other football freshmen to the beach. "Karl looked like he'd been in a POW camp," says John. "He'd lost thirty pounds. He was incoherent. We'd get to the beach and he'd just fall asleep. He seemed like he was on drugs."

But it wasn't until the night before the Wofford game that things just got out of hand. According to a criminal complaint filed last October by Brozowski, Rajewski had been visiting him nightly. Brozowski was polishing the floors of his room about 11 P.M. when Rajewski walked in with a toothpick in his mouth, liquor on his breath — though school policy forbids drinking — and hell in his eyes.

Rajewski ordered Brozowski to attention, says the complaint, took the toothpick out of his mouth and began poking Brozowski hard in the back with it. Then he walked around and started poking Brozowski hard in the nipples, hard enough to break the toothpick. He told Brozowski to swallow his lipful of chewing tobacco. To make up for that, he inserted an aerosol can of Cheez Whiz in Brozowski's mouth and squirted. Rajewski was just having a little fun, sort of a Tailhook-starter-kit type of thing.

Brozowski wanted to throw up, but Rajewski forbade it. Rajewski finally left, after which Brozowski spit in the round file. But Rajewski came back every twenty minutes until almost 5:30 A.M., when Brozowski had to be on the line for formation. This is not the best way to prepare for a 7 P.M. football game. Luckily Brozowski did not have to suffer any of the hell that went on after the Wofford loss. He quit.

"I had to," Brozowski says. "Under these conditions I was either going to flunk out or haul off and kill someone."

It wasn't until 1966 that the Citadel accepted a black cadet, and this inspired Pat Conroy's best-selling 1982 novel, *The Lords of Discipline*. Conroy, a '67 Citadel graduate, describes how a black cadet is tortured by a white-supremacist group, The Ten.

Twenty-five years later, in 1991, Charleston television reporter Angela Brown reported that a group known on campus as the Churchill Society contained within it a white-supremacist faction. Brown happened to be the girlfriend of the Citadel's starting quarterback, Jack Douglas, a black senior. And though the Citadel has said that the Churchill Society met only to discuss Western civilization, Brown stands staunchly by her story.

"All of my friends who went to it said it was a white-supremacy group," says Raymond Mazyck, a black who in 1991 was a senior. Mazyck, from north Charleston, was convicted by the school's Honor Court of encouraging a freshman to lie about how he had gotten a gash in his head a year earlier. What had happened was that a cadet had been forced to do bunk pushups, and the bunk had flipped and struck the freshman. It was Mazyck, an eyewitness to it all, who had taken the freshman to the infirmary that day. But a year later the freshman said Mazyck had told him to make up a story about the injury so that the freshman could not be racked for being a snitch. The Citadel code of honor says, "A cadet does not lie, cheat or steal nor tolerate those who do." Mazyck stuck to his original story, but the Honor Court believed the freshman. Mazyck was sentenced to be expelled, though he appealed the decision.

But what really went on in the Honor Court that day? Was it just a fluke that the head of the Churchill Society, Christopher Carrier, was also the Honor Court chairman? And was it just Lieutenant General Watts's sense of justice that caused him to

overturn the verdict and reinstate Mazyck, or could it have been
a lawsuit threatened by the Charleston chapter of the NAACP?

In 1986 five white cadets went into the bunk room of black
freshman Kevin Nesmith, the brother of the only black member
of the board of visitors. Wearing sheets — and pillowcases over
their heads — and holding a burning paper cross, they mumbled
Nesmith's name and uttered racial obscenities. The five were
convicted of violating the Fourth Class System, but it was Nesmith who left school and never got his degree. Today all five of
his assailants wear the Citadel ring.

"Race relations are not a problem at the Citadel," says Watts,
but the school's strategic planning report in 1988 found that 56
percent of black cadets — 7 percent of the student population is
black — said they were discriminated against "because of race."
Have things changed in four years? "I've heard guys call me
'boy,' " says running back Jason Pryor, a sophomore this season.
Wrestler Robert Reaves says he was called a "stupid nigger" last
year, when he was a freshman. The school formed a committee
to study race relations; it recommended that the playing of *Dixie*
and the waving of Confederate flags at football games be dis-
couraged.

Good luck. At the Citadel, Confederate pride still runs high.
At a Friday lunch last year a senior announced the Senior of
the Week award. It went to the cadet who had climbed seven
hundred feet up the Channel 2 tower in Charleston to hang the
Confederate flag. Cheers rocked the mess hall, but at one table
two black football players simply stared down at their plates.
They were Douglas, the quarterback, and Kelly Fladger, the star
cornerback.

You either believe in the Citadel wholly or you don't last. Five
days before the Wofford loss freshman Brian Alewine, a white
baseball pitcher, was in the shower room with a black freshman
he didn't know. Two other cadets came in and began taunting
the black cadet.

"Did you see *Mississippi Burning?*" they asked him. "How about
Lords of Discipline? Did you see the scene where they pour gaso-
line on the black guy? You know that — could happen right here
if you stay. You know that, right?"

The black cadet didn't flinch, but something inside Alewine couldn't take it.

"Why don't you back off?" Alewine snapped at them.

The two cadets pushed Alewine up against the shower wall.

"You got a problem?" one said. "We can settle it right here."

But nothing was settled until later. It was then, the next night, that things just got out of hand.

Alewine was running a message from his own H Company to the clerk's room at E Company. When Alewine got there, he says, "there was one kid standing in the corner just crying like a baby. And the E Company clerk was holding a broken-off stick, a transom stick." Alewine says that when the clerk saw him, he yelled at him to "brace" — to take the standard position for a freshman in the presence of an upperclassman: chin tucked tightly into the chest, shoulders up around the ears, a position that most resembles that of a child about to be struck.

"You're not bracing!" the clerk yelled.

Alewine braced harder, but it didn't seem to make a difference. The clerk took the jagged transom stick, walked behind Alewine and began jabbing him between the shoulder blades. "Shoulders up!" his tormentor kept yelling as he jabbed him.

Days later Alewine's father would be "shocked," he says, by the "big red lumps" on his son's back. Still Alewine did not report the incident. Unfortunately for him, somebody else did.

Four days later, the infamous night of the Wofford loss, Alewine stopped and braced at the bottom of the barracks stairs to let the upperclassmen down first. One of them was the clerk.

"Hey," a cadet yelled. "Do you know who this is?"

"Who is it?" yelled the clerk.

"It's Alewine," said the voice. "The rat."

The clerk asked Alewine if he had turned him in for the jabbing incident. Alewine said he hadn't. The clerk left, but another cadet ordered him to come to the darkened sally port near the trash cans and brace. Alewine did.

"You Alewine?"

Alewine could feel the cadet's nose in his ear.

"Sir, yes, sir!" said Alewine.

"You're the one that got those guys in trouble!" the cadet

screamed. "You called Colonel Dick!" (Colonel Harvey Dick is the assistant commandant.)

"Sir, no sir!"

"Were you hazed, Alewine? Is that what you told them?"

Alewine saw where this was heading, but what could he do? There are not many places a knob can turn in moments of terror. In each company there is one adult supervisor — one for every 118 cadets — but he goes home at night. Night in the barracks belongs to the boys.

"We're going to treat you the way we treat the rest of the niggers," the voice said.

Alewine tried to get past the cadet. He felt a hard right hand in the gut. Alewine swung wildly with his own right, smashed the cadet on the top of the head and ran. The next day he wound up in Charleston's Roper Hospital with severely bruised ribs and shortness of breath.

Three days later Brian Alewine stepped out of the Long Gray Line for good.

Around the Citadel the system is said to work. Don't you see? All the jocks and knobs who left, they never had the stuff it takes to be a whole man. The gate is always open. Only the wimps use it. Since nobody was expelled over any of these incidents, how could hazing have taken place? After all, if anybody had known about the hazing, the honor code would have obligated him to come forward, right?

Richard Varriale, last year's cadet regimental commander, the leading cadet on campus, says, "If somebody started poking me with a toothpick, I'd probably start laughing."

So Brozowski lied? And Davis? "No, I don't think they all lied," Varriale says. "I think they all exaggerated." And freshman football player Jess Fuller, who left claiming harassment and whose mother said she hadn't seen him that skinny since the ninth grade? And 1991 freshman soccer player Michael Lake, an outstanding student who left claiming hazing — the same Michael Lake who was once ordered not to cough in line even though he had bronchitis? "Lake was not well liked by his own teammates," says Varriale.

And Alewine? "Brian Alewine was not beaten," Lieutenant

General Watts wrote in a letter to the editor of the Charleston *Post and Courier,* which published Alewine's account of his night of terror. "[He] was hit one time by an unknown cadet. No beating took place." Watts wrote that the athletes who left had all "decided they would prefer a different life-style."

There will be no outrage among Citadel alumni over the bloody and torturous year of 1991. Forging good men has always been a little messy, hasn't it? Besides, Citadel men are mostly skin and a haircut wrapped around loyalty. They can be counted on to put their wallets where their hearts are. They chipped in $27 million over four years in a recent fundraising campaign. Not bad for a school that graduates only five hundred cadets a year.

But not all graduates are so generous. Mike Montei, a former Citadel baseball star, believes "the Citadel shot itself in the foot" over the Alewine incident. And Conroy wrote recently, "When the jocks start leaving early, it means the corps is out of control." Even quarterback Douglas, the alltime leading rusher among Division I-AA quarterbacks, is worried. "We need more adult supervision around here," he says. "This place can be crazy."

For the coaches the march never ends. Chal Port quit not long after the Alewine incident, ending twenty-seven years as a baseball coach. "I've never been in favor of hazing or harassment," he says. "There's a better way for leadership than to be negative all the time."

Football coach Charlie Taaffe shrugs when asked about the Fourth Class System. Every day he works with freshmen who can barely keep their chins off the ground. You can walk into the lobby of the football building any weekday and not be able to sit down. All the couches and chairs are filled with sleeping freshmen. Last season Taaffe lost four out of seventeen recruits to the Fourth Class System, and that's a waste of money and time and scholarships.

The coaches know that the Citadel would rather close its doors than give up the Fourth Class System. The breaking down of knobs is the backbone of the place. The Fourth Class System survives even though the Citadel's own 1988 report found that a vast majority of the faculty believe the system severely hurts freshman academics. "Our kids are exhausted when they come to class," says one English teacher. "As a result they are less competitive when it comes to grad school and ROTC commissions."

Watts bristles. "The Fourth Class System is time-tested," he says. "It's not a mean system. It's a demanding system."

And it might just be chasing out the wrong boys.

These days field goal kicker Davis does not feel nine feet tall and bulletproof. He feels terrified. Six weeks after leaving the Citadel, he was driving his car when he pulled over and went absolutely ballistic. He began screaming at his girlfriend — yelling at her as if she were a knob, saluting and marching back and forth. All he remembers is coming to on the hood of his car.

"I guess I went crazy," he says. "Like somebody in a war. I didn't know who I was or where I was. My girlfriend said I blanked out. I guess I'd gone back into [the Citadel]. It's funny, before I went to the Citadel, I never blew up at my girlfriend. Now I blow up at her all the time."

Davis is seeing a psychiatrist. He had a chance to kick for a small college, but he got only as far as the mailbox. "I didn't go because I'm scared of failing," he says. "I'm scared to make any kind of decision. I doubt myself so much." Davis's condition is just one of the achievements the sophomore class of 1990–91 can brag on. Smith, the cyclist, quit the Citadel soon after the saber episode. He and his mother got only $1,200 of his $13,000 loan money back. The Citadel explained where the rest went — to uniforms and meals and whatnot — but Smith never understood how he could have spent it all in three weeks.

Michael Lake has landed a soccer scholarship at Erskine College, in Due West, South Carolina. Jess Fuller is going to try to make the football team at Georgia as a walk-on. He has no scholarship. Karl Brozowski will play for Tennessee-Martin after fighting for six months to have the Citadel release him from his scholarship commitment. Brian Alewine is pitching for UNC Charlotte, but his scholarship is history. "All I know is, the two kids that beat my kid are still in school," says Alewine's father, Wayne, "and I'm here, paying through the tongue."

In fact, aside from the resignation of a cadet who beat a freshman golfer, not one cadet was expelled for hazing or lying about hazing in 1991. Rajewski was found guilty of violating the Fourth Class System and ordered to do 120 hours of marching, but he had the sentence forgiven by Watts amid the great good feeling on campus when the Citadel upset Army three games after the

Wofford loss. Because of its anger over the kid-gloves treatment of Rajewski, the Brozowski family pressed charges against him. Rajewski was sentenced to one hundred hours of community service as part of an agreement with the court.

And now the leaves turn again. The beaten, humiliated and spat-upon of last year will be beating, humiliating and spitting upon new freshmen. Things might just get out of hand, but a Citadel tradition is a Citadel tradition. Boys who love the ring will be driving out boys who love the ring just as much but who, for a bad sweep job here, a rifle called a gun there, will never wear it.

"I can tell you one thing," says the wrestler, Reaves. "I'm going to be *hell* when I'm a sophomore. I took a lot of crap. I've gotta get *somebody* back." Here's hoping they beat Wofford.

Postscript: Just before this story went to print, a black Citadel freshman told authorities he woke up on August 20 to find a string noose hanging from the bunk above him. Some say the noose was there because the freshman refused an upperclassman's demand that he sing *Dixie* in the barracks shower. The Citadel says that it has completed its investigation and has asked the South Carolina Law Enforcement Division to take over.

SEPTEMBER 14, 1992

Most of RICK REILLY's *recent work has been witty deadline stories on golf and pro football. This dark, brooding look into the Citadel football tradition demonstrates Reilly's range and makes us hope that, in the future, he will apply more of his time and talent to these substantial challenges.*
— F.D.

CRAIG MEDRED

Playing Back a Bear Attack

FROM WE ALASKANS

ALL THE DANGER and chaos came and went in the blink of an eye, and yet it transpired not so much like a videotape, but more like a series of vivid, still-life photographs.

At first, though, there were the sounds: the ominous woof of the brown bear sow, the thunder of the bear's feet thumping on the moss as she charged through the thick spruce forest, and then the all-encompassing silence which couldn't have been a silence at all for surely what came next had to make considerable noise, if only in the snapping of teeth, the breaking of branches and the explosions of the gun.

None of it registered. Only the pictures of the bear etched in memory — in glaring juxtaposition to how the day was supposed to have gone. This should have been a simple hike back to the moose muskegs. It was the next to last day of the September moose season. The plan was to set up a bivouac on the edge of an old burn and start reading Tom Clancy's new book, *The Sum of All Fears*. It was a perfect day for that.

Cold had come early, finishing off the white socks and gnats that can be a nightmare on the Kenai Peninsula in September. The leaves of the birch and aspen trees were a beautiful autumn gold. Fresh snow sprinkled the mountains above two thousand feet. The sky was blue, the sun warming the countryside by the hour.

A light breeze was blowing from the northwest, promising the fair weather would hold. It would keep my scent off the muskegs. There was a good overlook on a ridge at the southeast corner. You could sit there and read in comfort all day, looking up now and then to glass the openings and the nearby mountainside for moose.

Along toward evening, and again the next morning if necessary, a few well-called grunts in imitation of a mating bull would likely bring competitors. There was little question in my mind that I would see moose. The only question was whether one would have antlers wider than the legally required fifty inches.

There was a fair probability of that. I'd wandered back here a year before and seen a moose nearly that big. Expectations for this hunt were high. Two friends had already signed on to help pack meat if anything was killed.

Going in, thoughts were on finding a good route for packing loads out, and how bears could be kept off the meat pile, given that this area crawls with bears.

Along the Russian River that morning, there had been the fresh tracks of a blackie in the mud. That sign, like the moose sign that would be seen later on, was duly noted, but presented no cause for concern.

Many times I had wandered the surrounding country, prowling for moose, hiking cross-country over Bear Mountain toward Skilak Lake, following the Russian River Trail up through some of the most brown bear–filled habitat on the Kenai Peninsula. Sometimes I'd gone with friends. Often I went alone.

Solitary backcountry travel is not a practice I'd recommend, but there are a fair number of people, myself included, who do it regularly. Others might consider the wilderness an especially dangerous place, but I never have. I still don't.

When I stumbled into what at first appeared to be three yearling brown bears less than one hundred feet away in the dense spruce they registered not as a threat, but as a surprise. Bears had been expected back along the river or high in the tundra, where they would be dining on berries this time of year, but not in the spruce.

Seeing them there set my nerves on end, but no more so than any other chance meeting with brown bears. There'd been enough of those over the years that they were no longer cause for undue concern. Just a couple months before, I'd been within ten or fifteen feet of a pair of young browns on the nearby river, looking at their three-inch claws draped over the edge of a boardwalk along the trail and wondering why they didn't have the sense to treat humans with a little more respect.

Some Nervous Nellie, it seemed, was sure to get excited and take a shot at those bears if they didn't clean up their act, and that would be a shame. Bears seldom cause any problem for people; they are more threat than danger. They need to be treated with respect, but there is no cause for panic.

I was confident the bears off in the spruce wouldn't be a problem. They'd skedaddle when they heard a human voice. I started talking and angling away in a slow but even-paced walk.

The cubs followed.

That was unsettling, but not unprecedented. Cubs, like human juveniles, are curious, sometimes stupid.

"C'mon, Mom," I thought. "Round 'em up and get them out of here."

Meanwhile, I kept moving away, trying to keep an eye on the young bears and talking louder now, fully expecting them to turn and wander away.

And then it all went to hell.

There was the woof, the thunder of feet, and I turned to meet face to face with what I knew already was a charging bear, fully expecting this to be a bluff charge, fully expecting to find the bear coming to a screeching halt ten or fifteen feet away, fully expecting to see the bear swap ends and flee with her cubs in tow.

Only that wasn't the picture that materialized.

FREEZE FRAME: *The bear is at a distance of two feet. Her ears are back, her hair on end, her neck extended. She seems frozen in that position.*

In retrospect, of course, that was impossible, but the brain and the eyes did not know that at the time. They slowed things down the way they usually do in life-or-death situations, trying to provide the opportunity to hunt for a way out.

Observations, questions and conclusions all came and went in a nanosecond.

"Geez, you could reach down and pet this bear."

"What the hell is the matter with you. This isn't one of your Labradors coming up for attention."

"Hell, why wasn't this just a bluff charge like the ones before?"

"Now why did she have to go and do this?"

"Oh you're a beautiful bear. I don't want to have to shoot you."

"Get the gun up, get the gun up, get the gun up."

And by then it was too late.

The .454-caliber Casull handgun — carried in my right hand and ready because this had all begun as a hunt for moose — swung up only quick enough to catch the bear in the face. She grabbed it in her teeth.

FREEZE FRAME: *The bear has locked her jaws around the 2 × Leopold scope atop the pistol. She is a beautiful animal with a long, full coat of brown. Her hold on the gun positions the four-inch barrel perpendicular to her mouth. She has coal-black eyes.*

All of this was seen, digested and analyzed as if the bear were standing still, though she had to be still coming fast on the run.

Strangely enough, I felt no sense of danger, no panic. The speed of events buried any such reactions in the necessities of survival.

No thought was given to the critical need to hang on to the pistol or to the possibility of letting go. At some point, judging from the skin torn off my left hand, it must have come up to help grab the pistol grip. But I have no memory of that.

All that remains in memory are the detached observations and two thoughts that passed in that moment when the bear had total control of the situation.

The first thought was practical: "How the hell do you get the gun turned to shoot down her throat?"

The second was a strange flashback to childhood, a memory of an *Outdoor Life* story read as a preteen. It was about a hunter in Africa who saved his life by jamming his arm down the throat of a lion to prevent it from eating him.

"Can I get my arm down this bear's throat?" came my next thought.

Then the momentum of the bear's charge carried her over. I remember going down with the impact. Of the rest of her passing, there is nothing.

What happened then was reconstructed later based on an inch-long puncture wound that ripped an S-shaped scar along my jaw. That wound clearly came from a claw. The only way the bear could have inflicted such a wound was by stepping on my face as she went past.

There was no other time when her claws came into play. She never had a chance to take a swipe with her paws, for once the attack began, we were never more than an arm's length apart. At close range, her weapon was her powerful teeth and jaws.

Mine was the Casull.

Where and when it came loose from the bear's jaw is impossible to say, but somehow it did. It was again loose in the right hand, my thumb apparently moving without thought to cock the hammer on the single action, as the bear turned from the first charge.

FREEZE FRAME: *The bear has moved from my right side to my left, beyond me by half an arm's length and turning back. Her fur ripples above what looks to be five hundred pounds of muscle. Duff from the forest floor hangs in the air, torn up from her feet spinning in a high-speed turn.*

A new assessment flashed: "O.K., she's knocked me down. Now she's going to turn and go back to take care of her cubs. This is all going to be over in a second. We're all going to be O.K." And then she was in front of me, fur shaking on her body, jaws open, lunging to grab flesh. The gun was up, too. Cocked and ready to fire, though I have no memory of cocking it.

FREEZE FRAME: *I am on my butt on the forest floor, sitting up and in the middle of a roll to the left. The bear is in mid-lunge, mouth open. The gun has just gone off. The bullet has missed the bear clean on the right. It is obvious the gun was aimed at nothing but air.*

The bear simply was not in front of the barrel when the gun went off. Whether she'd been there and moved or whether I'd pulled the trigger too soon in the adrenalin of the moment is hard to say.

Thoughts were reverberating: "How the hell could you miss so big a target so close? Because you didn't aim the gun, idiot. You've got to point it at what you want to hit."

Then the bear made an amazing sideways leap. It was a stunning display of agility, like watching a house cat playing games on a kitchen counter. That an animal so big can move like this almost takes your breath away. Then she clamped down on my right leg just above the ankle.

FREEZE FRAME: *The bear is now below me on a gently sloping hillside. She has her head down, her jaws clamped on my leg. There is pressure but no pain. I am staring at her ears and the hump where her powerful shoulders join at the top of her back. She is no longer so pretty. She looks to be four feet wide.*

Simple thoughts rushed through my head: "Just point the gun at the middle of her body and pull the trigger. That's all you've got to do. Just point the gun at her and squeeze." There was no thought of aiming. No way to aim for that matter. The rubber scope covers had never come off the scope. Thus there was no way to sight through it, but it didn't matter. The target was fixed and inches away.

"Just point the barrel at it and pull the trigger." All of this was digested in the tiniest fractions of a second. The bear began to pull on the leg, dragging me along the forest floor, starting to shake her head. The jaws were growing tighter. I thought the bone would pop at any second.

"Shoot her now."

Somehow, instinctively and without any thought, the hammer had already been cocked again to rotate another bullet into firing position and prepare the gun to fire. All it took was a squeeze on the trigger. There was only one, last, quick and passing thought.

"Jesus, don't shoot yourself in the foot."

I pulled the trigger. The .454 Casull is the most powerful handgun in the world. The 260-grain slug it sends down the barrel carries with it close to a ton of energy. The reaction when this gun goes off is violent. There is a staggering amount of recoil with the Casull.

FREEZE FRAME: *The pistol recoils upward with the second shot, climbing inch by inch into the sky until it has covered a good two feet. There is dust or smoke in the air. There has been no realization of sound up to now, but suddenly the woods seem unearthly quiet.*

The bear lay on the ground two feet from my foot. The force of the impact from the slug had knocked her away. She rested on her stomach. Her eyes were glassy. The attack was finished.

The bear had begun this battle quickly. It had ended even more quickly with one shot from the gun.

I thought, in that moment, that the bear might be dead, that one unaimed shot might have hit her in the brain, miraculously and humanely killing her. Then came the sound of the bear breathing, blood gurgling in her throat or nasal passages. She was hit badly, probably fatally, but it was not an instant-killing shot to the brain. I thumbed the hammer to fire the gun again to finish her. The gun would not cock. The cylinder would not rotate another shell into firing position.

The bear moved. She had been down for seconds, maybe as many as fifteen, but she obviously was not going to stay down. The problem with the gun was obvious. The recoil of the first two shots had forced a bullet to jump the crimp on one of the cartridges. The lead tip of the copper-jacketed bullet extended beyond the front of the cylinder by a fraction of an inch. That fraction was just enough that the lead hit the frame of the pistol and blocked the cylinder from rotating into firing position.

I had seen the problem before. It happened two years earlier while deer hunting on Kodiak Island. All of the ammunition reloaded for the Casull after that had been double-crimped to prevent a recurrence. Dozens, maybe hundreds, of rounds had since been fired without a problem. Why now? I tried pulling back on the hammer and at the same time rotating the cylinder with the left hand in an effort to force the bullet into firing position. No go. The bear started to get up.

A tool was needed to smash the bullet back into the cartridge. The end of an unopened pocketknife would work, but the pocketknife was in the pocket of the jacket worn in the morning when it was cooler, and the jacket was in the backpack. Getting to the jacket would require struggling out of the backpack harness, removing the backpack, opening it and then finding the jacket.

Would all of this motion aggravate the bear to attack and finish what she had begun? But what good is a jammed handgun? Could I swing it hard enough to bash in her skull if she climbed back on top of me? What choices were there?

The bear tried to stagger to her feet. She got about halfway up the first time and fell over. The force of gravity pulled her downhill, away from me. The gap between us opened to ten feet.

She tried to rise again. And again she fell, moving even farther away. In the timber, the ground sloped down at no more than three to five degrees, but it was enough to force her away. She would have to come back uphill to resume the attack. She never did. Topography, in the end, was my saving grace.

Several times the bear tried to rise before she managed to stay on her feet and ramble unsteadily downhill toward where the brush was thicker. She was obviously thinking then about only one thing: getting away.

I lay there on the ground and watched her go. It was the worst moment.

From the first shot fired, there had been a deep sense of guilt at being forced to shoot a sow with cubs. Having done the job badly only made it worse. Now, on top of that, came extreme frustration at the inability to finish the mess once and for all in the way it should be finished.

In the chaos of the attack, the instincts of survival had controlled all thoughts. Now emotions began to surface. There was anger at the bear's bad judgment, the jammed gun, the wrecked moose hunt, the motherless cubs, the sow crawling off to die, the vagaries of fate.

"Why me?" I thought. "I don't need this." And then those thoughts passed, once more giving way to reality.

There were still problems to be dealt with. The first thing was to find out whether the leg worked. It was numb and the foot splayed outward, but it held weight when I stood. I thought it might be broken, but if it was, there remained enough adrenalin coursing through the system to mask any pain.

How long that would last was unknown. The trick was to get to help while it was still possible to move, before the pain became debilitating.

Off came the backpack that carried thirty pounds of gear for an overnight camp on the muskeg. No sense lugging that around; it would just put unnecessary weight on the leg.

Next I pulled out the jacket, got the pocketknife, smashed the jammed bullet back into the cylinder, rotated it, removed the offending cartridge and the rest — fearing there might have been more failed crimps — then reloaded.

By this time there were no signs of the bears. The sow had disappeared into thick spruce and alder undergrowth. The cubs that had been with her when the attack began were gone. They had disappeared from sight around the time she charged.

My injuries did not seem severe. My face was bleeding, but not badly. Likewise the leg. The polypropylene tights worn beneath the pants seemed to be maintaining good compression on the wound. There was, at the moment, no danger of bleeding to death.

The first thought then was that it was my responsibility to follow the bear and finish her. It was totally irresponsible to leave a wounded bear in the woods. The manly thing, the right thing, was to track her and kill her, but I couldn't bring myself to do it.

The rationalizations went like this:

"Look, you don't have much faith in the gun at the moment. What if the cubs (which looked to be between four and five feet tall) decide to get involved? You'll be lucky if you've got enough left to walk back to the truck. What if the bear's not hurt as badly as you think? What if the adrenalin runs out and the pain starts and you can't keep tracking her? If you have to stay back here, it could take days for anyone to find you."

Eventually, I decided to lean the backpack against a tree near the site of the attack and start hiking out. The pack would provide a marker for someone to come back, pick up the blood trail of the bear, track her down and finish her.

Then began an unusually long hike of only about a mile or a mile and a half. It was not so much painful as clumsy. The right foot did not work properly. It was a club. It had to be put down carefully before any weight could be placed on it. It had to be lifted over logs and obstacles.

It objected to crossing the river, balking at supporting weight when it had to on the slippery rocks. I began to worry that the Achilles tendon had been damaged. It was a struggle to climb the trail up the hill from the river to the pink salmon parking lot in the Russian River Campground.

My constant yells for help attracted no one. That was hilariously ironic. Here was the most popular fishing stream in Alaska, a stream where people stand shoulder to shoulder to catch salmon in June, July and August, a waterway where everyone has cussed the crowds at one time or another, and now, when I needed help, there was nobody.

"How the hell could this be?"

Why, just that morning, on the hike in toward moose-hunting country, radio disc jockey Rick Rydell had come walking along the trail from upriver and introduced himself. Where was he now?

Nowhere to be found. There weren't even any other vehicles left in the 100-slot pink salmon lot. That meant I'd have to drive the truck myself. For the first time in my life, I cussed a manual transmission. But somehow the truck was made to jerk its way the few miles to Gwin's Lodge in Cooper Landing.

It is always amazing how friendly and helpful Alaskans prove to be in a time of crisis. A lot of people intervened to help. One of the cooks got me down on the floor, propped my feet up to help prevent shock, and tried to squelch the bleeding.

Someone else called Fish and Wildlife Protection to report the wounded bear. A woman from the Forest Service carefully noted directions on how to find the backpack. Within a couple hours, I was in a first-rate emergency-care unit at Central Peninsula Hospital in Soldotna.

A couple hours after that, Fish and Wildlife Protection Trooper Brandon Anderson of Seward showed up to return the backpack and say he'd been unable to find the bear. Showing more courage than I, Anderson and officer Todd Sharp had tracked a trail of blood for a half mile into some blowdown before deciding the bear was headed for the mountains — away from any people — and letting her go.

What happened to her remains unknown. I still think about it — sometimes bothered by a Disney-esque vision of the yearling cubs following their wounded mother, hanging around confused while she slowly dies.

Nature doesn't work that way, I know, but I still feel guilty. There is something troubling about shooting a healthy and productive sow, even though wildlife biologist Sterling Miller, one of the country's top experts on bears, assures me the yearling cubs still have a good chance at survival.

Mainly, though, it is aggravating that the bear made such a stupid decision. All she had to do was ignore me, and we both would have been fine. The last thing I wanted to do was kill a Kenai Peninsula sow, further reducing the productivity of a brown bear population under increasing pressure from the encroachments of man.

What, I wonder, did I do to set this chain of events in motion? What could I have done to avoid it? The situation had seemed controllable enough when the bears were first spotted in the spruce. They were approximately one hundred feet away at about three o'clock on my right. They had sensed something, but they didn't seem sure of what it was.

A dozen or more times over the years I have encountered bears like this. Usually the bears have fled. A couple times there have been charges, but always those were bluffs. These bears did not seem overly aggressive or disturbed, just curious.

Judging by size, I thought at the time there were three yearling cubs and wondered at the whereabouts of the sow. She didn't seem to be with them, and that was somewhat worrisome.

Thinking about this since then, I have wondered whether there might actually have been a sow and two cubs — given the poor visibility and the terrain. The cubs could have been close enough in size to their mother that there was no immediately obvious distinction between them. I had concluded that they were three cubs because the one I could see clearly was a cub, and the others appeared to be of like size.

Whatever the case, the decision on how to handle them probably would not have changed. These were Russian River bears, after all. They had to have been exposed to people. They should have understood that if they didn't make trouble for humans, humans wouldn't make trouble for them.

Thus came my decision to begin talking to the bears in a normal voice while angling slowly away. I wanted the bears to know what I was, and where I was going.

A breeze of five mph or so was blowing from the bears toward me. They obviously hadn't smelled me, but they had heard something stumbling through the woods. They should have been able to clearly determine what that was once I started talking, and they would surely have seen me moving off, going uphill along a ridge at a sharp angle away.

The cubs must certainly have known what I was when they started following. One of them even stood to get a better look. I talked louder and kept slowly moving away, swearing under my breath. I thought about turning to confront the bears, but figured any aggressive act toward the cubs at that point would be unwise.

As it turned out, passive behavior didn't work so well either. The sow woofed once from behind the cubs and charged.

Based on a fifteen-foot streak of bear scat found on the far side of my backpack, Sharp later speculated that one of the cubs might have gotten behind me, putting me between the sow and cubs and sparking her charge.

There is probably even a remote possibility they were stalking me. I consider that unlikely, but no one will ever know.

Dozens of times on the long walk to the Russian River parking lot, in the ambulance on the way to Soldotna, in the Soldotna emergency room, and in later conversations with friends and wildlife biologists, I mulled over this attack.

It has left no great fears about bears. There have been no nightmares.

But part of me will always wonder what I might have done differently, how I might have avoided an encounter that left me with more than a dozen stitches in my face and leg, how I could have prevented a confrontation that ended with a bear wounded and now, in all probability, dead.

Where she was hit I'll never know. I thought at the time I'd shot her in the face, but when I look back on it now, that clearly was not the case. There was no blood visible when she lay on the ground looking at me, and there was the sound of her breathing blood, as if she'd been hit in the lungs.

From what Sharp saw in tracking her, he believes she was bleeding high on the shoulder. He found splatters of blood that looked to have been blown out through a blow hole. That leads me to believe that in thinking about trying not to shoot my foot, I hit her somewhere in the front of the chest, near where the shoulder joins the neck. It is possible to conclude that the bullet angled down through her lungs, possibly running the length of her body before running out of energy. There is no indication from the way she was bleeding that it ever came out down low, but given the angle at which I was shooting it had to have been headed in that direction.

Probably, she was bleeding into her lungs, and if that is the case, there is little doubt that by now she is dead.

I wish it were different. I wish there were some way this story could have had a better ending, but the truth is, I don't know that there was much I could have done differently.

That bothered me for a time. A friend finally helped me move past it with the simple words of a cliché.

"The one thing you keep forgetting," he said, "is that the only thing predictable about bears is that they are unpredictable."

And the wilderness wouldn't be the wilderness if they weren't.

OCTOBER 4, 1992

A few months after I read this agonizing account about a man being attacked by a bear, I was in Africa, where I was chased (in a car) by an angry herd of elephants. The incident made me appreciate CRAIG MEDRED's *story all the more — not just that he survived, but that he had the extraordinary presence of mind to remember so many details so vividly. — F.D.*

DONNA TARTT

Basketball Season

FROM THE OXFORD AMERICAN

THE YEAR I WAS A FRESHMAN cheerleader, I was reading *1984*. I was fourteen years old then and failing algebra and the fact that I was failing it worried me as I would worry now if the Mafia was after me, or if I had shot somebody and the police were coming to get me. But I did not have an awful lot of time to brood about this. It was basketball season then, and there was a game nearly every night. In Mississippi the schools are far apart, and sometimes we would have to drive two hundred miles to get to Panola Academy, Sharkey-Issaquena, funny how those old names come back to me; we'd leave sometimes before school was out, not get home till twelve or one in the morning. I was not an energetic teenager and this was hard on me. Too much exposure to the high-decibel world of teen sports — shrieking buzzers; roaring stomping mobs; thunderous feet of players charging up the court — kept me in a kind of perpetual stunned condition; the tin roof echo of rural gymnasiums rang through all my silences, and frequently at night I woke in a panic, because I thought a player was crashing through my bedroom window or a basketball was flying at me and about to knock my teeth out.

I read *1984* in the back seats of Cadillacs, Buicks, Lincoln Town Cars, riding through the flat wintry Delta with my saddle oxfords off and my schoolbooks piled beneath my feet. Our fathers — professional men, mostly, lawyers and optometrists, prosperous local plumbers — took turns driving us back and forth from the games; the other cheerleaders griped about this but though I griped along with them, I was secretly appalled at the rowdy team bus, full of boys who shouted things when you

walked by their table in the cafeteria and always wanted to copy
your homework. The cars, on the other hand, were wide, spacious, quiet. Somebody's mother would usually have made cookies; there were always potato chips and old issues of *Seventeen*.
The girls punched listlessly at the radio; applied Bonne Bell lip
gloss; did their homework or their hair. Sometimes a paperback
book would make the rounds. I remember reading one book
about a girl whose orphaned cousin came to live with her, gradually usurping the girl's own position in the household and becoming homecoming queen and family favorite. (" 'Why can't
you be more like Stephanie?' yelled Mom, exasperated.") It
turned out that Stephanie was not the girl's real cousin at all, but
a witch: a total surprise to the nincompoop parents, who had not
noticed such key signs as Stephanie failing to show up in photographs, or the family dog ("Lady") and the girl's horse ("Wild-
fire") going crazy every time Stephanie came within fifty feet.

   Now that I think about it, I believe I read *Animal Farm* before
1984. I read it in the car, too, riding through monotonous cottonfields in the weak winter afternoon, on the way to a tournament at Yalobusha Academy. It upset me a little, especially the
end, but the statement "All Animals are Equal, but Some Animals are more Equal than Others" echoed sentiments which I
recognized as prevalent in the upper echelons of the cheerleading squad. Our captain was a mean senior girl named Cindy
Clark. She talked a lot about spirit and pep, and how important
it was we work as a team, but she and her cronies ostracized the
younger girls and were horrible to us off the court. Cindy was
approximately my height and was forced to be my partner in
some of the cheers, a circumstance which displeased her as much
as it did myself. I remember a song that was popular around that
time — it had lyrics that went:

> We are family
> I've got all my sisters with me

   This had for some reason been incorporated into one of the
chants and Cindy and I were frequently forced to sing it together: arms around each other, leaning on each other like
drunks, beaming with joy and behaving in every way like the sisters which we, in fact, were most certainly not.

   Though there was a sharp distinction between the older girls and the younger ones, we were also divided, throughout our ranks and regardless of age, into two distinct categories: those of snob and slut. The snobs had flat chests, pretty clothes, and were skittish and shrill. Though they were always sugar-sweet to one's face, in reality they were a nasty, back-biting lot, always doing things like stealing each other's boyfriends and trying to rig the elections for the Beauty Revue. The sluts were from poorer families, and much better liked in general. They drank beer, made out with boys in the hallways, and had horrible black hickeys all over their necks. Our squad was divided pretty much half and half. Physically and economically, I fell into the category of snob, but I did poorly in school and was not gung-ho or clubbish enough to fit in very well with the rest of them. (To be a proper snob, one had always to be making floats for some damn parade or other, or organizing pot-luck dinners for the Booster Club.) The sluts, I thought, took a more sensible view of such foolishness; they smoked and drank; I found them, as a rule, much nicer. Being big girls generally, they were the backbones of the stances, the foundations from which the pyramids rose and, occasionally, fell; I, being the smallest on the squad, had to work with them rather closely, in special sessions after the regular cheerleading practices, since they were the ones who lifted me into the air, who spotted me in gymnastics, upon whose shoulders I had to stand to form the obligatory pyramid. They all had pet names for me, and — though vigorously heterosexual — babied me in what I am sure none of them realized was a faintly lecherous way: tickles and pinches, slaps on the rump, pulling me into their laps in crowded cars and crooning stupid songs from the radio into my ear. Most of this went on in the after-school practices. At the games they completely ignored me, as every fiber of their attention was devoted to flirting with — and contriving to make out with — various boys. As I was both too young to be much interested in boys, and lacking in the fullness of bosom and broadness of beam which would have made them much interested in me, I was excluded from this activity. But still they felt sorry for me, and gave me tips on how to make myself attractive (pierced ears, longer hair, tissue paper in the bra) — and, when we were loitering around after practices, often regaled me with worldly tales of various sexual, obstetric, and gynecological horrors, some of which still make my eyes pop to think about.

The gymnasiums were high-ceilinged, barnlike, drafty, usually in the middle of some desolate field. We were always freezing in our skimpy plaid skirts, our legs all goose pimples as we clapped and stamped on the yellowed wooden floor. (Our legs, being so much exposed, were frequently chapped from cold, yet we were forbidden to put lotion on them, Cindy and the older girls having derived a pathological horror of "grease" from — as best as I could figure — the Clearasil ads in *Tiger Beat* and *Seventeen* — this despite the fact that grease was the primary element of all our diets.) Referee's whistle, sneakers squealing on the varnish. "Knees together," Cindy would hiss down the line, or "Spit out that gum," before she hollered "Ready!" and we clapped our hands down to our sides in unison and yelled the response: "O-Kay!" At halftime there were the detested stances, out in the middle of the court, which involved perilous leaps, and complex timing, and — more likely than not — tears and remonstrations in the changing rooms. These were a source of unremitting dread, and as soon as they were over and the buzzer went off for third quarter the younger girls rushed in a greedy flock to the snack bar for Cokes and French fries, Hershey bars, scattering to devour them in privacy while Cindy and her crew slunk out to the parking lot to rendezvous with their boyfriends. We were all of us, all the time, constantly sick — coughing, blowing our noses, faces flushed with fever — a combination of cold, bad food, cramped conditions, and yelling ourselves hoarse every night. Hoarseness was, in fact, a matter of pride: we were accused of shirking if our voices weren't cracked by the end of the evening, the state to which we aspired being a rasping, laryngitic croak. I remember the only time the basketball coach — a gigantic, stone-faced, terrifying man who was also the principal of the school and who, to my way of thinking, held powers virtually of life or death (there were stories of his punching kids out, beating them till they had bruises, stories which perhaps were not apocryphal in a private school like my own, which prided itself on what it called "old-fashioned discipline" and where corporal punishment was a matter of routine); the only time this coach ever spoke to me was to compliment me on my burnt-out voice, which he overheard in the hall the morning after a game. "Good job," he said. My companions and I were struck speechless with terror. After he was gone they stared at me with awestruck apprehension and then, one by one, drifted gently away, not wishing to be seen in the company of anyone who had attracted the attention — even momentarily — of this dangerous lunatic.

There were pep squads, of a sort, in George Orwell's Oceania. I read about them with interest. Banners, procession, slogans, games, were as popular there as they were at Kirk Academy. Realizing that there were certain correspondences between this totalitarian nightmare and my own high school gave me at first a feeling of smug superiority, but after a time I began to have an acute sense of the meaninglessness of my words and gestures. Did I really care if we won or lost? No matter how enthusiastically I jumped and shouted, the answer to this was unquestionably No. This epiphany both confused and depressed me. And yet I continued — outwardly at least — to display as much pep as ever. "I always look cheerful and I never shirk anything," says Winston Smith's girlfriend, Julia. "Always yell with the crowd, that's what I say. It's the only way to be safe." Our rival team was called the Patriots. I remember one rally, the night before a big game, when a dummy Patriot was hanged from the gymnasium rafters, then taken outside and burned amid the frenzied screams and stomps of the mob. I yelled as loud as anybody even though I was suffused by an airy, perilous sense of unreality, a conviction that — despite the apparently desperate nature of this occasion — that none of it meant anything at all. In my diary that night — a document which was as secretive and, to my mind at least, as subversive as Winston's own — I noted tersely: "Hell's own Pep Rally. Freshmen won the spirit stick. Rah, rah."

It was on the rides home — especially on the nights we'd won — that the inequity of not being allowed on the team bus was most keenly felt by the cheerleaders. Moodily, they stared out the windows, dreaming of back seats, and letter jackets, and smooching with their repulsive boyfriends. The cars smelled like talcum powder and Tickle deodorant and — if we were with one of the nicer dads, who had allowed us to stop at a drive-in — cheeseburgers and French fries. It was too dark to read. Everyone was tired, but for some reason we were all too paranoid to go to sleep in front of each other; afraid we might drool, perhaps, or inadvertently scratch an armpit.

Whispers, giggles, sighs. We rode four to a car and all four of us would be crammed in the back seat; bare arms touching, goosebumped knees pressed together, our silences punctuated by long ardent slurps of Tab. The console lights of the Cadillac dashboards were phosphorescent, eerie. The radio was mostly static that time of night but sometimes you could get a late-night station coming out of Greenwood or Memphis; slow songs, that's what everyone wanted, sloppy stuff by Olivia Newton-John or Dan Fogelberg. (The cheerleaders had a virtual cult of Olivia Newton-John; they tried to do their hair like her, emulate her in every possible way, and were fond of speculating what Olivia would or would not do in certain situations. She was like the ninth, ghost member of the squad. I was secretly gratified when she plummeted — with alarming swiftness — from favor because someone heard a rumor that she was gay.)

Olivia or not, the favorite song that winter hands down was "You Light Up My Life" by Debby Boone. It must have been number one for months; at least, it seemed to come on the radio just about every other song, which was fine with everybody. When it came on the girls would all start singing it quietly to themselves, staring out the window, each in their own little world; touching the fogged window-glass gently with their fingertips and each thinking no one could hear them, but all their voices combined in a kind of low, humming harmony that blended with the radio:

> So many nights
> I sit by my window
> Waiting for someone
> To sing me his song . . .

Full moon; hard frost on the stubbled cottonfields. They opened up on either side of the car in long, gray spokes, like a fan.

Yes, I know. Girls cheering for boys competing is now terribly politically incorrect. But the animosities on DONNA TARTT's cheering squad mirror the same sort of divisions on football and baseball teams. Two, four, six, eight, this memoir I appreciate. — F.D.

KENNY MOORE

A Scream and a Prayer

FROM SPORTS ILLUSTRATED

THE EYE COULDN'T help but fasten on Noureddine Morceli and
Hassiba Boulmerka as they ran their respective 1,500-meter finals at the world championships in Tokyo last summer. They
stood out in their Algerian green, the green of mallards and
meadows, the green of Islam. Morceli, the indoor-record holder,
was the favorite in the men's race, but Boulmerka was virtually
unknown in the women's.

Morceli followed a strong, even pace and kicked early, with a
full 400 meters to go. He blasted into the lead so hard, burning
100 meters in a maniacal 12.8 seconds, that he seemed certain to
be exhausted well before the homestretch.

Boulmerka didn't claw out of the pack and into the lead until
late in the last turn. Behind her was world and Olympic 3,000-
meter champion Tatyana Samolenko Dorovskikh of the
U.S.S.R., famed for her kick and just beginning to open up.

Morceli covered the second 100 of his last lap in another extraordinary 12.8. His third 100 was yet *another* 12.8. He had just
run the fastest finishing 300 in the history of championship
1,500s, but he still had 100 meters to go and Kenya's Wilfred
Kirochi was only five meters back.

Boulmerka, in her homestretch, labored to hold on. She told
herself that now was the moment to believe. She had been strong
all season. She would be strong once more. And so she was.
Dorovskikh could sprint no closer.

Morceli, far from tightening, gained an astounding ten meters
in his last 100. He relaxed across the line in a meet record of
3:32.84. Barely ten meters past the finish, he sank to his knees

and placed his palms and forehead upon the track. There he prayed, motionless, a slender brown man in green, abruptly transformed from conqueror to supplicant.

As Boulmerka won her race by three meters in 4:02.21, she screamed. Slowing, she seized her hair with both hands and kept on screaming, as if her passion were so great that it might burst her brain. "I screamed for joy and for shock, and for much more," she said when at last she was able to explain. "I was screaming for Algeria's pride and Algeria's history, and still more." Boulmerka was the first female world champion from her country, which is divided over the very idea of female athletes. "I screamed finally for every Algerian woman," she went on, "every Arabic woman."

Morceli's performance capped an undefeated season that revealed him to be, at twenty-one, the most talented miler who has yet lived. He was humbled. "My prayer was just to God," he said, "to thank him for giving me the power for the victory."

No nation had ever before produced both the men's and women's world or Olympic 1,500-meter champions, and Algeria duly went wild. "At the airport," said Boulmerka, "it took the National Service to control the crowds. They threw *mountains* of bouquets." Boulmerka, overwhelmed, was borne through Algiers in an open limousine. "From the balconies the women threw out candies and wheat seeds. We do it at weddings. The wheat is symbolic of sweet life, basic life."

Boulmerka (pronounced bull-MERK-uh) and Morceli (MORE-sell-ee) were awarded the Medal of Merit, one of Algeria's highest honors. President Chadli Bendjedid was so moved at the ceremony that he kissed Boulmerka on the forehead. There were pledges of money and houses. "And," Boulmerka says, "several leaders of political parties told me, 'You did what we haven't been able to do for years. You brought us together.'"

Yes, but briefly. Boulmerka's victory for Islamic women was a fraying rope flung across a yawning social chasm. Many Algerians, even as they cheered, found their pride at odds with their religion. In public the devout female Muslim should be covered from head to toe. So having the bare-legged Boulmerka defeat the nonbelievers was wonderful, but for the strict it was a guilty pleasure.

Within a few months doctrinaire imams pronounced a *kofr*, or

denunciation, of Boulmerka as un-Muslim for "running with naked legs in front of thousands of men." Boulmerka, who had
worn modest boy's shorts in Tokyo while the rest of the women's
field pranced in Lycra briefs, shot back that she was indeed a
practicing Muslim but that the traditional Islamic woman's leg-
gings and head scarf might inhibit her stride.

Boulmerka, twenty-four, was hardly new to this. For years,
when she ran on Algerian roads, men had sometimes spat or
thrown stones to convey their contempt for her dress or endeavor. She had ignored them. But then Algerians began voting
Boulmerka's critics into high office. In late 1991 the Islamic Sal-
vation Front (FIS), the doctrinaire Muslim political party, won so
many seats in the first round of the country's first free parlia-
mentary elections that it seemed assured of taking control of the
government after the second round of voting in January.

Opponents of the FIS, including the army, believed that the
party would do away with the democratic process. "In Islam, the
people do not govern themselves by laws they make of their own,
as in a democracy," wrote the late Sayyid Qutb, leader of the
Muslim Brotherhood and mentor of the FIS. "Rather, the people are governed by . . . laws imposed by God, which they cannot
change." *Muslim,* in Arabic, means one who submits to the will of
God.

When Bendjedid indicated in January that he was willing to
share power with the FIS, the army had heard enough. It forced
Bendjedid to resign, canceled the elections, installed a ruling
council and outlawed the FIS. The party's followers rioted, and
hundreds of people died in the fighting. The government council declared a state of emergency for one year and empowered
the military to make arrests and conduct trials without observing
normal legal procedures.

It seemed just the time to visit a pair of Muslim milers.

It is not yet sunset in Algiers, but a thunderstorm has blown in
from the sea and made the afternoon night. Date palms, papy-
ruses, cypresses and day lilies all thrash together in the cold, wet
wind. Creamy buildings, which seem to have been lifted from
either Paris boulevards or Cairo squares, rise steeply from the
harbor into seething clouds. Hailstones shred banana plants but
bounce off rubber trees. Algiers, on the Mediterranean coast of

Africa, is barely 200 miles from the Sahara but is at the latitude of Tulsa. The city mixes climates, plants, architectures, histories, bloods.

A thunderbolt's oddly pink light momentarily reveals FIS graffiti spray-painted on the walls in curvaceous Arabic. The sound of the thunder echoes away until it is replaced by an amplified metallic voice, quavering and ancient. It is the muezzin calling from the mosque, calling that the sun is down, that the fast may be broken.

It is Ramadan, the ninth month of the lunar year, when the faithful abstain from food and drink from sunrise to sunset. It was during Ramadan in A.D. 630 that the prophet Muhammad won military and spiritual victory over the city of Mecca and established the first Islamic state, on the Arabian peninsula. The rhythm imposed by Ramadan is of hearty meals at dawn and dusk separated by wan, parched days and recharged, festive nights.

So after dinner, a freshly showered Morceli, with his manager, Amar Brahmia, and Brahmia's brother, Baki, take you out on the town. Amar drives through rain and dense traffic to a vast, dim parking garage where aged attendants, gesturing in the thick blue haze, enforce three-centimeter spaces between cars. The only exit is a stairway filled with twin torrents of Algerians urgently going up and down. Morceli, dressed in a loose black suit, black dress shoes and an audibly yellow and green shirt, directs you up and steadies you in the crush with a protective hand on your shoulder.

You emerge in . . . a shopping mall, a multilayered concrete complex of stores and restaurants, covered but open to the wind. It is thronged with promenading Algerian families. *"Riad Elfeth,"* says Morceli. "The Victory Garden. It's only like this now. After Ramadan, it goes dark at night again."

Morceli and the Brahmias stroll and mingle, letting you sense that the city is far from an armed camp. The mood is light. "Normal," says Morceli.

Well-wishers respectfully extend him a hand, giving Morceli the choice of taking it. Mildly, with a shy grin, he usually does. His face is an image of youth, of potential. "I don't come out much," he says.

Above the heads of the crowd, large TV sets show a sweating

orchestra and a ravaged old singer pouring out tinny *chaabi* music apparently so exquisitely heartrending that Morceli will hear no sarcasm about it. Soon you are at a table outside a café, sipping brick-red orange juice, getting back to beginnings.

Morceli was born February 20, 1970, in the small town of Ténès, 125 miles west of Algiers. His father, Abdallah, worked in a building-materials factory, and his mother, Kamla, took care of their six boys and three girls, one of whom, Zahia, is Noureddine's twin sister. Their house was 120 meters from the Mediterranean. As a child Noureddine loved fishing for sole from the beach, because he could jam his pole in the sand and sprint away with the wind whenever he could no longer endure inaction.

He cannot remember a time that he was not wholly and willingly subject to Islam's discipline. "All my family are very, very strong believers," he says. His religion's five basic duties are giving alms to the needy, saying prayers five times daily, fasting during Ramadan, professing the faith and, at least once in life, making a pilgrimage to Mecca. Morceli devoutly performs the first four duties, and he promises to make his pilgrimage, or hajj, when he can bring a "proper seriousness" to the mission.

His family, however, did not feel that simply observing Islam's fundamental practices would produce worldly rewards. "I was always taught," says Morceli, "that good is from God and that he says, '*Move* if you want to get something. Don't sit and wait.' "

So there was a second family discipline: running. "My most vivid memory is of when I was seven," Morceli says, "and watching on TV when my brother Abderrahmane placed fourth behind Steve Ovett in the 1977 World Cup 1,500 in Düsseldorf."

Abderrahmane, Noureddine's inspiration and intimate, has coached him ever since. What's more, Abderrahmane's best friend, who ran 3:36.50 in the 1,500 in 1981 and is an attorney and an agent for Algerian runners on the European circuit, also gives Noureddine advice. Who is this helpful man? The same Amar Brahmia who is now ordering everyone glasses of hot, bitter sugared tea with crushed mint leaves. "Abderrahmane and I even got married on the same day," says Brahmia, winking. "But not to the same wife.'

So Noureddine grew up never wondering what he wanted to do, or how to do it. "I am gifted by God," he says with arresting simplicity, "and I prove it by working very hard. From age eleven, I wanted to be world champion. I ran my first race at twelve, four miles of cross-country on the beach. I sprinted too hard at the start and came in fourth, and afterward my chest burned, and I thought, From now on I train seriously."

The young Noureddine seemed best suited to long distances. "At fourteen, I ran for five hours," he says proudly. "Three of us did. We just went for a run, and nobody wanted to stop, so we . . . kept going."

"They ran for two and a half hours, and then they had to get home somehow," says Baki Brahmia, twenty-nine, a 3:37.70 1,500-meter man who has about him a clarity appropriate to someone who just took his Ph.D. in solid-state physics from Warwick University in Coventry, England. Morceli is surrounded by remarkably capable people.

By osmosis, by example, by videotape, by making games of race tactics in workouts, Morceli's support group taught and toughened him. When he was sixteen, he had a bad race and finished sixth in the Algerian high school cross-country championships. "I got so upset that I trained three times a day," he says. "I was crazy. Two weeks later I beat all those guys in the Algerian youth championships and realized how good I could be." Solemnly, he announced to reporters his intention to become a world champion.

And so, as if ordained, it came to pass. At seventeen, Morceli placed second to Kenya's Kirochi in the world junior 1,500. At eighteen, in need of a good track, he enrolled at Riverside (California) Community College, where he ran the 5,000 for two springs, preparing for European summer 1,500s, almost all of which he won. At twenty he was ranked first in the world.

"No injuries," he says. "I would like to thank God for that." His tone is offhand, with a little nod down the table, as if God, too, were there chewing a soggy mint leaf. Amar Brahmia says some credit must go to Morceli's practice of taking recuperative breaks between the indoor and outdoor seasons and of using training camps in the United States, Mexico and Europe. "Algeria has its expectations," Morceli says, "and they grow. When I go outside this country, my mind is clean. I can focus just on what I want."

Undistracted, he won twenty-one straight 1,500s or miles, indoors and out, before coming in second in a 1,500 in Rome on June 9. Morceli ran the fastest mile (3:49.12) and 1,500 (3:31.00) of 1991. He believes he might have approached Saïd Aouita's 1,500 world record of 3:29.46 if there were now as much depth of talent in middle-distance running as there was in the early 1980s.

"When Aouita, Sebastian Coe and Steve Cram were at their best, they had close competition driving them to their records," Morceli says. "Last year I was by myself for the last half of most races."

By midnight the *chaabi* singer's voice is gone and the mall has started to clear. "Have to get some sleep before morning prayers," says Morceli, rising, and you are reminded of him crouched on the track in Tokyo. He was certainly right, back then, to count his blessings: talent, family, guidance and discipline. It was as right for him to pray as it was for Boulmerka to scream.

> Men have authority over women because God has made the one superior to the other, and because [men] spend their wealth to maintain [women]. Good women are obedient. They guard their unseen parts because God has guarded them. As for [women] from whom you fear disobedience, admonish them and send them to beds apart and beat them. Then if they obey you, take no further action against them. God is high, supreme. — The Koran (Surah 4:34)

After such a ferocious passage, there is a need for historical context. The Koran is mild compared with the desert tribes that the Prophet reformed. One of Muhammad's earliest prohibitions was against the then common practice of killing infant girls. But Islam still differs tremendously from many other religions in its treatment of women.

Hassiba Boulmerka grew up in Constantine, in the Atlas Mountains, 350 miles east of Algiers. The city is built upon a broad plateau and cut almost in half by a huge crevice that is spanned by a suspension bridge. The impression is of a collection of cliff dwellings.

"But the town was planned by the French," says Boulmerka. "It has all the amenities, a university and parks, so it was easy, physically, to run there."

Her French is clear and musical, her complexion as pale and

freckled as a Parisienne's. "I'm completely Arabic," she says. "My parents came originally from the remote countryside. But for ten years my father drove a truck in France and sent money home to our family."

As a teenager Boulmerka was hyperactive, vocal and in need of an outlet. When she won a footrace in school, her father, who had seen Frenchmen celebrating their daughters' athletic attainments, raised no objection. "My parents supported me all they could, emotionally and financially," says Boulmerka. "At first I really had no problems. All my classmates and I received a Muslim education, so there were rules, like no alcohol, no eating pork, no women going out dancing. We all lived by those rules, in harmony between men and women. We could do sport together, although the number of women in sport has always been small. At one point there was a move in the parliament to ban women's participation in sport, but the majority voted to keep it. Then, about when I started, the doctrinaire Muslims began 'working in the dark,' agitating against sport for women. It wasn't obvious, but I could feel it."

Here is the history that led to Boulmerka's plight. In the seventh century, Arabs from the Arabian peninsula invaded much of North Africa, spreading their culture and religion to the shores of the Mediterranean. They spent much of this time trying to subdue the Berbers, a warlike nomadic people, many of whom were blond and blue-eyed. But when the Berbers finally took up the green banner of Islam, they did so with a will. An Arab-Berber army invaded Spain in the eighth century and gradually overran the Iberian Peninsula. Because the Arabs adapted and preserved the science and culture they found in conquered lands, their empire became a light of human civilization while Europe was sunk in the Dark Ages.

Spanish Christians fought the invaders and slowly regained control of their lands, driving out the last Arabs in 1492. In the sixteenth century, Spaniards captured Algiers and other coastal cities of what is today Algeria. The Spanish in turn were expelled by the Turks, under whose rule the Algerians chafed for the next three hundred years.

Then came the final humiliation. In the nineteenth century, France colonized most of North Africa. The government in Paris came to consider Algeria a vast southern province, as French as

the mainland. So when, after World War II, Algerian pressure
for independence became irresistible, France resisted anyway,
fanatically. From 1954 to 1962, many Algerian women fought
beside their men in a savage war of independence, and when it
was won, some women refused to return to the subservience
symbolized by the veil. So Boulmerka was born into a plural-
ist society, which until lately seemed resistant to the calls for
government by the Koran that periodically sweep the Muslim
world.

"Algerian women are treated better than women in other Islamic countries," says Boulmerka. "Today, Algerian women can
wear swimsuits on the beach. But women don't always know the
force they have within them."

Boulmerka discovered some of her own extraordinary force in
1988 when she won the 800 and the 1,500 at the African Games.
After the Seoul Olympics, at which she did not advance past the
first round in either event, she and coach Amar Bouras made a
four-year plan for the 1,500 in Barcelona. "You can't be a champion in a week or a year," she says. "You must accept a time of
suffering."

In 1990 she moved to Algiers and intensified her condition-
ing in ways effective but mysterious. "We developed an Algerian method of training," she says. "It's very hard. It takes four
to eight hours a day." Since her eighty miles a week of running would take no more than two hours a day, you are quick
to ask what else she does. With a grin, she says, "It's a secret."
And it stays one, though she hints that she does much total-
body strengthening.

Like Morceli, Boulmerka trains for periods outside of Algeria,
but she vigorously rejects any suggestion that she might, or
should, emigrate. "When the FIS won the first round of elections," she recalls, "I said to myself, 'You can't be frightened of
these people, because the majority of Algerians voted them in.'
I'm not scared of Islam. It's there to facilitate the lives of the people, mine included. But I am scared of the fascists who hide
behind the veil of Islam in order to impose their political will.
These are the people you see in Iran. But Algeria won't be like
that. Our doctrinaire Muslims are too smart. They want to get
along with *all* the Algerian people. At least I hope they do."

And they brought him a coin. And Jesus said to them, "Whose like-
ness and inscription is this?" They said, "Caesar's." Then he said to
them, "Render therefore unto Caesar the things which are Caesar's,
and unto God the things that are God's." — The Bible (Matthew
22:19—21)

When you express the wish that Muhammad had said something
similar, and so had provided for the separation of mosque and
state, Baki Brahmia replies, "You have fundamentalist Christians
in the United States who don't separate God and the state. The
difference in Algeria is that the fundamentalists, as you call
them, are in the majority."

"What do *you* call them?" you ask.

"Why, Muslims," says Morceli. "Or we say, 'the more faithful.' "

Morceli and Brahmia are sitting with you this afternoon in the
lobby of the El-Djaazair Hotel in Algiers. Its densely worked tiles
and carpets are the more dizzying because you are sharing the
runners' fast.

"People in America told me that if they fasted, they'd die," says
Morceli, "but it's *good* to fast this way. It makes you very, very
strong. It's like a treatment for the stomach." He adds softly,
"You must respect traditions of religion."

Morceli could avoid the fast by staying abroad, because travelers are exempt, but he makes a point of being home for Ramadan, turning it into a break from hard training or racing. Yet devout as he is, Morceli is quick to support Boulmerka. "I think it's
normal for Hassiba to run," he says. "We, in the family of athletics, don't mind ladies running. It's no problem for most people
here."

"For some," says Brahmia, "it's a problem. The population is
probably 50—50, for and against. But it's easier for Hassiba to
resist the closed-minded people because there are a lot of open-
minded people. It must be hard in Saudi Arabia."

Asked what kind of Islamic state the FIS would have tried to
create in Algeria, Morceli says, "That's a good question. I don't
know." The issue is so heated that taking a position on it would
only subject him to an avalanche of reaction from both sides. So
you accede to his unspoken appeal to drop the subject.

Morceli reaches for your copy of the Koran and examines it
intently. "It is good to read the Book," he says. "Especially when

you are mad — if you read the Book, you feel good inside." He says his daily prayers at dawn, noon, 4:30 P.M., sunset, and ninety minutes later. The prayers consist of "reading the Koran only," he says, "asking strength and forgiveness."

"Just what," you blurt out, "do you need to be forgiven?"

"You never know," says Morceli with some firmness."You can do something wrong by your eye, by your hand or by thinking."

After a workout, Boulmerka perches on splintered wood bleachers in a field house in Vincennes, France. She has raspberry-colored fingernails, thoroughly chewed. There are eight shades of pink and plum on her sweatsuit and shoes."I'm here to settle down and train," she says.

It is harder for her than for Morceli to shut out everything but running. Much roils beneath her pastel surface. "When I won in Tokyo, I wasn't comfortable with being the center of attention," she says. "I like to keep things simple, not be a star. But I've become a representative of all Algeria, and of young women in particular. I've gotten so many letters wishing me courage. Often they ask for a photo, but when I send one, I mustn't write my name on the envelope if it is to get there." That's because the photograph might be confiscated by "the more faithful" postal workers, enforcing Islam's dim view of depicting the human form. The Koran, it happens, nowhere prohibits such visual representation. Not until the ninth century did Islam consider figurative painters and sculptors to be competing blasphemously with God the creator.

Boulmerka feels the Koran can be read far more liberally than doctrinaire Muslims have interpreted it. "When the Koran was written, there were no cameras," says Boulmerka. "And the Koran itself says you must work for science and technology, search it out. If the Prophet came to earth, he would accept TV, cameras, cars and planes, properly used."

And maybe even modern women, aching to be good. "I sometimes feel too selfish," Boulmerka says. "I have a relatively luxurious life, and I'm bound by my faith to help people who are poorer, less healthy than I am. I want to set up a group to help drug addicts and handicapped people. I'm looking for sponsors for it. No one has done that in Algeria.

Boulmerka clearly embraces her role as, if not a star, an exemplar. "I prove that Algerian young men and women can be athletes or doctors or engineers," she says. "That is so important to me that after my running career I'm tempted to get into politics."

She gets into them right away. "We've been governed by the National Liberation Front [FLN] since 1962. And in the last election, when people wanted change, all they had to vote for was the FIS, which would like to use the country as a toy. So I'd love to help create a new party. Seventy-five percent of Algerians are under thirty. I'd like to invite all young people to join in and show that they are aware of the real economic and educational problems of Algeria and that they can be responsible for solving them."

The soldiers outside a radio station in Algiers wear stiff new combat fatigues and carry AK-47 rifles with beautifully polished hardwood stocks. This is a place that the discontented might hit, so you are searched on your way in to watch Morceli do an hour on a talk show.

He takes off his jacket, puts on earphones and is asked about the challenge of Morocco's outspoken Aouita, who was injured in 1991 but recently returned to break the indoor 3,000 record. "He used to be my idol," Morceli says sadly. "But he talks too much, and he avoids racing the best athletes unless he's certain he'll win. All I can say is, if he wants to win the Olympic 1,500, I'll be on the track."

A little mouse quietly drops out of a hole in a wall and moves, unobserved save by a delighted Baki Brahmia, over a tangle of cables that crosses the dim floor like mangrove roots.

Before the show, a gentleman's agreement was reached that Morceli wouldn't be grilled on questions of politics or money. Now the interviewer breaks the agreement, asking if Morceli would accept were he to be named by the ruling council to a government position. Morceli says he would not. The interviewer immediately asks how much money Morceli makes. Morceli, his eyes widening at this rudeness, says that the most important thing is to perform one's best. The mouse appears poised to run up the interviewer's pant leg.

Amar Brahmia adds, on the air, that Morceli commands as
high an appearance fee as Carl Lewis, "and no athlete would
get more than that." The mouse turns and vanishes into a dark
corner. Decorum is preserved, which is a disappointment all
around.

This late-twentieth-century Islam appeared to raise political issues.
But it had the flaw of its origins — the flaw that ran right through
Islamic history: to the political issues it raised it offered no political or
practical solution. It offered only the faith. It offered only the
Prophet, who would settle everything — but who had ceased to exist.
This political Islam was rage, anarchy. — V. S. Naipaul, *Among the Be-
lievers* (1981)

Boulmerka, having bravely called for a practical approach, is
asked how she would structure Algeria's government. "I can't
project a precise shape," she says. "I'd have to know what the
people want, but I believe accommodation is possible, even if we
have to create a half-Islamic, half-secular government."

When she is asked to face the apparent contradiction in those
terms, to recall that the FIS believes that secular law — such as
equal rights for women — destroys the purity of Islam, she is
clear about where she takes her stand. "I know I want it to be
very democratic."

Paradoxically, Boulmerka says, the army's emergency rule is
good for Algeria — for now. "Thirteen million Algerians can't
read and don't know what politics are," she says. "These are the
people the FIS takes advantage of. It's going to be hard to estab-
lish any working democracy when they're not used to it." Boulmerka's speech slows under the weight of feeling. "I don't want
my country to fight for democracy, as some countries have for
centuries, without achieving it. The Algerian people aren't quite
ready. They could tear themselves apart. We can use this year to
teach. But democracy is not dead. The ruling council is protect-
ing democracy.

Driving his black Audi, Morceli and his nineteen-year-old
brother, Ali, escape Algiers. The hillsides are lit with mustard.
The land resembles Marin County, California, in March, but
with goatherds. After a half-hour drive, the Morcelis are run-

ning in a pinewood. The rain has stopped; the footing is duff
and loam. Ali, a deer, bounds away ahead. He is training for the
800 meters in the world junior championships. "In 1995, when
he's my age," Noureddine says, "he's going to run 1:39." Coe's
world record is 1:41.73.

Noureddine keeps turning to check on you as the pace inches
up. "This is running easy," he says, "just to keep shape, a little
bit, during the fast." When he trains in earnest, he says, he runs
only fifty miles per week, "but well paced, 4:48 per mile." He's
on a six-minute-mile pace now, his stride short and balanced,
with no hint of preternatural speed. After half an hour and some
further quickening, you slip back, faint and unfueled. Thus you
can watch from the side as Noureddine does a series of 100-me-
ter strides between closely planted pines. The passing trunks
give him a context, and he is revealed as a rocket.

He stretches his Achilles tendons by pushing against a tree.
The fragrant pine bark is smooth and yielding; he could
be pressing against a hand-tooled saddle. "We used to have
a golf course to train on," says Noureddine. "But the president took half of it for a house and garden. So we come to the
forest."

During the drive home, the rain resumes. Traffic is light. Noureddine says, "People are all inside, waiting to break their fast."
Not quite all. Occasionally, cars careen from behind and fishtail
around him. "Crazy, crazy," he says each time, cautiously making
his way through his city of hypoglycemics.

Boulmerka feels perfectly able to bring Algeria the Olympic
gold medal for the women's 1,500. But, ever the realist, she
doesn't believe she can break Tatyana Kazankina's twelve-year-
old world record of 3:52.47. "I can get *near* it, maybe," she says.
"But I don't know how many more years I will continue. Every
year it gets harder to balance my training, my friends, my other
interests and my duty to visit my parents and take care of
them."

Boulmerka can seem curiously shy for such a socially involved
person. That, too, is rooted in her religion. When she is asked if
she plans to marry or has a boyfriend, she blushes and says vehemently that such a question cannot be asked of a good Muslim

woman. Her embarrassment reminds you of her experience at
the gala IAAF awards banquet last year in Monte Carlo. "My race
at the world championships was the first time I ever felt complete
confidence in myself," she says. "I will never forget the emotion
of that day. But I'd never dared to look at my own film of the
1,500. I'd tried, but I couldn't. Then, at that banquet, with no
warning, they showed it, on a huge screen — me, winning and
screaming." As she did then, she puts her face in her hands, mortified by how much of herself she had revealed. "I couldn't face
it," she says. "I had to turn away."

Morceli, with admirable restraint, squeezes a wedge of lemon
into his *chorba*, a traditional soup of tomato, lamb and pasta.
Then he takes up a spoon and breaks his fast of fourteen hours.
Nourishment makes Baki Brahmia talkative as he tries to decide
who was the most prominent Algerian ever. "We have our history," he says, "but if you ask which Algerian most makes the rest
of the world vibrate with interest. . . ." He swivels to Morceli. "It
must be him."

Morceli says "second plate" and heads to the restaurant buffet
for a mound of couscous, fish, meat and potatoes.

"I'm proud of Noureddine for not allowing his success to
change his personality," says Brahmia. Several comely women at
a nearby table stop breathing when Morceli passes them. Brahmia immediately says, "The Koran may *permit* a man four wives,
but God discourages it if you can't be fair to them all."

Returning, Morceli says, "I only plan to have one wife." He
says that he may take her soon. "Maybe after the 1993 world
championships." This does not mean that he has made his selection. As he catches and returns a flash of dark eye, he says, "I
have to pick carefully. It's my future. But it's good to get married. It helps to avoid doing very bad things, like in Europe
sometimes. If you are not able to get married, you have got to
fast, fast, fast. God said that."

Asked how long he will race, Morceli becomes unexpectedly
animated. "It's possible to go on to thirty-seven, thirty-eight," he
says, almost defensively. "You can, if you are serious and dedicated each day. Look at Aouita at thirty-two. Look at John
Walker and Mike Boit. Age has *nothing* to do with it, running the

1,500." Morceli clearly dislikes talk of quitting his calling. Does one quit the faith?

A last talk with Boulmerka passes quickly from your control. "Algerian journalists always seem to have the same questions," she says. "There's no *evolution* to what they ask, so I make sure to mention what's important." That is, simply, her creed of sport: "In athletics, on the track, I learned to suffer, to love my country, to concentrate, to take responsibility. I believe you can express your *self* in sport maybe better than in any other field. All that, and it brings everyone together, too."

Boulmerka is caught in more than a struggle to be free of some patriarchal traditions. Her athlete's instinctive, childlike drive to improve and to find common ground with others in the process must inevitably war with the sectarian purity of doctrinaire Muslims. This is a great divide: between the religion of compassion and the religion of coercion.

Boulmerka and Morceli together, having gone into the world and returned victorious, face the question of how to explain our secular, fax- and CNN-wired society, for which there is no better symbol than the Olympics, to nearly one billion Islamic souls who see in it an ever more corrupt fall from the faith of the Prophet.

The Islam of the Prophet's time was open to learning and built upon it. The rigid religion of the FIS seems sterile by comparison, obsessed with making, in Naipaul's words, "abstract men of the faith, men who would be nothing more than the rules."

But Algeria's milers transcend the rules. They have used the discipline of Islam to fire extraordinary achievement, and they are not alone. It may be that the most renowned examples of personal attainment in the modern Islamic world, from Morocco to Kenya, are its runners. They are products of their culture's toughness and intelligence. They have not rejected the arena. They have mastered it. Let us hope that they shame the most zealous keepers of Allah's faith into accepting a thousand years of hard-won human civilization.

AUGUST 3, 1992

KENNY MOORE, *a marathoner-turned-writer, missed an Olympic medal in 1972, finishing fourth at Munich. Kenny possesses a natural affinity*

for runners, and he brings a curiosity for the world that helps him connect the athlete with his culture. I think Moore's story is the single most interesting one to come out of the Barcelona Games, a masterful example of the sports writer as sociologist. (In case you've forgotten, one of the two principals in the story won the gold, while the other won no medal.)
— F.D.

DAVID ROBERTS

A Mountain of Trouble

FROM MEN'S JOURNAL

CLIMBING HARD ALL DAY, Jeff Lowe forced the route through a wilderness of false leads and frustrating dead ends, but darkness caught him short of the ledge he had hoped to reach, stranding him in a vertical labyrinth. He was left with no choice but to carve a makeshift cave in a fan of snow plastered against the steep rock, then crawl inside. Wet, cold and physically spent, he lit his balky stove and began the task of turning pot after pot of packed snow into drinking water.

In the middle of the night the storm hit. A heavy snowfall poured out of the black sky, and as the snow gathered, it set loose spindrift avalanches that filled Lowe's cave and threatened to smother him. All night he lay in his sleeping bag, pushing and pounding the walls of his flimsy bivouac sack to maintain some breathing space inside the cave. A lifelong tendency toward claustrophobia compounded Lowe's distress. As he grew drowsy, he would be seized with panic, ripping open the door of the bivouac sack, he would gasp fresh air, allowing snow not only to spill inside the cave but to fill his sleeping bag, where it melted and soaked his clothes.

By morning, Lowe was in a perilous situation. It was February 28, his ninth day on the north face of the Eiger. He had climbed 4,500 feet over those nine days, but in the 1,500 feet of frozen limestone that still hung above him, he was sure he would find the hardest passages of all. His food was almost gone. He could not stay warm at night. And he was on the verge of exhaustion. This, Lowe knew, was how climbers died on the Nordwand. In just such a way the audacious Toni Kurz had come to grief, his rappel jammed on a knotted rope; or Stefano Longhi, left behind by his partner to freeze to death after a bad fall; or Max Sedlmayer, climbing hopelessly toward the avalanche that would pluck him from his life.

Getting down from so high on the north face, in the midst of a storm, would take a desperate effort, if it was indeed possible at all. At the moment, with avalanches thundering over the cliffs above and sweeping the fan of snow, descent was out of the question: Lowe could not even escape his snow cave.

Hunkered inside his claustrophobic hole, alone in a gray universe of nothingness, Lowe brooded on his predicament. During the last few days, with the weather holding, he had climbed so well, at last he had felt in perfect form, as success had dared to whisper in his ears. Now the prospect of failure loomed larger with every hour of snowfall. And if the situation got any worse, Lowe would be in a battle for his very life.

No, things were not going right — and the pattern was all too familiar. For a year now, things had been going wrong for Jeff Lowe. Major things, disastrously wrong. Bankruptcy. The failure of his marriage. Separation from his two-year-old daughter. He had scrambled to hold it all together, but his despair had peaked in late October, just after his fortieth birthday, leaving him sleepless, his antic mind tormenting him with a parade of furious creditors and disapproving friends. Out of the nadir of that depression had come the decision to climb the Eiger. A new route on the north face — a clean, direct vector between the Czech and Japanese lines. Solo. In winter. Without bolts.

If he could pull it off, it would be the greatest climb ever accomplished by an American in the Alps. And at a deeper, more personal level, the Eiger might somehow tame the internal voices howling of failure and loss. It would be a way for Lowe to return to his strength, to the thing he did better than almost anyone in the world.

Twenty-four hours after burrowing into the mountainside, Lowe was still stuck inside the inadequate snow cave. As he prepared to spend a second night there, shivering in a soggy sleeping bag, he got out his two-way radio and warmed the batteries against his body. Rousing his support team at the hotel far below,

Lowe spoke slowly, his voice seamed with fatigue: "I've got a decision to make. Whether to go up or down. It's a tough one." There was a long pause. "I don't know how hard it would be to get down from here," he said. "I figure it'll take three days minimum to reach the summit if I go up. And that's only if the weather's good tomorrow and Saturday."

Another pause: "I guess tomorrow's going to tell. If I go for it, I'll have to pull out all the stops."

Had Jeff Lowe been born a Frenchman or a German, he would be a celebrity, sought after for product endorsements, asked to write his memoirs. But in the United States, great alpinists remain as obscure as chess champions.

Lowe, moreover, is a purist. He makes a wry distinction between "expeditions" — large, highly publicized assaults conducted in the spirit of the Desert Storm campaign — and "trips with friends," on which, with from one to three cronies, he can attempt brazen routes on unexplored mountains. From his only Everest expedition, a massively funded attack on an easy route involving fourteen climbers, Lowe came home disenchanted. But on some of Lowe's trips with friends, he has performed splendid deeds on spectacular Himalayan mountains such as Tawoche, Kwangde and Nameless Tower; on his ascents of Pumori and Ama Dablam, the only friend was himself.

Climbs like Tawoche and Ama Dablam, however, do not make headlines in the United States. Since his early twenties, Lowe had been one of the two or three best ice climbers in the world. Names such as Bridal Veil Falls, Keystone Green Steps and the Grand Central Couloir — extraordinary ice routes that Lowe was the first to master — can bring an awed hush over parties of cognoscenti, but they mean nothing to the lay public.

In the last two decades, the cutting edge of mountaineering has become "good style" — and nobody's style has been cleaner, bolder or more prophetic than Lowe's. Says Michael Kennedy, editor of *Climbing* and a frequent climbing partner of Lowe's, "Beyond a shadow of a doubt, he's the most visionary American Himalayan climber who's ever lived."

In a family of eight children growing up in Ogden, Utah, Lowe and his three brothers were pushed hard by their lawyer father to excel in sports. He was climbing seriously by fourteen, quickly developing his skills and managing to survive the usual near disasters of adolescent ambition. After he spent three years at unaccredited Tahoe Paradise College on a ski-racing scholarship, Lowe became a full-time climber; meanwhile, he scrounged a living from the kinds of marginal jobs most American climbing addicts resort to: pounding nails, teaching at Outward Bound and tutoring beginners in the sport.

In 1968, Lowe's older brothers Greg and Mike launched an outdoor-equipment company called Lowe Alpine Systems, which quickly gained cachet for its innovative packs and began turning a robust profit. Fifteen years later, Jeff Lowe started his own company, Latok — named for a mountain in Pakistan that was the scene of one of his most memorable climbs — which sold technical climbing gear. His first full-scale business venture, it began to collapse in 1987, and Lowe's brothers took over the company's debts to bail Jeff out.

Looking back, Lowe says: "I think part of my business problems stemmed from a feeling that I had to be more than a good climber, that I had to do something more 'meaningful.' And that may come from my father."

As if remounting the horse that had thrown him, Lowe soon joined with Texas entrepreneur Dick Bass to organize the first international climbing competition on American soil, at Snowbird, Utah. Contests on artificial walls had become one of the hottest new spectator sports in Europe, and Lowe was gambling that Americans would similarly embrace the spectacle. In the end, Snowbird '88 was an aesthetic success, but far fewer people than anticipated were willing to fork over twenty dollars to stare at the inch-by-inch progress of European climbing stars they had never heard of.

Undaunted, Lowe incorporated himself as Jeff Lowe Sport Climbing Championships Inc., attracted sponsors and investors and laid plans for an ambitious nationwide series of climbing competitions to be held in 1989 and '90. Thus began the downward spiral that in two years sucked Lowe into a whirlpool of failure. None of the events came close to breaking even, and Lowe's debts piled up to vertiginous heights. He began borrowing from future projects to pay off past ones. By the time the final compe-

tition of 1990 approached — an event organized by the late Bill
Graham, the legendary rock promoter, to be held in Berkeley,
California, in August — Lowe was teetering on the brink of fi-
nancial ruin.

In need of a quick infusion of cash just to pay his personal bills,
Lowe concocted a trip with friends to Nameless Tower, a soaring
tusk of granite in the Karakoram Range of Pakistan, to be filmed
for ESPN. The big draw for European sponsors would be a summit push pairing Lowe with thirty-one-year-old Parisian Catherine Destivelle, the most famous woman climber on the planet.

The Berkeley competition, which took place while Lowe was
out of the country, turned into yet another financial fiasco
plagued by dismal attendance. Lowe persuaded the North Face,
a purveyor of high-end outdoor gear, to lend its name to the
event as the leading sponsor. In order to keep the competition
from sullying its good reputation, the company claims it was
forced to cough up $78,000 to cover Lowe's bills. "We believed
that when Lowe went to Pakistan, he'd secured his loans," says
Ann Krcik, director of marketing operations for the North Face.
"Three days before the event, it became evident that Sport
Climbing Inc. didn't have the money." Bart Lewis, an entrepreneur who helped market the competition, claims that when the
dust cleared, Lowe owed him $40,000. Lowe counters: "That's
absolutely insane. I owe Bart not even close to $40,000." Other
creditors emerged, clamoring for payment. Says Lowe: "I always
emphasized the risks involved. Those who were misled, misled
themselves."

On the other side of the globe, meanwhile, Lowe and Destivelle managed to climb a difficult route on Nameless Tower. The
film was broadcast on ESPN, but several European sponsors had
backed out at the last minute. The upshot was that Lowe came
home from Pakistan deeper in debt than ever, owing money
even to close friends and fellow climbers who had worked as his
support party. For two decades Lowe had been one of the most
admired figures in the tightknit fraternity of American climbers;
now, around certain campfires, in various climbers' bars, his
name began to elicit bitter oaths and tales of fiscal irresponsibil-
ity.

By the fall of 1990, Lowe had been married for eight years to a woman he'd met in Telluride, Colorado, where she was a waitress. The couple settled in Boulder, where Janie Lowe became her husband's full-time business partner. In 1988 they had a daughter, whom they named Sonja.

On Nameless Tower, Lowe was deeply impressed by Destivelle's performance. As their teamwork evolved, Lowe realized that with only one or two men had he ever felt so confident climbing in the great ranges. At some point, he and Destivelle began an affair. Because her private life is intensely scrutinized in France, and because she had a longtime partner of her own back in Paris, Destivelle urged Lowe to be discreet about their relationship.

When Lowe returned home from Nameless Tower, "he seemed very angry and distant," says Janie Lowe. "It was as if he wanted nothing to do with me. I asked him if he was having an affair with Catherine. 'No, no, no.' Finally, it came out. I asked him, 'Why did you lie to me?' That hurt me so bad. He said, 'I'd promised Catherine.' I said, 'After twelve years, you tell me your loyalty to Catherine is greater than your loyalty to me?' "

On September 13, 1990, Lowe turned forty. He was deep in a whirlpool, clutching for flotsam. At the end of October, Lowe declared bankruptcy. As his business partner, Janie took an equal brunt of the misfortune, and their relationship grew more troubled. As she tells it: "Jeff would come home and go straight into his study and close the door. Sonja would say, 'Mommy, why doesn't Daddy want to talk to me?' " In mid-December, Jeff moved out of the house, and they began the process of getting a divorce.

"I fell apart," Jeff says. "I felt hopeless. All I knew was that I couldn't stand it after a couple of weeks. I had to start dealing with things one by one."

By early February, Lowe was in Grindelwald, Switzerland, staring up at the north face of the Eiger.

Beguiled by the shape of this unfolding drama, Jon Krakauer and I had come to Switzerland as well, to serve as Lowe's support team. Lowe's business woes were common knowledge in the climbing community, and word of his Eiger project had spread far and fast. More than one observer suggested that Lowe might be on a suicide mission. Boulder writer and climber Jeff Long, a loyal friend of Lowe's, later admitted, "With all the pressure he had on him, I was afraid he was going to use the Eiger as some kind of exit."

Suicidal or not, the scheme — a new route, solo, in winter, without bolts, on the most notorious face in the Alps — seemed wildly improbable to most climbers. Destivelle later told Lowe that her French friends were of a single mind: "He'll never do it. It's too cold in winter, and too hard."

Jeff Lowe does not look like a climber: an accountant, you might guess on meeting him, or maybe a viola player. He stands five feet ten, weighs about 150; his slender physique seems more wiry than muscular. Clean-shaven, he has an open face, on which alertness struggles against a natural placidity. He wears the wire-rim glasses of a professor. The long, straight blond hair conjures up the hippie he once thought himself to be. Though his hairline is receding, he combs his locks straight back, as if daring them to retreat further. When he smiles, his eyes crinkle shut, and incipient jowls shadow his jaw. To call his low, cadenced speech a drawl is to suggest a regional twang it does not possess: His voice is rather that of a tape recorder whose batteries are running low.

"For the first five years, we were extremely happy," Janie had told me. "I think our problems had a lot to do with having a daughter. When Sonja came along, things changed."

Now Jeff Lowe commented obliquely on marriage and business. "It's a lack of freedom," he said. "I'm trying to get my freedom back. I could have saved my marriage if I had chosen to. But when I was forced to take a new look, I realized, 'Hey, it's not what I really want.' If I do what I really want — it's a weird thing, but climbing is still at the center."

Lowe paused. "The Eiger — even if I succeed — isn't going to make all the other shit go away. I don't expect this climb to make everything right." A grin spread across his face. "It'll just feel real good."

The hotel at Kleine Scheidegg near Grindelwald is a rambling Victorian masterpiece, festooned with tiny rooms supplied by elegant if quirky plumbing, with linen wallpaper and richly varnished wood wainscoting, cozy reading nooks, eighteenth-

century engravings and oak floors that creak and undulate like a
glacier. For fifty-six years the hotel has been the headquarters
for Eiger watching. As he prepared for his ascent, it became
Lowe's base camp.

The hotel is owned and run by the legendary Frau von Almen.
She is a handsome woman of seventy with an imperious manner
and a constant frown of disapproval on her brow. Checking in
for the three of us, I told her about Lowe's plans. The frown
deepened. "This is insane," she announced. "It is more than insane — it is mad." She turned and walked away. "I do not like
the accidents," she nattered. "Because they are so unnecessary."

To stay in the hotel is to put up with Frau von Almen's tyran-
nical regime. There was a lengthy codex of unwritten rules, a
good portion of which we managed to break. I wore my climbing
boots upstairs, Krakauer and Lowe brought sandwiches from
outside and ate them in her café; I foolishly asked her to unlock
the front door of the hotel before 8 A.M., and Krakauer had the
nerve to wonder if he might move and photograph a portrait of
the pioneers who had made the first ascent of the Nordwand in
1938.

There was no way to get on her good side. After dinner one
night, I complimented her fulsomely on the four-course repast.
"And did your friend enjoy the dinner, too?" she asked ominously.

"Oh, yes," I answered.

"Because he will not eat like this up on the mountain."

Only Frau von Almen's longtime guests — those who had
come every winter for more than a decade and skied innocuously
each afternoon — seemed to bask in her approbation. The truth
was that she was down on climbers. And this was sad, because her
husband, Fritz, who died in 1974, had been the climbers' best
friend, watching them for hours through his telescope, exchanging flashlight signals with their bivouacs each night. The Frau
still had the telescope but would unpack it, she said, "only for
emergency." An old-timer told us that a few years ago some
climbers accidentally knocked over the telescope and broke it,
then ran away.

On February 11, Catherine Destivelle arrived from Chamo-
nix. Five feet four inches tall, with curly brown hair, a conquer-

ing smile and a formidable physique, she is a superstar in France, yet fame has left her relatively unaffected. Though they could hardly disguise the fact that they were staying in the same room, at first Lowe and Destivelle maintained a demure propriety. Gradually the handclasps became less furtive, the kisses semi-public.

For a first-rate climber, Lowe seemed woefully disorganized. For days his gear was spread all over his hotel room, but as he inventoried it, he discovered that he was lacking essential items. From Krakauer he borrowed a headlamp, pitons, first-aid supplies and a crucial pair of jumars for ascending ropes; Destivelle brought him foodstuffs (she swore by powdered mashed potatoes) and a two-way radio.

Destivelle was scandalized by Lowe's preparations. "I can't believe he is climbing with equipment he has never used before," she told us again and again. "I would never do this." Lowe dismissed the problem, omitting one of its causes. He was so broke he had had to sell much of his climbing gear and now was dependent on the largess of European companies intrigued with his Eiger project.

On the night of February 18, Destivelle joined Krakauer and me in the bar, where she chain-smoked half a pack of Marlboros. (Ordinarily, she goes months without a cigarette.) At breakfast the next morning, she said she had dreamed obsessively about an all-out war in which everybody was hunting Lowe. She had spent a fitful, miserable night, while beside her Lowe had slept soundly. In the morning, Destivelle rode the cog railway up to the Eigergletscher station, where she kissed Lowe goodbye. He put on his skis and headed for the base of the wall.

On February 19, his first day on the Nordwand, Lowe waltzed up 2,000 feet in only two hours. The going was easy but dangerous, a matter of planting the picks of his ice axes in a steady rhythm, of stabbing the crampon points strapped to his boot soles into brittle ice overlying steep rock. He soloed without a rope. If he slipped, he would die. But Lowe was in his element on this nerve-stretching ground. The speed and precision that had made his technique famous among a generation of American climbers spoke in every swing of his axes.

It was, however, still the heart of winter, and this was the Eiger. Over the last six decades, it was the easy start on the north face that had seduced so many alpinists: Between fifty and sixty of the best climbers in the world had died here, in a variety of gruesome ways.

The names of the Eiger's most storied landmarks — the Ice Hose, the Death Bivouac, the Traverse of the Gods, the White Spider — are canonic touchstones to alpinists everywhere. Whether or not they have ever seen the notorious wall, all climbers grow up with a keen awareness of its history. Eight of the first ten men who set out to climb the Nordwand were killed trying. The first man to attempt a solo ascent backed off prudently, only to die on a subsequent attack with a partner. The second, third and fourth solo attempts all ended in death. Early on, the wall acquired its punning German nickname, the Mordwand.

Accounts of these disasters built up the Eiger mystique. Every climber knows the tales, as visceral as tribal legends passed on around the campfire: Hinterstoisser falling to his death as he tried to reverse his traverse on iced-up rock. Angerer strangled by his own rope. Toni Kurz expiring when the knot jammed in his carabiner, only a few feet above his rescuers, as he spoke his last words, *"Ich kann nicht mehr"* ("I can do no more"). The last words of Longhi, borne on the wind from the ledge high on the face where he froze to death: *"Fame! Freddo!"* ("Hungry! Cold!")

At the foot of a sheer 350-foot rock cliff called the First Band, the climbing abruptly turned hard. As Lowe used his rope for the first time, his pace slowed to a vertical crawl. In three and a half hours, he gained only 110 feet. On the second day, a dogged and ingenious struggle over nine intense hours won Lowe a mere eighty feet more.

On other great mountain faces, clean vertical cracks, good ledges and solid rock abound. The Eiger, however, is notorious for limestone knobs that crumble as you grasp them, for down-sloping ledges covered with ice and for a scarcity of good cracks. The severity of the terrain brought out the best in Lowe, as he used tiny metal hangers and the tips of his ax blades to "hook" his way upward.

But already there were problems. Lowe had what he called

fumble fingers, dropping three or four of his most valuable nuts and pitons, and the pick on one of his ice axes had worked loose. He climbed on anyway, adjusting his technique to the loose wobble of the pick, which meant he could never really swing the ax hard and plant the blade securely into the ice. It was a bad compromise, like driving at 30 mph on a flat tire.

Late on his third day of climbing, he had put most of the First Band beneath him, but the climbing was the most frightening yet. The storms of the last few weeks had glued snow and ice onto vertical and even overhanging rock. Lowe had to shift back and forth between rock and snow, from spidering with bulky plastic boots and gloved hands among the limestone nubbins to crabbing his way up the hollow snow with crampons and axes. When he could, he placed protection — a machined nut or piton in the rock or a screw in the ice.

At 2:50 P.M., Lowe clung to a particularly flimsy patch of rotten snow. Two thousand feet of cold, empty air fell away beneath his boots. He doubted whether he could reverse the moves he had made above his last protection eight feet below and had no idea whether he could find protection above or climb through the looming overhang that blocked his view of the rest of the gigantic wall. For all he knew, he was creeping into a vertical cul-de-sac.

The boldness of Lowe's choice to go without a bolt kit was now manifest. Throughout his efforts to surmount the First Band, he had been stymied right and left by blank, unclimbable rock. With bolts, it is possible to drill the rock and build a ladder through the most featureless impasse. Every other new route on the Eiger in the last thirty years had employed bolts; the Japanese who had pioneered the imposing line just to the right of Lowe's had placed 250 of them.

Bolts also bestow a huge bonus in safety. When a climber is "running it out" — leading into uncertain terrain, with bad protection — he never knows whether he can find a reliable anchor before he reaches the end of his rope. With bolts, a solid anchor can be manufactured where nuts and pitons are useless. Without bolts, the process is like creeping farther and farther out on a lake covered with thin ice.

Lacking bolts, Lowe fiddled with a tiny nut, trying to wedge it into a crooked, quarter-inch crack that split the First Band. Suddenly the snow broke loose beneath his feet. He was falling.

In conventional climbing, with two people on a rope, one anchors himself to the precipice and feeds out the rope as the other leads above. If the leader falls, he plunges a little more than twice as far as he was above his last protection, until his partner "belays" or stops him by holding tight to the rope. For a soloist, the belayer is a mechanical apparatus. As one might suspect, solo self-belaying is far less reliable than the kind afforded by a human partner.

As he had started up the wall three days before, Lowe carried a new kind of self-belay device he had never used. Before his first hard pitch, he had not even taken the contraption out of the plastic bag it was sold in. The question now, as he fell through the air, was whether the device would work.

An abrupt jolt gave him his answer. The rig had done its job. Lowe was unhurt. He had not even had time to be scared, but now the delayed adrenalin started to surge. In response, he edged his way back to his high point, where he found another plate of snow to try. Gingerly he moved up it, anticipating another fall with each step, until he stood beneath the rock overhang.

The only way to proceed was to angle left through a weakness in the browing cliff. Lowe made a series of delicate moves on rock, until he could plant the picks of his axes on snow above, the left pick wobbling in its disturbing fashion. But here the snow was worthless, sloughing loose under the slightest touch. For a full hour he struggled in place, patiently probing the terrain for its arcane secrets. At last he found a small patch of more reliable snow. He planted both axes, moved his feet up and stabbed the front points. The snow held. He moved a few feet higher, then surged upward.

He was over the First Band, but by now it was getting dark. Lowe placed three ice screws at his high point, then rappelled back down to the snow cave he had slept in the night before. He crawled into his thin sleeping bag and pulled the frosty bivouac sack over him. Tired though he was, sleep escaped him. His problems danced mockingly in his mind, their shadows darting from wall to wall inside the cave of unhappiness in which he'd lived for a year. The loose pick on his axe nagged at him, and at the rate he was burning stove fuel, he would run out of gas canisters long before he could reach the summit. And he needed those nuts and pitons he had dropped.

In the morning Lowe turned on his walkie-talkie and called down to Krakauer and me at the hotel. "Guys," he said in his slow, gravelly voice, "I'm thinking about a slight change of plans." He had decided, he told us, to leave his rope in place over the most difficult parts of the First Band and, while he was still low enough on the wall to do so, descend briefly to Kleine Scheidegg, where he might fix his malfunctioning ice axe, replenish his supply of food and fuel and replace the hardware he'd dropped. Then, in a day or two, he could go back up the wall.

Lowe reached the hotel before noon. "Why did you not tell me before the weekend that you were coming down?" Frau von Almen complained, fingering her room charts. It happened to be Friday. "Now I have to put you in eighty-eight, way up on the fourth floor."

"That's fine with me," said Lowe.

"I know," said the Frau as she walked away. "But you are very simple."

A stack of faxes was waiting for Lowe at the hotel, most of which were from furious creditors demanding payment. These did not appear to rattle his composure, but a long missive from Janie seemed to trouble him deeply.

Having come to admire and like Lowe, I was puzzling over the vehemence of his detractors. Jim Bridwell, who claims Lowe still owes him $3,000 for Nameless Tower, had said: "I think of Jeff as a climber and what that used to mean. You used to be able to trust climbers. But Jeff'll say one thing and do another. I just think he's disturbed. Either he doesn't know he's lying, or . . ."

Janie Lowe thought Jeff's problems had been compounded by his pride. "He can't say he's sorry," she told me. " 'Hey, I really fucked up.' Just a few sentences would resolve his debt with his friends."

One voice in Lowe's defense, however, was that of Jeff Long, who insisted: "These people want Jeff's professional corpse swinging in the wind. I think what they did in investing in Jeff was to invest in his vision. What collapsed, they thought, was a whole vision they shared. The brotherhood of the rope. But what was going on was really just business."

For all her sorrow, in any case, Janie was determined to keep the channels open. "We'll always be parents," she said. "We have a wonderful little daughter. For Sonja's sake, I hope we can keep our own bullshit in the background."

One night in the hotel, Lowe had watched the three-year-old daughter of a guest carrying her plate heaped with food from the salad bar. The sight had brought tears to his eyes. "Yeah, I really miss my daughter," he admitted.

As Janie had pointed out, though: "Yes, he totally loves Sonja. But you know what? He doesn't love her enough to be with her."

In his own way, Lowe acknowledged that stricture. "I think I know now," he said in a reflective moment, "that I can't do this sort of climbing and have a domestic side. You're not a practicing father if you're not there. You're maybe a visiting father."

There had been a snowstorm on the morning of Lowe's descent, but by the following day the precipitation had ceased and the weather had stabilized. The temperatures were strangely warm, however — well above freezing at the 6,000-foot elevation of the hotel. That was better than brutal cold, except it meant bad avalanche conditions. In the weekend prior to his start on the Nordwand, thirty-one people had died in avalanches across the Alps.

There were, in short, plenty of reasons to give up the climb, excuses lying ready to be seized. But Lowe spent the evening in room 88, sorting his gear in his slow, fastidious fashion. Early the next morning he returned to the foot of the wall, and by noon he was back at his bivouac cave, at the lower end of the ropes he had left in place. By the time evening fell, he had reascended the ropes and wrestled his one hundred pounds of gear up to his previous high point.

Then, boldly, he led on into the dusk. It was not until three hours after dark that he suspended a hanging tent from a pair of ice screws and crawled into his sleeping bag. He was halfway up the Nordwand.

"Good morning, Vietnam," he radioed us in the morning. "I just woke up from one of the best sleeps I've had in a long time." When he started climbing again, his route coincided for a few hundred feet with the classic 1938 line. This section of the route, known as the Ice Hose, had been a formidable test to most of the expert climbers who had attempted the Nordwand over the years. For Lowe, with his impeccable ice technique, it was almost like hiking. He raced up the Ice Hose and across the Second Icefield and at day's end was bivouacked at the base of the summit head wall.

Only a little more than 2,000 feet of climbing remained, but it promised to be severe and unrelenting. And as he inched his way up into the dark, concave head wall, it would grow increasingly difficult to retreat. Somewhere on that precipice, he would reach a point of no return, after which descent might well be impossible, and the only escape would be up and over the summit.

It was Monday, February 25. The forecast from Zurich was for continued good weather through Wednesday; then a warm front bearing heavy snow was predicted to move into the area. A fiendish scenario began to propose itself. With two days' steady climbing, Lowe might well find himself near or at that point of no return, only to get hammered by a major snowstorm.

Krakauer and I were using the coin-operated telescope at the gift shop next to the hotel to follow Lowe's progress, but he was so high now that we could tell little about his individual moves. On Tuesday night we took a walk. There was a full moon directly behind the Eiger. We caught sight of a pinpoint of light, impossibly far above us, three-fifths of the way up the wall: Lowe's headlamp, as he dug his bivouac site, a lonely beacon of purpose in the mindless night.

Later, his voice came on the radio, raspy with lassitude. "Watch that forecast real carefully," he said. "It's going to be a strategy-type thing. If it comes in hard and I'm not in a good place, it's not going to be good."

On Wednesday night, the storm indeed came in hard, forcing Lowe to hole up in the claustrophobic snow cave he'd dug in the vertical fan of snow. It was from this pathetic shelter that he'd wondered aloud over the radio "whether to go up or down." After a long, pregnant silence, he confessed: "I don't know how hard it would be to get down from here. I figure it'll take three days minimum to reach the summit if I go up. . . . If I go for it, I'll have to pull out all the stops."

Lowe's miserable snow burrow proved to be a poor place to ride out the tempest. On Thursday morning, he remarked over the radio: "I've never been so pummeled in my life. There's a big avalanche coming down every five minutes. I couldn't move if I wanted to."

At noon Lowe radioed again. He had managed to get out of his snow hole, but a search for a better bivouac site had been fruitless. The avalanches were still rumbling down, his clothes were soaking wet, and he was cold. It seemed that Lowe had little choice but to descend, and even that would be exceedingly sketchy. Much to our surprise, however, he declared, "I'm going to sign off now and try to get something done." He had resolved to push for the summit.

More than a week before, I had probed Lowe's motives by alluding to the suggestions I had heard of a suicidal impulse. "I think everybody has had thoughts about checking out early," he said. "But I wouldn't do it this way. I'd do it a lot simpler."

Even if Lowe could complete his route, what lasting difference would it make in his life? Magnificent though the climb might be, was it little more than a superstitious gesture, a way of lashing back at the furies that bedeviled his path? The finest climb ever accomplished by an American in the Alps could indeed bring with it a huge bestowal of self-esteem. And in the chaos that his personal affairs had become, self-esteem might be what Lowe needed most.

He had said: "For me there's no future. All I'm interested in is now." In the hotel, that had sounded like wishful thinking. Divorce and bankruptcy turned *now* into a crumbling wall between the flash floods of the past and the future. But up on the Eiger, all that changed. The past was the piton ten feet below; the future was that handhold three feet above and to the left. *Now* was what held him to the world, and the trance of grasping its ledges and cracks gave it a glorious breadth. It expanded and became the ocean of all that was.

Friday, March 1, marked the sixth day of Lowe's second attempt on the Nordwand, his tenth day of climbing overall. A south wind sent hazy wreaths of fog sailing over the mountain, but the favorable weather that had blessed the first week of the climb

had returned, although another storm was forecast to arrive by
Sunday. If he didn't reach the top before it hit, his prospects for
survival might be grim. By noon, Lowe had hauled all his gear
up to a distinctive ledge called the Central Band. Only 1,200 feet
remained.

Here the wall was scored with ice-glazed ramps leading up and
to the left, most of which led nowhere. The protection was mini-
mal, the climbing nasty. Lowe was aiming for the Fly, a small ice
field five hundred feet above. But now, when he needed to move
fast, with the threat of the next storm hanging over him, he was
slowed drastically by what turned out to be the most difficult
climbing yet.

Watching through the telescope, I could gauge how steep the
cliff was when I saw him knock loose chunks of snow that fell
forty feet before striking rock again. At one point it took him
more than an hour to gain twenty-five feet. The rock had turned
loose and crumbly; stone towers, teetering like gargoyles, sat
waiting to collapse at the touch of a boot, and pitons, instead of
ringing home as he pounded them, splintered the flaky limestone and refused to hold. Bolts would have been a godsend.

Yet on these pitches, Lowe's brilliance came to the fore. He
thought of one particular stretch of fifty feet as a kind of never-
never land: It was the crux of the whole route to this point. A
more driven, impatient alpinist might succumb to dizzy panic
here, where the slightest misjudgment could rip protection loose
and send him hurtling into the void. With his phlegmatic dispo-
sition, Lowe inched his way through his never-never land in a
cloud of Buddhist calm.

On Saturday, Krakauer started up the west ridge — the easiest
route on the Eiger and the path by which Lowe would descend.
Krakauer wanted to camp near the top to greet Lowe and, if
need be, help him down. As soon as he skied above the Eigergletscher station, however, Krakauer realized the venture was a
mistake. A few days before, he had cruised halfway up the ridge
in only two hours; but in the interim, the conditions had completely changed. The storm had blanketed the slope with deep,
unstable snow; without skis, Krakauer sank to his waist, and even
with skis on he plowed a knee-deep furrow as he zigzagged la-
boriously upward.

At the fastest pace Krakauer could sustain, it would take days

to get to the summit. What was worse, the slopes were danger-
ously close to avalanching; indeed, as he climbed slowly up the
ridge, his skis periodically set off small slides.

At two o'clock Krakauer came over the radio. "I'm getting the
hell down," he said in a jumpy voice. "The hundred feet just below me is ready to avalanche. Watch me carefully. If it releases,
it's going to be massive." With a series of slow, deliberate turns,
he skied down as delicately as he could. The slope held.

When Lowe next radioed, I had to tell him about Krakauer's
retreat from the west ridge. He took the news calmly, even
though it raised the specter of serious danger for his own descent. For the first time we talked about the possibility of a helicopter's picking him up on the summit.

Lowe climbed on. By early afternoon clouds had gathered
around the upper face, where it was snowing lightly, even
though the hotel still baked in sunshine. Pushing himself beyond
fatigue, again well into the night, he managed to set up an uncomfortable bivouac just below the Fly. His two-day push from
the Central Band had been a brilliant piece of work, but the Sunday storm was coming in early, and 700 feet still lay between him
and the summit. He was well past the point of no return.

That evening he slithered into his dank bivouac sack and tried
to sleep. Lowe had two gas cartridges left to melt snow, but his
food supply was down to a couple of candy bars. His hands were
in terrible shape — the incessant pounding, grasping and soaking had bruised the fingertips until they swelled into tender
blobs, and the nails had begun to crack away from the cuticles.
Each morning, his fingers were so sore and puffy that merely
tying his boot laces was an ordeal.

Worse, his sleeping bag, thin to begin with, was soaked like a
dishrag: It provided almost no warmth at all. That night Lowe
got not a wink of sleep. For fourteen hours he shivered, waiting
for dawn, as the snow fell outside his cave.

On Sunday morning it was still snowing. "Where I am," he radioed, "it's hard to even peek out of the bivy tent without dis-
lodging everything. I'm going to sit here and hydrate." He faced
an acute dilemma. If he hunkered down and waited for the
storm to end, he could run out of food and gas and succumb to
hypothermia. If he pushed upward prematurely, on the other
hand, the storm itself could finish him.

By noon he had not moved. At two o'clock, through a break in the clouds, we saw him climbing slowly above the Fly. As he started to climb, however, he grew deeply alarmed. Something was wrong. He felt weak all over, weaker than he should have from fatigue alone. He had been going on too little food, not enough liquids, insufficient sleep. This was how climbers died on the Eiger. This was too much like what had happened to Longhi and Kurz. After stringing out three hundred feet of rope, Lowe returned to his bivouac hole of the night before and spent the rest of the day resting and hydrating and trying in vain to get warm.

Once more, sleep was impossible. Lowe shivered through another night, even though he lit the stove and burned precious fuel in an effort to heat his frigid cavern. The weather had cleared late Sunday afternoon, and the sky was now sown with stars. There was an odd acoustic clarity: Toward morning he could plainly hear dogs barking in Grindelwald, miles away and 10,000 feet below. And he thought he heard something else: a humming, crystalline, harmonic music in the air. Was it an aural hallucination? Was he beginning to lose his grip?

Monday dawned luminous and clear, a perfect day, of which he would need every minute. Good weather had been forecast to last through the evening, but a major storm was due on the morrow. We called REGA, the government-run rescue service, and alerted it to a possible need for summit pickup. Then we watched Lowe climb. At 9:15, he turned a corner and disappeared into a couloir we could not see. Two hours later, there was still no sign of him, no murmur over the radio. Though we did not admit it to each other at the time, Krakauer and I each separately trained the telescope on the base of the wall, where we swept the lower slopes. In just such a way over the decades, the fate of several Eiger victims had been discovered.

Lowe had hoped that once he was above the Fly the going would get easier. But in icy chimneys broken by bands of brittle rock, he was forced to perform some of the hardest climbing yet. Normally he never let himself be rushed on a climb: It was one of the secrets of his sang-froid and his safety. Now, however, he kept looking at his watch, and his brain hectored, *Oh, no, hurry!* Ever so slightly, his technique lost some of its famous precision.

He felt less weak than he had the day before, but the sense of struggling to meet a terrible deadline oppressed his efforts.

It was hard to place good protection anywhere. Lowe found himself hooking with front points and axe picks on rounded rock wrinkles that he had to stab blindly through the snow to locate. His balance was precarious, and then, just before it happened, he knew he was going to fall.

The picks scraped loose. He was in midair, turning. Twenty-five feet lower, he crashed back-first into the rock. The self-belay had held, but he was hurt. He felt as though someone had taken a baseball bat and slammed it into his kidneys.

Oddly, instead of panicking him, the long fall calmed him down. *Okay,* he said to himself, *you've done that. Don't do it again.*

He pulled himself together, started up again and found a through the dicey hooking sequences despite the pain pound in his back. At last he surmounted a buttress and reached a go ledge, only four hundred feet below the summit.

But here he faced a problem. The warm sun had loosened the summit snowfields. Every chute and depression became an avalanche track. One swept right over Lowe, filling his goggles with powder snow, buffeting his body as it tried to knock him from the wall.

He was moving faster now, as slides shot down all around him. For two hours he climbed doggedly on. During that time, three more avalanches engulfed him. One of them knocked his feet loose, but he managed to hang on with his axes. At 3:20 he called.

"God, Jeff, those avalanches looked bad," I said.

"Yeah, they were pretty horrendous." His voice was ragged with strain. "I got really douched. I'm totally wet. Am I about a pitch from the west ridge?"

"A pitch and a half, maybe."

"I'm going to call for a pickup. I just want to get up this thing."

We signed off and called REGA. They were waiting in Grindelwald, ready to fly the moment Lowe emerged on the west ridge, a few feet below the top. But a stiff wind had begun to blow a steady plume off the summit. The wind could prevent the helicopter from approaching close enough to execute a pickup or even cause it to crash.

To our dismay, Lowe disappeared once more into a couloir. The minutes ticked by. At 4:15 he emerged, fighting his way out of the top of the gully, spindrift hosing him at every step. He was only forty feet below the crest of the ridge.

We prepared to call REGA, then watched in distress as Lowe stopped at a mottled band of rock and snow, only twenty feet below the ridge. For ten minutes he thrashed in place; we saw him grabbing chunks of black limestone and tossing them into the void below.

In the hidden couloir, Lowe had found it impossible to get in any protection. He had dashed upward, aiming at the mottled band, but when he got there, he found only a skin of ice holding together rocks that were as loose as a pile of children's blocks. When he flung stones aside and dug beneath, he found only more of the same. He could engineer no kind of anchor — neither piton, nut nor ice screw would hold.

Only twenty feet short of safety, he had run out of rope. His own anchor, three hundred feet below, was imprisoning him. In despair, he realized that he would have to climb down at least forty feet to the previous rock band, try to get some kind of anchor there, rappel for his gear and jumar back up. He was not sure he could make that down-climb without falling. What was more, he was running out of daylight.

Lowe got on the radio. Krakauer said what we were both thinking: "Jeff, if you just dropped your rope and went for it, could you free solo the last twenty feet?"

"No problem," said Lowe. "But are you sure the helicopter can get me?"

If we urged Lowe to abandon his gear and the helicopter failed, he would be stranded near the summit without ropes, sleeping bag, food, stove or even his parka. He was soaked to the skin. The wind was whipping hard, and the sky had grayed to the color of lead. Tuesday's storm was arriving early.

Krakauer said, "I'm almost positive they can pick you up."

"Let's do it," said Lowe.

He untied his rope and draped the end over a loose rock. He was abandoning all the gear that he had fought for nine days to haul up to the 6,000-foot precipice and, with it, deserting his own last refuge.

We called REGA; the helicopter took off from Grindelwald. To be picked up on the summit of the mountain was not a true rescue; more than one previous Eiger climber had resorted to flying from the top when he was far less strung out than Lowe was. It would, however, be a kind of asterisk attached to his great deed. It would not be the best style, and that would bother Lowe. But it was survival.

He sprinted up the last twenty feet. All at once, Lowe had escaped the north face. He stood on a broad shelf of snow on the west ridge, just below the summit. The helicopter spiraled upward toward him.

Still talking to us on the radio, Lowe couldn't keep the shivering out of his voice. Krakauer instructed him: The helicopter would lower a cable, which he was to clip on to his waist harness.

Now the chopper was just above him, hovering in the stiff wind. Suddenly it peeled off and flew away toward the Jungfraujoch. For the first time, Lowe seemed to lose it. He wailed, "What the hell's going on?" Nervous about the strong winds, the helicopter pilot, we later learned, decided to drop off a doctor and a copilot who had been on board, so he could fly as light as possible when he made the pickup.

The helicopter reappeared and hovered above the summit, its rotors straining against the wind. The steel cable dangled from its belly. We saw Lowe swipe for its lower end, miss once, then seize it. He clipped in, and the helicopter swept him into the sky. Down at the hotel, the guests and skiers cheered wildly all around us. Lowe was off the Eiger.

The cable wound upward as he rode it toward the open door. The winch man reached out his hand. Lowe climbed through the door and crawled back into the conundrum of his life.

MAY/JUNE 1992

It's rare in journalism — sports or otherwise — to find a self-contained story that really is a story *— plot and character, both. What raises this tale far above the usual mountain-climbing fare — the theater of because-it's-there — is that* DAVID ROBERTS *has made us understand the climber as well as his quest. —* F.D.

MITCH ALBOM

A Tragedy Too Easy to Ignore

FROM THE DETROIT FREE PRESS

THE INSTRUCTIONS are taped to the wall above his bed. They show diagrams of hands and feet, with arrows pointing left and right. His mother pulls on his limp right arm, forward and backward, forward and backward, as if rowing a boat.

"He couldn't move nothing at first," she says. "Now he can do some on his own. Show him, Damon."

The young man in the blue pajamas turns his head and squints. He is nearly blind now. The room is dark, the air stale, the one window closed. The rails along his single bed keep him from falling out.

Now he looks at his arm and concentrates. It does nothing at first. Then, finally, it jerks in the air as if yanked by a puppeteer's string. It stays up for one second, two seconds, Damon Bailes, the most tragic currency in the city of Detroit, a young black male with a bullet hole in his head, smiles briefly, then lets go.

His arm drops, dead as air.

"We got next!"

It was a warm May night and the basketball game was moving up and down the asphalt.

"We got next!" The kids were sweating as they waited. They dribbled in place. Damon, whose nickname was "Smooth," looked around. He had never been to this court before, outside old Bentley High in Livonia. He and four friends, Lawrence Poole, Torrin Cottrell, Kevin Franklin and Terrill Malone, had started the afternoon in the city, but they lost their first game, and the line was too long to wait for another. There are not enough playable courts in Detroit. And far too many kids with time on their hands.

Poole said he knew a place in the suburbs where the competition was pretty good. So they got in the car and drove to Livonia. Five black kids in a Ford Escort. They were not there long before a police car stopped them.

"Your plates are expired," the officer said. When he ran their names through the computer, one of them, Kevin Franklin, was shown as delinquent on child support payments. He was arrested and taken to jail.

"Let's just go home," Torrin said.

They almost did. But Damon wanted to play ball, and Poole did, too. So now they stood under the floodlights at Bentley, four city kids, waiting for the suburban rims.

"Check the guy in the red shorts," Poole said to Damon as they watched the game.

"Uh-huh."

"There go the shorts we want, the long kind."

"Yeah, they nice. We should buy some of those."

That was it, they claim. Nothing more. The guy in the red shorts, Tyrone Swint, also from Detroit, might have seen them looking and pointing. He would later tell police he thought Damon was "a guy who jumped me" at a Detroit nightclub. Whatever. Something set him off.

And he had a gun.

"Bring the car around," he told a friend.

"What for?"

"We might have a fight."

The suburbs were about to meet the city.

"O.K., let's play," Torrin said, and he bounced an inbounds pass. They ran up and down the court several times. Damon, a six-foot-two, baby-faced guard who had dropped out of high school but starred in church leagues and was hoping to get to a small college if he could pass his equivalency exams, tossed in a couple baskets. Now he dribbled the ball upcourt. He loved this part of the game, when everything was open, everyone was moving, and he was in control. He felt special. Maybe this was the only place he ever felt special.

He was about to make a pass to his best friend, Poole. Suddenly, witnesses say, Tyrone Swint, guy in the red shorts, came up behind Damon and pulled out a gun. He shot Damon in the back of the head. This was before anyone had the chance to yell, "Look out!" This was while Damon was dribbling a basketball. The bullet went through Damon's brain and lodged between the skull and the skin. He went down. The ball rolled away.

"Everyone started running," Cottrell says. "I saw the guy shoot Damon and then he shot again at someone else. As I was running, I saw him go jumping into the window of this black car and they drove away."

The black car was the escape horse, and Tyrone and his buddy were cowboys heading out of town. They drove down Five Mile Road and turned onto Middlebelt. Tyrone threw his gun out the window. It landed in the dirt. Later, Tyrone jumped out of the car and ran through the streets alone.

Back on the court, under the suburban floodlights, Damon Bailes was lying in blood. One of the players was trying to take his pulse. Poole was yelling at the oncoming EMS workers: "My boy's lying here shot! He's shot!"

Torrin was crying. He had known Damon since they were kids. They played in church leagues together. The summer before they had gone to Saginaw for an all-day tournament, and they won the whole thing and everyone got trophies. On the bus ride home, Damon was laughing and talking about how good they were. He had scored all these points. They waved their trophies at each other.

Now Damon was flat, not moving, his head was swollen and bloody, and there was a big knot on the forehead where he had hit the pavement. Torrin and Poole couldn't stop crying. They were still kids, really. They had never been in trouble like this. They ran to the school and found a pay phone. They called Damon's aunt.

"Damon been shot!" Poole said. "Damon been shot!"

Inside the quiet A-frame house on Greenlawn in Detroit there is a small, white, plastic Christmas tree. Velma Bailes, Damon's mother, a woman who looks too young for nine children, no husband, and an ominous pile of hospital bills, bought the tree last year, at Shoppers World, for $25.99. She walks around its needles, and says Damon wants a small TV for Christmas, so he can watch programs from his bed.

"Will he get what he wants?"

"He'll get what he needs."

"What does he need?

"He needs boots for the snow."

It has been seven months since the bullet, which was taken from Damon's brain and given to the police. Damon was in a coma for the first five weeks. Velma would try to talk to him in the hospital, as the doctors had suggested.

"Damon, we need you to come back," she would say. She would hold his hand and look at the tubes in his throat, nose and arms. She would go home.

One night, a nurse called and said to come down quickly. The patient next to Damon was saying, "Damon can't see."

"How do you know?"

"He woke up yellin', 'I can't see! I can't see!' "

The bullet had hit the lobe that controls vision. It also had left Damon paralyzed on the right side. In the months that followed, he would regain a slurred speech, partial vision and some feeling in his otherwise dead right leg and arm. The vision bothered him most. He would cry for hours over his near-blindness.

"He was always saying, 'How can I play basketball if I can't see?' " recalls Mary Roy, who manages the brain-injury program at the Rehabilitation Institute of Michigan. "We tried to tell him, 'Damon, there are other things you can do that are more important than basketball.' "

This, of course, is wishful thinking. The truth is, for a kid like Damon, there was only basketball. He was never college material. He couldn't get through two different high schools. He never held a job. He lived at home, he had a baby with his girlfriend. Maybe he foolishly figured that little leather ball would someday lift him up above all this, the welfare checks, the food stamps, the porch that is falling apart.

If he was stupid, so be it. He is not the first. But he did no wrong. He committed no crimes. The tendency in well-to-do circles is to dismiss a kid such as Damon as hopeless, destined to a bad finish, as if this were some kind of birthright as an urban baby. But if we think like that, we cut the veins out of our city, and, don't kid yourself, our suburbs, too. Young black males. Wounded by gunshot. Young black males. Killed by gunshot. This is all our story. This is where we live. Detroit. A place where, this year alone, 266 children under the age of seventeen have been shot.

We are dying, one bullet at a time.

"I don't know what parents are thinking when they let kids have them, guns," Velma Bailes sighs. "If one of my children had a gun in the house, they got to go. I don't care. All they ever do is get you killed."

Damon, lying in bed, is looking at the ceiling. He is asked whether he ever fired a gun. He snorts a breath and closes his eyes.

"Nuh-uh," he whispers.

It didn't take police long to find Tyrone Swint. They found the gun. They found the car. He still was wearing the red shorts when they pulled up several hours later in Detroit. Swint admitted to the shooting. He claimed self-defense, although how you do that and shoot someone in the back of the head is still a mystery. Why did he do it? Did he even know Damon? Is it true, as Damon's friends claim, that the two had never met? The trial, already postponed once, is now scheduled for February.

Meanwhile, the basketball courts at Bentley have been closed since that night. The gates are padlocked, the rims removed. Signs reading "NO TRESPASSING" are posted. This is a quick suburban reaction: you have trouble, cut off its food supply.

"It's a real shame," says Sergeant Lawrence Little, who works in Livonia and made the arrest. "They had a nice setup at that school, nice courts and all. But you can't have bullets flying near a subdivision.

"We asked those kids why they came up from Detroit to play basketball. You know what they said? They said, 'You can't play down in Detroit. You get shot.'"

Damon Bailes is still waiting for Medicaid to approve his much-needed physical therapy. It could take weeks, even months, the rehab center says. Meanwhile, he sits in bed, and his mother and brothers must bathe him, exercise him, walk him down the hallway, and help him to the bathroom. He is twenty-one years old.

Tyrone Swint, who is twenty, sits in the Wayne County jail. When a verification call is made, a worker there is intrigued.

"Swint? What'd he do?"

"He shot someone on a basketball court."

"Yeah? He shoot one of the Pistons?"

"No, nobody famous."

"Oh. Well. Yep, he's in here."

"Thank you."

"Merry Christmas."

"What can you remember?" Damon is asked.

He looks at his arm. He speaks in a whisper. "Can't . . . remember nothing."

"What do you see when you close your eyes?"

He closes his eyes. He tries.

"Don't . . . see . . . nothin'."

"What do you see when you dream?"

He sniffs. He slowly smiles.

"I see . . . me . . . playing ball . . ."

Damon Bailes can be easily ignored. He can be ignored in a backlog of police reports. He can be ignored in a backlog of Medicaid requests. He can be ignored because he lives in the lowest strata of our city, and, at times, he might as well live in a cave.

But he counts. He may not be William Kennedy Smith, but he counts. On the wall of his tiny bedroom is a note from Poole: *"Damon, you are a precious part of my life and I won't ever forget you."*

He counts. And we cannot solve his problem with a padlock and a sign. We are linked to the city, whether we work there, live there, or even go in for a meal. There is no moat around Eight Mile Road. Their problems are our problems. They bleed, we all bleed.

"All we were doing was playing basketball," says Torrin Cottrell, almost pleading. "You don't expect someone to run up and shoot you. It's like, if basketball is doing something wrong, then what are we supposed to do?"

What *are* we supposed to do? The future of our city is being taken down, gangland style, one ambulance after another. We have to do something. Tonight is Christmas Eve, they are talking flurries, and that should make our suburbs pretty and white. But try to remember, while you open your presents, that somewhere, not far away, Damon Bailes is struggling to see the drawings on the wall, the ones teaching him how to walk again. For what, you keep asking yourself? For what? For what? For what?

For nothing.

And the snow falls.

DECEMBER 24, 1992

MITCH ALBOM *has practically become a cult figure in Detroit. There they have named sandwiches after him, and hardly a month goes by when he is not rumored to be taking on a column in New York or Los Angeles. Most columnists are straitjacketed to a set length, but I much admire the* Free Press *for allowing Mitch's columns to play out. This tragic little story is a classic of the newspaper sports columnist's art, bringing sport and his city together.* — F.D.

WILLIAM NACK

True to His Words

FROM SPORTS ILLUSTRATED

LATE OF AN APRIL evening in 1974, Rubin Carter was sitting at the small desk in his five- by seven-foot cell in Rahway (New Jersey) State Prison, reading the manuscript of his autobiography, when he picked up that faint, familiar scent of menace in the incarcerated air. The man had spent nearly half of his thirty-seven years behind bars — the past seven for a triple murder that he vehemently insisted he had not committed — and in the course of time he had learned to read, like a second language, the quietest shifts in mood and rhythm inside prison walls.

Carter looked at his watch. It was past ten. He went to the door of his cell. Outside, the lights were still on in his wing. Rahway ran like a timepiece, and one of the things a man could always count on was the dimming of the houselights at ten. In the second language, lights off beyond that hour was good; lights on, bad. "It meant that something extraordinary was going on," he says.

Carter was the leader of the Rahway Inmates Council, a group of jailhouse rockers working for prison reform. That very day Carter had presided over a peaceful, if unauthorized, meeting in the prison rec hall, urging inmates to air their grievances through the council. He sensed he was in trouble for that. Indeed, Rahway was preparing to ship him back to Trenton State — the maximum-security prison where he had previously done time — on charges of inciting a riot.

"I *knew* they were coming to get me," he says. "I didn't have to hear rumors."

That left him but one thing to do.

Quietly he picked up his footlocker, his standing locker, his desk — every movable object in his room except his bed — and stacked them against the door of his cell. He then stripped off his shirt and denims and pulled on his sweatpants and sweatshirt, the one with the hood to cover his shaved head. Fearing an attack of Mace, he uncapped a jar of Vaseline and swabbed his neck and face with jelly, spreading it in thick gobs around his nose and eyes. He was ready.

It was surely no wonder, in this hour of maximum danger, that he should choose to face the enemy on the terms he understood best, gleaming and hooded in a very small space. Back in the mid-1960s, Rubin (Hurricane) Carter had been the number one–ranked middleweight fighter in the world — a fierce, unembraceable attacker with a hard body, a mastiff's courage and a left hook that whistled as it worked.

Carter lost his only shot at the middleweight title on December 14, 1964 — a fifteen-round split decision to champion Joey Giardello. Nearly two years later he was training for his second chance, against champion Dick Tiger, when he and a former high school track star named John Artis, a college-bound nineteen-year-old who had never been in trouble with the law, were arrested in Paterson, New Jersey, for the June 17, 1966, slaying of three whites in Paterson's Lafayette Bar & Grill.

For all the years that Carter would spend in prison for that crime — from 1967 to '85, from the first day of his confinement at Trenton State through his extraordinary metamorphosis at Rahway, through two demonstrably tainted trials to his final vindication and walk to freedom — he would proclaim his innocence by living in contempt and defiance of his keepers. On first entering Trenton he refused to surrender his wristwatch and ring; to shave his goatee, as prison rules required; to work at any of the prison jobs. As punishment he spent three months in The Hole, his first of many descents into that airless, sepulchral dungeon. When they finally raised him up out of The Hole, he refused to wear prison clothes. He refused to undergo psychiatric evaluations. An angry recluse, he ate his meals alone in his cell, heating up cans of soup with a small copper coil. Late into the night prisoners could hear him tapping at his antediluvian type-

writer, a manual Underwood left to him by a parolee, pecking
out his story in the long, impassioned cadences of his rage.

Now, on this April night in 1974, he sat on his bed, looking like
some deranged warrior peering out from the hollow of his cowl,
his black face smeared with translucent war paint, listening for
the sound of boots marching along the tier. They came about
three o'clock. "With Mace and chains and shackles," Carter recalls. "Fifty of them, all lined up out there. Guards in their full
riot gear."

Carter froze. From inside a helmet, a muffled voice boomed:
"Come out, Carter! Come out!"

"I mean this," Carter warned them. "I ain't going with you. If
anybody comes in here to get me, god forbid. You'll need twenty
men! First come, first served."

At that moment Bobby Martin, a sergeant of the guards, arrived on the scene. He had just rushed back to Rahway from his
house and was on a mission to save a man he regarded as a
friend. "I never met anybody like him," says Martin, a captain
now in the New Jersey prison system. "I used to go in the cell and
talk to him during lunch. You're not supposed to do that, but I'd
do it." Martin owed Carter one, too. One day when Martin was a
rookie, he had found himself trapped by two thugs on the tier in
Four Up Wing. Carter came to Martin's rescue, knocking out the
assailants.

Martin came to the door and looked inside. "Ever see Rubin's
eyes when he's mad?" says Martin. "His eyes get real small — like
a mad cat's eyes. I looked at him and said, 'Good lord. Help me
now.' He was going to war."

Martin asked Carter to let him in. Carter removed the barri-
cade and opened the door. Inside, the two men huddled quietly.
Martin told Carter that they were taking him to Trenton State.
He assured Carter that nothing bad would happen to him. "Let
me hook you up, and *I'll* take you down to Trenton," Martin said.
"Eventually you're going to have to go, whether you beat fifteen
of us. Or twenty of us. There'll be a hundred more."

The promise of Martin's escort was all Carter needed. "I'll go,"
he said, and he rose to leave. Before he left, though, Carter
scooped up the manuscript of his book and stuffed it into his
sweatpants. Holding the sheaves of paper to his body, Carter left

Rahway in the dead of that terrifying night. "If they had stripped me naked," he said, "I would have taken that manuscript. It was a little thread of hope. The hope that somebody, someday, would read it and understand what had happened to me. What *was* happening to me. It was my lifeline — my message beyond the walls."

Six years later, one September day in 1980, a sixteen-year-old black youth named Lesra Martin arrived at a used-book fair being held in a warehouse in Toronto. Lesra was accompanied by what he would call "my new Canadian family" — eight white entrepreneurs who had plucked him out of the Bushwick ghetto of Brooklyn the year before and brought him north to live and study in their tree-shaded house in Toronto. Lesra was extremely bright, and the Canadians had taken him to the fair to feed his increasing appetite for books, encouraging him to find works by black writers as a way of learning about the culture and history of his people. While roaming the warehouse, Lesra saw a black face on the cover of a hardback. He picked up the book — *The 16th Round: From Number 1 Contender to Number 45472* by Rubin (Hurricane) Carter.

Lesra paid a dollar for it.

That afternoon in his room, Lesra curled up with the book. *The 16th Round*, published to general acclaim in the fall of 1974, was an angry, eloquent indictment of growing up black in America, of the New Jersey judicial system that had arrested Carter and locked him up and of the medieval prisons that had so long confined him. Lesra became engrossed in Carter's tale of his life: his youthful days as a gang leader in New Jersey and his arrest at age twelve for attacking, with his Boy Scout knife, a man he accused of sexually assaulting him; Carter's six years in the Jamesburg (New Jersey) State Home for Boys, his escape from there and his enlistment in the Army in '54; his discharge from the Army and his quick arrest for the Jamesburg escape, for which he spent ten months in the Annandale (New Jersey) Reformatory; his arrest in '57 for purse snatching ("the most dastardly thing I've ever done," Carter would say) and the four years he served in Trenton State for that crime; his release from Trenton; and his rise to fame as a prizefighter.

Early in the book, where Carter described how a policeman

had hassled him as a boy, Lesra — who had experienced the same thing in Brooklyn — so identified with the story that he started reading it out loud to his Canadian friends. They too got caught up in the tale, and for the next few nights they took turns reading it to each other.

They learned, among other things, that at 2:30 in the morning of June 17, 1966, two black men walked into the Lafayette Bar in Paterson, opened fire with a shotgun and a pistol and instantly killed two people: the bartender, James Oliver, and a patron, Fred Nauyaks. A second patron, Hazel Tanis, died of her wounds a month later. A third customer, William Marins, suffered a head wound that partially blinded him. That night Carter and Artis were drinking and dancing in a local club, and, accompanied by a third black man, John Royster, they left the club and went driving in Carter's white Dodge Polara about the time of the Lafayette Bar shootings. Carter let Artis drive.

At one point a policeman stopped the three men, but when he saw Carter in the backseat — Carter was probably the most recognizable citizen of Paterson, a nationally known fighter with a signature shaved head — he waved them on, telling them that the police were looking for "two Negroes in a white car." After Artis dropped off Royster, he and Carter suddenly fit the police description, and they were stopped again. The police whisked them off to the scene of the crime and then to a hospital, where Carter and Artis were placed before the wounded Marins. Asked by police if these were the men who had shot him, Marins shook his head no. Marins and Tanis agreed that the killers were light-skinned blacks, about six feet tall, and that the man with the shotgun, whom the state would later claim was Carter, had a pencil mustache. Carter was five foot seven, very dark, with a thick mustache and goatee; Artis was light-skinned and six-one.

Carter and Artis were given lie-detector tests, and each passed. The police then released them. Two weeks later, during a grand-jury hearing at which both Carter and Artis testified, the city's investigator in charge of the case, Vincent DeSimone, testified that "the physical description of the two holdup men is not even close [to that of Carter and Artis]." Furthermore, DeSimone said, both killers had worn "dark clothing." Carter had worn a white jacket, Artis a light-blue V-neck sweater. The grand jury returned no indictment.

Carter and Artis were arrested four months later, on October 14, for the Lafayette Bar murders. What had happened during the interval to turn Carter into a light-skinned, six-foot black with a pencil mustache? The state had produced two eyewitnesses, Alfred Bello and Arthur Dexter Bradley, who would testify that Carter was one of the gunmen; Bello would also identify Artis. Both witnesses were repeat offenders, but their testimony was the key to convicting Carter and Artis, even though the state suggested no motive for the crime. Bello testified under oath that the state had offered him nothing for his testimony but protection. On June 29, 1967, Carter was given one concurrent and two consecutive life sentences, Artis three concurrent life terms.

While in prison Carter focused all his energy on resisting his jailers and fighting for his freedom. "I don't belong here," he told members of the prison board. "I am *not* a criminal. You are not going to treat me like you treat other people here." In prison he lost his right eye in what he called a "botched operation" to correct a detached retina. (It was to seek improved medical treatment for inmates that he then joined the Inmates Council.) Though his schooling was limited, he read Plato and imagined himself communing with Socrates. He was respected by fellow prisoners because he was a man of his word. "When he said he would do something," says Bobby Martin, "he did it."

When Lesra and his Canadian friends finished *The 16th Round*, they were convinced of Carter's innocence and curious about his fate. They searched through newspaper files at the Toronto Reference Library for information on him.

What they learned stunned them: Late in 1974, just weeks before the publication of Carter's book, Bello and Bradley recanted their testimony identifying Carter and Artis as the Lafayette Bar killers. They told both a public defender and reporter Selwyn Raab of *The New York Times* that Paterson police had pressured them into lying in exchange for reward money and lenient treatment for crimes they had committed.

"I was twenty-three years old and facing eighty to ninety years in jail [for robbery]," Bradley told Raab. "There's no doubt Carter was framed. . . . I lied to save myself."

Carter's case became a cause célèbre among civil libertarians and the political left, new and old. In the autumn of 1975, radio stations across the nation began playing Bob Dylan's new song, *Hurricane*. One of the verses went like this:

> Now all the criminals in their coats and their ties
> Are free to drink martinis and watch the sun rise
> While Rubin sits like Buddha in a ten-foot cell
> An innocent man in a living hell.

During the recantation furor of 1974, a tape recording surfaced of a DeSimone interview with Bello on October 11, 1966. The New Jersey Supreme Court, to which Carter and Artis had appealed their convictions, listened to the tape. The transcript, the court stated, "shows that in the beginning Bello was unable to identify Artis as one of the two men and was not sure of Carter. He was also uncertain of the make of the white car used by the gunmen, which he had seen driving slowly through the area and later parked on the street. However, as the interview progressed, and after DeSimone had given assurances that Bello would receive favorable or sympathetic treatment, Bello became positive in his identification of Carter and Artis and the car in which they had been riding."

Not only had the defendants not known about such inducements, which they could have used to discredit Bello's testimony during their trial, but also Bello had not disclosed the fact that he had been offered more than protection. The New Jersey Supreme Court, in a 7–0 decision, overturned the 1967 verdict on the grounds that the state had violated the U.S. Supreme Court's Brady rule, which requires prosecutors to give exculpatory evidence to the defense.

Carter and Artis got a second trial, in the fall of 1976. By then, however, Bello had reversed himself again. He testified once more that he had seen Carter and Artis leaving the murder scene carrying guns. This time, with an admitted perjurer as its key witness, the state offered a motive for the Lafayette Bar killings, portraying them as an act of "racial revenge." The alleged motive, presented at a time of widespread racial tension and fear of urban riots, was baseless in fact and prejudicial in nature, but the jury did not see it that way. On December 22, Carter and Artis were convicted a second time of the Lafayette Bar murders. Their prison sentences from the first trial were reinstated.

Once the Canadians had caught up with all these developments, they were more intrigued than ever. They tracked down Carter by telephoning Trenton State, and then Lesra composed the first letter he had ever written. It began "Dear Mr. Carter" and ended with "Please write back. It will mean a lot." The letter described how a kid from one of the meanest ghettos in New York had ended up reading *The 16th Round* with a "family" of white folks in Toronto.

This is, in its fashion, a tale of two cities. Most of Lesra's Canadian friends had first met in the 1960s as students at the University of Toronto, where some were involved in social work and in helping expatriate Americans dodge the draft during the Vietnam War. The Canadians came from a salad of backgrounds. Sam Chaiton, who studied modern languages and literature, was the son of Jews who had immigrated to Canada after surviving the German death camp at Bergen-Belsen. Terry Swinton and his sister Kathy were the children of a wealthy Toronto business executive. Lisa Peters, divorced and with a young son, Marty, had emerged from a life of poverty to study psychology at the university. She would later become involved in drug rehabilitation work.

They and a few others eventually went into business together, importing batiks from Malaysia, and in 1976 they bought a house to share in Toronto. In '79, weary of long trips to the Orient, they began looking for something else to do with their restless energy. Chaiton and Terry Swinton went to work testing a device intended to reduce pollution in automobile engines. Their experiments took them that summer to Brooklyn, where the U.S. Environmental Protection Agency had a lab. It was there that they met Lesra, who had a summer job at the lab. Fascinated with these foreigners — "Dere go Canada!" he would say when they passed him — he started hanging around them.

"We responded to his spark and light and curiosity," says Chaiton. "He responded to us, and we became very friendly. We loved him right off the bat."

"They trusted me," Lesra says. "That meant a lot."

The boy lived with his parents, Alma and Earl, and five of his seven siblings in a fourth-story apartment with no railing on the top staircase and no knob on the door. They were churned in poverty. Earl had once been the lead singer in a popular doo-wop group, the Del Vikings, but the group had long ago disbanded, and he had been disabled since falling in a factory accident. Lesra's oldest brother, Earl Jr., was in prison for breaking and entering, and Lesra earned money for the family by bagging and delivering groceries and working at the lab.

When Chaiton and Terry Swinton returned to Toronto, they invited Lesra and a friend to visit them there. The boys spent three days playing in Toronto's parks and gamboling about town, and when the Canadians invited Lesra back a few weeks later, he fairly leaped into their arms. By the end of his second visit, the Canadians had grown so fond of him that they offered to make a home for him in Toronto and send him to school there. "We want to give you a chance to have a good education," Chaiton told Lesra. Lesra was eager to join them.

The Canadians approached Alma and Earl with their plan, and Earl flew to Canada to see where his fifteen-year-old son would live. It did not take him long to decide. Bushwick was a war zone. Lesra "didn't stand a chance if he stayed in Brooklyn," says Chaiton. "There was no way he would get anywhere."

When Lesra moved to Toronto in the fall of 1979, the effects of his ghetto life were manifest. He was malnourished and suffering a chronic infection that made his nose run and his eyes bloodshot. Antibiotics cured the infection; the Canadians' plump refrigerator, the malnutrition. But nothing would touch Lesra more deeply than being taken to an ophthalmologist and being fitted for eyeglasses. "I was blind," Lesra says, "and I didn't even know it. I had nothing to compare it to. The world was a blur."

His poor eyesight mirrored the state of his education. It was apparent that he could not attend public schools in Canada. "He was almost illiterate," says Chaiton. So he began tutoring Lesra at home. Since black ghetto English was Lesra's primary tongue, Chaiton says, he began teaching Lesra the King's English as if it were a second language. "I got a textbook instructing how to teach English to a foreigner," he says.

The Canadians read to Lesra from books such as Claude

Brown's *Manchild in the Promised Land,* about the author's life in Harlem, and within a year they began urging him to read, on his own, the autobiography of Frederick Douglass. Lesra literally cried in fear of such a book, with its long words and serpentine prose, but the Canadians kept after him until, in the summer of 1980, he somehow was able to finish reading it. "The problem we had was not one of his intelligence but of the overwhelming feeling of inferiority he had," says Chaiton. "Overcoming those psychological barriers was awful."

Down in Trenton, meanwhile, Carter had been going through a sea change of his own. After his second conviction, he says, "I wanted to die." He had turned his face to the wall and withdrawn even further into himself. "I was looking down a long, dark tunnel," he says.

Carter saw and talked to almost no one, in prison or out. At his insistence, his wife, Mae Thelma, had stopped coming to see him. (They were divorced in 1984.) Carter hibernated with his books for three years. Then, on a sweltering afternoon in 1979, the summer that Lesra met the Canadians, Carter did something that he hadn't done in years. He went outside, to the yard, to escape the prison heat. "I was looking at the big wall, thirty feet high, with gun towers, and suddenly a light lit up, and I could see through the wall," he says. "No, it was not a hallucination! I was amazed. As suddenly as it appeared, it disappeared. I had heard about these things. So I began reading about Eastern religions. And I began growing my hair, something I hadn't done in twenty years. And I cut off my beard."

That was the Carter, softened around the edges, to whom Lesra wrote his letter in 1980. "I was leaving me, and I didn't even know it," Carter says. "I was opening up. And suddenly this letter came. How could I not respond? His letter had so much energy! There was a feeling there. . . . I typed a reply."

Thus began a relationship tying the man to the boy and the Canadians, a relationship that would ultimately change Carter's life. He and Lesra exchanged several letters that fall, and Lesra suggested visiting Carter when he was home in Brooklyn over Christmas. Carter hesitated; at Trenton visitors met prisoners in the abandoned cells of the former death row, next to the execution chamber where Bruno Hauptmann had died after being convicted of killing the Lindbergh baby, and Carter did not want to expose Lesra to this unearthly grimness. "This face is *trying* to get *there* and not bring another face here," he wrote to the family. "So if Lesra wishes to come — he will."

For Lesra it was haunting to step inside that tomb. He had a powerful sense that this was the world he had escaped when he went to Canada. "When I heard those steel gates closing behind me," he says, "I thought, I could be in here." Carter could feel him trembling when they embraced. The boy told the man about his family in Brooklyn and his new life in Canada, about his studies and the books he was reading. He was working on weekends, sending money home to his relatives, but he felt guilty for leaving them and accepting the chance he had been offered. "How did I deserve escaping that?" he asked Carter. "Why me?"

"You never deserved to be there in the first place," Carter told him, "so you don't have to feel guilty about getting out."

The two connected. Carter heard a boy's laughter that he had not heard in years. "Lesra was in a state of joy," Carter says. "You could feel it. It was like a son coming to see me. He was just so effervescent, and I loved the way he spoke, so precisely, and the way he laughed, even in this death house. The way Lesra was gave a lot of credibility to the Canadian family. I knew then that this was not a hoax. These were not people playing with our lives. It made me listen to them, and at that time I wasn't listening to anybody."

Early in 1981, at the Canadians' urging, Carter began calling them collect, and that February, Chaiton, Peters and Terry Swinton drove to Trenton to see him. No one knew it at the time, of course, but the freeing of Hurricane Carter had begun. The Canadians were shocked at Carter's appearance. "He looked almost fragile," Swinton says. "A hundred and thirty-five pounds. He wasn't eating. A can or two of soup a day. He looked to us like a really gentle person, more like a writer than a prizefighter."

They teased Carter at once about his soft demeanor. "We don't believe you were ever the Number One contender," Chaiton said. "Come on!"

Carter turned on his "baleful stare," the one he had learned from hanging around and sparring with Sonny Liston, but the

Canadians laughed at him. Peters's father had been an amateur fighter, and whether it was because of that or the poverty she and Carter had both experienced when they were young, the two began forming a strong attachment.

Over the next few months, in visits, phone calls and letters, the Canadians learned a lot about Carter's life in prison. "Don't you go to parole meetings?" Terry Swinton once asked.

"You have to admit guilt and be remorseful," Carter said. "How can I do that? I don't want a parole. I want to be exonerated."

"Do you need anything?" asked Swinton.

"I've got everything I need in my cell," Carter said. "Jesus, Socrates and Buddha. I fill the voids in my life with figures in history. I don't need anything else."

"Man, that's a shame," Chaiton said. "If you've got everything you need, then it's not too bad a place."

Carter snapped off his words: "If you need anything, if you want anything, then this place has a hold over you because they can deny you that. The least painful thing is not to want anything. All I want is my freedom, and they deny me that every day, every hour that I am here. Do you understand?"

They soon understood a lot of things, and they liked what they saw of Carter. Indeed, Carter quickly became another member of their family, one who happened to be living far from home. The Canadians began by visiting him once a month for long weekends, staying in cheap motels near Trenton, and by the spring Carter was calling them collect several times a week. He wrote them a letter in which he said, "For the first time in my life . . . I can truly say that I trust somebody. I trust you. And without reservations."

That letter deepened the Canadians' resolve to help Carter find his way out. "If you had a brother in jail for something he didn't do," Terry Swinton says, "wouldn't you do everything possible to help him?"

For the next four and a half years, that is precisely what the Canadians did. At the end of 1981, using money they had made selling batiks, they turned their business efforts to renovating houses in Toronto. They also began spending ten days a month in New Jersey, visiting Carter and becoming immersed in the history of the Lafayette Bar case. On December 5, just before Artis was released on parole after serving fifteen years, Carter was exiled to Trenton State's dreaded Vroom Readjustment Unit for the system's incorrigibles. Artis, a model prisoner, had attended Glassboro (New Jersey) State College while doing his time, leaving prison unguarded in the morning and returning at night, and had taught adult-education courses for inmates; Carter, meanwhile, was sent to Vroom for ninety days for refusing to stand up in his cell for a head count.

He spent the first fifteen days in The Hole, "where you are like dead," he says. "No air, no ventilation. They turned on the heat in the summer and turned it off in the winter. Do you know what it's like to be powerless? Totally and utterly powerless? I never knew a prisoner who did not go to his cell at night and cry. Not every night, but every prisoner. You could hear them. You could hear everything. I still hear everything. Only this time I had Lisa, Lesra, Terry and Sam to hold on to. They were my anchors."

In January 1982, with Carter calling Toronto for several hours a day, the Canadians' long-distance telephone charges were $4,238.39. By then the Canadians had broken Carter's resistance to accepting their gifts of food, clothing and appliances. Peters had argued, "You are denying yourself stuff before [the guards] have a chance to take it away. You are helping them keep you kept. If they want to take it, let them."

Now Carter was walking around in a pair of sheepskin slippers, wearing a velvet robe and watching television in his cell. Moreover, every month the Canadians sent him a twenty-five-pound box of his favorite canned foods, chiefly exotic nuts and date breads. The only time the Canadian anchors were not there for him was when he quietly cut them loose in the fall of 1982, a few months after the New Jersey Supreme Court, by a 4–3 decision, rejected his appeal for a third trial on the grounds that the defense had not adequately demonstrated that suppressed evidence might have affected the outcome of the second trial. "It was just crushing," Terry Swinton says. Carter was inconsolable over the decision, despite a strong dissent by Justice Robert Clifford, who wrote that the prosecution's chief witness, Bello, was "a complete, unvarnished liar, utterly incapable of speaking the truth."

Retreating into his carapace, Carter did not call his friends for nearly eight months. The house in Canada went into mourning. "I was getting ready to settle back into prison — absent good food, absent love and companionship," Carter says. "Lisa used to send me great big novelty cards. I had those pasted on those walls. I used to look at them. I felt helpless." He finally called the Canadians late in the summer of 1983. "I need you guys," he told them.

A few weeks later the Canadians decided to make one final push. They put their house on the market, and three of them — Chaiton, Terry Swinton and Peters — moved to New Jersey. The others moved into a smaller house in Toronto, where Lesra had graduated that year from high school with straight A's. He had just enrolled at the University of Toronto, where he would major in anthropology. The Canadians' commitment staggered Carter. "I was astounded," he says. "They set up house!"

Carter asked for, and received, a transfer from Trenton to Rahway, and the Canadians took an apartment near the prison, which was closer than Trenton State was to the New York offices of Carter's and Artis's lawyers, Myron Beldock and Lewis Steel, and those of Leon Friedman, a renowned constitutional scholar who was assisting them with the case. For nearly two years the Canadians scoured New Jersey searching for new evidence and witnesses to exonerate Carter and Artis. They set up shop in Beldock's law firm at Forty-sixth Street and Fifth Avenue.

"The Canadians did the one thing that impresses me," says Beldock. "They did their homework." They had sent ahead a black case containing a three- by nine-foot chart in which they had painstakingly detailed how the testimony of various state witnesses had changed over the years. "It was like a jump-start," says Beldock. "Very exciting."

Chaiton and Terry Swinton sat in the office surrounded by documents, and they pored through papers and folders. "It was like there were two law firms up there," Steel says. "One was Beldock's and the other was This Thing, across the hall, with the Canadians. You could go in there and ask one of these guys, 'We think in such and such a hearing that such and such was said. Do you know what I mean?' Twenty minutes later, they would come across the hall with a transcript open to the page: 'Is this what you're looking for?' "

The Canadians "heightened our awareness and our ability to

handle even small issues, which all got woven into these briefs," Beldock says. Friedman was in charge of writing the legal sections of the briefs, and he recalls a day when he saw an unfamiliar statement in a draft of a brief. "Where did this come from?" Friedman asked Ed Graves, another attorney working on the case.

"The Canadians put it in," said Graves.

"Are you *sure* it's right?"

"Leon," said Graves, "if the Canadians say it's right, it's right."

What all the parties remember, as they were preparing the papers seeking a writ of habeas corpus from U.S. District Court Judge H. Lee Sarokin, was the crackling energy that went into the work — and the panicky sense that this was Carter's last chance to be freed from prison.

By the fall of 1985, Carter's transformation was so dramatic that he was almost unrecognizable. His cell looked like a yuppie pad. He was growing an amaryllis bulb in a pot, padding around on a Persian rug, listening to Otis Redding on his tape deck, hanging Manet prints on the walls, drying his hands on monogrammed towels and eating everything from crab béchamel to beef Wellington — all offerings from the Canadians, who were determined to grease his transition from prison to the outside world. He was greeting fellow prisoners with a smile and a nod and giving fatherly advice to rookie guards.

Two weeks before Sarokin's decision, convinced he would soon be free, Carter started giving away all of his belongings — his typewriter and clothes, his 125 books, his prints and his copper coil. Terry Swinton visited him in prison and asked him where he had gotten his raggedy haircut. "My hair's falling out in clumps," Carter said. "The tension, I guess."

On November 6, 1985, Beldock called the Canadians' apartment to tell them that Sarokin's decision was coming down the next day. The veteran judge had studied voluminous files — by his own reckoning, Carter's is the most important case he has ever decided. "I have seen some very good briefs," Sarokin recalls, "but this was about the best set of briefs I've ever seen. A remarkably good job."

The next day the Swintons went to Sarokin's chambers and waited; Peters stayed at the New Jersey apartment, waiting for

Terry Swinton to call, while she talked by phone with Carter. Chaiton, Lesra and the others were at home in Canada, sitting in silence. At about eleven o'clock, Graves walked out of Sarokin's chambers holding the opinion over his head, a smile wreathing his face. Swinton grabbed the papers and read:

"The extensive record clearly demonstrates that [the] petitioners' convictions were predicated upon an appeal to racism rather than reason, and concealment rather than disclosure. . . . To permit convictions to stand which have as their foundation appeals to racial prejudice and the withholding of evidence critical to the defense, is to commit a violation of the Constitution as heinous as the crimes for which these petitioners were tried and convicted."

Terry Swinton called Peters. She and Carter heard the click of call waiting. Peters hit the button. "We did it!" screamed Swinton. She hit the button again. "We won!" she told Carter.

Stunned, Carter raised his eyes. Then he shouted: "We won! We won!"

Paulene McLean, a friend of Lesra's, called Canada. "A complete silence fell over the house," says Lesra. "We were stunned. It was as if, after holding our breaths all those years, we finally could exhale."

In minutes, word had swept around the prison, and then radios were carrying the news. Prisoners flocked around Carter, patting him on the back, while others came running.

"Rube, you've won!"

"Rube, you're on the radio!"

"Way to go, Rube!"

Sarokin ordered Carter released the next day. The state appealed the judge's decision for twenty-six long months, right up to the U.S. Supreme Court, but it lost at every level. Finally, on February 26, 1988, a Passaic County judge formally dismissed the 1966 indictments. The twenty-two-year odyssey of Rubin Carter and John Artis had ended. It had touched many people in many ways, and it had left the two defendants changed beyond their memories.

For Artis, an only child raised by doting parents to be respectful and live responsibly, prison was a long nightmare that robbed him of his freedom, his wish to raise a family, his dreams of a career as a professional football player. He says it is not easy to confront a prospective employer, who always gets around to asking him what crime he was convicted for. "Ah, triple murder. But. . . ." It's a stigma to this day. And given the tortuous history of the case, it's difficult to explain away.

The state had tried hard to get Artis to testify against Carter. Officials took Artis to his father's house at Christmastime in 1974 and promised him freedom the next day if he fingered Rubin. He refused. "It would have been a lie," Artis says. "I wasn't brought up like that."

He could not help himself one day in 1973 when he was out on furlough. He was in Paterson, and he had to see the bar where the three people were murdered. He had never been in there. "It was no different than any other bar I'd ever seen," he says. "People kept lookin' at me. I stood inside the door and just looked around. I was trying to place what happened there, from the testimony in the trial . . . and then I left."

Artis lives in Portsmouth, Virginia, and works with troubled youths. "Being in prison is like being dead, and I want these kids to know that," he says. "And you know what? When we were cleared, no one even apologized."

Lesra Martin still goes back to Bushwick to visit his siblings and see the old friends who have escaped the usual traps. There are not many left. "I will never forget where I came from," he says. "Ghetto life will always be a part of me. I do not want that feeling to go away." He is further away from it today than ever. After graduating with honors from the University of Toronto, he went to graduate school in sociology at Dalhousie University in Halifax, Nova Scotia — a last stop on the Underground Railroad, which spirited slaves out of the South. He was drawn to the black community there. Last year, after getting his master's degree, Lesra entered the law school at Dalhousie. He is interested in constitutional law.

"I enjoy where I am now," Lesra says. "It's frightening that there are still hundreds of thousands of people in the ghettos who can't read or write. I'm no genius. I was just given access and resources. When you're going through what I went through, you don't realize how miraculous it is. But it *is* miraculous."

And Carter is where he is because Lesra was where he was. The former inmate number 45472 moved to Canada in 1988, after the state dismissed the charges against him, and for the last four years he has spent much of his time reading, writing and lecturing. He also got married. Lisa Peters is Lisa Carter now.

"I love it up here," says Carter, who intends to remain a U.S. citizen but has applied for landed immigrant status in Canada. He helped Chaiton and Terry Swinton write a book about their shared experience, called *Lazarus and the Hurricane,* using Lesra's Biblical name. Now, having also written a screenplay based on the book — it has been making the rounds in Hollywood — Carter and the Canadians are doing research on a proposed book about the kidnapping and murder of the Lindbergh baby in 1932.

They work out of a six-bedroom half-timbered house on ten acres of land about twenty miles north of Toronto. They leased the house in a state of disrepair three years ago and converted it into the European hunting lodge that it resembles today. Carter also helped build the two-stall barn behind the house, and in fair weather he likes to spend his leisure riding his horse, Red Cloud, along the trails that wind through the woods and fields for miles around. "I always loved to ride horses, even back in my days as a fighter," Carter says. Horses certainly suit his new lifestyle. Carter has been given the name Badger Star by a medicine man in the Lakota Indian nation, whose culture and traditions Carter regularly studies. He has also been adopted into the family of a local Cree elder, Vern Harper.

Carter has been a willing speaker at colleges and law firms, and he was recently asked to deliver a lecture next fall at Harvard Law School before a student conference on the writ of habeas corpus. Says Judge Sarokin, "I can't think of anybody, with all the opposition now to habeas corpus, who better symbolizes the need for it than Hurricane Carter."

The Great Writ, as legal scholars call it, has been coming under heightened attack from the political right, and civil libertarians view it today as a kind of endangered species, particularly given the ultraconservative cast of the U.S. Supreme Court. Leslie Harris, chief legislative counsel of the American Civil Liberties Union in Washington, D.C., says that the Bush administration has made elimination of habeas corpus the centerpiece of its efforts to look tough on crime. The writ is the only instrument by which the federal judiciary can correct abuses of the Bill of Rights at the state-court level, according to Harris, and the Carter-Artis case shows how vital an instrument it can be.

It is now more than twenty-five years since Carter was arrested in Paterson, yet wherever he speaks, he tells a tale of a past that will not let him go. "It is not finished," he says. "I still feel the loneliness. I still feel the pain. I feel it now. I feel *everything*. The day you get out of prison is the day your sentence begins."

APRIL 13, 1992

Any list of our most versatile writers must put BILL NACK *at the top. He can cover horseracing like a handicapper, write chess so the layman can follow it, turn out newspaper columns on deadline, and write long, reportorial investigative series. Still, this jack-of-all-trades stuff pales before the quality of his profiles. This heartwarming saga of Hurricane Carter follows past years' selections in* Best American Sports Writing *about other subjects as diverse as Sonny Liston and Secretariat. Bill also ingratiates himself to other writers by remembering* their *best lines and quoting them back.* — F.D.

SCOTT RAAB

Asphalt Junkie

FROM GQ

CLEVELAND STATE UNIVERSITY hired Kevin Mackey to coach men's basketball in 1983, the summer I graduated. No one gave a shit, me least of all. The team had gone 8-and-20, and Mackey was some no-name Boston College assistant. Besides, like a lot of CSU students, I was older, married and working for a living. We came to campus for classes, bolted coffee at the snack bar, and took the bus to the job. For us, that was college. There were no dorms, unless you counted the flophouses a block away on Prospect Avenue, where fraternity boys jeered at the working girls in their spike heels and buttcheek-high skirts.

We did have two student newspapers, one for blacks, one for whites. The most active on-campus social group was the local branch of the American Nazis. They wore brown shirts with swastika armbands while they signed up new members in the student center. Every year, on Rudolf Hess's birthday, *The Cauldron* — the white paper — ran their letters to the editor asking the Allies to release Hess from Spandau Prison. My most memorable moment at CSU, besides the day I met my wife, came when I took a piss in a University Tower john and looked up to see the twin lightning bolts of Hitler's SS inked onto the wall above the urinal, beneath the words "WE ARE BACK."

What I'm saying is that CSU was a fine place to get out of for a muddling Jewish boy from Cleveland Heights. And it was the perfect setting for an Irish guttersnipe like Kevin Mackey — who'd made his bones recruiting hungry city kids no one else could find or would take — to begin his head coaching career.

What he did his first three seasons at CSU was win sixty-four games. By 1986, his Vikings were 27-and-3 and in the NCAA tournament for the first time; I was a teaching assistant in Iowa City and Mackey's only fan west of the Cuyahoga River. On the day CSU played Bobby Knight's Indiana Hoosiers in the tournament's opening round, I canceled "Forms of Comic Vision" and invited the class to watch the game with me. The few who showed up at my house — all corn-fed, small-town, blond-haired Big Ten pinheads — looked smug, too polite to laugh, when I told them that CSU was bound to win.

That day — March 14, 1986 — the rumpled-suited, fast-talking Mackey dealt Knight his first loss ever in an opening-round game and made me proud to be from CSU. Afterward — after the all-black Vikings outshot, out-rebounded, outhustled and outsmarted third-seeded Indiana; after the plump and shining Mackey shook the dour Knight's hand, raised both fists, and punched the sky; after my students went home — I drank myself full of beer, lit my victory joint and cried for joy.

On the evening of Friday the thirteenth, July 1990, Kevin Mackey is passed out on a couch inside a crack house on Edmonton Avenue. His party started the night before as it always did, just him and a cooler of Lite iced down in the back seat of his Lincoln Town Car as he cruised the Cleveland ghettos, scouting summer-league games and getting drunk.

Somewhere in the previous night, he recruited a couple of strawberries — young crack whores — and the next morning, before heading back to the house on Edmonton, they all drove to campus together to snag Mackey's paycheck, the first issued to him under his brand-new, two-year, $350,000 contract, announced only two days before.

Now, after nine hours at the crack house with his fast new friends, Mackey is unconscious. It isn't only the beer and the wine and the crack and the women. Mackey (who says he faints during blood tests) has two big venipunctures — needle pokes — in his upper thighs.

Meanwhile, acting on a phone tip, the Cleveland Police Street Enforcement Unit has been staked out at the corner of Eddy Road and Edmonton for nearly five hours, and Sergeant Ray

Gercar has a headache so piercing that two years later he will recall asking one of the women stumbling out of the two-story house at 12406 Edmonton if she has any aspirin.

Gercar calls in the plates on the Lincoln at the curb: It's Mackey's. No reports of its having been stolen.

Farther up Eddy Road, near St. Clair Avenue, a news crew from Channel 8 waits too. They've got a camera on the scene, and their handsome young reporter, Martin Savidge, dispatched by the head of the station's "I-Team" after another mysterious phone tip.

No one rings Mackey's wife, Kathy, and their three kids, at home in Shaker Heights, but somebody does phone Alma Massey, Mackey's longtime lover, to tell her that her boy's in deep shit. Massey, a heroin user and former prostitute whose police record dates back to 1974, knows where to find him. But rather than go directly into the house when she arrives, she instead pretends to slash the tires on Mackey's Town Car.

Gercar figures Massey's just playing it safe, trying to lure Mackey out. Maybe Massey smells cop. The crumbling house has been a known drug nest for some time, and Mackey, according to Gercar's sources, is a frequent patron.

Everybody waits in the summer twilight, waits for Mackey.

Finally, the coach wobbles out, pasty-faced, disheveled, in an aquamarine polo shirt, khaki pants and white sneakers, a blinking, fucked-up, forty-four-year-old leprechaun groping in the dark heart of Cleveland's Third World. As he and Massey climb into the Lincoln, Mackey behind the wheel, it's 8:25 P.M. They turn north up Eddy, inching toward St. Clair.

The next thing Mackey knows, he's up against the side of his midnight-blue ride, hands on the roof, as Gercar arrests him. The Channel 8 camera is already close enough so that on the videotape you can hear Alma Massey say "Would you mind gettin' that out of my face?" in a polite, cold voice.

Mackey peers into the lens, deadpan, the skin slack on his chipmunk cheeks, jowls sagging, eyes lighting up as he struggles to outline a play in his mind.

At Sixth District headquarters, Mackey fakes two puffs into the Breathalyzer, reaches into his pocket and fires a hit of Binaca into his mouth, ruining any accurate breath analysis. Perfect.

The defining moment, the sum and essence of Kevin Mackey, distilled into one Homeric act — Mackey the Gamin from Boston's Somerville, Mackey the Spewer of Blarney, the Comber of Projects and Savior of Ghetto Youth, Mackey the bottom-line, ninety-four-foot, balls-out, how-many-fucking-games-have-YOU-won motherfucker.

Foxed them again.

Then Gercar hands Mackey a plastic cup, asks him to take a leak, and there it is, all of it, pissed away: the cocaine; the $350,000 contract, complete with new car, radio and TV shows, membership in the University Club, and 500 season tickets for inner-city kids in "Kevin's Korner"; the chance to prowl the sidelines in the new $55-million, 13,000-seat arena they call "the House That Mackey Built"; the thirteen-room Shaker Heights mini-mansion with the pretty blonde wife and the swimming pool; and any prayer of Kevin Mackey's ever again passing for someone young and on his way to the top.

Mackey holds an "I led two lives" press conference, a sullen, teary public confession with wife, son and brother beside him. His lawyer negotiates with the school for a medical leave of absence, but six days after the arrest — plenty of time for local and national media to gnaw the carrion from the bones of the beer-swilling, crack-addled white coach and his black junkie hooker gal pal — CSU shitcans Mackey.

Mackey does better in the Cleveland courts: Sentenced to ninety days treatment in lieu of conviction, he splits his time between the Turning Point in Cleveland and former NBA star John Lucas's Houston-based recovery program. After an additional few months in Houston, Mackey uses Lucas's connections to get back on the coaching trail.

His first job is a $300-per-week assistant's gig with the Atlanta Eagles of the United States Basketball League, with a contract stipulation that requires him to be tested at random for drugs.

After one USBL season, Mackey is named head coach of the Fayetteville Flyers of something called the Global Basketball Association. In February 1992, I rent a white Cadillac and drive to North Carolina. Mackey lives in a team sponsor's motel room, hauls in thirty grand a year, and drives a Hyundai Sonata owned by a local car dealer. Sober since the day after his arrest, Mackey works off another chunk of his debt to sports and society via exile to this hardwood Elba, where the penitents suffer poorly laundered uniforms, chubby cheerleaders in washed-out spandex, and all-night bus rides between road games.

Spread from Albany, Georgia, to Saginaw, Michigan, the GBA is a touring hoops halfway house full of head cases, addicts and full-court lifers, guys whose dream of driving hard to the hole ended somewhere between the prison gym and a massage parlor. The salary scale for players begins at $9,500 for the sixty-four-game season and tops out at $25,000.

Fayetteville itself is pure GBA: Half the waffle houses, pawnshops, and strip malls in America are laid end to end here, crammed with soldiers, rednecks, and women with hulking, tortured hair. A blue GMC pickup parked in front of Uptown Undies and Stimulants sports a bumper sticker that reads "MY WIFE — YES. MY DOG — MAYBE. MY GUN — NEVER."

Over at the Cumberland County Civic Center, hard by the Charlie Rose Agri-Expo Center, I find Mackey sitting alone at courtside and introduce myself.

"This is only about basketball, alcohol, and drugs, right?" he says as we shake hands.

The old twinkle in Mackey's eyes has splintered into shards of blue and black. He's pale, blotchy, thinner than in the CSU days, back when he loved to tell writers that "the modern game of basketball is a game of short, fat, white coaches and big, black studs." He's aged twenty years in two, the lines in his face etched too deep for a man of forty-six, even one whose entire adult life passed in gyms and barrooms.

What Mackey doesn't want to talk about, I quickly learn, is his wife and family, his relationship with Alma Massey and the mystery of who set him up with the police and the TV station.

Which omits all the why of Mackey's life, how he got to this 4,300-seat dung heap with its photo-montage tributes to Elvis and Alabama near the ticket window, a million miles from glory.

"Home is where my job is," Mackey says. "I'm very grateful to be here, to have this opportunity."

Sure, but Kathy Mackey still lives in the house in Shaker, and the bank is foreclosing fast. Back in August 1988, Mackey forged his wife's signature on an application for a $75,000 line of credit, using their home as collateral. According to Mackey's attorney, the money went to Alma Massey and her seven children. Officially, the Mackeys are still husband and wife. Unofficially?

"My family is very supportive," he says, "and that's the end of that."

How about Alma Massey?

"Look, I'll give you plenty of stuff on the basketball, the alcohol, and the drugs. You'll get everything you need."

Fine. How about who phoned Alma from the crack house?

"I can't give you that because that would open it up too good for you. She was called, and she put herself in jeopardy to come down and get me out of there and probably save my life, O.K.? She didn't know anything. The worst thing that ever happened to Alma Massey was to meet Kevin Mackey."

It's not unfriendly, this game of keep-away, not without smiles on both sides. Savvy with reporters, Mackey needs his name in print, lest he be forgotten long before he gets another shot at the big money; there are plenty of younger coaches around with records just as good who've never been arrested on-camera after exiting a drug den. He also knows that I'm an addict too and a CSU grad, a native Clevelander undyingly grateful for every nanosecond of hometown sports glory.

As his players gather, Mackey shuffles onto the court and runs a light practice for an hour or so, hands the players their paychecks — something you won't see Chuck Daly or Pat Riley do — and gives them some mild grief about the fact that they're 2-and-4 in games played the day after payday.

"Ah, you guys put those checks in the bank. You don't need to be out spending that money the same night you get it."

Everyone laughs except Stu Gray, a seven-year NBA journeyman backup center who's drawing half a million dollars from his last Knicks contract. Gray, the only white on the Flyers, smirks.

Mackey suggests a Hardee's not far from the Civic Center when I ask him where we can go to have a bite and talk.

I tell him I'll gladly buy him dinner somewhere nice.

"Nah. I just need some diet Coke."

We drive the 500 yards or so to Hardee's. Mackey digs the white-on-white Caddy.

"This yours?" he asks.

"No, no. I take the bus."

"Nice. That's all right. Where you staying in town?"

"Same place as you."

A grunt. He doesn't like that at all.

At Hardee's, Mackey sticks to soda while I drink coffee—just two clean, sober men of the nineties, trapped in a frieze of fast-food orange, sparring over the details of his botched career. Mackey speed-raps from 5:30 until 10, pausing only to visit the men's room to void the diet Coke. In the two ticks I once needed to chop and pop a brace of fat lines on a mirror, Mackey dashes off a thousand words, half of them variations of "fuck"; another couple hundred are the phrase "off the record," tossed into the mix at irregular intervals as his rasp waxes into white noise.

The voice is all cracked Boston blacktop and broken glass, with an "ah-ah-ah" stutter he uses like a dribble as he darts from sentence to sentence. Asking Mackey a question is like passing the ball to a shooter with no conscience: Once he's got his hands on a thought, you'll never see it again.

To Mackey, coaching is war, a test of strength, smarts and guts, and may the most ruthless urban gangster win. The college game is a "fucking farce": Behind the scenes, millions of dollars flow from booster to assistant coach to player, everyone knows it, everyone's a pimp or a whore. Even Catholic high school coaching, where he began, demands outlaw recruiting. That's what makes whipping the Hall of Fame guys, the coaches who get the All-State players and most of the acclaim, so sweet to Mackey.

"How'd I feel after beating Indiana? Like I could've done that years ago if someone had given me the chance. Who the fuck is Bobby Knight? You see me running off the court? I couldn't wait to go get fucked up. I couldn't wait to get to the fucking bar. I resented there were coaches making more money than me, who had better players to work with than me, who had better cooperation from the university, better facilities. But that's just another excuse to medicate yourself. Twisted, insane thinking. Once addiction kicks in, it takes anyone you love and anything you love and starts to eliminate it. In the end, it's just gonna be you and the addiction. Then it takes you."

Mackey's down with this addiction talk, his full-court press built on programmed self-disclosure, honest self-abnegation and, in his case, relentless self-promotion. Each phrase he mouths across the booth at Hardee's pops up in every article about him: His monkey is "baffling, cunning and powerful," his life "a descent into hell," his journey "a collision course with disaster." If addiction is at root an ego problem, a need to keep the furnace of the self red-hot, Mackey is Etna.

But back to Cleveland, Mackey, Cleveland. I mention the late, great Sterling Hotel, the seediest of all the Prospect Avenue flea-bags, and Mackey recalls it with a grin. Nearby was the New Era burlesque house, a square barracks of downscale sin where the distaff stars of the dripping screen appeared in the flesh. I saw Marilyn Chambers there once, flashing her nether lips and then hurling herself from the stage into the mucky sea of Neander-thals who'd paid $20 a head for a whiff of her fabled cooz.

"You sound like you miss it," Mackey notes.

Of course I do — burning at nostalgia's heart is always a core of loss, and where Ms. Chambers and her nipples once rose now stands the CSU Convocation Center in white-piped glory, its rafters hung with the banners Mackey's teams earned in tiny Wood-ling Gym. He never coached a single game at the Convo Center. And there have been no tournament appearances, no new banners, since Mackey left.

I tell him that some folks say CSU was raring to fire him, that the talk of his alcoholism and philandering, added to a history of recruiting violations, made him easy to kiss off, despite all the wins and banners. One source at the school told me back in 1990 that "the university has a fairly thick file on such activities, in-cluding the drinking and numerous arrests for DUI."

Mackey claims he was never actually arrested.

"There's nothin' on the record except a few speeding tickets, maybe seven," he says. "You can look it up."

When the cops did stop him — he admits he was pulled over a lot, "rushing to a bar" — he'd offer up a pair of sneakers or a basketball from the Lincoln's trunk, throw in a fistful of game tickets, and party on.

"While you're winning, you're the king," he says. "Nobody says anything, nobody sees anything, you can do no wrong."

Then I ask Mackey about crack, what it feels like. I myself quit

using everything in Iowa in 1988, threw out the Stoly and the
three hits of blotter in the freezer, the bong and the one-hitter,
the single-edged blades and the amber vials, even the rusty ni-
trous-oxide cartridge dispenser. For eighteen years, I'd done
everything I could touch but the needle. But stuck in Iowa, I'd
never smoked crack, and even now it kills the addict in me that I
might have missed something even more crippling than angel
dust.

"Beam me up, Scotty," Mackey laughs. Then he pauses.

"I'll tell you what it's like," he says. "What I went through? I
didn't hit bottom. 'Bottom' is a guy in the crack house with nothing to offer but himself. I've seen it, O.K.? Do you understand
what I'm saying? He's got no money, nothing else to pay with.
And he's gotta have it. You understand?

"I can go to bars to meet people or whatever — no problem,"
Mackey adds, "but I know if I was around the crack again, it
would suck me in. I can feel it inside me at any time. It's almost
like there's another person inside. It just waits."

Kevin Mackey grew up an altar boy and a playground rat in Somerville, a blue-collar Irish-Italian enclave just north of Boston
proper. Both parents were teachers, and Mackey was the first of
four kids. He says now that he was an alcoholic from age sixteen.

Mackey's academic priorities were "basketball and cheerleaders." At twenty-one, he was already married and coaching at Cathedral High in Boston's black South End, where his first teams
didn't even have a gym to play in. No problem — he not only
made the situation work for him, he discovered the key to the
coaching highway: ghetto ball.

"I had to go beg, borrow, or steal places to play, and I had to
find my own way around there. I got to see for myself what these
people were going through, their dreams and aspirations, and I
saw the talent — so talent-rich. I coached inner-city schools, and
I became known as kind of an inner-city coach."

Mackey's flair for finding raw black talent in risky places
quickly became legend. And if by chance you hadn't heard of his
reputation, he would gladly, loudly, fill you in.

"I go into the projects," he would boast, "and they see a white
guy in there, he could be one of two people, a cop or a coach. If

you tell 'em you're a coach, you're welcome. If you're a cop, you gotta look out. They don't bother me in the inner city."

As Mackey hustled up Washington Street from Cathedral to Don Bosco, a New England high school basketball powerhouse, and then to Boston College as player procurer for head coach Tom Davis, his reputation defined his limits. He worshiped talent, especially small guards — the word comes out "gods" in Mackey's dialect — landing current Celtic John Bagley and NBA All-Star Michael Adams for BC. Adams he discovered in a Hartford gym; no one else had even offered the kid a scholarship. "I got goose bumps, I started to sweat, I hadda go to the bathroom, I was gettin' chills," says Mackey. "I wanted the kid outta the game. I wanted him to get hurt, not badly, just bang his knee or something. I didn't want anyone else to see what I was seeing."

But while big-time schools need super-recruiters, when it comes to the man who runs the show, few risk choosing a street guy, a braggart, a tightrope walker. Everyone seemed to know that, except Kevin Mackey.

When Tom Davis left Boston College in 1982, Mackey, his assistant for four years, fully expected the promotion to head coach. Not only was he passed over, according to one Boston sportswriter, "he was never seriously considered. He was viewed as a bandit, a renegade, a guy who could get you in trouble down the road."

Down the road, of course, was my alma mater, a state institute of semi-higher learning with an open-admissions policy, the academic reputation of *Romper Room,* and a silver-haired prexy with matched black poodles named Amos and Andy. Like many another urban college — Memphis State and UNLV leap to mind — Cleveland State in 1983 figured it would be simpler, cheaper and more fulfilling to build a high-profile basketball program than an actual university with a decent library and all that stuff.

Quicker, too.

According to the NCAA and to CSU officials, Mackey's recruiting violations began within weeks of his arrival. Three years before his arrest and firing, he landed CSU on probation for recruiting Manute Bol, a seven-foot-six Dinka tribesman from the Sudan who spoke no English.

"They sniffed around for four fucking years, and that's all they could come up with," says Mackey. "I told the motherfuckers 'Look at my guys — they're wearing fake gold and driving old cars. For Christ's sake, go find a program with real money.' But they had one guy on the committee who was all upset because the Africans were taking scholarships away from American players.

"Besides," Mackey goes on, worked up now, "Manute never played one fucking game for Cleveland State. We knew we couldn't get him into school, but what were we supposed to do, send him back? He refused to go. His people were starving back there. The bottom line is, we got zero competitive advantage, none, and they hit us with three years fucking probation."

No, I say, the bottom line is that the NCAA report says that CSU fed and housed Bol for a year, paid thousands of dollars to his English tutors and worked him out with the team, all serious violations. Which makes Mackey sound like a bank robber bitching that he got tossed in jail even though he didn't get to spend the dough.

"But we got *no* competitive advantage," he insists.

The administrator who says he knew Mackey best, Jan Muczyk, claims that the people who hired him received fair warning "from a very reliable source that in three years he [would have us] in an NCAA playoff and in four years he [would have us] on probation."

As with every CSU person I spoke to, in and out of the athletic department, Muczyk's memories of Mackey mingle a willful innocence with expressions of loss and betrayal you might hear on *Divorce Court*. Muczyk himself is a College of Business professor, who negotiated Mackey's contracts. According to a faculty member close to the 1990 negotiations, it was Muczyk who "referred to Mackey's taste for African-American women as a 'perversion.'"

Muczyk admits "there were rumors, including drugs, rumors that he'd hang around with sordid women." When he confronted Mackey, Muczyk says, the coach assured him that these women were the mothers and the aunts of prospective players.

"I didn't hire a private eye," Muczyk continues. "I didn't have the budget for that." As for the citywide stage whispers about Mackey's drinking problem, Muczyk says he tested the coach himself.

"I deliberately took him to a number of watering holes and offered to buy him strong alcohol — bourbon, scotch, whatever."

The wily Mackey tricked Professor Muczyk by refusing anything stronger than Miller Lite. Case closed, except for the photo that Muczyk wants me to see.

"Look at this," he says, holding it across the desk. "This one will bring tears to your eyes."

There stand Mackey and Muczyk at a postgame party. Mackey looks fine, crisp and smiling, clear-eyed, a whistle around his neck. Muczyk is obviously shitfaced.

"I went to battle with him everywhere, everywhere. It took me a while to get over the feeling I was betrayed," he says, and it's plain that he never has. "Hell, the guy's more sober than I am. *He's* not wearing the stupid booster hat, you don't see him holding a drink in *his* hand. Who's got the problem in that picture?"

Mackey can't remember the nine hours in the crack house, he says, because he was unconscious. Needle holes? Yeah, but who, what, and how, he just can't recall. What's left of self-disclosure is a twelve-step pablum cooked up for the straight reader, weak cheese that'd be stuffed back into his face if he tried it at an NA or AA meeting. And Mackey hasn't seen a meeting room for a while.

"Nah," he tells me, "I haven't gone of late, which is not good as far as recovery goes. I've been very busy. But I believe in the meetings. My thing is to do the best I can with each day, and don't pick it up. That's worked very, very well for me."

Maybe for him, but not for the people he hurt. Contact with his family is sporadic. In Fayetteville, he has no friends, only players. The younger brother who stood by him at the post-arrest press conference won't discuss him now, refuses even my question about their age difference; they got into a fistfight upon Kevin's release from the rehab program and haven't spoken since. Mackey's twenty-three-year-old son, Brian, a commodities trader in New York City, muses on his father as "tragic hero," a man whose "dark spot started to grow larger and larger."

Still, it's the women in Kevin Mackey's life who bear the ugliest scars. Alma Massey spent her weekends in jail for two years after the police found heroin in her purse at the Edmonton Avenue

SCOTT RAAB   447

bust. Mackey's relationship with Massey dates back to at least
four years prior to the arrest. Channel 8 revealed an audiotape
from July 1986, when Massey's distraught mother phoned the
station to claim that Mackey was funneling Alma $2,000 at a time
for drugs and that the police wouldn't do anything about it.

Massey, too, is sober now, and it's clear from one brief conversation that she's a bright, complex human who was distorted by
the local media to fit the ghetto-wench stereotype. Offered thousands of dollars by the local media to tell her story, she refused.
Now, she says, she's struggling to get and keep her life and family together.

She's also frightened. At first, she seems willing to talk — if we
meet at her lawyer's office, and if I'll sign an agreement to quote
her in full. What exactly do I want to know? But as soon as I pose
a few questions about her and Mackey, she asks if I've been
watching her house and tapping her phone. Then she's gone.

Mackey's wife, Kathy, is a small, brittle blonde who works as a
jailhouse nurse-supervisor in the Cuyahoga County Corrections
Center. She says she threw her husband out of their house when,
on the morning after the arrest, he left to visit Alma. For Kathy
Mackey, the betrayal continues: Her husband lied and kept on
lying, even after his public scouring. To this day, she says, he
hasn't come to terms with his real problems or the pain he
caused.

"Kevin has his own agenda," she concludes, her voice, like his,
a street-corner snarl, a cross between Betty Boop's and Ma Bar-
ker's. "My life was cut open and spread out on Euclid Avenue.
The thing is, I would have lived with that man anywhere. I would
have lived with that man in a tent on Public Square. It wasn't the
money. It wasn't the fame. I loved him."

The house at 12406 Edmonton still stands, barely, next to a vacant corner lot. No house number, but I know the place from the
tapes: two slumped stories, a caved-in brick porch piled with garbage, peeling pale-green paint browned by filth. At high noon, a
bare bulb burns in a ceiling fixture on the second floor; I stare at
it from the street, safe inside the Avis Cadillac.

According to Sergeant Gercar, the place is back in business; at
the Justice Center that morning, he warned me not to approach

it even in daylight. So I sit a while, listening to Lou Reed, wondering what Mackey saw two years ago beyond that blank plywood door.

Later, I phone Mark Johnson, an Edmonton Avenue resident who saw the coach on the morning of his arrest, buying beer and wine at a little corner grocery on Eddy. Johnson spotted the two girls, too, waiting for Mackey out in the Lincoln.

Johnson admits that he's the guy who tipped Channel 8 to Mackey. He says he was worried about the coach's safety in that neck of the woods.

"He looked like he was ready to pass out. I called Cleveland State, also — [Merle] Levin. He told me there's nothing he could do about it. I says, 'Well, I thought maybe you guys would want to know.' He told me he was busy."

"Did you call the police too?" I ask Johnson.

"No way. I wasn't the only one who saw him that day. I mean, he's very visible down here. I called everybody I thought I could, and then I thought to myself, Well, nobody seems to care."

Merle Levin's title at CSU is sports-information director and assistant athletic director for marketing and communication. When I ask him about Johnson's call, he skips a pass to John Konstantinos, the athletic director, hired only two weeks before Mackey's firing.

Konstantinos says Johnson phoned him — three times.

"The first message I got was early afternoon. I had been out. It just said 'Mark Johnson re basketball.' " Konstantinos doesn't recall the second note, but says that he came home to find an unforgettable message on his machine.

"It said 'Good news about basketball,' and I couldn't imagine what that was all about because I was supposed to meet with Kevin that afternoon and he didn't show up.

"I called the guy, and he went through the whole spiel about how he had seen Coach Mackey earlier that morning, buying liquor. He said he checked and it was the blue Lincoln. There were two young ladies in it. He even gave me the license number. He said, 'Is this your coach's car?'

"Well, no sooner do I get off the phone with him than Merle Levin calls me — he was probably trying to call me while I was talking to Mark Johnson — to give me the news of what had happened, that Kevin had been arrested.

"I remember asking Merle, 'Is this his license number?' And he said 'Yes,' and I said, 'Then the guy knew what he was talking about.' I've never spoken with him since. I have no idea what he looks like. He sounded sincere."

So does Konstantinos when I suggest that his account hints of, um, a peculiar lack of concern about the basketball coach he'd inherited.

"Let me tell you, I did not welcome his demise. It created problems for me that I'm still living with."

But isn't he the guy who decided to dismiss Mackey rather than give him a medical leave?

"Yes, I recommended that he be fired. How could we maintain our image? What would I tell my thirteen-year-old son? How could we then go out and recruit? How could we get into a front room with Mom and Dad to sell them on the idea that they should send their young person to our care?

"The other thing was, no one could tell how long it would take to rehabilitate him. What were we supposed to do, put our whole program on hold?" But isn't there at least the appearance of a setup put in motion by the same crew who'd just inked Mackey to a new deal?

"There was so much going on, and who knows what the truth of the matter is? Sometimes I think I don't really want to know. I give 'em an old Lou Holtz quote — 'The good Lord put eyes in front of my head instead of behind so I can see where I'm going instead of where I've been.'"

After the GBA season ends, Mackey will be named head coach of the Albany, New York, franchise of the Continental Basketball Association. It's another step up — this is where Phil Jackson coached before he got the call from Michael Jordan's team — but Mackey had loftier hopes. His old friend and role model Jerry Tarkanian might have taken him on as an assistant with the San Antonio Spurs, but when Tark phoned Mackey to pick his brain, Mackey told him straight out that the team had holes, serious holes, and Tark never called back.

"[Mackey's] never gonna be an NBA head coach, no way," says a Boston writer. "That's too bad in a way, because he'd probably win 'em a lot of games, but it's exactly the same reason BC didn't hire him when Tom Davis left. He was too dangerous."

Sweet music to Mackey, a tune he can't resist. Mackey in the NBA? Only a matter of time, he says. He's got connections, a sexy winning percentage and no doubt about the warp of his whole life.

"All you've got to do is tell me I can't do something, and I won't stop until I do it. It's a burning thing in me, it's like a fire, to do well. Some people know how to win, know what it takes to win. I think I've demonstrated that throughout my career."

In Fayetteville in February, with little for Mackey to work with, the Flyers' record is 28-and-13. Mackey pockets an extra ten grand if the Flyers win the league, but the odds are long despite the current standings. His top three scorers have fled — one to the Philippines, two to Australia — for longer green. The schedule is grueling, and the players, desperate for a first or last shot at the League — that's how one and all refer to the NBA, just the League, spoken with a pilgrim's awe and reverence — are selfish, fierce, and angry on the floor.

The bush-league referees can barely trot and blow a whistle at the same time, much less control the game, but Mackey hardly baits them anymore. In one game, he shouts "This isn't girls' junior high!," which draws a technical foul, but mainly he just seethes and silently takes another pull on his diet Coke. He's still wound tight on the sidelines, never sitting, but he's calmer than in the old days.

"I have to be careful because of what I went through," he says. "I have to watch the way I conduct myself."

Still, he's not above illegally substituting one player for another at the free-throw line, knowing that these officials will never catch it. Neither will the opposing coach.

On an off night in Fayetteville, I drive Mackey to the WFNC-AM studio for a guest spot on *Fanfare,* an hour-long sports chat.

"Your segment is twenty minutes," host Alex Lekas tells him, but forty-five minutes later, Mackey's still on caller number two, swigging soda from a Big Gulp cup, cracking ice with his teeth. The pitch of his monologue makes the mike superfluous: If the caller turned off his radio and flung open his windows, he'd surely hear Mackey rumble against the sky.

"I'll tell you," Mackey spumes, "I'm grateful for the chance to coach in this league. The GBA is only a bounce away from the NBA."

It's maybe the tenth time I've heard Mackey use this same line — to his players, at a press conference in Raleigh, during a postgame radio interview, in the Hardee's booth, and in my room at the Marriott. After practice the next day, I ask Stu Gray if it rings true.

Seven years spent trading elbows and riding the NBA pines from Charlotte to Indianapolis to New York left Gray short on front teeth but equipped with a rugged, war-tempered stare into the middle distance. He averaged only 2.3 points and 2.6 rebounds per game in the big show, but he was there.

"Sure," Gray says after a while. "One bounce, or one million."

Still, listening to Mackey in the darkened studio, it's not so hard to believe. Just a stutter-step through the circle, a flex of the knees, an uncoiling of spirit and fast-twitch muscle and up they go, up from this outlaw outback, up into the League, all these men-children who, as Mackey says, have "come through the test of fire" that burns in the projects and the gyms and the bars and the straight glass pipe.

Won't they need a coach?

"Hey," he croaks to the caller, winding to full torque, "test me, test me. Anyone. Anyone who wants to pay me, who wants to give me an opportunity. Test me. Write it in the contract ad infinitum. What more can I say?"

For Kevin Mackey there's always something more to say, about pressure defense, the Olympic team, his all-time starting five, you name it, so long as it's basketball. The station break on the half-hour is long past due, but Alex Lekas just sits there, struck dumb while Kevin Mackey smolders on, belching diet Coke and the smoke of his soul into the far blue midnight.

OCTOBER 1992

SCOTT RAAB *has written what is surely the grittiest (even ugliest) story in this collection. The dark side of sports — especially college sports — is certainly nothing new, but Raab's personal connection to Cleveland State, the institution in question, is what gives the grim piece a special flavor — all the more so that Raab inserted his own relationship in just the right proportion.* — F.D.

MIKE LITTWIN

A Fan Again,
After All These Years

FROM THE BALTIMORE SUN

DO YOU WANT to know the weirdest thing about being a sports writer other than, of course, the requirement that you spend much of your time talking to naked men? The other weird thing is that you don't get to be a fan.

The difference between sports and ballet is that in sports you root for somebody. Nobody yells at one of the ballerinas to "break a bleepin' leg, ya bum." You're a fan from somewhere deep down in the gut. The funniest thing about the old *Saturday Night Live* bit about Da Bears is that it was exactly true to life. For the real fan, sports are life — and death. That two Latin American countries once went to war over a soccer game can't surprise anyone. The surprise is that it doesn't happen more often.

I miss being a fan.

Oh, I'm a fan of certain players. Julius Erving and Magic Johnson are 1 and 1A. My all-time favorite sports event, by the way, was not the N.C. State win over Houston or the Bucky Dent home run or Mike Devereaux climbing a wall. It was watching Dr. J and George Gervin play one-on-one each day after practice for the Virginia Squires back when I was a cub reporter and they were cub superstars. Duke Snider was my first childhood hero. I dropped him for Sandy Koufax. Koufax for Muhammad Ali. Ali for Jane Fonda, who just got confused when they asked her to pose in a tank top.

But sports writers don't root for teams. The first rule you

learn, even before the one about never eating airplane food, is no cheering in the press box. Usually, you're not tempted. Say you're a sports writer covering the Atlanta–Toronto World Series. Everyone else is going nuts because — to the players, fans, and every other life form in the stadium — winning that game is as important as breathing. Your priorities are a little different. In fact, the sports writer's primary concern at such times is finding a place to plug in his computer.

Sure, you enjoy the great moments. You get excited as anyone when Francisco Cabrera turns the world upside down.

But it's not *your* moment. When the hit comes, all you're thinking about is how to capture the moment for someone else.

The moments used to be mine. Like most sports writers, I grew up in love with the games. I grew up a Dodgers fan, a religion handed down from father to son. My first dog's name was Dodger (he was followed by Duke and Campy and Sandy), and I would often fall asleep listening to the games on a radio tucked under my pillow to hide the sounds from my parents. Just my luck to be born before headphones.

The most told story of my childhood involves my grandfather, a devout Yankees fan all his life. Dodgers fans, of course, hate the Yankees. He and I were watching a game on TV in the bottom floor of his tri-level house. The Yankees were batting with two outs in the bottom of the ninth, down a run or two, a couple of runners on and Mickey Mantle at the plate.

"Pop one, Mick," my grandfather screamed at the TV.

"Yeah, pop one up," I chimed in. (Yes, a wise guy even in my youth.)

The Mick popped up. The game was over. The Yankees lost. And my grandfather stormed out of the room, up the stairs past the kitchen where my grandmother and mother were sitting, and up more stairs to his bedroom, from where I heard the thundering slam of the door.

My grandmother asked me what happened. I told her Mick popped up. She understood. Having seen these tantrums before, she went to my grandfather's room to try to calm him down.

"Sadie," he said, each word slowly and fiercely delivered, "I don't ever want that damn kid in this house again."

I was ten — and exiled because I had made the Yankees lose. I had to apologize. But the hated Yankees had lost. That was my moment.

I went on to become a sports writer and would be lucky enough to cover many of the great events of the past two decades. I even covered a Dodgers–Yankees World Series, and, as much as I wanted to root, the stories came first. The stories and the deadlines and the outlet for the computer.

Somebody once wrote — another wise guy — that the only thing dumber than a grown-up playing a little kid's game is a grown-up writing about grown-ups playing a little kid's games. Maybe there's truth in that. All I know is for twenty years I could never imagine doing anything else.

OCTOBER 18, 1992

MIKE LITTWIN *is one of our finest sports columnists, and when I saw this lovely and charming valedictory to sports writing in the* Baltimore Sun, *I immediately saw it as the most appropriate finale to this year's collection. The only negative is that it means Mike is leaving the game.* — F.D.

Biographical Notes

Notable Sports Writing of 1992

Biographical Notes

MITCH ALBOM has won more than one hundred awards as a sports columnist for the *Detroit Free Press*. He is the coauthor of Bo Schembechler's autobiography, *Bo,* and is currently working on a book featuring the University of Michigan's men's basketball team.

ROGER ANGELL is a writer and editor for *The New Yorker*. His contributions to the magazine include fiction, humor, editorial comment, reviews, light verse and reporting. His latest book about baseball is *Once More Around the Park*. Mr. Angell graduated from Harvard and served in the Air Force in the Pacific during World War II. He lives with his wife in New York City.

MICHAEL BAMBERGER has been a reporter for the *Philadelphia Inquirer* since 1986. He is a frequent contributor to *Golf Digest* and has written two books, *The Green Road Home* and *To the Linksland*.

DAVE BARRY is a native of Armonk, New York. He joined the *Miami Herald* in 1983 and subsequently won a Pulitzer Prize for commentary in 1988. His popular column is syndicated in hundreds of newspapers throughout North America.

ROY BLOUNT, JR. is a contributing editor to *Spy*. He was named a "Literary Lion" by the New York Public Library in 1987. His latest book is entitled *Camels Are Easy, Comedy's Hard*.

JENNIFER BRIGGS was the first batgirl for the Texas Rangers. She is currently a major league baseball columnist for *The Fort Worth Star-Telegram*, where she has worked since 1980. She is the coauthor of *Nolan Ryan: The Authorized Pictorial Biography*.

AMBY BURFOOT won the Boston Marathon in 1968 and still runs the race every five years. He began thinking about the article that became "White Men Can't Run" while stationed as a Peace Corps volunteer track coach in El Salvador. He has been executive editor of *Runner's World* since 1986.

RON FIMRITE lives in San Francisco and has been a writer for *Sports Illustrated* since 1971. He is the author of the collection *Way to Go!* and *The Square,* about San Francisco's venerable Washington Square Bar and Grill.

CORY JOHNSON is a twenty-seven-year-old staff writer for *FYI,* Time Life, Inc.'s house organ. He graduated from New York University with a degree in Music Business, Metropolitan Studies and Journalism in 1989 and has written for *Men's Journal, People, Rolling Stone, Sports Illustrated* and, of course, the *Village Voice.* At age eleven, he fell off his skateboard and landed on his face. Now he is a runner.

BEN JORAVSKY has covered politics and education as a staff writer for the *Chicago Reader* since 1990. He is coauthor of two books, *Against the Tide* and *Race and Politics in Chicago.* He lives in Chicago with his wife and two children.

PAT JORDAN is currently at work on Bobby ^{2}, a novel about a South Florida minor league drug dealer. A portion of the novel has appeared in *Playboy.*

DONALD KATZ is a contributing editor for *Esquire, Men's Journal, Outside,* and *Worth.* He is the author of *Home Fires: An Intimate Portrait of One Middle-Class Family in Post-War America* and *The Big Store: Inside the Crisis and Revolution at Sears.*

HOWARD KOHN is a contributing editor for the *Los Angeles Times Magazine* and *Rolling Stone.* His book *The Last Farmer: An American Memoir* was a runner-up for the Pulitzer Prize in general nonfiction in 1989. He is currently writing a book about the civil rights movement.

MARK KRAM was born and raised in Baltimore, where he first worked for the *Baltimore Sun.* He was a senior writer for *Sports Illustrated* for fourteen years and is currently a contributing editor for *Esquire* and an active screenwriter.

MIKE LITTWIN was a sports columnist for the *Baltimore Sun* for seven years, where he is now a features columnist. He previously worked for the *Los Angeles Times,* the *Virginian Pilot,* and the *Newport News Times Herald.*

CRAIG MEDRED's story "Across the Burn" appeared in *The Best American Sports Writing 1992.* He is outdoors editor for the *Anchorage Daily News* and is a past recipient of the American Society of Newspaper Editors Award for deadline reporting.

KENNY MOORE finished fourteenth in the marathon at the 1968 Olympics in Mexico City and fourth in the marathon at the 1972 Olympics in Munich. He has been a senior writer with *Sports Illustrated* since 1980 and is the author of *Best Efforts: World-Class Runners and Races.* He has appeared in two films, *Personal Best* with Mariel Hemingway and *Tequila Sunrise* with Mel Gibson, Kurt Russell, and Michelle Pfeiffer.

WILLIAM NACK has been a senior writer for *Sports Illustrated* for thirteen years, during which time his coverage of thoroughbred horseracing has won him six Eclipse Awards. *True Heart,* his story on the death of Secretariat, appeared in the first collection of *The Best American Sports Writing.*

CHARLES P. PIERCE is a contributing writer for *GQ* and *Boston Magazine.* His piece on the market for Negro League baseball collectibles appeared in the 1991 collection of *The Best American Sports Writing.*

SCOTT RAAB attended Cleveland State University and the University of Iowa. His short stories and articles have appeared in the *North American Review, Sport, Seventeen, Self,* and *Philadelphia.*

RICK REILLY worked for the *Boulder Daily News,* the *Denver Post,* and the *Los Angeles Times* before joining *Sports Illustrated* in 1985. He has coauthored two books, *The Boz: Confessions of a Modern Anti-Hero* and *Gretsky.* He is currently at work on a screenplay, a comedy about a 1920's professional football team.

PETER RICHMOND, while on staff for the *National Sports Daily,* contributed two stories to the inaugural collection of *The Best American Sports Writing.* He is a staff writer for *GQ.*

DAVID ROBERTS is an experienced Alaskan mountaineer with many ascents to his credit. He is the author of *Once They Moved Like the Wind: Cochise, Geronimo and the Apache Wars.*

E. M. SWIFT joined *Sports Illustrated* in 1978. Since 1986 he has primarily covered figure skating. His novel *Each Thief Passing By* was published in 1981. He lives in Carlisle, Massachusetts.

DONNA TARTT is the author of one of the most talked about novels of 1992, *The Secret History.* Her short stories have appeared in *The New Yorker* and numerous other publications. She lives in Mississippi and New York City.

Notable Sports Writing of 1992

SELECTED BY GLENN STOUT

JOHN DEREVLANY
Up Shit's Creek. *The Village Voice*,
   October 13, 1992.

MARTY DOBROW
o and 15. *Hampshire Life*, December
   4–10, 1992.

JOHN DORSCHNER
The Greatest Living American. *Tropic*,
   April 5, 1992.

MIKE DOWNEY
Living for Each New Day. *The Los
   Angeles Times*, August 3, 1992.

JACK ETKIN
Brett Accepted the Challenge of
   Greatness. *The Kansas City Star*,
   October 2, 1992.

PAUL FEINBERG
Down with DDP. *LA Weekly*, March
   13–19, 1992.

TOM FERREY
Hope and Pain. *The Seattle Times/
   Seattle Post Intelligencer*, August 30,
   1992.

WILLIAM FINNEGAN
Playing Doc's Games. *The New Yorker*,
   August 24 & August 31, 1992.

STEVE FISHMAN
The Needle Boys. *Details*, October
   1992.

TOM FITZPATRICK
Memories of Leo and Willie. *New
   Times*, March 11–17, 1992.

BOB FORD
Leaps of Faith. *The Philadelphia
   Inquirer Magazine*, November 8,
   1992.

LEW FREEDMAN
King of the Seven Summits. *Anchorage
   Daily News*, May 31, 1992.
Nick Randazzo's Return to Life.
   Anchorage Daily News, May 3, 1992.

PETER FREDERICI
Hawking. *The Chicago Reader*, June
   12, 1992.

SHAV GLICK
Glory Came Fast, Didn't Last. *The Los
   Angeles Times*, May 17, 1992.

MICHAEL J. GOODMAN
Fernando Valenzuela Goes South. *The
   Los Angeles Times Magazine*,
   September 13, 1992.

CINDY HAHN
Surviving Stardom. *Tennis*, October
   1992.

CATHY HARASTA
A Fighting Chance. *The Dallas
   Morning News*, June 28, 1992.

DONALD HARRISON
The Devil Drives. *Fairfield County
   Advocate*, February 27–March 4,
   1992.

TOM HAWTHORN
Born to Be a Boxer. *The Province*,
   December 20, 1992.

DOUGLAS HEUCK, BILL HELTZEL
AND DAVID TEMPLETON
Mel Blount: Putting a Long Time
   Dream in Order. *The Pittsburgh
   Press*, May 10, 1992.

JOHNETTE HOWARD
Though His Heart Is Aching. *Detroit
   Free Press Magazine*, September 6,
   1992.
A Woman's Place. *Detroit Free Press
   Magazine*, February 9, 1992.

MARYANN HUDSON
The Cannon Is Quiet. *The Los Angeles
   Times*, January 26, 1992.

DAVID JACKSON
Jordan's Acquaintances in Shadowy
   World. *Chicago Tribune*, March 29,
   1992.